# organizing
# for
# whole language

# organizing
# for
# whole language

*Edited by*

YETTA M. GOODMAN

WENDY J. HOOD

KENNETH S. GOODMAN

**HEINEMANN**
*Portsmouth*
*New Hampshire*

IRWIN PUBLISHING
*Toronto*
*Canada*

**Heinemann Educational Books, Inc.**
361 Hanover Street     Portsmouth, NH 03801
*Offices and agents throughout the world*

Published simultaneously in Canada by
**Irwin Publishing**
1800 Steeles Avenue West     Concord, Ontario, Canada L4K 2P3

Thanks to the Upper Arlington City School District, Upper Arlington, Ohio, for permission to quote from their K–12 Language Arts Graded Course of Study in Chapter 27.

Every effort has been made to contact the copyright holders for permission to reprint borrowed material where necessary. We regret any oversights that may have occurred and would be happy to rectify them in future printings of this work.

Library of Congress Cataloging-in-Publication Data

Organizing for whole language / edited by Yetta M. Goodman, Wendy J.
  Hood, Kenneth S. Goodman.
      p.   cm.
    Includes bibliographical references (p. ).
    ISBN 0-435-08541-7
      1. Language experience approach in education.   I. Goodman, Yetta
M., 1931-   .  II. Hood, Wendy J.   III. Goodman, Kenneth S.
LB1576.076   1991
372.6—dc20                                                    90-21918
                                                                  CIP


Canadian Cataloguing in Publication Data

Main entry under title:

Organizing for whole language

Includes bibliographical references.
ISBN 0-7725-1888-2

1. Language experience approach in education.
I. Goodman, Yetta M., 1931-   .   II. Hood,
Wendy J.   III. Goodman, Kenneth S.

LB1576.074 1991   372.6   C91-094546-2

Designed by Wladislaw Finne.
Prepress production services by G & H Soho Ltd.

Printed in the United States of America.
91  92  93  94  95  9  8  7  6  5  4  3  2  1

*To all the hardworking teachers*
*inventing the wheel*

# CONTENTS

## EMPOWERING TEACHERS AND LEARNERS

# ABOUT THE AUTHORS

**Carol S. Avery** is a primary-grade teacher in Manheim Township School District, Lancaster, Pennsylvania. She is an active member of the National Council of Teachers of English.

**Lois Bridges Bird** is a whole language consultant and editor in Palo Alto, California. She is co-editor of *The Whole Language Catalog*.

**Deborah Landwehr Bosnos** was a Chapter I Mathematics Resource Teacher in Tucson, Arizona, for many years. She is now teaching kindergarten and attending graduate courses at the University of Arizona.

**Phyllis E. Brazee** is Professor of Reading and Language Arts at the University of Maine in Orono. She worked there with science education Professor **Warren C. Tomkiewicz** until his recent move to Plymouth State College, Plymouth, New Hampshire.

**Fredrick R. Burton** is an elementary principal in the Dublin City Schools, Columbus, Ohio. He has been active in effecting policy change in his district.

**Richard E. Coles** is a Grade 8 teacher in an inner-city area of Toronto, Ontario. He is interested in the literacy development of young adolescents and whole language in middle school education.

**Caryl G. Crowell** teaches bilingual third grade at Borton, a magnet school in Tucson, Arizona.

**Toby Kahn Curry** and **Debra Goodman** helped to found the Dewey Center for Urban Education, a magnet school, in Detroit, Michigan, where they both now teach.

**Karen Sabers Dalrymple** recently moved from Eagle County, Colorado, to Ashland, Oregon, where she is an assistant superintendent. Her position in the Ashland Schools allows her to continue learning together with students, teachers, parents, and other administrators.

**Deborah Nash Dodd** has been a middle school teacher in Tucson, Arizona. Recently married, she is moving to Denver, Colorado, where she is looking forward to networking with other whole language teachers.

**Linda Dorn, Micki Orian, Pam Pearce,** and **Dianne Taylor** have taught together at Stephens Elementary in Little Rock, Arkansas. They have been instrumental in reorganizing their school to facilitate whole language.

**Jean F. Dunning** teaches middle school students in multicultural, urban British classrooms.

**Dana Fox** recently completed her doctorate in English Education. She has been the Assistant Director of Undergraduate Education, and Coordinator of Field Experiences in the College of Education, University of Missouri, Columbia.

**David E. Freeman** is the Director of Secondary Education and Co-Director of Language Development at Fresno Pacific College, California.

**Yvonne S. Freeman** collaborated with **Samuel D. Nofziger, Jr.,** in his second-grade bilingual classroom in Fresno, California. Yvonne is Director of Bilingual Education and Co-Director of Language Development at Fresno Pacific College, California.

**Kenneth S. Goodman** is Professor of Education in the Department of Language, Reading, and Culture at the University of Arizona. He is the author of *What's Whole in Whole Language?*

**Yetta M. Goodman** is Regents Professor of Language, Reading, and Culture at the University of Arizona. She is co-author of the *Reading Miscue Inventory: Alternative Procedures.*

**Lynne Griffiths** is a special education teacher at Fair Oaks Elementary School in Redwood City, California.

**John Hardcastle** is a former London secondary teacher who is now on the faculty of the Institute of Education, University of London.

**Susan W. Haynes**, from Bar Harbor, Maine, functions professionally as a literacy tutor, adult education teacher, special education teacher/consultant, reading specialist, and teacher educator. She holds master's degrees in special education and reading/language arts.

**Wendy J. Hood** teachers second grade at a whole language school in Tucson, Arizona. She is co-editor of *The Whole Language Evaluation Book.*

**Debra Jacobson** is a Chapter I reading teacher in Tucson, Arizona. Debra is founder of the whole language newsletter, *Teachers Networking*, and Executive Director of Tucson TAWL.

**Wendy C. Kasten** collaborated with **Joni R. Ramer** in Joni's kindergarten in Bradenton, Florida. Wendy is a professor at the University of Southern Florida, Sarasota.

**Mary M. Kitagawa**, formerly of Tucson, Arizona, teaches middle-grade students in Amherst, Massachusetts. She is co-author of *Making Connections with Writing*.

**Constance J. McCarthy** teaches middle-grade students at China Elementary in China, Maine.

**Alex Moore** teaches high school students in multicultural, urban British classrooms.

**Dorothy Watson** is a professor at the University of Missouri, Columbia. She is editor of *Insights and Ideas* and the first president of the international Whole Language Umbrella.

**Joni Weed** is a second-grade teacher in Rockport, Maine. She has taught undergraduate language arts at the University of Maine.

**Sari Windsor** is the instructional assistant in a whole language classroom in Fresno, California. She writes with the parent support group from her classroom.

# PREFACE

**Wendy J. Hood**

You open the door. The fluorescent lights hum as you enter the room. There are four walls around you. A light flickers. You take in your surroundings. The linoleum floor, though recently waxed, shows the wear of many years. You hear traffic rumbling past on a nearby street. The pastel painted walls are smudged and dirty. Upon closer inspection you can see the masking tape marks left by the previous tenant. You sit down on a hard, worn chair that seems a little too short for you and think of what to do next. Your choices are . . .

Is this really a piece of interactive fiction? No, not really. Proceed.

One of the grungy pastel walls is covered by a large board. Through the shining surface of the newly washed board, you can see the vague marks and outlines of lessons of days gone by. A large desk sits askew near one corner of the room. A hideous greenish brown trashcan decorated with vintage glue, glitter, and bubblegum looms out at you from another corner. Up near the top of one of the translucent windows, dangling mysteriously from a yellowed piece of cellophane tape, is a tiny piece of what proves, upon closer inspection, to be a remnant of a paper snowflake.

By now you know that you are not in the Twilight Zone or a Choose-Your-Own-Adventure come alive. This is your classroom. It is too small, poorly lit, run down, and lacks sufficient storage space. All the good furniture has been removed by senior teachers who turned into bookcase vultures the moment the previous tenant was transferred. You scan the room once again.

The pencil sharpener (if there is one) is either missing the shavings catcher or mounted too high for the students to reach. There is a locked cupboard you hadn't noticed before. Fumbling with your recently acquired keys, you move slowly toward it. Cautiously, you open the door. A cockroach scurries away. Your eyes first come to rest on three boxes of spirit masters and twenty-seven reams of ditto paper. A second shelf is full of pre- and post-test booklets for three different subjects. A colorful box on the top shelf grabs your attention. You reach up, blow off the dust, and slowly lift the lid off the box. It contains 1,023 flash cards, copyright 1943. You put the box back and flop down into another short, hard chair.

Your task is to transform the space within these walls into a warm, comfortable, literate, nurturing environment that will motivate, encourage, support, and enhance students' learning individually and cooperatively. You contemplate this.

As you sit, the door opens. A friendly but unknown person rolls in a squeaky cartload of books. "I was picking up my basal readers and spelling workbooks so I picked yours up, too. I used to team with the teacher who was here before you. We divided the students by reading ability. She took the low readers and I took the high ones. Did you find all the phonics charts in the cupboard?" You courteously thank your new neighbor for the help and mutter something about being new and not ready to team yet. He leaves.

The students will be entering in two days. How do you create a whole language classroom environment in such a sterile setting? Where do you begin? And once the physical environment is in place, how do you reorient students who may well have come from very traditional classrooms? And once they are oriented toward your whole language setting, how do you encourage the risk taking, the cooperation, the thinking that you want to see happen? And once the kids begin thinking differently, taking risks, and working together, how do you empower them to take charge of their own learning?

These are some critical questions all whole language teachers have to ask themselves. They do not always get resolved in the limited days before the students show up, but whole language educators, whether new teachers or experienced teachers who have reconsidered traditional methods, work through these and many other questions before they begin to be satisfied with themselves as educators. Besides working toward personal resolution of the questions they face, all whole language teachers have other things in common.

1. Whole language teachers share a common philosophy that helps them persevere.
2. Whole language teachers develop their own personal whole language classrooms. Each is unique.
3. Whole language teachers are constantly learning. They aspire to do more, to be better, to be more like that *other* whole language teacher they consider their mentor.
4. Whole language teachers enjoy their work.

# ACKNOWLEDGMENTS

When we first started this book, there was no way we could antici-pate the overwhelming response we'd get to our call for proposals about organizing for whole language. It was tremendously exciting for us to read about all the whole language experiences being organized by thoughtful professionals. The hard part for us was selecting only enough articles for ONE book. (There could easily have been two or three.) Along the way, many people worked hard and wrote well but are not among those finally included.

We specifically want to thank Alex McLeod of the Institute of Education, University of London, for recruiting and enabling us to include the chapters by the three British classroom authors. We also would like to thank Phyllis Brazee, Wendy Kasten, and Dorothy Watson for encouraging many classroom teachers to find their voices in professional writing.

There were many individuals, especially classroom teachers, who have used this opportunity to take a risk and write professionally for the very first time. We hope that their writing has found an audience through other publications, and we encourage each of them to con-tinue sharing their visions.

Yetta, Wendy, and Ken

# beginnings

beginnings

# 1

# YIPPIE-AYE-AY: PLANNING AND ORGANIZING HOLISTICALLY

## Kenneth S. Goodman

"Home on the range" has taken on a new meaning in recent years. A movement has been developing that brings environmentalists and ranchers together to examine their interests in the context of the whole range. It's called "Holisitic Resource Management" (HRM). What its advocates believe is that in the past people have looked at ecological issues from narrow vantage points: how many head of cattle to graze per acre, whether to let hunters "harvest" excess deer, whether to put out range fires or let them burn, and so on. The holistic view says that you must start with a whole: a backyard, a ranch, a national forest, the Navajo Reservation, a state, a country. Then you consider what it has: people, animals, plants, climate, natural resources, institutions, traditions, a society, an economy, a government. You also consider how these relate to each other and what might be needed to achieve the optimal benefit to the whole (those that live there and those that have a vital interest). From this a holistic plan is developed.

If there is a need to take a holistic view in planning and organizing range management, then there is certainly a need to apply the same holistic principles to organizing education. Start with a whole: a group, a class, a grade, a school, a school system, a state or province, or a nation. Then consider what must be present (space, facilities, furniture, equipment, time, materials), who lives there (pupils, teachers, other professional and nonprofessional staff, administrators), who has vital interests (parents, community, boards, cultural groups).

We also need to put the whole school into a larger sociocultural context. What is the relationship of the school to the community?

3

What is the history and what are the traditions? What's there now and what needs to be there? Who are the kids and what can they do? Where do they come from and where are they going? What interests and doesn't interest them? Who are the teachers and the other staff? What are their abilities and needs? And what do we want to happen—all of us: kids, teachers, community, decision makers? What objectives do they have and what priorities do each of those interested have among these objectives? What kinds of people does our culture want us to be and to become?

When we have some sense of the whole, we can start to plan and to organize the time and space, energy and effort, materials and participants.

For the HRM people, the goal is a functioning, productive whole—one that produces what's necessary to support and renew itself, its people, animals, and plants, one that is healthy and capable of sustaining the life cycles of each participant.

In organizing for whole language, we have our life cycles too. We also want a healthy, dynamic, and functioning whole—one that maximizes opportunities for learning, that facilitates teaching and that gets the benefits for the time and energy and resources expended. We want self-renewal too: a continuous cycle of intellectual, physical, and social growth and development. We want a healthy whole and we want happy, healthy, productive individuals—both teachers and learners. Pupils, teachers, and other professionals spend a big chunk of their lives in classrooms; they ought to be pleasant, productive places to be in. Teaching and learning are hard work; both require commitment to be successful; they require supportive environments, policies, and resources to be fully productive.

Both the range and the school are dynamic. They change continuously. And every change in one element causes changes to the whole, to the other elements, and to the relationships among them. Climates change for both ranges and schools. In both we can make the mistake of trying to avoid change and to preserve the status quo in some kind of static state. In neither case are there some unchanging basics to go back to. We need to organize, not only to maintain the whole but also to keep it dynamic: growing, advancing, developing, improving. We need to understand change, plan for it, and cherish it as it happens.

## TAKING A CLASSROOM AS THE WHOLE

Let's consider the nature of a classroom as a whole. As a case in point, we'll imagine a second-grade classroom in Rosewood School, which is open to innovation and supports it. Let's indulge ourselves and say that, within the limits of available time, energy, people, and resources, we can organize any way we choose. Let's assume that all those involved are working sincerely to achieve the optimal education. These are all, of course, conditions that don't always exist and in the real world much of our energy may go to fighting for optimal, and sometimes even minimal, conditions for education to have a chance.

We discover we have thirty children at the start of the school year ranging in age from not yet seven to well past eight. About half are boys, and half are girls. Ours is a big-city magnet school, so we have half neighborhood kids from the multiethnic working-class community and half multiethnic middle-class kids whose parents bring them for the whole language program we're offering. The kids vary considerably in language background. Some are bilingual; a few speak another language and have only limited English. Several American English dialects are present. This is only the fourth year of the whole language program in Rosewood School, and only about half of the teachers are comfortably into whole language, though this year almost everyone is showing some movement.

Now, the fact that we have thirty children assigned to one room and that they all fall within a narrow age span implies some decisions have already been made at a school level: Children are assigned to grades by age levels; the size of each class is about thirty. These are not the only possible ways of organizing assignment of pupils to classrooms. There could be multiage groups, and there could be smaller or larger class sizes. Ratio of pupils to teachers, available space, traditions, and many other factors go into these decisions. Team teaching might mean that there are groups of teachers working with larger groups of pupils. Or each teacher might be assigned a subject and pupils might move from teacher to teacher, as they do in many high schools. Each of these alternatives involves value judgments, but it also changes all the other relationships. The decision to offer a magnet school for pupils from outside the immediate neighborhood is related to complex social, political, economic, and demographic patterns in the community. And it is a political decision, as are all school organization decisions.

As they begin second grade, some of the pupils are reading confidently and writing comprehensibly. Others have just made a beginning as readers and writers. The rest are spread in between. A school policy is to have heterogeneous grouping in assigning pupils to classes. Another is that *every* teacher expects a range of abilities and achievements and plans for it. There is no sense in which a child could be considered "failing" in achievement or fail to be "promoted."

The pupils vary considerably in the range of experience they have had. Some have been read to a great deal at home and own a large number of children's books. Others have had only their first-grade experience with books. But these come from homes where reading and writing are related to getting on with everyday business of the world: getting and keeping a job; reading forms and ads; planning for and going shopping; participating in church; coping with the establishment. Some have never been out of the neighborhood. Others have lived in several countries.

Just to make things more complicated, about half had both a

whole language first grade and kindergarten. The rest had a mix or a range of more traditional experiences. For some pupils reading has been largely basals, workbooks, worksheets, skills, and words. Writing for them has been handwriting: practicing letter formation and copying, carefully, from the board or from worksheets. For others, reading and writing have been merged through predictable books, journal writing, big books, and thematic units. Some are self-reliant—ready to make their own choices, and ready to move around the room as they need to; others expect to do what they are told to do. They may mistake the relative freedom of a whole language classroom for absence of rules and objectives for a while.

Ms. Johnson, the teacher, is in her mid-thirties. She has taught a variety of grades in her eight years of teaching. She's always been child-centered, but three years ago, after two years at home to have a baby and finish her master's degree, she began experimenting with whole language. Two years ago she dropped the basal entirely in her fifth-grade class. Last year, when she switched to teaching second grade, she decided, with the advice of members of her whole language teacher support group, to do without the basal there, too. Ms. Johnson is particularly interested in music and art. She's decided this year to do more with math and science. If you ask Ms. Johnson whether she's a whole language teacher, she'll say something that includes words like *becoming*.

SPACE

The building was built circa 1965 under pressure by civil rights groups to replace antiquated and inadequate facilities in the inner city. Ms. Johnson has scrounged an assortment of tables and chairs to replace the chair-desks she found when she moved into this room last year. She felt the chair-desks were not flexible enough to organize her class for whole language. The room space itself is a challenge: not enough storage, not enough display space, too much chalkboard space, and too little floor space for the flexible arrangements Ms. Johnson and her class would like to try. It seems to have been designed for the arrangement she found when she first entered: a teacher's desk up front, with rows of chair-desks all facing front. In an earlier period, they would have been bolted to the floor.

To facilitate whole language, she and the class, with the support of parents, have made the following adjustments: a rug that is big enough for the whole class to gather on is in one corner. It's used for class meetings and doubles as a work and reading area when pupils spread out with a book or a project. Ms. Johnson had a loft in her fifth-grade room in an older school, taking advantage of the high ceilings and the generosity of a pupil's dad who built it. However, here in this room, lower ceilings preclude a loft, but there is a library alcove created by free-standing bookcases. It's furnished with bean bag chairs and pillows on the floor. The backs of the bookcases provide more display space. By grouping tables, work areas can be created and changed periodically to facilitate current class interests and needs. Some of the unneeded chalkboard space has been covered to create more display space for pupils' work. Often committee work spills over into the corridor outside the room, and special displays adorn the hallway walls.

Both pupils and teacher treat the building maintenance staff very well; they know that it's easier for the staff to clean a room where everything is neat and tucked away and that the maintenance staff needs to understand that their room is orderly but full of finished and ongoing projects. There are class-established rules for cleanup and use of materials. The room belongs to all of them, and they take responsibility for keeping it in good shape. They invite maintenance staff in frequently so they will understand why ongoing projects need to be left out sometimes, why space is used innovatively, and how the janitors can support their efforts. They leave room arrangement maps and thank-you notes for the cleaning crew. The faculty and the principal consider the nonprofessional staff as part of the team. They involve them in planning and respect their expertise in their jobs and in their life experiences.

There are also class-established rules for how and when pupils may move around the room or leave the room, and where particular kinds of work and activities are to be conducted. Ms. Johnson wants them to feel free to obtain materials or books, sharpen pencils, consult references, go to the rest rooms, or get drinks of water as they need and want to. She spends a good deal of time early in the year building a sense of responsibility in her pupils as they get used to this independence.

## CURRICULUM

The curriculum is dynamic and developing, too. Ms. Johnson is continuously evaluating and revising it in the context of state and district policies and guidelines. These holistic guidelines, produced by professionals, including teachers like Ms. Johnson, with the help of a broad range of community representatives, set the priorities and the broad goals. The school's policies are more specific than the district's and state's policies, because they take into account the nature of the community, the pupils, their cultural and educational backgrounds, and their particular values, interests, and needs. But it is in each classroom that the curriculum becomes real: rich, authentic experiences, developmentally appropriate for a particular group of learners.

Ms. Johnson considers herself a learner, too. There is a strong emphasis in her class on problem solving and inquiry. She and her pupils collaborate and negotiate the curriculum together. They learn collaboratively, too. She's not afraid to admit that she doesn't know all the answers.

Ms. Johnson sees development of knowledge and concepts as important for her second graders, as she did for the fifth graders she taught before. But she also sees the development of language and thinking strategies as equally important. So each experience or thematic unit is planned and evaluated to achieve knowledge, thinking, and language growth. Furthermore, she accepts responsibility for social goals as well. In the process of learning, planning, playing, and being together, the pupils form friendships, develop attitudes of respect for others, and become comfortable in using language to achieve mutual goals. These social goals are as important as any of the others in Ms. Johnson's classroom. Pupils are expected to share their abilities and their knowledge and to support each other. Ms. Johnson works hard to build a sense of community in her classroom. The pupils understand that at some time during the year they will be working with every other class member but they will also have choice in any given situation of which classmates they will work with.

To achieve the broad goals of her school and district, Ms. Johnson plans thematic units around problems, issues, and interests. Her goal is to provide her second graders with rich experiences with science, social studies, math, literature, art, music, and drama. Much of this is integrated in these units. A discussion among her second graders on the contrast between city and country has led to a unit which contrasts farm life and city life. It includes inquiry into why these contrasts exist, what the features of their community are and how they got that way, how people meet their needs, how they keep their environment clean and healthy, what real problems they face. Ms. Johnson will read to them, they will read to each other and by themselves. And they will talk to community people to learn. They'll take trips to the country, hear parents and visitors describe their lives and work, and walk through their neighborhoods to see them more fully. And they'll write as they observe, synthesize their understandings, and narrate their experiences. They'll be involved in a wide range of oral and written language in all its many forms and functions, and they'll begin to control the use of all these genres. They'll brainstorm, web their existing knowledge, and frame questions. Each child will build on his or her own experience and feel comfortable using his or her own language in presenting and discussing it.

Ms. Johnson has some ideas of the units she might develop with her class and what resources will be needed, but she is open to alternatives or modifications as her students respond and she senses their interests and needs in the context of world events. Whether it's the geranium dying on the windowsill, an earthquake, or a local political event, Ms. Johnson is ready to respond to the immediate interests of her pupils. She knows she can build broad concepts and strategies for learning on the basis of specific interests. And there will be room for pupils, individually and in small groups, to explore personal interests and develop expert projects which they will share with the class.

In Ms. Johnson's class, both product and process are important. She expects invention of spelling and punctuation in her pupils' writing. She expects miscues in their reading. She expects misconceptions as they move toward understanding. She encourages risk taking, celebrates progress, and mediates learning. Ms. Johnson is a professional kidwatcher: she knows the signs of growth, interest, problems, and hang-ups. She helps her pupils to self-evaluate and to appreciate their own progress; at appropriate times she encourages them to polish and to edit their final products and to move toward written language conventions when necessary. She and her pupils celebrate both growth and excellence, as the work displayed in her room demonstrates.

RESOURCES

Ms. Johnson takes her resources where she can find them. Like generations of teachers, she hopes that they will be provided by school authorities but she is ready to buy, make, borrow, scrounge, beg, or "steal" them, as the need arises. Her criteria is that she wants a range of materials that serve the needs of her curriculum and are suitable for her pupils. She can find useful resources in textbooks and commercial kits, but she is selective in what she takes from them and how they are used. In becoming a whole language teacher, she decided that the texts were resources for her and her kids. She has vivid memories of being forced to follow a teacher's manual, and she's not going to let herself go back to that again. She uses the textbooks rather than letting herself be used by them.

She and her pupils consider the real world rich in resources which can be used or adapted for use. Parents are asked to participate and save milk cartons or shoe boxes to be used for mailboxes, juice cans for paintbrush and pencil holders, and trophies and photographs from vacation trips to illustrate class reports or to decorate displays.

The classroom library grows every year. Ms. Johnson encourages parents to contribute books rather than sweets to honor birthdays. Paperback book clubs also help to provide reading resources. In this school, the librarian helps to provide books and keeps up with units each teacher is planning so that resources can be provided.

THE CLASS AS A LEARNING COMMUNITY

Ms. Johnson's class has named itself "Narnia." It came up naturally when she was reading them *The Lion, the Witch and the Wardrobe.* They've participated in making the rules, named the centers to fit their overall name, and do a good deal of the ongoing work of the class: taking attendance, passing out lunch tickets, taking care of the classroom library. They create the bulletin boards and displays. Discipline is intrinsic. There are no artificial schemes—no assertive discipline. Actually, there is very little use of discipline or punishment at all. When general problems occur, a class meeting is devoted to the matter. Usually the kids are so involved and busy with the ongoing learning that there is little of the misbehavior that comes from boredom and lack of involvement in many classes.

This is not to say that none of the children have problems that they bring into the classroom. But Ms. Johnson tries to deal with such problems before they would lead to confrontations. She has arranged that Mary, who often comes to school sullen and angry because of trouble at home, can go to the kindergarten class to help the teacher for a half hour during the morning if she's gotten her own work started well and hasn't had problems with her classmates. She has Leroy, who always seems to know what to do, checking up on George, who never seems to be confident about what to do. She tries to be close to Carlos as he's settling into a new activity. He's a happy, energetic kid who gets into tussles because other kids take his playful pokes and jabs too seriously.

The kids will tell you that in Narnia "We all help each other." Ms. Johnson has worked hard to establish the value that the class must be a place where they can all feel safe and accepted. They understand that it is their obligation to help others and that at some time during the year they will all have worked with every other class member. Committees are organized for the operation of the class and the conduct of the units with this idea firmly in mind. Ms. Johnson understands that language is the medium of both communication and learning, so she encourages the kids to discuss their solutions to math problems, to try out their understandings on each other, and to present their conclusions when they are ready. They work in pairs, in informal ad hoc groups, and in more formally organized committees. Even in "quiet" reading and writing times there may be an undertone of conversation. Ms. Johnson is aware there are times when a funny line or a touching event in a book must be shared, when advice on an idea for a story is sought, or when collaboration is useful. Her second graders are learning to be aware of other people's need for privacy and to balance it with their own need for response or help.

As a kidwatcher, Ms. Johnson is always seeking insights that will help her help them. She welcomes parents into the classroom and tries early in the year to visit each home. She is not satisfied to simply note superficial behavior. She wants to know why it happens and how to build on the strengths, interests, and experiences of the children. Ms. Johnson expects her pupils to treat each other respectfully, and she treats them respectfully.

## TIME

Time needs to be used productively so there is time for real reading, and real writing, and real involvement in authentic learning. But there also needs to be time for thinking, planning, and socializing.

Time is planned on a long-term, medium-term, and short-term basis. Her thematic units are planned for periods up to three or four weeks in second grade. In fifth grade they were longer. Once the unit is in operation, the kids always know what to do next; they pick up on one day what they were working on the day before. There are regular rules for how they may use their time during work periods.

And, in most cases, they can negotiate to continue reading a book or writing a story. They are also always free to continue to work at home at something they began in school. Ms. Johnson watches how kids use their time. She adjusts her expectations, and she helps the children plan their time and become comfortable with their choices.

Ms. Johnson helps her pupils develop their sense of time and time-telling as she involves them in planning their use of time. One rotating responsibility for pupils is reminding her and the class when it is time to stop work or activities, to clean up, to get ready to go home or to recess. Weekly and daily schedules are constructed and prominently displayed. Time lines for units are also developed. Ms. Johnson wants pupils to have a sense that time must be used wisely and productively, but she doesn't want them to feel oppressed by having too much to do in too little time.

## GONE BUT NOT FORGOTTEN

Let's consider some traditional things that aren't happening in Ms. Johnson's classroom: She doesn't organize around textbooks and basal readers. If there are any in the room, they are used as resources. In the country/city unit, some of the pupils might choose some stories with farm settings to read from the basal. A science activity on planting seeds and observing their development might be used by a committee. But the workbooks, black-line masters, and drill sheets are gone. Ms. Johnson keeps hoping she'll find some useful suggestions in the teacher's manuals, but she always comes away turned off by the command form of the language there and the triviality of the exercises. In their place are a wide range of fiction, nonfiction, and informational books, as well as magazines, newspapers, and real-world print matter, like signs, cereal boxes, and forms.

The part language curriculum with separate periods allotted to spelling, handwriting, grammar, punctuation, and phonics is gone. Ms. Johnson and her class deal with those in the context of their reading and writing. If their writing is to be published, they edit it. In reading and writing conferences and in mini-lessons or strategy lessons, Ms. Johnson calls attention to strengths and needs.

To the extent that she can, Ms. Johnson minimizes the impact of standardized tests and report card grades on her pupils. She has a wide range of ongoing informal evaluation techniques which she uses. She uses more formal devices, like miscue analysis, when she needs more in-depth information about individual pupils. She keeps portfolios of the pupils' work and anecdotal records of their progress. She summarizes each conference with a pupil in terms of growth.

## SELF-DEVELOPMENT AND SELF-EVALUATION

In her holistic planning, Ms. Johnson recognizes that she must plan for her own development, too. That's why she joined a whole language teacher support group, why she belongs to other professional organizations and reads their journals, and why she attends local, regional, and national professional conferences. Some of her best ideas have come from what other teachers have written in books like *Organizing for Whole Language, The Whole Language Evaluation Book* (Goodman, Goodman, and Hood, 1989), *Workshop 1* and *2* (Atwell, 1989, 1990), and *Ideas and Insights* (Watson, 1988).

She expects her administration to support her professional growth through useful staff development programs and through release time and travel expense support.

Ms. Johnson has found her own voice in writing and in presenting her own ideas at conferences. The recognition her risk taking and innovations have been given encourages her to keep planning for her own growth and that of her children. She's begun to make presentations at local and regional conferences. Her classroom is open to visitors, and they come with increasing regularity. She's written for the local whole language newsletter, and she and Ms. Perez, her principal, will have an article in *Instructor* on Rosewood's curriculum soon.

## ORGANIZING THE SCHOOL HOLISTICALLY

As I discussed how a second-grade classroom is planned and organized as a unified whole, it was impossible to avoid bringing in characteristics of the organization and policies, and planning of the school in which the classroom would be found.

Principals, like teachers, have considerable latitude within state and central curricula, policies, laws, and regulations in planning for the whole, in this case the school. In Rosewood Elementary, our hypothetical magnet school, Ms. Perez considers herself a team leader whose responsibility is to insure the optimal education for the pupils. One advantage she has, as principal of a magnet school is that many parents have chosen to send their children to Rosewood for its whole language program. They expect the program to differ in important ways from traditional programs.

Ms. Perez takes advantage of this level of parental interest by involving parents, both from the neighborhood and from outside the neighborhood, in planning at all levels. They are welcome to visit classrooms and are encouraged to help the teachers and offer their expertise and resources to the school. With a parent-teacher committee, a regular newsletter keeps parents and the community aware of what's going on and particularly what's new. A parent with some newspaper experience makes sure that the media hear of special events and programs and of the exciting ongoing activities in the school. The principal invites state legislators and school board members to school functions whenever it is appropriate.

Ms. Perez never misses an opportunity to demonstrate her respect and appreciation for the teachers and pupils in the school. She's ready to hear a third grader read a book he's just published, attend a book tea in a fifth grade, take a first-grade teacher's class so he can attend a district committee meeting, or hear what a committee of fourth graders are planning for a field trip and consider their requests. Ms. Perez is in and out of classrooms all the time. She knows the pupils by name; she takes an interest in the personal lives of her staff, both professional and nonprofessional; and she makes a serious effort to know the community. She attends community functions, often with several teachers.

None of this suggests that Ms. Perez does not have the responsibilities which divert many principals from such endeavors. But, like Ms. Johnson, Ms. Perez delegates responsibility and thereby shares it. She has an efficient school clerk and office staff who can handle much of the responsibility for filling out forms, ordering and delivering supplies, answering the phone, and responding to emergencies. Because everyone in the school is treated with respect, they tend to respond by acting responsibly. Policies are made collaboratively, so everyone from lunchroom manager, to crossing guard, to janitors know what the school policies are and what their responsibilities are.

Ms. Perez delegates particular responsibilities to her teaching staff or committees of teachers. They plan and organize a school-wide thematic unit every year (this year it was "Finding Our Roots"). They plan special assemblies. They determine the staff development needs and resources. (Ms. Johnson and another teacher, Mr. Rapoport, have agreed to do three sessions on integrating music and art in the curriculum.) They establish the needs for supplies and equipment. Teachers in Rosewood are careful about making demands or complaints: they know they're likely to end up on a committee.

The year before Rosewood became a whole language school was spent with Ms. Perez and a committee of teachers and parents developing a long-range plan for making Rosewood a whole language school. Staff development began that year. With financial support from the district's alternative schools office, Saturday workshops introduced basic concepts of whole language to the staff and community. Teachers from other schools in the district were invited to attend as well. The staff development involved some local university faculty and teachers in the district, including a few from Rosewood already into whole language.

By the end of the year, a few teachers chose to leave Rosewood, opting not to "go whole language," as they put it. But there were many others eager to take their places. The district bent its rules to facilitate the transfers. The union, consulted on the plans, agreed to the modified procedures. Parents involved in the planning held special PTA meetings to bring the community in on the changes that would occur. Some parents took the option of shifting to other open schools in the district, but there were more than enough parents eager to have their children in a whole language magnet school to take their places. By the second year of the whole language program, the school had a waiting list, which grows each year.

Key, ongoing aspects of the long-range plan include changing curriculum, resources, use of staff, space, and time. In no case did the plan call for immediate changes. Careful transitions were planned. Staff development programs were planned to facilitate all changes. At the end of each year, when the plan is evaluated, it is modified to take into consideration new insights and needs.

The school district contracted with the local university for 40 percent of Dr. Leroy Elston's time to work with staff in developing the whole language program. Dr. Elston works with a number of schools in the district and coordinates, with Ms. Perez, the Rosewood staff development. He often meets with committees working on curriculum, resources, space, and time. He also spends time in the classrooms at the request of teachers. Several of Dr. Elston's graduate students are working with teachers on collaborative research studies in their classrooms. Undergraduates are in Rosewood classrooms doing field assignments and student teaching. Three of these have subsequently joined the Rosewood staff.

The school, under Ms. Perez's guidance, plans its use of time carefully. With the support of the parents, Ms. Perez negotiated with the central administration to reorganize the school week. Four days a week, school hours were extended by thirty minutes. This makes it possible to dismiss school at 1:30 P.M. on Thursdays so that the rest of the afternoon is available for staff development and staff committee meetings. This small change was not easy to achieve. Bus schedules had to be carefully negotiated; the extended day-care program, which operates at the school for children of working parents, had to be persuaded to offer extra hours on Thursdays. Even crossing guards had to agree to change their hours. But the staff planned well, and the community gave its support.

There are no pull-out programs at Rosewood. All special staff work with the teachers in their classrooms. Mr. Chinn, the Chapter 1 resource teacher, works with his target population in each classroom. He plans with the teachers and supports their reading and writing programs in creative and holistic ways. The same is true of Ms. Cervantes, the ESL/Bilingual teacher and the special education staff. Besides supporting the holistic philosophy of the school, there are no longer the time disruptions that plague so many schools.

Though the physical plant of the school is traditional, several creative changes have taken place in the use of space. Ms. Perez successfully lobbied the district administration so that some walls between rooms could be replaced with sliding doors. Already some kindergarten and first-grade teachers are teaming, using the space and furniture more flexibly with the sliding doors fully or partially open. There are tentative plans for some cross-age teaming, which will require minor remodeling of two or three adjacent rooms. An artist in residence, funded by a humanities grant, is working with a team of upper-grade children to create a mural for the building entrance depicting the history of the community.

Space outside rooms in school corridors has been arranged to facilitate student group activities and display of pupils' work. This requires a few tables and chairs, some bulletin boards, and some judiciously placed waste receptacles. The PTA has provided some live plants to make the corridors look less institutional. Outside the school, a series of campus beautification projects have been conducted by teachers and pupils. The goal is not only a more attractive school site but to provide the children and the community with a sense of pride, ownership, and participation. Incidents of vandalism have dropped dramatically.

Ms. Perez is firmly committed to the whole language curriculum and resources, but she recognizes the need for planning transition away from traditional programs. No new basals have been purchased, but teachers are free to use the old ones to the extent they wish, as long as they plan time to include real literature and have begun to develop classroom libraries. Use of reading and spelling workbooks has decreased notably each year, as has the use of commercial worksheets. Ms. Perez and Ms. Johnson are on a district committee lobbying for every elementary school to have a library and a professional librarian. Right now Rosewood shares a librarian with another school. But, through parent volunteers and the student library club, Rosewood's library continues to grow. By not buying basals and workbooks, Ms. Perez and the staff have several thousand dollars every year to spend on trade books and other resources.

Dr. Elston has helped teachers who had not gotten a writing program started to make some good beginnings. The school now holds a noncompetitive young authors' celebration every spring, and a poetry magazine is published every two months. A technology team has developed a plan for bringing computers into every classroom for use in the writing program.

Ms. Perez facilitates her staff visiting each other's classrooms. She frequently asks teachers to demonstrate particularly innovative whole language activities for the whole faculty or for grade-level teams. She welcomes visitors to her school and uses the opportunity to showcase the innovation going on and give some visibility to the teachers. Hardly a week goes by without visitors coming to Rosewood. Groups of teachers have presented at local TAWL, IRA, and NCTE conferences, as well as state, regional, and national conferences. There is a sense of participation in a dynamic, exciting, and successful program on the part of the staff, the pupils, and the community. This year the school will host a district-wide whole language fair.

The district, as part of its holistic plan, is moving away from its traditional report card and letter marks to a narrative report that goes out three times a year to parents. Each report will be accompanied by parent-teacher conferences. Ms. Perez was quick to volunteer Rosewood as a trial site for the new reporting system. Though the district still uses standardized achievement tests, there is growing recognition that the tests are incompatible with the holistic curriculum and the proposed new reporting system. As the district changes how it treats teachers, it is coming to recognize that the evaluative judgment of informed professional teachers is far more useful than information from machine-scored tests. Next year the achievement tests will be dropped for kindergarten through second grade. And plans exist to phase the tests out gradually in elementary and secondary schools.

## WHOLE LANGUAGE FOR WHOLE DISTRICTS

I've tried to lay out the holistic organization and planning that go into developing whole language classrooms and schools in some detail. I believe strongly that the only real change in education is what takes place at the chalkface where pupils and teachers meet in the classroom. On the other hand, no classroom is an entity unto itself: The policies of the school strongly limit what may happen in classrooms. Though many strong whole language teachers have succeeded in building whole language in their classrooms without support from their colleagues, ideally we need whole language schools for whole language classrooms.

I've suggested how schools can be planned to support whole language and to facilitate change toward whole language for teachers. One good way for a school system to begin its evolution to whole language is to support pilot school programs where administrators and teachers are ready to move with the support of their community. That's why I've discussed a hypothetical magnet school. There are now many—perhaps hundreds—of such pilot whole language schools all over North America. In some school districts, there may be one such school; in others, several. A few are described in this book.

There is a very different set of problems when a school district, state, or province decides, as a matter of policy, to move to whole language. There is no way that whole language can be mandated or required of teachers who do not understand it and are not committed to it. Where it has become the prevailing model, as in New Zealand, that change was accomplished through a gradual, carefully planned transition—an evolution over many years' time. In some of the Canadian provinces and in some of the Australian states, it has been possible to achieve whole language policies which are widely accepted. But changing what happens at the chalkface, that is, turning policy into classroom reality, requires time, holistic planning, and real respect for the professionalism of teachers. Australia has developed teacher-teaching-teacher staff development programs to disseminate whole language.

When the administration of a school district commits itself to whole language, it must be ready to plan holistically. It's not enough to get rid of basals, run some large-scale, one-shot staff development programs, or adopt a beautifully phrased policy that says all the right things. Every change leads to the need for many others. Too much happening too fast brings insecurity and defensiveness on the part of teachers who need some time to get used to being treated like professionals. So there needs to be plenty of time to fully achieve the transition. Here are some steps I think school systems could take:

1. Develop a holistic plan that involves all of the people who have a stake in the system. Consider not only where the system wants to go but also where they're coming from. Be careful to consider what institutional changes would be needed, such as staff and pupil assignment policies, distribution of funds and resources, text and other resource acquisition and distribution policies, line and staff structures, and distribution of decision making and authority.
2. When a draft plan has been completed, circulate it as widely as possible so that professionals, pupils, parents, and community people all have a chance for input.
3. Support teachers and administrators who are ready, willing, and able to make their shifts to whole language. Don't rush anybody, but don't hold back those who are already moving forward. Use them as much as possible as models, for demonstration and pilot centers, and as key participants in the planning.
4. Establish a time line that allows for steady, deliberate change with sufficient time for all the professionals to make their own transitions.
5. Commit the resources necessary for staff development, in-class support services, and the cost of moving to more appropriate use of time, space, resources, and people.
6. At all levels from classroom to district, systematically evaulate the program and gather data to document the benefits and continue the dynamic process.

Evolution or revolution—the change to whole language is a basic and pervasive one. It is in essence, a move to bring today's schools in line with today's wisdom on the most effective education for our society. It can't work if it's only lip-service or an attempt to achieve the benefits of whole language without the systematic changes it requires. That's why it requires holistic planning.

> *Whole, whole in the school.*
> *Where there's language and thinking at play,*
> *Where seldom is heard,*
> *A discouraging word,*
> *And the kids are productive all day.*

# 2

## A CELEBRATION OF LITERACY: ONE SCHOOL ORGANIZES FOR WHOLE LANGUAGE

Linda Dorn / Dianne Taylor / Micki Orian / Pam Pearce

Is that Shakespeare you hear in the fourth-grade room? Are those sixth graders telling the tale of the Twistmouth family? Are those dog biscuits being wrapped in bright red paper?

If you had visited Stephens School during our celebration of literacy, you would have seen and heard all this and more! We are a community of literacy learners, and it is appropriate to celebrate our learning!

To celebrate literacy is to celebrate our humanity. It is to celebrate the growth that all of us have experienced this year. Many events happened during our weeks of celebration.

Children's work spilled from rooms to hallways. Visitors participated in our celebration as they stopped and shared books we had written and heard the "goings on" of our day.

One resource student who designed an invitation to school board members, our superintendent, and other officials discovered that, truly, "reading transforms your life" (Figure 2-1). We are certain that those who came to join our celebration agreed.

On the day our special visitors came, a cake decorated with balloons was served by students using their best "company" manners.

Clifford, the Big Red Dog, joined us to celebrate his birthday. Each classroom came forth to present Clifford with a unique gift. The man who volunteered to wear that heavy, hot costume was properly appreciative of all the presents brought forth. We could tell that his favorite was the Big Book written by the first graders.

The storytelling festival Stephens hosted was another highlight of the year. Five Little Rock, Arkansas, elementary schools participated, as well as high school and university student storytellers.

The dragon kite, made of decorated paper plates and tissue streamers, was our celebration's official "mascot." Stories, poems, skits, and dragon research abounded as together we brainstormed a name, where he came from, and how he liked hanging in our front hallway.

Now . . . the kids are gone; the memories linger. Empty halls still echo the sounds of Shakespeare and tale telling. Is that Clifford barking?!

It was truly a celebration befitting a community of learners! We reflect on how we got here.

## GETTING IT ALL TOGETHER

Stephens Elementary School is an inner-city school with a 99 percent black population in Little Rock, Arkansas. Most of our children are labeled at risk. A couple of years ago, our staff began to look seriously at our reading and language instruction. We began to study the whole language approach as an alternative to the traditional basal reader. We were convinced that the heavy emphasis on isolated

**Figure 2-1** *Kelly's Invitation*

skills through workbook pages and drill sheets had failed our children. We believed children could learn to read from all kinds of materials if those materials were meaningful and appropriate to their experiences and their language.

In the 1987-1988 school year, our school had been designated a literature specialty school by our district and had been issued class sets of trade books to be used as a part of our reading program. With our specialty label, several of our teachers began using literature exclusively and supplementing literature sets with library books and student-written books. Several other teachers were using their basal readers in limited ways, mostly as a supplement to their literature program. Everyone was using literature to some degree. Most of us were whole language teachers long before we ever acknowledged ourselves as such. The more we read about whole language, the more we identified with its beliefs. With this realization, we were ready to commit ourselves to becoming a literature-based whole language school.

With the decision to become whole language, we started planning and organizing toward that goal. The actual planning stages began over the summer months with the implementation of a core literature planning committee comprised of the principal, the reading specialist, and a representative sampling of classroom teachers. The committee's primary function was to outline an effective, whole language program built on a theoretical base. We believed that teachers must have knowledge of the reading process and how children learn and be able to make decisions about their own teaching practices based on theory. The committee proposed several initiatives over the summer: the EYE (Expand Your Experiences) reading program was one, and the adoption of literary themes was another.

The literature planning committee also initiated groups to deal with particular aspects of the program. There were five subcommittees of classroom teachers, focusing on themes, materials, evaluation, in-service, and public relations.

**Themes.** We decided early during the first year that monthly themes would revolve around literary styles. Our purpose for using literary themes was based on the belief that story structure plays an important role in children's understanding of a text (Smith, 1986; Adams & Bruce, 1982; and Ferreiro and Teberosky, 1983).

One of our main criticisms of the basal reader is that stories tend to jump from type to type and children are not allowed enough time to note relationships within story patterns. Research studies (Pearson, Hansen, and Gordon, 1979) support the belief that readers who develop schemata for a particular pattern appear to understand more.

The theme committee's major function was to organize theme materials for each upcoming month. Packets of relevant materials— with suggestions for activities, projects, and book lists—were put together by selected teachers (of the month) and distributed to all classrooms. It was understood that these were just suggestions, and teachers and students were free to explore and expand on their own. It should be noted, also, that classrooms were not restricted by the themes. Everyone was encouraged to participate on a school-wide level in the themes, but the degree of participation was controlled by the individual students and the teachers. This procedure was based on the philosophy that children are intrinsically motivated to learn if they are interested and involved in decision making; therefore, if students and teachers in any class felt they had outgrown a particular theme and desired to work on projects outside the theme, this was encouraged.

**Materials.** Because of the special needs of our children, our school received special funding from the state. We chose to spend the money on additional class sets of trade books, predictable Big Books complete with student copies, a bookbinding machine, and a storeroom full of bookmaking and publishing supplies. We started out somewhat hesitant about purchasing workbooks, but we decided that a workbook which emphasized comprehension might be a good transitional tool for teachers who were moving from the basal reader to the whole language approach. We carefully selected workbooks that included DRTA predicting procedures through short story selections, mapping activities, and follow-up writing lessons. Interestingly enough, by midterm of the first year, our teachers decided that the workbooks were no longer needed or wanted: their reasons were that "workbooks are still workbooks, regardless of their format, and re not a substitute for real reading." Needless to say, by the end of the school year, we decided that workbooks would not be a part of our reading program for the second year. It was evident that the more teachers were learning about reading theory, the more this theory set them free to teach in the way they wanted to.

**Evaluation.** The problem most stressed at meetings was the issue of evaluation. We realized that since state funding had financed much of our program, documentation was crucial. The committee's job was to present an evaluation program that would include informal measures for teacher and student purposes, but would provide, as well, standardized measures for administrative purposes. Since most teachers considered other measures more valid and relevant, particular attention was given to researching and studying different types of evaluation used in whole language programs. Several types of evaluative measures were presented by the committee, and the following were adopted by most of our classroom teachers: (running) reading and writing records; assessments of reading strategies employed by students; tape recordings of children's oral readings; evaluation of reading miscues; writing samples with writing evaluations by both students and teacher; conference logs; attitude scales; interest inventories; and teacher observation.

**In-service.** The in-service committee's primary responsibility was to discover what the teachers and administration wanted and to implement identified in-service. Teachers' concerns fell into four categories:

1. How to evaluate
2. Effective ways to implement the program
3. How to teach skills
4. How to motivate (students and teachers)

The first planned in-service of the year had to do with evaluation. Informal measures were explained, checklists were handed out, and teachers worked together in small groups to discuss the procedures. Professional books and articles about whole language evaluation, reading strategies, miscue analysis, and kidwatching were purchased by the school and became the foundation for a new professional whole language library. As the year went on, the issue of evaluation began to resolve itself as teachers became more comfortable with themselves and the growth of their students.

The second concern, which dealt with implementation, was addressed in several ways. One of the most significant was bimonthly sessions during which teachers shared successful experiences from their classrooms with each other. Videos on whole language were added to our professional library, and a whole language consultant (Virginia Pearce from Texas) was hired to conduct a two-day workshop to help teachers implement their program. The greatest contributions, however, came from the teachers, as they excitedly shared the many wonderful things they were doing with their students in hallways and lounges and after school.

The issue of skills and keeping motivation high began to take care of itself. As teachers became more knowledgeable about reading theory, they began to see how the learning of skills was happening as part of the holistic reading and writing experience.

**Public relations.** We realized that positive publicity concerning the whole language approach and the success of our children would help to insure its acceptability in the community. The school, as a whole, began an all-out campaign to advertise our whole language approach. During the school year, we encouraged visits by students from the University of Arkansas' Education Department, teachers and principals from neighboring school districts, and the district superintendent (who personally visited classes and invited us to the school board meeting for a special presentation). Because we realized the importance of educating the public on whole language, the press was invited to the school to observe the approach in action. The result was a wonderful feature article: "NEW APPROACH INSPIRES STEPHENS STUDENTS TO READ: Hundreds and Hundreds of Books Read!" Throughout the year, our principal continued sending invitations to schools, school board members, district personnel, a state representative, and the governor. Public relations was viewed as a shared responsibility among the staff; however, it was felt that a PR committee helped to funnel newsworthy events to the proper sources.

**Parental involvement.** A major component of any school's public relations is with parents. First, we created a literate school environment so that parents, upon entering the school, were immediately immersed in print. Student-written books of all sizes and shapes hung on cuphooks lining every available space inside and outside classrooms. Stories, which showed children's invented spellings, as well as writing projects which clearly identified the writing process with its multiple drafts, were available for parents to read and become a part of the whole language movement.

Monthly newsletters sent home kept parents informed of the myriad of reading and writing events within classrooms. Other happenings, such as storytelling sessions, school plays, career day, and field day, not only involved parents but also allowed them to experience the excitement of whole language learning.

Second, we decided to help our parents understand the whole language approach. A September PTA meeting addressed our move to whole language, what it meant to our students, how parents could help, and the types of evaluative measures that would be used in the approach. Preschool meetings were held to educate parents about emergent literacy. Collections of articles were compiled into a handbook with suggestions on how parents could create a literate home environment for their children. All parents and visitors, upon entering the school, were given a handbook stating our philosophy of how children learn and the whole language approach as it applies to these beliefs.

Knowing that the link between home and school is important for a child's literacy development, we each took seriously our responsibility to involve parents in the school.

Parents' literacy skills were addressed through a collaborative project between Stephens and the Literacy Council of Pulaski County. Bo Montgomery, Director, assigned tutors to any parents who expressed a desire to strengthen their literacy skills. This became an intergenerational literacy project, which has grown into our Family Literacy Project with an on-site tutoring center. One special success story resulting from the project is about a grandmother who asked to be tutored so that she could read stories to her kindergarten grandchild, a student at our school. You can imagine the pride we all felt at the end of the year during a Flexible Friday session when she took the stage to read *King Louie Katz* while the kindergarten class enacted the story.

These things—ordinary and extraordinary—give parents the opportunity to become involved in the school. In spite of our best efforts, low parental involvement remains a problem. However, we believe that the books, the warm feelings, and the success stories our students carry home will, in time, positively affect parental involvement.

### AND WE BEGIN TO GROW . . .

As our program developed, we expanded our emphasis to all aspects of language development. We organized Flexible Friday, a school-wide bimonthly event, to be a shared oral experience. Student language projects ranged from reciting a poem to enacting a play to singing a song to sharing a favorite book. One of the greatest rewards of Flexible Friday was that our students became more willing to take risks and accept responsibility for their actions. Children have gained confidence in their ability to speak in front of their peers and their teachers. Overall, Flexible Friday provides authentic literacy events for our children and enables our teachers to move toward a language-based program in a nonthreatening way.

One of our "beary" special success stories last year came about as a result of our first venture into a theme—"Bears." "Beary" special events included:

1. Research projects on bears
2. Writing activities growing out of "bear experiences"
3. Bears in literature
4. Math activities—"The Bear Facts"
5. Vocabulary—original crosswords, puns, "bear" lists
6. Original skits and plays
7. A mascot for the month—a huge bear complete with a Stephens School T-shirt

Our principal added to the fun and the learning with his "beary" special morning announcements, which were liberally sprinkled with puns which became almost "unbearable."

This "beary" special month ended with a Flexible Friday event—a parade covered by the press. Children and teachers brought teddy bears from home and paraded from classrooms to the cafetorium where they shared "bearographies." This was presided over by a panel of bear dignitaries, which included Paddington Bear, Papa, Mama, and Baby Bear, Corduroy Bear, and the Biggest Bear. Some children simply shared the origins of their own teddy bears, while others had dressed their bears to represent famous personalities. One child's bear became Mean Joe Green—"the meanest, baddest bear to ever play for the Pittsburgh Steelers."

In evaluating Flexible Friday at the end of last year, it was decided that, while it had served as a transitional springboard, sharing was now occurring between the classrooms regularly. Flexible Friday had served its purpose.

At the end of our first school year, the theme concept was evaluated. We decided that themes had a motivating effect on the students and teachers and that they tended to pull the school together in a positive literacy experience. We decided, however, to abandon the themes of literary styles. This was not done because our beliefs had changed; in fact, the year's successes had convinced us even more strongly that a child's knowledge of text patterns may be the basis of comprehension and that the role of story structure is crucial in our reading program. Instead, the change was brought about as teachers' knowledge of reading theory grew and they realized they no longer needed a literary theme to enable them to teach relationships and characteristics of story patterns. Broader themes, such as giants and animals, were adopted for the second year.

**Our EYE is on you.** In organizing our program, we always came back to our basic beliefs about reading. We believe that reading is language based and agree with Frank Smith that "children learn to read by reading, just as they learn to talk by talking." We also believe that meaning is derived from a child's prior knowledge or background experiences. It is therefore our responsibility to provide our children with a wide range of background experiences and endless opportunities to read and share.

The classes file into the cafetorium. It is the end of an old month and time to embark on a new school-wide reading adventure. As the Stephens' students settled comfortably on the floor, adults—aides, teachers, and principal—one by one take the spotlight to advertise their book of the month. This scene forms the setting for our EYE (Expand Your Experiences) reading program. EYE was designed to bring all students and all adults in our school together in a shared reading experience and, at the same time, expose all involved to a wide range of good literature in small-group settings.

Our delight at the involvement in and response from teachers and students to our themes led to the suggestion that the EYE readers be encouraged to carry the monthly theme concept over to their groups.

The program has not been without problems; it was altered several times during the course of its first year. One major concern of the program has been the time factor. EYE was designed to take place during the first twenty minutes of the school day. Unfortunately, this was the time during which teachers were busy taking attendance and lunch count. Of greater significance, the time previously reserved for Uninterrupted Sustained Silent Reading (USSR) was now being replaced by EYE. Since EYE was not designed as a substitute for the silent reading period, teachers had to make additional adjustments in their already too-tight schedules to accommodate USSR. These were problems teachers worked out on individual terms; however, in the final evaluation, it was concluded that the advantages of EYE outweighed the disadvantages. The rewards were obvious; for with the implementation of EYE, not only were students being read to each day but teachers and students across the grades were getting to know one another through the sharing of books.

The attitude throughout Stephens School is that everyone can read and write and that reading and writing are fun. In the following sections, four Stephens teachers share how they organize their own classrooms within the whole language school.

---

# NOW THAT I AM IN MY ROOM, WHAT DO I DO?
**Linda Dorn,** *Grade Three*

"The basis of comprehension is prediction" (F. Smith, 1982, p. 68), prediction cued by a reader's prior knowledge or background experiences. Since prediction forms the basis of my reading instruction, I begin the school year by conducting prediction awareness sessions where my students discover the relevancy of prediction in their everyday lives. For example, our classroom is across the hall from the lunchroom and we are always tantalized by smells of food cooking. This simple incident becomes a vehicle for prediction awareness. Questions such as, "What do you predict we will have for lunch today?" serve to cue the students into thinking about using prediction as a problem-solving technique. Prediction is an ongoing, stable component of my reading plans.

The following dialogue illustrates the beginning of my lesson on prediction.

T: (*Holds up a large poster board with the word PREDICTION written across the top*) Who can read this word?

S: *Prediction.*

T: Who can tell me what the word PREDICTION or PREDICT means?

S: I'm not sure.

T: Let me put it this way. Who can "predict" what the word PREDICTION means? What do you think I want you to do?

S: You want us to guess what it means?

T: (*Writes "to guess" on the poster board next to the word PREDICTION*)
(*The discussion continues.*)

T: Sometimes you can predict based on something that has happened to you before or something that you already know. (*Writes "to make a guess based on something you already know" on the chart next to the meanings for PREDICTION*)

S: Yeah, that's like I know my little brother is gonna' cry every time I go out to play. He always wants to go with me and he always cries, so I know I'm gonna' have to sneak out before he sees me.

T: All of you are using predictions. How are you able to predict these things will happen?

S: We're using clues??

T: Sure, you are using things you already know about to help you make new predictions. Think for a moment what it would be like if you were unable to predict. What if you were unable to predict that Thomas would be on the phone, or that you would win the ball game, or that your little brother would cry to go with you?

S: That would be weird.

T: OK, let's try this. (*Shows the cover of the book* Jumanji *to the students*) What kinds of clues can you use to help figure out what this book might be about?

s: Well, the picture and the name of the book can tell us.

t: Sure, you are using the title and picture clues to help you predict what the book is about before you have even read it. The important thing is that you are willing to make predictions; because it is as you said, if you can't make predictions about something, it would be really weird, or hard to understand what is happening.

Prediction strategy lessons help children to become aware of the role of prediction as a reading strategy and guide them to discover its relationship to comprehension.

This year there are twenty students in our class; six attend Chapter I reading, and two attend special education. It is important that all children in our class feel successful; therefore, I provide all children with successful reading experiences. Everyone participates in cooperative learning. Students are paired as student teachers, reading partners, proofreading teams, and artists-in-residence.

At the beginning of each month I organize the materials and resources I plan to use for each particular time or theme. These resources become only a small part of what I will eventually end up using to launch the children into the theme, or they may constitute a necessary component of my reading program. My lesson plans are a collaboration between my theory of reading and the resources which my students and I choose to use. As other whole language teachers have stated: "Theory sets you free to teach the way you want," and I am able to teach the way I want because I have a theory to operate from.

For instructional purposes, I generally have four heterogeneous reading groups that are changed regularly, organized according to the need of the moment. My primary purpose for grouping is to allow small-group interaction between the students. However, grouping is not a "law" in our classroom, and students are encouraged to participate in additional groups of interest to them. Today is October 1, the beginning of mystery theme month. I have gathered *my* materials for the week and outlined *my* lesson plans. I have chosen *my* groups according to *my* purposes for the week and have decided that I will teach reading using selected mystery books from the library.

## GROUP 1

**Day 1.** I tap the children's prior knowledge by having them tell me what they already know about mysteries. I record their information on a chart. I give each student a copy of the story guide for mysteries to be used while reading their book. We read over the questions and discuss them. We talk about mystery books (or movies) they have read (or seen) and relate them to the mystery guide. Then I show the children the mystery books I have read ahead of time and invite or encourage students to select one book for reading and sharing with their classmates. I always have extra books on hand to allow the students a wide selection. I then share the schedule for the week with the students and they begin reading their books.

**Day 2.** The children continue reading their mystery books. I conference individually with the children about their books assessing the students' understanding of the book and of the underlying structure of the story. I also use conference time to have the students predict the rest of the story. I remind the students that the books should be completed by Wednesday and the story guide should be filled in.

**Day 3.** The children come to the reading group with their books and completed story guide. In the meantime, I have a story guide on a large sheet of butcher paper for recording information. As the children, one by one, share about their book, I write this in the appropriate section on the chart. The children must support their statements with quotes from the book: For example, if a student describes a character as being selfish, the child is encouraged to prove this statement with evidence from the book. During this activity, the students are guided to discover the relationship between the mysteries and to form conclusions that mysteries have many of the same internal characteristics (Figure 2-2).

**Day 4.** The students begin preparing projects that relate to their books. I keep a variety of supplies from which the students choose to use in creating projects: hanging book mobiles; book jackets; dioramas of scenes or events from the book; student-made books which have been rewritten and published; maps, mazes, and crossword puzzles; riddles and comic strips of the book; murals,

---

**Figure 2-2** *Mystery Guide*

### MYSTERY GUIDE

1. Who is the main character from your story?
2. What are the qualities of the main character? Which ones are stated in the story and which qualities do you have to infer? (Find a passage from the story to prove your answer.)
3. Who are the other characters?
4. What are the qualities of the other characters?
5. What is the setting of the story?
6. What is the mystery to be solved?
7. What are the clues which help to solve the mystery?
8. How is the mystery solved?
9. Who helps or hinders in solving the mystery?

paintings, clay sculptures, and character masks; puppets, character dress-ups, and plays; and poems and films. If supplies are unavailable for a particular project, students are encouraged to choose another until materials can be located. Students are also encouraged to work together on projects or to enlist the help of class members from outside their group. The fourth day is a day of preparation, and students learn to organize their time wisely to be ready for sharing their projects the following day.

**Day 5.** The members share their projects with the class.

## GROUP 2

For group 2, I collected copies of the witches' chant from Shakespeare's *Macbeth* (Martin, 1973, pp. 300–301). My plans were to have the students read and learn the chant, do extension activities, and share their work with their classmates on Friday. I called the group to the table and tapped their prior knowledge by having them tell me some of their favorite recipes or dishes and to predict some of the ingredients that might be contained in them. Next, we predicted the ingredients a witch might put in her recipe or brew. I recorded the students' responses on the chalkboard and then instructed them to listen carefully to the ingredients in the witches' brew from the witches' chant. After the reading, the students added the new ingredients to the list, and I recorded them on the board. Then I passed out student copies of the book, and we practiced reading the chant together in our "witchiest," scariest voices. Imaginations soared as animals from pages were cut into tiny portions and unidentifiable masses were labeled as brains and guts. The ingredients were glued to a large poster-size black kettle and labeled. Extension activities for the week were to create recipes using the pictured ingredients. Measurements used in various recipes were studied and applied to the witches' brew. The chant was rehearsed in small groups, and props were made as students prepared for our Flexible Friday presentation (Figure 2–3, p. 30).

In organizing the reading program, my ultimate goal is that students will become independent learners willing to take risks and be responsible for their own learning. To accomplish this objective, my reading plans are organized in a redundant, predictable fashion that directs students toward independence. Since specific activities are designed to meet the needs of individuals within the group, students can anticipate the sequence of events. The first day's lesson is generally teacher guided, but lessons from that point on are student directed, with my role shifting more to that of facilitator.

Writing conferences are held as needed, and evaluations become a collaborative effort between the student and the teacher. Unfinished work is filed in individual storage compartments, and students work on these projects daily. Before publication of any written work, students undergo proofreading sessions, evaluations, and final drafts.

**Figure 2-3** *Witches' Brew*

October 12, 1988

# Witches Brew

Ingredients:

1 qt. blood and guts

5 Vampire eyes (found at midnight in an abandoned cemetary.)

1 chopped-up snake (big pieces)

1 cat scull (found at midnight on night of full moon.)

1 chopped-up chicken

one set of fangs of a rattle snake

one mummy's hand

one skinned swamp monster

one nest of roaches

10 qts. of water

1 tep. of spider spit

2 teaspoon of salt

2 teaspoon of pepper

one pinch of suger

two pinches of cinnamon

## Directions

1) Pour in 10 qts. of water
2) Mix it with one quart of blood and guts
3) Bring it to a boil over a hot fire.
4) Stir with a mummy's hard and cook for 1 hour.

A whole language classroom gives the appearance of running "almost by itself," but within every whole language setting, there exists an underlying structure of supreme organization—a day centered in theory and directed by children.

## BUT READING LABS AREN'T SUPPOSED TO BE FUN . . .

**Dianne Taylor,** *Chapter I Reading Specialist*

Amelia's mother was concerned because she felt Amelia was not reading as well as she should. Rather than tell the mother her expectations for a second grader were unrealistic and not based on experience, I evaluated Amelia. She used context beautifully to figure out unknown words, a strategy that, I suspect, her mother did not value. Her reading strategies were mature for her age. I was able to show the mother, both through informal and formal measures, that Amelia was progressing, and the mother relaxed, thereby enabling Amelia to.

I have been a whole language teacher for many years. In fact, I went into the reading specialty area so that I could move away from the confining basals and workbooks so prevalent at that time in the regular classroom.

As the Chapter I reading specialist at Stephens Elementary School, my job involves not only helping the children to become fully literate but also believing in them until they can believe in themselves. Our reading lab is a learning lab—a place to take risks and to learn from mistakes. Years of kidwatching have taught me that reading, writing, speaking, listening, and thinking are best taught interrelatedly.

My reading lab is a busy, cheerful place where kids are surrounded by print. Their work is displayed with honor. Books, magazines, posters, and a myriad of other reading materials abound. The clear message is that reading is important. Many of my students do not always "shine" in the regular classroom, but with individual help and patience they are stars in the reading lab. When I plan for their instruction, I make sure to emphasize their strengths while we work together on their weaknesses. I show them that reading is not only fun but it is also the way to know "the latest." Many of my students believe that reading is sitting around the table answering questions or doing workbook pages.

Now, all of us at Stephens must work to undo these effects of former years of reading instruction.

I structure for success. I make sure that the child basks regularly in what I call the "hero effect." This means making sure that peers see the projects and performances—the successes. This not only promotes authentic literary and speech events but also helps each child see a purpose for becoming literate. Often kids lose the sense of this after years of being exposed to the subskills approach. I also make sure that parents and regular classroom teachers know of each student's progress.

As part of my accountability to the school district and Chapter I, I keep a folder on each child containing pertinent information—both formal and informal assessment measures. I add to this anecdotal entries, interest inventories, writing samples, taped oral readings, and other significant data. I engage in kidwatching. I often ask children about their own reading strategies. Kids are honest and can usually tell you what is giving them problems. This constant interplay of planning, teaching, and evaluation guides my decision making.

My reading lab serves a maximum of eighty students. I see a different group of ten children every thirty minutes for a total of eight classes per day. While I enjoy the interaction a small group affords, I also must work within certain time constraints. I do not meet each class every day; therefore, projects are more difficult to "finish." With only thirty minutes per session I must begin and end on time. Any pull-out program also carries with it other negatives: there is always the worry that my kids are missing other learning. Thus, I feel I must make their time with me really count. The children know I will listen, will help them with each task, and will expect cooperation among them. Since the lab is always full of good things going on, I rarely have to correct anyone. High expectations communicated both in word and deed empower my students as they succeed, and "success breeds success." Learning to revalue themselves takes time and a teacher who won't give up—no matter what. The children take responsibility for their own learning. I serve as facilitator, coach, cheerleader, and teacher. The children know I am there when they need me. Discipline problems rarely arise because the children are interested, busy, and in control of what is important to them. To coordinate with October's mystery month, I chose Mercer Mayer's *There's a Nightmare in My Closet*. Children in grades 1 through 6 participated. I was able to interest the older children under the guise of "doing some special things for the little kids"—a tactic I often employ with success.

With every group, regardless of age, we began with a brainstorming session on our ideas of a nightmare. Tapping background knowledge in this way helps the children feel the anticipation of success. They already know a great deal about the subject. I, of course, participated and shared my own idea of just what comprises a nightmare! At the primary level, I read the book with the children after enjoying Mayer's cover illustration. At all levels, we followed our reading with discussion and a comprehension aid such as a circle story or a story chart.

One of the special things the older kids did was to create a sign that warned of monsters inside the lab. Cooperative learning occurred as older children worked with younger children in cutting out large nightmare shapes based on each child's original nightmare.

The shapes were stapled together and stuffed with newspaper wads to make them "come alive." Bits of fabric, yarn, lace, buttons, glitter, and other junk were used for adornment. The shapes, hung from the ceiling, created quite an eerie effect. This effect set the stage for all our performances and projects. Each day as we began class, we dimmed the lights and set the mood for our "nightmarish" work.

Using a Venn diagram, we compared nightmares with dreams (Figure 2-4). We discussed likenesses and differences and mounted these diagrams on wallpaper for display. It was interesting to see that younger and older children used the same words and feelings to describe nightmares.

We took a random survey of fifty students to determine whether a monster, alien, or animal was the most common main character in a nightmare. Our compiled and published statistics showed that monsters are, by far, most "popular" in Stephens students' nightmares.

Each primary child drew a picture of his or her "worst ever" nightmare and "best ever" dream. These we did while listening first to loud, unsettling music and then to soft, soothing music. We talked about how the music affected our moods and our work. These pictures were bound into a book which was shared with each child's regular class. Several teachers reported that this sparked some very interesting and, sometimes, revealing discussions.

The older children brainstormed how they could get rid of a nightmare. They wrote stories based on their ideas. One group of fifth graders was particularly creative in their imaginings: "How about setting twenty-four mouse traps that go "snap, snap, snap, . . . (to 24!) as the nightmare comes into the room?" As students shared their stories in their regular classrooms, they all felt the "hero effect." As always, afterwards, many of the other children clamored to come to

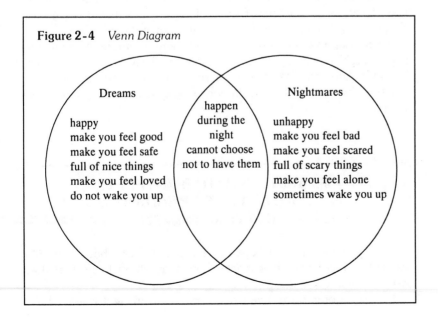

Figure 2-4   *Venn Diagram*

the lab "so I can tell you how I'd get rid of a nightmare." My kids felt very important as they were looked to as "authorities" on nightmare extermination!

When fifth and sixth graders paired off with second graders, they brainstormed together on the same topic. The younger children dictated stories one on one to the fifth and sixth graders, sharing completed stories with the entire group. Later, the older students compared their own stories with the younger children's stories using a Venn diagram. We particularly looked for elements of plot, character, setting, and whether or not a "method" was realistic or fantastic. The older group discovered the maturity of their writing as we discussed how they, not so long ago, had been second graders. They found pride in their growth and process. Self-evaluation can also be revaluing.

Primary children created stick and paper bag puppets of Mercer Mayer's characters. A puppet show traveled throughout the building. Invitations were written and sent "RSVP" so that we could keep track of our schedule. The show was a huge success—not only did it foster quite a "hero effect" but also the necessary reading and writing involved became incidental.

One of the most special things we did was to interview the book's nightmare. After we had brainstormed, all children had a chance to hand in a question they would like to ask the character. Older children compiled the questions and wrote a television script. They chose "Barara Waaah" to host the show, "Night with the Nightmare." The children, working collaboratively, made puppets and painted them to look lifelike. The younger children again wrote invitations to send to each classroom, delivering them with much pride and anticipation.

Showtime arrived, the lights were dimmed, and "theme" music was played as the audience filed in. The cast, assembled behind the puppet stage, questions in hand, was excited and ready to go.

From "Barara's" first question, "Are there anymore like you, Mr. Nightmare?" our audience was spellbound. They even enjoyed Ms. Waaah's slight lisp! We clearly soared in the Nielson ratings (or at least the Stephens)! Once again, whole language teaching worked its magic!

---

## JUMPING IN WITH BOTH FEET: CONTENT AREA READING
### Micki Orian, *Grade 5*

In August when school began, I jumped in with both feet. My students knew I was their teacher, but they didn't know that they would do the teaching.

My classrooms have never been organized in neat rows. I have always grouped my students, usually putting talkers with nontalkers, and moving students randomly when I deemed it necessary. This year I grouped for a purpose. The purpose may vary with the subject being taught, the objective of the lesson, and the interest, gender, behavior, and ability of the students. Sometimes I limit the number per group, sometimes the students choose groups, and sometimes the group size varies. Usually three or four are in a group, but one can also be a group.

I spent last summer immersed in professional reading and became convinced that whole language is for me and the students I would have in my fifth-grade classroom this year.

Although reading has been separated from the content areas for many years, it has been my belief that reading should be a part of *all* subject areas. Reading, writing, speaking, listening, and thinking are all interrelated. You cannot do one of these language components at a time, nor can you just teach one at a time. They are each used continually throughout a day, in all subject areas.

Over the years, I have experimented in teaching my science and social studies classes. Some years I was able to be flexible and try various ways of teaching these subjects. Other years I was not allowed any freedom at all. Each administrator has had a method that I've been required to follow. Last year I was able to experiment by teaching reading throughout the curriculum. I tried many different things. Some things I tried worked and others fell flat.

When I started, we used tables for our groups. Our desks were arranged for large-group activities. Now we use tables, desks grouped together, and the floor. Our classroom may have a different arrangement from class to class as well as day to day. I've become flexible. It is my belief that a busy classroom is not always a "neat" classroom, or a quiet one, but it is a fun one and an interesting one!

During past years, I always informed my students what they already knew. For example, I would say, "You know that birds have feathers and are vertebrates." I never asked my students what they actually did know. I took for granted knowledge my students may or may not have had. This was very dangerous, since I was actually setting up some of my students for failure before they even began.

This year I use KWL as my strategy for teaching reading in the content areas. The letters K, W, and L stand for What I *K*NOW, What I *W*ANT to know, and What I have *L*EARNED. When we begin a new topic, I ask my class, "What do you know about . . . ?" Sometimes the list of what they know is short. When we studied "Animals with Stinging Cells," all we knew was that they are invertebrates. Sometimes the list is very long. When we began a unit on birds, we almost filled the chalkboard. To my surprise, my students knew that birds have hollow bones, feathers, and wings, are warm-blooded, and *much* more.

When we begin a KWL, I use the chalkboard, overhead projector, or a large sheet of paper for the list. I like the paper best because we can hang it up and refer to it often. When we use the chalkboard, it is often necessary to erase before we finish. The overhead is good but sometimes inconvenient during other class times. There are times I do the original KWL using the overhead, then project onto paper to "record?" (Students could do the recording onto paper, tracing words and lines.)

After we reflect on what we already KNOW, we decide what we WANT to know about our topic. I ask, "What do you want to know about . . . ?" Usually this list is long. Some of the most frequent "want to knows" on our lists are: What do they eat? How do they reproduce? How big do they get? I make this list on paper so it can also be used for referrals.

We then break into groups. The students take their textbook, science or social studies, to the group. The lesson is read aloud from the textbook, unfamiliar words are discussed and looked up, and questions are asked and answered by the students. Sometimes I give each group comprehensive questions. The answers are not found in the book, but by reading, discussing, and thinking, the answers can be found.

I have the students do the reading aloud activity for science and social studies for several reasons: 1) Everyone in the classroom will have a common foundation for the lesson. The students do not all have the same prior knowledge. 2) I find when my students read aloud the group's comprehension is improved. When the students are, for example, researching animals in science or states in social studies, I want them to have a broad understanding of the subject. (Later the groups will focus on the topic that has been assigned to them or chosen by them, and they will become experts on that particular topic.) 3) The students can practice oral reading without being assigned to a specified reading group. 4) The other students in the group can stop the reader at any time to ask a question or to have the material clarified either by the other students or by me.

A simple web (Figure 2-5) is used by the group, using information from the textbook. The information for the web can come from the book or be written in their own words. The web helps students see relationships between text material and their KWL. It also helps some groups fine tune their topics.

Finally, our research begins. We use a variety of resources, such as *Ranger Rick, National Geographic, World Book*, library books, trade books—anything available. After reading and discussing what has been found, new information is added to the web. During this activity, the students may refer back to the "I WANT to know" list that has been posted. The group organizes the web facts into paragraphs, using their own words. A draft of the report is turned in to me, along with the completed web. I read it and meet with the group for final discussion. I ask the group questions to be sure they know their topic. First, we go over any unclear areas of their report, and then we make sure all spelling and punctuation is correct. The group makes the corrections. The report is written up by me. A copy is made for each student in the group, and one copy each for the

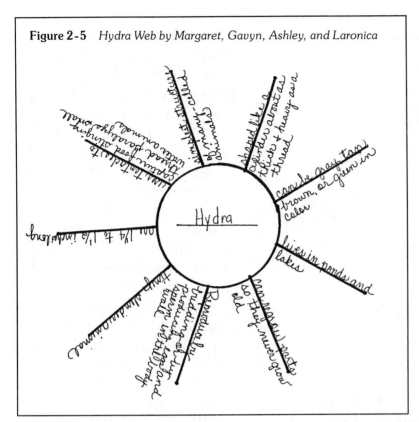

**Figure 2-5**  *Hydra Web by Margaret, Gavyn, Ashley, and Laronica*

classroom and the library. Each student illustrates his or her own copy. The reports are laminated and bound (Figure 2-6, p. 38).

During the group activities, I meet with groups and check their progress, answer questions, help find additional information, and also assist in proofreading the paragraphs.

After we have finished our writing process, we look back to our K and W—what we KNOW and what we WANTed to know. We then discuss what we have LEARNED. We do this in a variety of ways: through large-group discussions, presentations to other classrooms, Flexible Friday presentations, oral reports to the class, compare/contrast charts, and tests. At the end of a study on frogs, we made frog puppets and practiced a Bill Martin skit on frogs. Then we presented the skit to a class of third graders and gave each student and the teacher a frog puppet. My students really enjoy making oral language presentations to other classes in our building.

For science each child has written a book on invertebrates, vertebrates, and experiments we have done. We have rewritten a large portion of our science book. Our science book is written at a difficult level for fifth grade. For my students to learn the concepts in our science book, we had to get it to their level of understanding. We have not covered the entire book, but what we have covered, the

**Figure 2-6**   *Hydra Book*

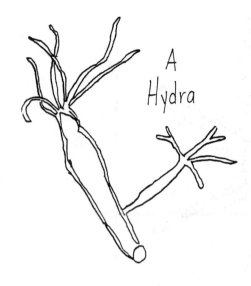

A
Hydra

shape like a cylinder — it is about as thick and heavy as a thread. It is about ¼ to ½ inch long.
    The hydra can be gray, tan, brown, or green. A hydra uses its

tentacles to capture food. The stinging cell or thread paralyzes other small water animals.
    Hydras reproduce by budding or by producing eggs and sperm in the

A hydra is a tiny, slender animal that lives in ponds and lakes.
    The hydra has one of the simplest structures of the many celled — animals. The hydra's

body wall.
    Hydras can regrow body parts — so they never grow old.

students know and enjoy. They take pride in their books and show them off every chance they get.

In social studies we have a class-made book about explorers. We have written biographical sketches and traced their journeys on world maps. We are also working on a book about all fifty states. We are also making a book of maps tracing the history of our state— Arkansas. In our reading class we are reading seven of Laura Ingalls Wilder's books. We combine social studies and reading. We have studied many aspects of pioneer life, and we have many interesting projects going. We have churned butter from whipping cream and eaten it with fresh homemade whole wheat bread. We are in the process of designing and making both a sod house and a log house. We have studied the states Laura and her family lived in and traced their journeys on a large U.S. map.

Everything we do is put up for display. We've put books we have written in the library, and we have hung them on hooks in the hall and from clotheslines in our room. We've taken some to our school's business partner for display in its lobby. The kids love seeing their work displayed and printed in the newspaper.

This method of teaching is really fun for me. My students walk in at 8:00 A.M. and want to know what we're going to do today and when we can begin writing. As a result of their enthusiasm, grades have improved, creativity has been given a shot in the arm, and discipline problems have decreased. Although I'm the teacher, I'm really the facilitator of learning experiences. My students are taking the responsibility for their own learning. They are proud of what they can do and I'm proud of them! Teaching just keeps getting better!

## CAN HAMSTERS TEACH READING?

**Pam Pearce,** *Grade Four*

It's party day. Martin has brought the punch. Charea has brought the chips. Katherine has brought the cookies. John has brought the candy—three bags. We're going to be hyped today! It's Christmas. Surely I can get through this last day before vacation. I have stashed all our goodies safely behind the box labeled Christmas. My various holiday inventories are kept in boxes along the shelf in my class-room. The current holiday box is always just an arm's reach away so that we can add or discard anything we are not interested in.

After attendance and lunch count, we check on our most interest-ing inhabitants, a female and male hamster. Usually one of the children takes control at this juncture, reassuring the class that there is plenty of food and water in the cage. To attend to their emotional needs, Mark coaxes the hamsters down the cage tube into his eager little hands. Big Daddy, the male hamster, runs to Mark willingly. However, Big Mama is not as anxious to visit the little humans. We are all puzzled by her behavior but decide to let her alone. Mark informs us, "She gonna have babies today."

Like a good teacher, I check our calendar of "hamster happen-ings" and say matter-of-factly, "No, I believe it will be a few days. In fact, I'm afraid we will miss the birth of Big Mama's babies. We're going to be out for vacation."

"No, Ms. Pearce, she gonna have those babies today," insists Mark.

As I agree that she might, I notice several children checking our books on hamsters, rodents, and gerbils to confirm the gestation period and due date.

Our morning goes quite well. Two of the girls are involved in writing their book, *How the Hamsters Meet.* It is a love story with soap opera possibilities. John and Stevie are really into poetry with a beat; it pulsates as they work it out using the tape recorder in our "studio." Antonio loves to make puppets. (I love his simple little puppet shows. He knows he'll have at least an audience of one.) So it goes, with everyone reading, talking, or writing as I circulate, watch, admire, and participate with my fourth graders.

All of a sudden Mark yells, "She, Big Mama, Mama laid the babies! And here come another one!"

In one gigantic movement we all seem glued to the cage to see this miracle. Mark cautions us to be calm so we don't make Mama nervous. I absolutely cannot believe my eyes when I see six tiny, pink-skinned hamsters in this little wad of a nest. Then, as we watch, the seventh is born. All I can think is, "Please let that be all." Someone suggests that we write down what Mama is doing in our *Hamster Journal*. Some children grab chairs, some sit on the table, but all, as if by magic, have pencil and paper in hand as they busily watch, "ooing" and writing. There is awe in their remarks as they watch and record Big Mama taking care of her seven babies. They seem to feel it very important to get the details.

One child says, "What that white thing I see through they skin?"

Another child says, "I don't know. They all have it. Write it. Draw it."

Then, unexpectedly, Mama begins to eat one of the babies. The children are horrified. They turn to me and plead, "Do something!"

I reply, "Didn't we read something about this?" Ronnell reaches for a little handbook on hamsters that is on the table. He flips nervously through the book.

"Yip! Right here it say she eats the babies if she have too many to take care of or if she gets nervous." Several children feel she is definitely nervous. Others think seven babies are too many.

"Mark, where is Big Daddy?" I ask.

"Oh, he in my pocket. I told you she gonna have those babies today. I put Big Daddy in here so he won't be messing with 'em. The book say to take Daddy out when the babies come 'cause he like to eat 'em."

All I can say is "Hmmm," and nod my head approvingly. The recess bell rings. The children are anxious to spread the birth news to all their friends. Several children run outside. But what to do with Big Daddy during recess? We cannot put him in a box because he can gnaw right through a box. Big Daddy can even gnaw through plastic. Someone suggests the wastepaper basket would be a safe place for Big Daddy. Good idea! Mark deposits Big Daddy, a little food, and some cedar shavings in the wastepaper basket.

As the day progresses, we watch Big Mama cuddle up with her five (she ate another one) babies. They nurse continuously. Mama licks them and nudges them as if she were assuring herself that they are alive and well. Big Daddy plays in the wastepaper basket. He seems to love it there with bits of crayon and wads of paper.

Of course we can't leave Mama and five babies all alone in the classroom during the holidays. Mark offers to call home to see if he can take them home for the vacation. His mother gives permission for them to reside with Mark during the Christmas holidays. I volunteer transportation and include extra food. Everything is finally under control. What a day!

As always, the custodian comes in to empty the trash just before dismissal. All of a sudden someone yells, "Where Big Daddy?" "He gone!" "The trash gone!" "Mr. Anderson! Mr. Anderson threw Big Daddy away!" As I quickly run with my class to the rescue, several children run ahead, trying frantically to explain about Big Daddy, the babies, the trash. Mr. Anderson is completely confused. Very puzzled, he stammers, "What they talking about?"

Just as excited as the children, but a little calmer, I reply, "Mr. Anderson, one of our hamsters was in our wastebasket. When you emptied the trash, you also emptied Big Daddy, the hamster. I'm sorry, but . . . ." About this time the children are digging in the trash, saying, "Come on, come on . . . Big Daddy, come on . . . ."

With a befuddled Mr. Anderson and an exhausted Ms. Pearce looking on, Big Daddy scampers out from under a punch cup. He is almost smacking his jaws because he's had such a great Christmas party.

After I say my good-byes and take Mark, little sister, and the hamsters home, I return to my very quiet, messy classroom. My thoughts wander to my students, as they so often do. I think of the children who didn't even like the idea of writing a sentence at the first of the year. Reading for them *had* meant completing a worksheet.

We had such a long way to go, and somehow I thought we needed a new stimulus. Since children are interested in animals, I decided on hamsters for the room. It worked! The hamsters became our springboard. The entire class has become so motivated to know all there is to know about hamsters that they read, write, illustrate, tell cute little stories, and compare bits of factual information (Figure 2–7, p. 42). Even journal entries reflected hamster-itis (Figure 2-8, p. 42). The excitement never dwindled.

We're keeping individual journals, as well as a class-dictated journal recorded on a chart tablet used for shared reading.

4-20-89

Today at 11:00 A.M. the hamsters had babies! This is the second litter. Mark was the first one to discover the new arrivals. He said, "Ah! She had those babies!" He quickly put the babies and Momma in the little nursery. Everyone was excited. Everyone wants a baby. They will be able to adopt their baby when it is about 3 weeks old. During lunch Mark gathered celery and carrot sticks for Momma. Momma made a nest for the babies in the nursery while she busily dug in the cedar shavings. When she was comfortable, she gathered her babies around her and went to sleep. When she woke, she put a baby in her pouch! We were afraid she would eat it. It was a relief to see the baby fall out of her mouth and wiggle under Momma to nurse.

**Figure 2-7** *"Hamsters" by Antonio*

<u>Questions</u>

What is some hamsters? brown + white
Who is the care taker? michael + threet
What color is the hamster eye? black
Who got the hamster? mrs Pearce +

<u>Hamsters</u>

Some hamsters bite and they also eat food. Some have babies. Some hamsters clean their hands. Also their eyes are black. Sometimes hamsters are brown and white.

Writer and Illustrated by Antonio Earnest

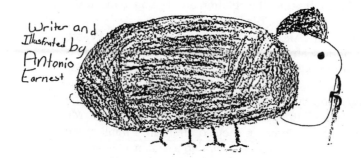

---

**Figure 2-8** *Michael's Journal*

<u>Michael Threet     1-5-88</u>

Today we will clean The Cage Mrs Pearce brought a camera. She will take pictures of our baby hamsters. She will take my Pcture.

---

4-21-89

We decided to keep Momma and the babies in the big cage so they would have plenty of room. When we put Momma in the big cage she ran all around as if she were checking every corner for anything that would hurt her babies. She gathered the babies in a huddle and covered them with cedar shavings and paper towels. She was hiding them. Next Momma seemed to be searching for food. She found some celery and carrots and put those in her nest—like going to the grocery store, bringing the groceries home, and putting them in the cabinets. Daddy is asleep in the little cage. He doesn't seem too concerned about the babies. He doesn't help Momma. She is so busy, she doesn't seem to care if Daddy doesn't help her right now.

4-24-89
After the weekend the babies looked the same—a little fatter, a little more active, and they squeak for Momma. Their tail is longer. They still do not have fur. They look like wads of pink bubble gum.

4-25-89
We took a baby out to measure. We noticed they have light fur. We can still see their skin. We really need to clean the cage, but we hate to disturb Momma and the babies. We watched Momma move the babies. She carried them in her mouth like a cat. She covered them with cedar shavings to hide them for protection. Their ears are more pointed. Tails are longer.

4-26-89
Big Daddy has run away. Sheree discovered cedar shavings on top of his cage (little one) and the paperweight was pushed over. The boys think he is in the vent; some think he is in the box by Ms. Pearce's desk, he could be in the closet, he could be behind the bookshelf or he could be in someone's desk. We will keep searching for Big Daddy.

4-27-89
When we got to school Daddy had not eaten the food we left. He had not slept in his little cage. He is still gone. Momma and the babies are fine. The babies are pulling themselves with their front legs and dragging their back legs. They really get around now. When we measured the baby hamster, he wet on the paper. These hamster babies make us think of our baby sisters and brothers. Ms. Pearce told Mark that one of her twin daughters crawled like the baby hamsters. Mrs. Callaway came to our class to ask for some help with making fossils. Ms. Pearce looked in the cabinet under the sink for some things to make fossils. There was Big Daddy crawling over the plaster of paris. Ms. Pearce said, "Howdy, Big Daddy." She picked Big Daddy up and gave him to Derrick. Derrick put him in the cage. Our class is so glad to have Daddy back. But Little Mama, "She don't like him," said Mark. "Little Mama bit him where she shouldn't. He bit her on her lip. It ain't bad what he did to her, but she did something terrible to him. We ain't gonna have no more babies 'cause she bit it off."

Encouraged with their acceptance, the children were willing to risk more writing, reading, and even word cards for their word banks. They also enjoyed rehearsal reading, choral reading, and reader's theatre. I noticed more independent reading and writing happening spontaneously.

We think the hamsters taught us to read and write! After these nurturing language experiences, it was as if the children had been given wings and were ready to fly.

## IN CLOSING . . .

Our school is fortunate. We suspect we have encountered fewer problems than most schools in making such a "radical" conversion from a skills-driven approach to a whole language program. Our principal, Stan Strauss, has been instrumental in this movement. He has empowered teachers to teach as they believe they should, and he has provided for teachers many workshops, professional literature, and videos, as well as funding for national professional conferences concerned with reading and language. Because of the concerns for the at-risk students in our school, the district has been "open" to our beliefs. Dr. George Cannon, District Superintendent, has publicly demonstrated his support for our program. Reading superintendent Dr. Mary Mosely has provided leadership and guidance in implementing our program. Dr. Anna Heatherly of the University of Arkansas, a mentor and teacher to many of us at Stephens, has long advocated whole language. Our program has flourished with the leadership and support of these forward-thinking professionals.

In this atmosphere, whole language teachers in our school have grown in knowledge and experience, and the students in this environment are exhibiting early signs of becoming lifelong readers and writers. We realize we have a long way to go, but we greet our days with more excitement than we have experienced in a long time. In an era when so many teachers are feeling the negative pressures of their profession, whole language has given us a new lease on teaching.

# 3

# "BOY IS FOR *B*": LIVING IN A WHOLE LANGUAGE KINDERGARTEN

## Wendy C. Kasten / Joni R. Ramer

On one particular Wednesday, the routine in Joni Ramer's classroom was disrupted because the long awaited repainting of her room had finally been scheduled. Joni and her class spent the day in the school library, making the best of an unusual situation. As Joni was working with several students on number concepts, Nick, the smallest and least mature student in the class, approached her. Nick suddenly realized in this new environment that he didn't know where the bathrooms were, and so he asked his teacher. Before Joni could respond, Robert, a more mature student, gave Nick directions for finding the bathrooms. Nick seemed tentative and unsure, and so nearby classmate, David, added for reassurance, "Boy is for *B*." Several nearby students chimed in to reassure Nick that he would be able to find the right bathroom.

In this whole language kindergarten, there is more than one teacher. All the students are responsible for teaching each other what they already know. Learning exists in an environment of cooperation and collaboration. There are high expectations for students in this kindergarten: not expectations to fulfill grades or to complete piles of worksheets, but expectations to be responsible for oneself and for others in the class. Expectations that *everyone* in the class is a reader and a writer, and that *everyone* is doing their best; expectations that *everyone* is a capable individual with important qualities to share and to respect. Everyone who shares this environment on a daily basis works together like a family, mindful of humanity and compassion. The manner in which Joni organizes for whole language is as important as the content she teaches.

You will hear four voices in this chapter: the voice of the researcher, Wendy C. Kasten, who visits the classroom; the voice of Joni Ramer, the teacher, who shares her ideas about why she believes this classroom works; and the voices of two children, Robert and Nick, who work together a great deal. Their frequent partnership is typical of the way collaboration works in whole language settings. Nick gravitates toward the resource and the security of Robert, a more articulate and mature kindergarten student.

## BACKGROUND

Advocates of whole language often hear others propose that whole language is appropriate only for more mature, perhaps even gifted, students. It is important that we dispel this particular myth. We believe that all children benefit from whole language, but especially those learners who have exposure to literacy different from middle-class children will find whole language experiences most supportive to their success in school. Musgrove (1987) found after a year-long study in her own kindergarten, for example, that three children who had arrived at school with little exposure to print and no exposure to connected discourse never figured out that letters, sounds, and words were supposed to have meaning. In her conclusions, Musgrove called for a whole language curriculum to supply the necessary context for literacy learning.

The students in Joni Ramer's class, also from South Florida, have backgrounds and issues that are similar to those Musgrove studied. Joni describes her class as she recalls it in September when the school year began. The family background of the students includes agricultural field workers, blue-collar workers, or parents who are unemployed. Some children have little or no prior experiences with books, and little experience with print in general.

## STARTING POINTS: JONI

After teaching in a more affluent setting, coming to my present school was a big shock. Literacy was not a basic need in their first five years. Approximately one-third of the kids had experience with Head Start and nursery schools, but the majority were experiencing the joys of literature, books, and writing for the first time. I wasn't sure what to expect.

I hesitated to begin with a mass bombardment of language. The children were hesitant to speak at all about any experiences they might have had. They didn't come forward to share with the class. I began my journey into literature and exposed them to books through the theme, "I'm Me, I'm Special." When I read aloud to them, they were very comfortable, but they found it difficult to converse about the story afterwards. They seemed not to care much about the sequence of the story or comprehension activities but immersed themselves in the visual effect of the books. Their favorite book was

*Spot* by Eric Hill (1980). The predictable answers from the animals hidden in the story helped them to feel secure, and so they began to chime in.

I assure you that only a handful of children attempted to "read" books aloud in the reading corner during center time. Others enjoyed looking at the books but didn't attempt to recite a story line. They were more interested in games and puzzles. After about three days, I began to spend fifteen or twenty minutes in the reading corner modeling storytelling from picture cues. With five or six children, I persuaded them to give it a try and I asked questions which I knew they could be successful at answering. Although they were open-ended questions and I tried to reinforce thinking skills, they stuggled to predict and to respond with logical answers.

I became frustrated with the lack of participation during sharing time. I wasn't sure if they didn't have the vocabulary or if they were insecure about sharing. I began to think about things they might have encountered in their short lives. It soon became clear that the reality of neighborhood events and television were the mainstays of their experience.

I modeled by sharing things I did after school and on weekends, even though I felt they were insignificant. For example, I might have shared my experience of going to the mall and visiting the pet store. As I continued to share orally each day, more and more children came forward to tell about going to the grocery store, riding their bikes, or visiting grandma.

I continued to invent situations and stories for sharing time also. After about two weeks of school, I decided that music would open up our lines of communication. I started using Raffi (1977) songs to show how we could enjoy talking together and playing together. We danced and talked. We moved to rhythmic songs and marched with our band instruments easily. They became closer as a group and were more comfortable. Gradually, this enthusiasm spread to other areas. Center activities had to remain simplistic, however. I was unable to provide appropriate, more complex, independent activities. I became frustrated and worried about whether or not they would achieve very much.

I found that art was a powerful medium in which the children seemed to excel. They enjoyed the experiences with paint, glue, paper, scissors, and talking about what they were doing. A month into school they began to self-initiate art projects, creating products that they were proud of, no longer dependent upon my specific instructions.

WENDY: What Joni Ramer describes constitutes some basic principles that are practiced by whole language teachers. She evaluated her students from where they were and tried to find common ground upon which to create literacy experiences. She was a kidwatcher (Y. Goodman, 1978) searching for as much information as possible about the values and culture of the children. She used their experiences and focused on what they knew, instead of on what they were lacking.

JONI: The environment I tried to create is one that is closely related to a family network. Just like a parent does, I watch, I listen, and I gather information about each child. This is important to me. I continue to observe their daily learning, including the way they use language, how they communicate with their peers, their learning styles, and abilities to cope with new experiences.

WENDY: Joni's class operates smoothly because the accumulated responsibility that students assume for their class increases their sense of ownership. The process of learning becomes as important as the thematic content. Learning respect and to be kind to each other are priorities along with academic achievement. Children learn each others' strengths, as well as their vulnerabilities, and they use this information to function as a family-like unit. They discuss, for example, that if a student is particularly sensitive, they should not tease him or her.

JONI: Organization of the classroom is important, and many daily routines are handed over to the children. Children know they are responsible for taking down the chairs in the morning, putting art supplies at the art center, getting paper for the writing table, and refilling paper towels, soap dispensers, and toilet paper holders within the room. Within a basic structure, the students learn to accommodate interruptions in the daily schedule and to be flexible when new things arise.

WENDY: Sometimes, to an outsider, a whole language classroom appears unstructured or haphazard. What is not always evident to an observer is how intricately structured a whole language classroom must be in order to function smoothly. One difference is that, in a child-centered curriculum, some of the structure is organized and maintained by students. Their vital role in the daily routine helps provide a sense of ownership in their class. Whereas a teacher might feel the burden of all classroom tasks in a more conventional setting, the whole language teacher is freed of unnecessary, trivial tasks, while teaching pupils responsibility, and heightening children's self-esteem. The organization in Joni's kindergarten serves both to help people live together in the classroom and to address the content of the curriculum, such as foundations of literacy learning.

JONI: Process is my focus for reading and writing. I give the children the chance to succeed and to gain confidence. Patterned language big books has become a daily part of reading. I encourage them to use their imagination and to relate everything we learn, as much as possible, to their past experiences. I read aloud to them five or six times a day. It is important for me to model that reading is fun and exciting and that we can learn things in books. I want to turn them on to reading. Trelease (1983) advocates that teachers advertise good literature by reading aloud frequently. He uses the metaphor of doing a "commercial" about good books. Hearing quality literature read aloud over and over again sells the idea that reading is worthwhile.

On the first day we wrote, I wrote in front of them. Although they all "wrote" that first day, their attempts were varied. Most of them drew a picture and wrote their name, but some did nothing at all. I asserted that everyone could write something—even a picture. At first they drew houses, rainbows, trees, and suns. Eventually, all of them would be drawing, and also looking around to see what others might be doing. Several copied letters from environmental print in the room, but most of the actual writing consisted of letter strings containing letters of their names.

WENDY: What happened in those early days in Joni's room formed certain important foundations. First of all, modeling is fundamental—the idea that teachers do the same things that they ask children to do. There is an important message that is communicated during such teacher demonstrations. It must be important if the teacher does it.

Another foundation is acceptance. Everyone's attempts at writing are viewed as positive steps, again focusing on what children know, and not on what they might be lacking. Allen (1974) writes that "Learning is risk taking." Risk taking becomes another important foundation. Children are made to feel secure, successful, and accepted. Any barriers to learning are removed, and so there is absolutely no reason for the children not to try out things that might be difficult. There are no reprisals of harsh correction or humiliation if they attempt difficult things. No one laughs at their mistakes, because mistakes are viewed as a natural part of learning. Children in Joni's room learn that it is OK to try again and to ask someone for help.

JONI: The foundation of my classroom is structured around learning centers, which are designated work areas. They facilitate small group activity centered around our current theme. For example, during the month of October, our theme is "Octobearfest," a celebration of both live and storybook bears. The children enjoyed circulating to the different centers such as the art center, the listening center, a math center, the reading corner, a science center, and a game and puzzle center. The children also choose to visit the paint easel, the water table, or the puppet theatre, which were very popular activities.

In the early part of the year, the children hurried around anxious to try out all the new experiences at once. At times, I would need to direct them to centers where they were more apprehensive about participating in the activity. I began to realize that I needed to limit their options to only two or three activities in order to make it easier for them to make choices. I reinforced certain rules that guided each center, such as the completion of tasks, asking peers for directions and assistance, and for cleaning up their space when they were finished. I continued to circulate from center to center, talking to them, asking questions, and listening. I found that during play they relaxed, began to communicate more, and explored their world through language.

After about two to three weeks, the routines were secure and literature was becoming a vehicle for language development, art, math, science, social growth, and enjoyment. The children gained confidence and began taking new risks each day. For most of them, cutting with scissors, holding crayons, and using glue was entirely new. I repeated successful activities and continued with similar strategies that would ensure success. Day by day they grew in their own ways. I continued to nurture their weaknesses as individuals and to use their strengths to help others learn. I saw bright, receptive, eager little minds and realized that, once they could understand how and why they learn, there seemed to be nothing to keep them from growing.

## A VIEW OF JONI'S KINDERGARTEN: WENDY

School at Samoset Elementary begins at 8:30 A.M. By 8:45, attendance has been taken and Joni is listening to the children share orally anything important that they have to say. On March 15, 1989, I visited the class for most of the day. The children I observed seemed very different from the immature kindergarteners that Joni had described in September. This is how the daily schedule looked:

| | |
|---|---|
| 8:30–8:45 | Opening |
| 8:45–9:00 | Sharing, Choral reading, etc. |
| 9:00–9:45 | Language Arts, entire group, with shared reading experience |
| 9:45–10:30 | Center time |
| 10:30–11:00 | Read aloud to the children |
| 11:00–11:35 | Lunch |
| 11:35–12:00 | Playground |
| 12:00–12:50 | Author's Circle (Monday, Wednesday, Friday) Sustained Silent Writing (Tuesday, Thursday) |
| 12:20–12:50 | Rainbow class (Art, Music, etc.) |
| 1:00–2:00 | Centers, continue morning activities, special events, etc. |
| 2:00–2:15 | Read aloud |
| 2:20 | Dismissal |

When I entered Joni's room that March morning at 9:00 A.M., Joni and the students were reading *The Grouchy Ladybug* by Eric Carle (1977). Students were participating by joining in on the familiar, repetitive lines, "If you insist," "You wanna fight," and "You're not big enough anyway." Joni would stop at intervals and ask them to predict text, or notice punctuation marks. Students were obviously enjoying a story they had heard before. At 9:28 A.M., the teacher directed everyone to get up and take a stretch. Leading some exercises, Joni was reinforcing number concepts as they counted repetitions of certain tasks. Balance activities were included, such as standing on one foot. Then children were paired and took turns holding each other's legs while one of them did sit-ups. Children now chose partners easily, and this exercise time went along smoothly with no management difficulties.

In discussing how they felt and how their pulses had increased, Joni used the word *oxygen*. She asked the students to guess what *oxygen* meant. Finally, one child said it was "air." Joni brought this child forward, encouraging his good thinking. "How did you come up with 'air'?" Joni asked. "I just came up with it," the student said, giggling somewhat with delight, "I just thinked."

Joni grabbed a marker and an index card and asked the children how they might write *air*. They discussed letters that might be found in the word *air*. Joni modeled how to invent a spelling, listening for sounds in the word. She allowed the children to predict the spelling. They came up with *A-E-R*. She wrote their prediction on a card and placed it on the board with tape. She then discussed how close they were to the conventional spelling and wrote the conventional spelling next to their invented one, adding that they both could say "air."

The theme around which curriculum had been woven during the past few weeks was "Wild Animals," and this week's topic was "Elephants." They had already written a class-dictated language experience story, which was displayed on large paper on the bulletin board in the group activity area. This original text became the focus of this day's shared reading experience. First they read the story chorally. Joni asked, "Who thinks they can read this all by themselves?" Several children volunteered enthusiastically. Dante was selected to go first. He had difficulty getting started, so Joni suggested that he start again, and they read the first line together. Then Dante went on to read most of the rest of the story by himself before the group. He was nearly accurate, with minor miscues that did not disrupt the meaning. At one point, Dante got a little lost and confused in the text, and Joni read the next few words with him. Dante was then able to complete the rest of the story solo. Joni exclaimed, "What a reader!" with a hug, and the rest of the students applauded.

Melissa took the pointer next and read accurately, pointing to the print as she read. Terry read next. The class prompted him somewhat, supportively, as they were aware that he has less confidence in himself as a reader. Terry did some self-correcting as he read and became more accurate at reading this story as he proceeded. Several more volunteers had turns.

Joni asked who in the group could find the word *elephant* somewhere in the story. Kristi got up and used her hands to define the beginning and ending boundaries of the word, showing the word *elephant*. Some more students read, and at the end of the session, the teacher asked them to get up and take a bow before the class. They did so, congratulating each other with handshakes and applause. They were celebrating their success as readers.

At 9:50 A.M., Joni called the group together to discuss directions for the centers. She reviewed directions for making Easter cards and reiterated that it would be important to listen to the directions, because she would not be available to repeat them once centers had started. She reminded all students that, if someone needed help during a center, they would be in charge and would need to find a way to help solve any problems, including assisting other students who might need help. She reminded them that she is not in charge of the centers once they begin, so they should ask questions before beginning.

Centers began at approximately 10:12 A.M. Two children were in the reading corner. There were four other centers, including the writing center, which is where Joni would be primarily stationed. Some students, such as Robert, were writing on their own at this point. Other students were more reliant on peers or, occasionally, on dictation written by the teacher. Most students wrote something. Robert's text was now mostly readable with invented spellings. Nick's papers had letter formations, word boundaries, and punctuation, but there were only occasional grapho-phonic correspondences.

## ROBERT AS A READER AND WRITER

I had occasion to talk with Robert about what it was like to learn to read and write in his kindergarten class. I began by getting some basic facts.

WENDY: How old are you, Robert?
ROBERT: Six.
WENDY: Six! When did you become six?
ROBERT: About a month ago.
WENDY: What's it like being six?
ROBERT: It's fun.
WENDY: It's fun, why?
ROBERT: Because you're bigger.
WENDY: Why is that a good idea to be bigger?
ROBERT: Learning how to read.
WENDY: Do you know how to read? (*Robert nods*) How did you learn to read?
ROBERT: Miss Ramer taught us.
WENDY: How did she do that?
ROBERT: Reading books to us.

Robert, like all of the students in his class, already thinks of himself as a reader and a writer. I asked him some questions about writing.

WENDY: Do you like writing? (*Robert nods*) What's the part that you like about writing?
ROBERT: How the words look?
WENDY: Is there a part of learning to write that's easy?

ROBERT: You know how the letters are. But some people who don't know the alphabet, don't know what the letters are.

WENDY: How can you help them?

ROBERT: You could play letter bingo.

Robert says that he likes to write, but that it is hard at times. In an interview with Robert, Joni asked him, "What's the easiest part of writing?"

ROBERT: The imagination.

JONI: What's the hardest part of writing?

ROBERT: Sounding out the letters. And the pictures.

JONI: What do you do when you come to a part of your story that's hard?

ROBERT: I say, um . . . I think a little bit about it . . . and I see if I can sound out the letters . . . and if I can't and it gets too hard . . . I stop writing and . . . um . . . I think about it again.

Progress can be observed in Robert's writing. Figure 3-1 shows some early evidence of letter-sound correspondence in Robert's written "string" (Clay, 1975). Note the presence of a *D* and *V* for the nouns in his sentence.

In February, Robert wrote, "The dinosaurs are fighting" (Figure 3-2). Now letter-sound correspondence appears, along with some word boundaries. This phonetic writing (Gentry, 1981) shows a great deal of growth in a short time. In March (Figure 3-3), Robert wrote: "The army man is shooting their gun." Robert now uses word

---

**Figure 3-1**   *Robert: January 3*

## tDOAYOXUVToD

*Translation:* The dinosaur is climbing up a volcano

---

**Figure 3-2**   *Robert: February*

## THEDNS RFT.

---

**Figure 3-3**   *Robert: March*

## The AEIT.Me.St.EAr.ThR.GiN.

---

**Figure 3-4**  *Robert: April 18*

## He.Man.iS.Look.KEN.For.Sclotor.
## Fo.He COM.He WLE. FILe. HM.

---

boundaries more conventionally, and there is evidence of phonetic understanding in each separate unit. He may be overgeneralizing a rule about periods, with which he is experimenting, or, like many beginning writers, he may have invented his own word boundary marker. He continues to experiment with periods. On April 18, when Robert wrote, "He-man is looking for Skeletor. If he comes, he will fight him," he regularly utilized both uppercase and lowercase letters, although not necessarily conventionally (Figure 3-4). His writing has become transitional or invented (Gentry, 1981). Robert came up to read his story to Joni. After he read it, they had the following conversation.

JONI: Robert, what are all these marks?
ROBERT: Periods.
JONI: What are they used for?
ROBERT: They tell us to stop at the end of the sentence.
JONI: Oh, so, if I read your story, I should say "He (pause) Man (pause) is (pause) . . .
ROBERT: No, no. (*Robert interrupts, a huge grin on his face. Robert rereads his text and thinks for a while.*) There should only be a period after *Skeletor* and *him*.
JONI: Okay, that makes more sense. Let's read it together. (*They read the story together, and Robert seems to understand how to use periods as punctuation.*)

NICK AS A READER AND WRITER
Early in the year, Joni found time to chat with Nick about his beliefs about reading and writing.

JONI: Nick, why do you come to school?
NICK: Because . . . to learn.
JONI: What do you like about school?
NICK: It's good.
JONI: What's good about school?
NICK: You get lots of good things.
JONI: What kinds of good things?
NICK: Like games and puzzles.
JONI: Do you like to write?
NICK: Yeah.

JONI: What's hard about writing?

NICK: You have to use your brain.

JONI: Is it hard to use your brain? What do you mean by that?

NICK: Like, you have to work hard.

JONI: How do you know how to write?

NICK: My brother teaches me.

JONI: What's easy about writing?

NICK: It's good, and you can learn.

JONI: Is it easy for you to learn to write? (*Nick nods*) Why is it easy?

NICK: Because I use my brain.

JONI: How did you learn to write in Miss Ramer's class?

NICK: You teached me.

JONI: How did I do that?

NICK: Looking at you and seeing what you was doing.

Nick is the youngest of three children in a two-parent blue-collar family. He is very small for his age and appears immature. Nick relies a great deal on other members of the class, but especially on Robert, his more mature friend. Nick requests help from Robert in all areas of kindergarten life, not just reading and writing.

On May 2, for example, Joni had just made Nick a blank book for his theme book on "Wild Animals." This was their topic of study in April and May, and the blank books would be used daily by students to contribute both a picture and text about something they learned about animals. When Joni handed Nick his book, the following conversation took place.

NICK: Does Robert have to help me?

JONI: Do you want Robert to help you?

NICK: Yeah.

JONI: Okay, go ask him if he'd like to help you.

NICK: Okay.

Nick seemed relieved. Robert is the person Nick is most comfortable going to. On April 6, Nick brought a toy from home that had a rotating cannon attached to it. He was talking with some classmates in line while returning from recess. Another boy had said that Nick's toy was "twisted." Nick went up to Robert and asked, "Robert, what does *twisted* means? Is it broken?"

Robert's answer was, "No, it means it can turn around. Don't worry, see." (Robert demonstrated *twisting* to Nick.)

On May 11, Joni asked Nick if he knew how to read. "No," was Nick's reply, "You have to be bigger." Joni brought out a favorite Big Book, *The Meanies* (Cowley, 1983), and asked Nick to read it. Nick read the entire book flawlessly. Joni asked him how he could do that, since he had just said that he didn't know how to read. Nick replied, "I listened to the tape, and I got to read."

"Do you mean you learned to read this book by listening to the

---

**Figure 3-5** *Nick: May*

# The ElePhants

# isdoirin.kwalk

# aed Serteton Drre

# bickS.

---

tape?" Joni asked. Nick nodded in agreement. "You must be pretty smart to do that, huh, Nick?" Nick again nodded in agreement, this time with a giggle.

As a writer, Nick is less experienced than Robert. In March, all his entries consisted of letter strings, produced from left to right. There was no evidence of grapho-phonic correspondence. In April, his strings of letters were longer, often with more than one line of print. There was still no real evidence of any correspondence between letters and how he read it to his teacher.

In May, he began to make entries into his "Wild Animal" theme book (Figure 3-5). His first entry read, "The elephant is drinking water and squirting it on his back." According to Nick, Robert helped him with writing this. Subsequent pages were less sophisticated than this one, so Robert and Nick probably did collaborate on the first page. In a whole language classroom, collaboration is encouraged and nurtured. This collaboration, which under other circumstances might be viewed as Robert doing Nick's work for him, is recognized by whole language teachers as valuable because students are helping and learning from each other.

Vygotsky (1978) termed this type of collaboration, "The Zone of Proximal Development." He recognized that learners can do more in collaboration with peers or with adults than they can accomplish in isolation. Other studies demonstrate powerful collaborations taking place between students (Kasten, 1984; Kasten and Clarke, 1986), just as Nick and Robert often do.

## THE "READING BUS"

We have looked at several unique aspects of the organization of one whole language kindergarten. Some of these aspects include the supportive climate that nurtures risk taking, an immersion in reading and writing activities, and a focus on living together as a family and sharing responsibility for the classroom. In a child-centered class, the ideas of the children become the focus of the curriculum because children's ideas are viewed as worthwhile and valuable.

On May 3, the children were washing their hands after recess and then going to the water faucet for a drink. They migrated toward the book corner to spend a few extra minutes looking at books. Some-one pulled a chair into the open space, in order to sit down and read. Soon, several other children decided they needed a chair also, and there were suddenly several chairs all lined up in the reading corner, inhabited by classmates reading.

One child piped in all of a sudden and said, "It looks like a reading bus!" So, enthralled with the idea of having a "reading bus," several more children brought chairs over, making the line even longer. One child moved his chair to the front of the row and declared, "I am the bus driver!" For the next several weeks, every day, "the reading bus" became a regularly scheduled classroom event, with every member of the class riding the bus, reading their favorite books.

On my last visit to Joni's room, she had just explained to the class that she and I were writing a story about their classroom and that was why she would be taking pictures with her camera. The children were excited about having their pictures taken. She explained to them that she would show them the story when it was all done but that it would be a story written for grown-ups, so they would not be able to read very much of it. I asked them, as a group, "Do you think your kindergarten is the same or different than other kindergarten classes?"

"Different," they all said in unison. I asked further, "Now think about this before you answer, and remember to raise your hands, if you have something to share. What do you think makes your kinder-garten different?"

"We write lots," said one classmate.

"We illustrate," added another student.

"Sharing and caring," one little boy said rather quietly.

"We're *friends*," said another child.

This is what it is like, living in a whole language kindergarten.

# 4

## ARE WE LISTENING?

### Carol S. Avery

On a June morning, after school was out, I lounged on the deck of a motel in Cape May, New Jersey. Two eight-year-old girls sat down beside me and opened a writing folder made from an old book cover.

"Let's see," said one, "what shall we write today?"

"Check the menu," suggested the other.

They began to go through a list of topics written on the inside of the folder. Some items had large checks beside them, indicating that the girls had written on these subjects. When they were unable to decide on a writing topic, one girl said, "Let's read some of our other stories first." Her friend concurred, and they selected several pieces for reading.

I began talking to the girls, and they eagerly shared their writing with me, taking turns reading aloud. The stories were basically two kinds. One genre the girls called "pretend stories": fiction pieces revolving around a central character (frequently an animal) who needed a friend, was lost, or perhaps had been naughty. The second genre, which the girls labeled "grown-up stories," consisted of lines of dialogue between adults. The subject matter included a shopping trip to buy an expensive dress, a couple making plans to go out to a bar and deciding what to wear, and conversations at a cocktail party. The writing integrated rich imaginations with the reality of actual experiences. The girls were using written language to form meaning from experiences in their lives.

I assumed that their engagement with written language was an extension of classroom activity—that these girls were involved in the writing process and had developed a variety of strategies in the context of a writing workshop at school. But I was wrong. When I asked them about their writing folder, I got blank stares. They had not heard of a writing folder. To them, writing in school meant copying the teacher's words from the board. "See," they said, "the teacher writes a story on the board, and then we copy it. Later, she writes the words you don't do right on your paper, and you have to keep trying to get them right next time."

The girls resumed reading to me until a mother came to call them to breakfast. "Wait," they protested, "we're reading to her."

"Oh, I see," said the mom. "Is she a teacher?"

"No," they replied, "*she wants to listen.*"

This statement, which came so easily, so readily, from these children, left me stunned by its implications. The girls implied that, from their experience, at least, teachers are not listeners. As I reflected upon this incident, I had to agree that the girls were right. The traditional role of the teacher is not to be a listener in the classroom. Traditionally, the teacher has been the authority, the speaker, and students are the designated listeners.

In classrooms adhering to whole language philosophies, the traditional roles of teacher and student are changing. These changes were addressed during July of 1987 at a conference convened by the Coalition of English Associations. In the conference discussions, participants recognized the changing populations of students, reflected upon recent research on the teaching-learning process, and discussed directions for the future of language arts/English studies. They defined the classroom as a *community of learners* where the role of teacher and the role of learner are intimately related, each defined in terms of the other.

The final report of the Elementary Strand at this conference addressed the role of the teacher:

> The teacher is an expert and authority on learning and pedagogy, and in some subject matter fields as well. She is a researcher working both theoretically and practically. She is herself a skillful user of language—a reader and a writer as well as a speaker and listener. Even before the children enter the classroom, she plans, organizes, chooses materials, considers teaching strategies. She sets up a structured learning environment to ensure that the desired academic and social interactions are fostered. These activities become on-going ones, occurring throughout the school year.
>
> When the teacher works with the children, his role is delicately balanced between that of a manager-director and an enabler-interactor with them and their learning. Interactions involve individuals, small groups, or the whole class. As children read, write, talk and listen, the teacher accepts and affirms their language. He also helps them extend and expand their language by having them use it—in all modes—to make meaning in all areas of the curriculum. The teacher provides information and direction. More often, he responds thoughtfully to children's efforts—with questions,

statements, or even laughter and hugs. The teacher also models appropriate actions and attitudes by sharing his personal interests, his curiosity, his affections and respect for children. He also systematically observes children in informal ways in order to assess their progress toward desired ends. (Lloyd-Jones and Lundsford, 1989, pp. 7-8)

This description of the teacher's role presents an ideal, a model, which we can keep before us as we work with students and as we grow as professionals. To strive toward this ideal is to make a commitment to being a learner both outside and inside the classroom and to organizing the classroom to facilitate learning for students and teacher.

To maintain expertise and authority on learning and pedagogy, we keep ourselves informed through professional reading and attendance at conferences, workshops, and conventions. We are readers, writers, speakers, listeners, and learners. We continuously revise, rethink, redo the ways we plan for and carry out instruction in our classrooms.

As we plan our classroom structure, we allow *time* for children to think and talk, and build a classroom routine which creates daily opportunities to listen to each student individually. In this way, we can learn what the child knows and then respond appropriately. Writing and reading workshops are set up with conference times where we randomly move among the children, stopping to listen to individuals as they are engaged in writing and reading activities. When we read aloud to children, we take time to pause and listen to their responses to the text. We slow down the pace of the traditional classroom to incorporate children's ideas. The school day is full of talk, but it is not just teacher talk. Children talk too, and teachers listen.

We learn by listening to our students. To *accept and affirm* a child's language, to *extend and expand* that language, to *respond thoughtfully*, to *model appropriate actions and attitudes* require that we abandon our traditional role. Rather than being the authority who holds all answers, we listen to our students, to set aside preconceived ideas and to postpone judgments in order to learn from children. When we do this, we are able to respond to individual learners in meaningful ways and to facilitate learning. When we understand what the learner understands, we can use our professional expertise more effectively as we respond to that learner. We are better able to engage the learner in an active, lifelong process of learning.

The researchers and experts in the literacy development of children repeatedly point us in this direction.

- Donald Graves (1978-1981), in the final report of his study on children's writing development, advocates a "waiting responsive style of teaching."

- J. Harste, V. Woodward, and C. Burke (1984) speak of the "child as informant" and urge teachers to listen to the "intentions" of the child.
- Yetta Goodman (1978) suggests "kidwatching," which involves observing, interacting, documenting, and interpreting.
- Tom Newkirk and Nancie Atwell (1988) state that it is essential for teachers to question and seek answers in the classroom setting. "Informed observation" is the term they give to this inquiry process.

In my own classroom, I have discovered the importance of listening to, and learning from, children. During a writing workshop in the first week of school, one student, Marlene, drew a rainbow with a person standing under it. Above it she wrote "OOSOORB OB SOT" (Figure 4-1).

When I first looked at Marlene's writing, I saw little indication of a correlation between sounds and letters. (She had been told to say the words she wanted to write to herself and then to write the letters she heard.) I asked Marlene to read her writing to me. "I am outside, under a rainbow and beside a tree," she read as she moved her finger under the letters in a very precise, deliberate fashion.

**Figure 4-1** *Marlene as Informant*

"Tell me about these O's," I responded.

Marlene looked at me and giggled because I did not see what was obvious to her. "Those aren't O's," she said. "They're circles."

"Circles?" Now I was really puzzled. "Well, why did you decide to put circles in your writing?"

"Because. See, I couldn't tell what letters make those sounds, so I just put circles for what goes there, because something goes there, only I don't know what."

Marlene read and pointed her way through the line again. "I am— oops, I forgot to write *I*." Her finger landed under the first circle as she said "am." She continued on, and I saw that she had correctly written *S* for side, *RB* for rainbow, *BS* for beside, and *T* for tree. Marlene was unable to identify vowel sounds, but she was able to develop a strategy to deal with this.

When I set aside my first perceptions of Marlene's writing and *listened to her* explanation, I understood that she could distinguish the sounds of vowels in words but did not know what letters represented those sounds. By listening to Marlene, by allowing her to teach me what she knew, I was better prepared to provide "information and direction" to her. I could also acknowledge and celebrate her successful thinking with her. The result was an empowerment that enhanced risk taking and learning.

On the same day, another child, Wendy, produced the piece of writing shown in Figure 4-2. Had I looked at her work after Wendy left the classroom, I probably would have been able to read her written message: "I am making a picture." My understanding of her efforts would have been limited, however. When I invited Wendy to

**Figure 4-2** *Wendy as Informant*

tell me about her work and when I *listened* to what she had to say, I learned much more.

Wendy told me that this was a picture of Wendy painting a picture of Wendy painting a picture of Wendy painting a picture. She added that this idea came from seeing it in one of her books at home.

The creature wandering through the paint and making tracks across the bottom of the drawing was neither a dog nor a cat, but a mouse. At this point, Wendy told me a story about the mouse that got in their home, how frightened her Mom was, and how she herself thought the mouse was cute. "You see," Wendy explained, "he's up close, and he'll look bigger because he's closer, and so that's why I made him bigger." The yellow object in the upper right-hand corner was not the sun (as I first thought) but the lights in our classroom. By listening to Wendy as she was engaged in writing, I came away with a more profound understanding of her thinking processes, her knowledge and experience levels, and her ability to observe her environment. Wendy extended and expanded her language as she told me about her work, and she wrote longer, more complex pieces in subsequent writing workshops.

When I came to Chris's desk, I saw him furiously coloring the picture in Figure 4-3 with his *black* crayon. Primary grade teachers

**Figure 4-3** *Chris as Informant*

know that first graders usually prefer bright colors—reds, blues, yellows, fuschias. When a child uses black as intently as Chris was doing, we often become concerned. The more I watched Chris and the intensity of his efforts with that black crayon, the more alarmed I became. When I asked him to tell me about his picture, he said, "We went to New York," and continued coloring.

"Hmm, New York? You mean the city?"

"Yeah," Chris answered without looking up.

"Well, why is New York so black?" I asked.

Chris looked up, startled. "Black??" he said.

"Yes, why is New York black?" I thought of the pollution and grime of the big city and began to anticipate what Chris might say.

"You mean this dark?" he said. "Well, this is the *shadows*. These big buildings make *shadows*, and you can't see the sun down here, so that's why it's dark." He pointed to the sun in the corner of the picture and added, "See, the sun's up here, but it's still dark down here because of the *shadows*."

My assumptions were wrong. When I stopped to listen, Chris explained and clarified *my* thinking. The teacher must be a learner within the context of the classroom, as well as outside its doors. We learn from our students as well as from books and courses. Thus, we organize our classroom to allow time for listening to children, we wait for the child to inform us, we question and listen, *and we learn*. We become reflective practitioners—theorizers who are continuously learning. Then we can best:

Accept and affirm, extend and expand children's language
Provide information and direction
Model appropriate actions and attitudes
Respond thoughtfully to children's efforts

We also demonstrate listening to our students and, in the process, establish communities whose members learn to listen and to care about each other. Perhaps our students, unlike the girls on the New Jersey shore, will know teachers as people who *want* to listen.

# 5

## WAlkM To RnM 33:
## Vien Vinidos al cualTo 33

Yvonne S. Freeman  /  Samuel D. Nofziger, Jr.

During a discussion in a graduate class on bilingual education at the end of the semester, Sam Nofziger commented on changes in his classroom: "My classroom works better now because it is more structured." We looked at each other surprised, and I asked him to repeat what he had just said. We made a discovery we didn't know we were making. The impression many people have of whole language classrooms is that there is no organization, no structure. The opposite is what we discovered to be true.

The whole picture of how to organize a whole language classroom was coming into focus for us. The students in Room 33, a first-second combination bilingual classroom in Fresno, California, have become more empowered every day as they have been given more choices. They have begun to take more and more responsibility for their own learning. Old routines, such as daily journal writing and literature discussions, have become more organized as they have become more meaningful. By centering ideas around a theme and beginning new writing activities, including pen pal letters, literature response logs, and content journals, Sam has converted his class-room into a place where students move from activity to activity in an orderly, self-directed, and purposeful way. Structure seems to be one key to organizing the whole language classroom.

When Sam and I first met, we were strangers with two common interests: whole language and bilingual education. I had been searching for a bilingual classroom to work in, and Sam had been experimenting with whole language but wanted someone to support what he was trying to do. We both decided that the only way for us to learn was to plunge right in. We embarked on a joint venture that would lead to our new insight about whole language and bilingual education.

### ORGANIZING OUR IDEAS: YVONNE

On the day of my first visit to Sam's classroom, I was nervous. I worried that my convictions about whole language for second lan-guage learners might not really work with these bilingual children. After school that first day, we sat and talked for over two hours, discussing our philosophies about learning for bilingual students and considering where we might begin. Sam and I agreed that our goals for the classroom would be centered around the following whole language principles:

Learning proceeds from whole to part
Activities should be learner centered, drawing on students' back-
grounds and interests
Lessons should have meaning and purpose for the students
Learning involves social interactions
Oral and written language can be acquired simultaneously
The potential of bilingual students is expanded through faith in them
as learners (K. Goodman, 1986; Harste, Woodward, and
Burke, 1984; Goodman, Goodman, and Flores, 1984; Free-
man and Freeman, 1988; Rigg and Hudelson, 1986)

Sam was already using literature written in English and Spanish instead of basals, and he had his children doing daily journal writing and also writing stories in the language of their choice. However, he wasn't comfortable with the organization of his classroom and wasn't sure how to begin working on that. After some discussion, we decided to see if working with a broad theme that included com-parison and contrast would give us a start. Since we lived in Fresno, a city of 350,000 people, and since many of the children had come from rural homes, we decided that a broad theme, "La Ciudad y El Campo"/"The City and the Country" would be a good place to begin.

## ORGANIZING OUR IDEAS: SAM

When Yvonne's visit began, so did our adventure. I was flattered and excited that she was interested in working with me and the students in our classroom. Although I was using some activities that were consistent with whole language, I knew that I did not completely understand the philosophy behind whole language and that there was more that needed to be done.

That first day, Yvonne saw the class reading and writing, singing, sharing, and learning together. Our discussion of the day helped me focus on some options for improving my classroom. The organization of my whole language classroom was a place I decided to begin. I wanted a unifying organization that would allow my students more choice and more responsibility.

I knew the children in my classroom were already doing activities seen in most whole language classrooms, but I also knew that I wanted some kind of unity to those activities. My students were writing in journals, creating their own stories, and reading literature, but I was not satisfied with any of those three activities. As I attempted to respond to twenty-six or more student journals daily, I found myself literally running around in an attempt to get to every student. Our story writing process included writing a first draft, sharing the draft with peers, and then putting the story in a class library. The content writing the students did was limited to a line or two on a teacher-assigned topic that was based on a social studies or science lesson. I needed some advice on how to enrich, to "brighten up," the writing experience for my students.

My literature studies, which were limited to books on the district's literature list for my grade levels, consisted of reading a book a week together, doing teacher-assigned projects around concepts in that book, such as character, plot, and setting, and having students read and reread the book alone or in pairs. Although some of the students enjoyed the fact that they could read the books with ease, others found the books too difficult, and still others got bored reading the same stories over and over. I believed the activities I planned for the children were more enjoyable than using a basal and worksheets, but I also knew that interest in the activities varied from week to week because they were not always learner centered. The children were not being given enough choice in what they read or in how they responded to the literature.

While there were parts of our classroom schedule I was anxious to work on, there were areas during the day that Yvonne and I decided not to modify, because I felt that these were important times for the students. I was not willing to change the morning opening time, the time spent in small groups with the bilingual aide, Mrs. Romero, or our daily share time.

Since one of my concerns was that isolated activities did not seem to hold the students' interest, Yvonne suggested that we try unifying the curriculum with a broad theme. I had already been using themes. At the beginning of each year, I would examine our district's "Standard Expectancies" for my grade level. Then I would plan units that would include as many expectancies as possible in a unit. However, there was little, if any, connection between units. One month was "Weather and Space/El tiempo y el espacio" and the next "Maps/ Los mapas." I also found that the units were tied more to the teaching of facts than to the learning of concepts and that we did little writing or reading of literature within the unit themes.

## THE FIRST STEPS: YVONNE

Once Sam and I had decided what direction to take, we had to agree on how to get started. This involved planning, collecting materials, and deciding how to approach the unit.

### MATERIALS

When we discussed materials, we both had concerns about the availability of resources in Spanish. However, when we pooled ideas for books, songs, and poems and consulted with the bilingual resource teacher, we found there were quite a few resources available in Spanish as well as English that related to our theme.

### AN ORGANIZATIONAL PLAN

As beginning work on the theme, I suggested that we use the "Wonderfilled Lessons" (1984), by Don Howard, a teacher in Glenville, Illinois. Howard has suggested that teachers involve students in the process of organizing units by following six basic steps:

**The Wonderfilled Lessons**
Step 1: Ask the students: "What do we know about . . . ?"
Step 2: Ask the students: "What do we wonder about . . . ?"
Step 3: Ask the students: "How can we find out about . . . ?"
Step 4: With the students work out a plan of action and at the same time work school/district curriculum requirements into the unit.
Step 5: Plan some kind of celebration of what all of you have learned together.
Step 6: Learning is continuous. From any unit more topics and questions come up. Begin the cycle again.

By using the steps of the "Wonderfilled Lessons" as a guide, we could apply the principles of whole language we'd agreed upon earlier: draw upon students' background knowledge and interests; get the students actively involved in the decision making; ensure that their involvement was meaningful; get them reading and writing about what they were doing; and give them more choice and responsibility.

I also suggested we incorporate comparison and contrast into the theme. I had been intrigued by Egan's (1986) idea of using binary opposites in developing units to help students develop concepts and make connections. Sam and I decided that, by brainstorming about what his students knew about the city and the country, we could see what kinds of comparisons the children could make and we could capitalize on their strengths and interests.

## THE FIRST STEPS: SAM

OUR UNIT

Getting started was by far the most frightening aspect of the entire process for me. I had to trust that the students would guide us through the unit, that they would provide the base upon which we would build concepts. Allowing the students so much choice was an additional gamble. I wasn't sure it would really work. I was beginning to read about this kind of teaching in books, and I had seen a few examples of it in other classrooms, but I was still unsure whether or not it would actually work for me. Would my students be ready for such changes? After all, most of the successful whole language classrooms I had seen were not bilingual classrooms.

Following the first step of "The Wonderfilled Lessons," we began with a brainstorming session one morning. Because we live in a city and so that the children would have somewhere to start, I asked the children to tell me everything they could think of that had to do with the city. I wrote their responses on a large sheet of butcher paper as they dictated.

### The City
it's big
many persons
more things than in the country
big buildings
lots of cars
raggers fight
noise
houses
sometimes they don't allow pets
lights
zoo
grass

The list showed what the students knew about the city. They drew upon their personal experiences and shared their perceptions. The addition of items like "sometimes they don't allow pets" reflected common experiences of the children at our school where living in rented homes or apartments is the norm and the transiency rate is high. I was especially intrigued and saddened that these first and second graders were so aware of the rival gangs, "the blue raggers" and "the red raggers."

I left the list hanging low so students could reach it easily, and I invited the students to add to the list as they thought of additional items. That same day a police car and five big buildings were drawn on the butcher paper. Next to the buildings one child wrote "GOT BIG BIDES" (got big buildings). Over the next few days, we added more words to our list as things related to the city came up in songs, literature, and conversation.

The Little House didn't like it.
Too noisy
lights are too bright
She (*The Little House*) couldn't see the seasons.
London
New Orleans
Dover
Harlem
Fresno

The first four additions came after we read Virginia Lee Burton's *The Little House*. *London, New Orleans, Dover,* and *Harlem* were suggested by the children after we had sung "Yankee Doodle," "Great Big House in New Orleans," and "I've Been to Harlem" during our morning opening time. What was exciting for me to see was how the children were already making the connections. The list was something that they were in charge of, and they were coming up with things I never would have thought of.

After a week of exploring what the children knew about the city, we then brainstormed what they knew about the country. The children naturally came up with contrasts with the city, such as "little bit of people" and "little bit of houses." They also listed crops such as grapes and vegetables, grown in the countryside around Fresno, and animals commonly found on a farm, like pigs, goats, and chickens. As with the list about the city, their personal experiences were again reflected in suggestions such as "little food," "good people," and "old trucks."

During these first few weeks, some quite exciting things began to happen with the activities we were doing. Several students chose to write stories about the city or the country. It seemed that many things that happened in the classroom or that we read about or discussed had connections to our theme even when I hadn't planned them. In fact, the children were constantly telling me, "Mr. Nofziger, that's in the city" or "That's like in the country." The students were doing things I had hoped for but had not necessarily expected.

I have since found that the children are always eager to share what they know and that they make connections that go way beyond my expectations. One day, for example, the students and I made lists of places we knew in our city, Fresno. We categorized the lists into types of places, like restaurants and stores. When we got to "skating rink" and "school," Margaret, one of the students, suggested we put the two together. I asked her why they went together. She said, "They both have rules." Her answer was incredible to me. I began to realize how important it was to draw on the children's knowledge. Before I tried activities such as this one, there didn't seem to be any opportunity for this kind of sophistication to shine through. As with the previous lists, the children's own experiences and perceptions were expressed clearly. I began to see how much I was learning about and from the children, how much they knew, and how they thought.

As we have explored our theme of "The City and the Country," I have continued to learn from my students. As Howard suggests in his "Wonderfilled Lessons," I have tried to draw upon what the children wonder about and have included the children in helping to decide how we can find out about the things we wonder about. The children have continued to compare and contrast naturally, and one project has led to another. We have made maps of our school, our neighborhood, and our city. We have gone on field trips. We have done art and science projects. All of these activities have related in some way to our theme and have involved the children in reading and writing.

CHOICE

While I was organizing my curriculum around a theme, I was also making other changes in my classroom. I remember the first week I allowed students free choice during their reading and writing time. Yvonne came that day for support. I explained the organization carefully to the students:

> While some of you will be in a book discussion group with me and others will be working with Mrs. Romero, the rest of you can choose what you want to do. I won't assign you an activity anymore. Each center will have only so many people at a time. Everyone will have a chance to read to each other and write a response, to send messages, to work on our class mural about the city, to paint, or to play with clay.

The students listened attentively. When I asked, they showed me that they had understood the different choices they would have and the rules about the number of children allowed at each center. Once I began giving students choice, there was stress.

That first day, with Yvonne's help and the help of the aide, all went quite smoothly, even though two or three children could not make their own choices. However, by the third day, I felt that the classroom was out of control. Students in some centers were involved, but at others they seemed to get bored quickly and relied on me to make their choices for them.

At this point in my learning, I realized a very important thing: Too much change too quickly hurts the students as well as the teacher.

I knew that it was important for the children to make choices, and I did not want to give up on the idea. By watching the children, I could see which activities were not interesting to them. I thought about activities that had engaged them in the past and replaced some of the choices with those. By following the lead of the children and their interests, I was able to create a classroom where students really had choice and accepted responsibility.

After the first few weeks, I found that the children were making choices well and that the classroom was running more smoothly.

## ORGANIZING FOR BILINGUAL CHILDREN: YVONNE

Sam and I knew there was another aspect of a bilingual whole language classroom that needed consideration: more balanced use of the two languages. In Sam's classroom, children were allowed and encouraged to write in either Spanish or English, and the whole class sang songs and read poetry in Spanish, but Sam had not read books in Spanish to the whole class, and Spanish-speaking students did not share in Spanish in the large group as freely as both of us would have liked. However, we have been able to make significant changes. By reading in Spanish to the whole group, showing kids that the adults speak Spanish in the classroom, and continually developing the theme around all the children's strengths and interests, we have been able to convert Room 33 into a true bilingual classroom.

### GETTING STARTED WITH MORE SPANISH

Sam had hesitated to read to the whole group in Spanish because he was a little concerned about the monolingual English speakers in the class and their reactions. However, when Sam and I discussed these concerns, we reasoned that monolingual Spanish speakers had to cope daily with most reading done in English, their second language, and, as a result, were learning English. The monolingual English speakers could be enriched by listening to more Spanish.

Soon after the class had begun their theme and had been brainstorming about what they knew about the city, I volunteered to read *La Ciudad* (*The City*) by M. Rius and J. MaParramon (1986) to the whole class during the opening time. Before I read to them, I told the children that we were going to read a book in Spanish and showed the children the cover with a picture of a city. I asked the Spanish speakers to explain the meaning of the title to the other children, and then the children predicted in English and Spanish what they thought we would see in the book. When I began reading the book, all the children were involved. By using pictures and their own background knowledge of books, the monolingual English speakers were able to predict what the Spanish on each page said.

From that point on, Spanish reading and discussion has seemed almost as natural as English. As the year has progressed, both languages have been used freely in readings and discussions. Monolingual English-speaking students not only used Spanish themselves occasionally but also became more accepting of others when they used Spanish. Brainstorming and class discussions have included more use of both languages.

PEN PAL LETTERS

Another activity that has supported Spanish speakers in Sam's classroom has been the pen pal letter exchange. I was excited about what was happening in Sam's classroom, and I wanted my teacher education students at the college to be part of the excitement. Over the course of one semester, students in my reading and writing course exchanged letters with Sam's students so that they could learn about the development of children's writing and have the experience of getting to know one child well. My students exchanged letters weekly with Sam's students and visited his classroom twice. My five bilingual education teacher candidates wrote in Spanish to ten of Sam's bilingual kids. This exchange reinforced for Sam's students the importance and legitimacy of their native language and allowed them to share what they were learning in class with their pen pals. During one visit, one of Sam's students, Andrea, shared her feelings about the country with her pen pal and gave her the picture shown in Figure 5-1.

**Figure 5-1**  *Andrea's Pen Pal Letter*

*A mí me gusta el campo. Yo vivo en el campo.*
(I like the country. I live in the country.)

Both the children and the college students benefited from the exchanges. The children learned from the written demonstrations of others and enjoyed making new friends and telling their own stories in writing both in English and Spanish to others. The children had a purpose for writing weekly, because their audience was real and, for the Spanish speakers, their audience communicated with them in their native language. This sense of purpose and audience was definitely also felt by the college students. They all took a real and very personal interest in the children who were their pen pals. In our class on campus, they shared letters they received with me and the others in our class and pointed out the children's progress, which was often dramatic. They were amazed at how all the children used the letters they had written to their pen pals as models. They also noticed how the content of the children's letters improved in quality and quantity over the few months they exchanged letters.

## READING AND WRITING IN TWO LANGUAGES: SAM

By organizing around a theme, drawing on the students' strengths, including their first language, and providing more choice, I have been able to make my classroom a place where children are engaged and excited. The reading and writing activities I was concerned about at the beginning of the year, including daily journals, story writing, content writing, and literature studies, have all evolved and expanded naturally and are part of our routine activities. A look at each one of these activities gives an idea of how they are organized and how children learn when they are involved in them.

### DAILY JOURNALS

Daily journal writing has continued in Room 33, but, because of all the other writing we do and the responsibilities that the students now take, it is less hectic than it once was. In January, a student teacher, Miss Camargo, joined our classroom. Miss Camargo has helped respond to journals in a whole group setting. Students can also share their journals with others if there is not enough time for me or Miss Camargo to get to each student daily. As students have taken on more responsibilities, our job has become easier.

I have been especially interested in how my bilingual students choose the language they write in. They feel free to write in both Spanish and English and move comfortably back and forth between the two languages. Benito, for example, most often chooses to write in Spanish but is also comfortable experimenting with English. During Fresno Fair, his journal entries appeared in both languages (Figure 5-2, A through E). Though I have not specifically encouraged the children to write in both languages, they seem to do it naturally.

**Figure 5-2**  *Benito's Journal, October 11–17, 1988*

*Today is October 11 1988
Iho a La ferilla Otop*

**A.** Today is October 11, 1988.
*Yo a la feria*
(I to the fair.)

*Today is Octoper 12 1988
Otra ves voi a La ferilla*

**B.** Today is October 12, 1988.
*Otra vez voy a la feria*
(Again I go to the fair.)

*Today is October 13 1988
I like The Fari it
esz fian.*

**C.** Today is October 13, 1988.
I like the fair   it is fun.

*Today is October 14 1988
I like TheFari it
ess fiun.*

**D.** Today is October 14, 1988.
I like the fair   it is fun.

*Today is October 17 1988
yo esta va canatano
ne la Ferilla.*

**E.** Today is October 17, 1988.
*Yo estaba cantando en la feria.*
(I was singing at the fair.)

STORY WRITING AND CONTENT WRITING

As the year has progressed, I made some changes in process writing. In working with the children, I have tried to help them set specific goals and identify audiences for their writing. As a result, the children have purpose for their writing, and their writing is more important to them. My students not only share their pieces more freely now with each other in groups and with their pen pals but also read their stories to the vice-principal and preschool children at their school.

**Figure 5-3** *Manuel's Story*

A. I Like the Contry. There is A House.

D. I Like the House. My Ant Lives there.

B. I like the Lake. It is cool.

E. I love the Contry. Morc then the city.

C. I Jumped on the Water. It was Fun.

The more the students feel that they have a specific audience for their writing, the more they are willing to write.

The topics for the children's writing began to change as we began reading and discussing our theme. Children who had previously never done any content writing beyond labeling a picture began writing whole stories which showed their understanding of the content we were studying. Although it was never suggested, students began to choose to write about the theme in their story writing time. In his story (Figure 5-3, A through E), Manuel not only talked about the country and described his personal experiences in the country but also ended his story by making his preference for the country clear to the reader. Though both the city and country were being discussed in class, he clearly did not confuse the two.

Elena created an interesting mixture of content and fiction when she shared what she knew about the country and interspersed it with a story of romantic conflict in which she used the names of class-mates (Figure 5-4, A through K, pp. 78-79).

It is interesting to note that Elena used the English word *farm* but for the rest of her story used Spanish words. This kind of written codeswitching was often evident in the children's writing. Olga, for example, wrote a story in Spanish but codeswitched in the first two pages of her story using the English word *cantri* (country).

Edelsky (1986) found that codeswitching in the writing of bilingual children was rare and that when it was done it was usually because the writer had learned the term in the other language. In the writing of Elena, Olga, and the other children who wrote in Spanish, we also found this to be true. Elena and Olga seemed to use the words *farm* and *cantri* because we had been discussing those ideas with our units in class. They understood the concepts discussed and put the English words into their Spanish stories.

Another example of using content in stories came from Juanita. Her story, written in Spanish, is an especially delightful example of her understanding of how plants grow (Figure 5-5, A through H, p. 80).

With all the content writing the children were doing naturally during story writing, I decided to further encourage content writing by using content journals. Sometimes we have had to encourage the students to share what they know in writing. After a recent discussion that Miss Camargo and I held on photosynthesis, Jay wrote two sentences. Miss Camargo encouraged Jay to write more in his journal by engaging him in a written dialogue. As a result, Jay was able to share more of what he had learned. He shared the definition of *photosynthesis* he and another student had written earlier: "The plant need the sun to bloom." He even explained the function of chlorophyll: "It therms (turns) the plant's green" (Figure 5-6, A, p. 81).

Others in the class naturally shared what they remembered about plants without any probing, but did not reach the scientific detail Jay provided. Rachel's journal is an example of this (Figure 5-6, B).

**Figure 5-4**  *Elena's Story*

**A.** *el campo*
(the country)

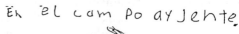

**D.** *En el campo hay gente.*
(In the country there are people.)

**B.** *El campo es bonito y tiene un río.*
(The country is beautiful and has a river.)

**E.** *Hay árboles en el campo.*
(There are trees in the country.)

**C.** *Una señora había pasado por el country.*
(A woman had gone through the country.)

**F.** *Ariana fue con su novio al campo.*
(Ariana went to the country with her boyfriend.)

Ariana y Simone Fue toli
al campo y peliaron
y aria na gaho.

**G.** *Ariana y Simonea fueron al campo y pelearon
y Ariana ganó.*
(Ariana and Simonea went to the country
and they fought and Ariana won.)

Juliana Fue al
campo.

**H.** *Juliana fue al campo.*
(Juliana went to the country.)

En el campo
a bi an casas.

**I.** *En el campo habían casas.*
(In the country there were houses.)

Eh el campo
ay un Farm.

**J.** *En el campo hay un farm.*
(In the country there is a farm.)

En el campo ay
Pajaros.

**K.** *En el campo hay pájaros.*
(In the country there are birds.)

**Figure 5-5** *Juanita's Plant Growing Story*

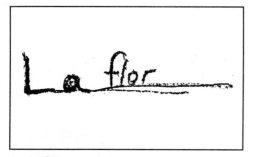

A. *La flor*
   (The flower)

E. *Y más.*
   (And more.)

B. *Un día planté una flor.*
   (One day I planted a flower.)

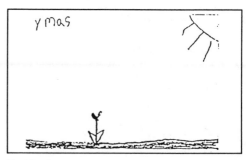

F. *Y más.*
   (And more.)

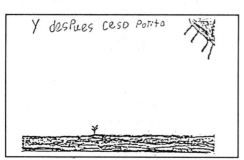

C. *Y después creció un poquito.*
   (And afterwards it grew a little bit.)

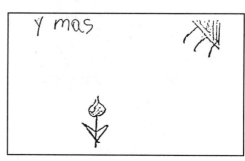

G. *Y más.*
   (And more.)

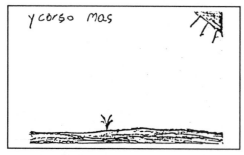

D. *Y creció más*
   (And it grew more.)

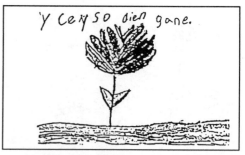

H. *Y creció bien grande.*
   (And it grew really big.)

**Figure 5-6**  *Content Journals, Jay and Rachel*

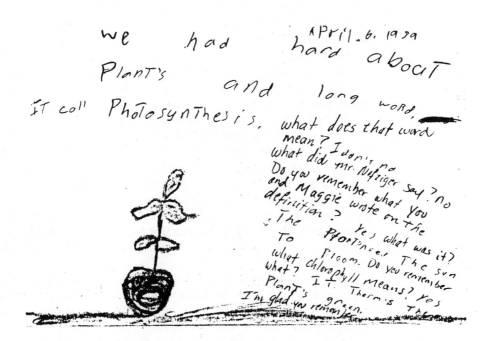

we had ^April.6.1989 hard aboaT
PlanT's and long word,
IT coll PhoTosynThesis. what does that word
mean? I don't no
what did mr. Nofziger say? no
Do you remember what you
and Maggie wrote on the
definition? The
The yes, what was it?
To PrønTsnser. The sun
what? Ploom. Do you remember
what chlorophyll means? Yes
PlanT's IT. Therm's The
I'm glad you remember green.

**A.** We had heard about plants and a long word. It's called Photosynthesis.

Mr. Nofsinger Brang
a plant. It was a
green and white
plant. It was Buttfuy
plant. I LiKe hes
plant. Miss. Rosenbergs class
Let us use then plant

**B.** Mr. Nofziger brought a plant. It was a green and white
plant. It was beautiful plant. I like this plant. Miss
Rosenberg's class let us use their plants.

## LITERATURE DISCUSSIONS AND LITERATURE LOGS

We have been able to give our students a good choice of books in both Spanish and English. We made trips to the district resource center and several libraries to provide the children with books they would never had had access to otherwise. In this way, Mrs. Romero, Miss Camargo, and I have been able to provide the students with as much literature related to the theme as resources allowed. As a result, our book-sharing times have gone well.

Because of all the discussions and the writing going on in the classroom, I decided that the next logical step was to do literature response journals. I began by asking kids to write the title of the book they had just read, to write a short message about the book, and then to draw a picture of their favorite part. I then responded by writing questions to encourage the students to write more. What was most exciting about doing this was that from the very beginning the children were able to respond to the literature with only a little encouragement.

Now the children respond without the question probes and make very insightful observations about their readings. Through readings, written responses, and interaction, the children are able to respond very personally to what they have read.

When I read *The Patchwork Quilt* to the class, I began to cry because I was comparing the grandmother in the story to my own grandmother.

Laura began her written response to the book by relating the story to her own life: "I like the story I like the part when the cilenien (children) saw there grandma because I go vitet (visit) my grandmother." I wrote Laura that the story made me sad because it made me think about my grandma, too. She wrote asking me why and I explained that my grandmother was very old and I was scared she would die soon. Then Laura wrote, "I fell (feel) verry sad." After I wrote her and told her that I was not sad anymore, she replied, "Now Im happy" (Figure 5-7).

Maria was watching and listening to our conversation, and her response to *The Patchwork Quilt* reflected this. She wrote: "I heard you and Laura talk because I think that will I never saw my grama. She died befor she said goodbye. And I was mad because she didn't say goodbye but I still love her."

Laura and Maria were not only sharing their story but also sharing their lives with me. The literature logs have expanded our understanding of each other as well as of what we read.

## ENDINGS AND BEGINNINGS

At the end of our year together, Sam reflected on how the students had grown over the year. The students were writing. The students were reading. The students were drawing. The students were painting. The students were solving problems together. The students were making choices. Miss Camargo, Mrs. Romero, and I happened to

**Figure 5-7** *Laura's Literature Response Journal*

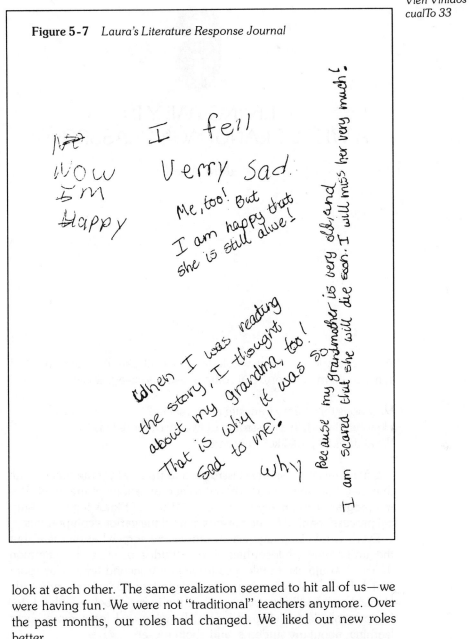

look at each other. The same realization seemed to hit all of us—we were having fun. We were not "traditional" teachers anymore. Over the past months, our roles had changed. We liked our new roles better.

Sam and I do not pretend that we have solved all of the problems of organizing the whole language classroom. The school year is coming to an end, but Sam is already looking forward to next year. He wants to try a new theme, one that will encompass the use of more children's literature. As he reads more professional books and talks to other teachers, he gets more ideas about new things he wants to try. What he has learned this year will serve as a basis for what he does for years to come as he continually revises the organization of his whole language classrooms.

# 6

## LIVING DAILY IN
## A WHOLE LANGUAGE CLASSROOM

**Joni Weed**

As teachers learn about whole language, it usually makes a lot of sense to them in theory. But some questions always arise:

How does this theory translate into practice?
How can it work in a classroom of twenty or more kids?
What does it "look like" in progress?

Often teachers visit my classroom and frantically write notes on all that they see, sometimes without asking questions of me at all. But my program can't really be understood without knowing the "thinking process" behind it, the reasons behind the various components.

Every whole language classroom will be somewhat different, but the underlying philosophies and attitudes provide the common thread. I would like to take you through my second-grade classroom and "show you" what my whole language classroom presently "looks like." I will also try to explain the purpose behind what I do. My program is evolving and ever changing as I learn more about learning, about my students, and about myself.

### ORGANIZING THE PHYSICAL ENVIRONMENT

As you come into our classroom, you see desks in groups, shelves and dividers providing "corners," walls filled with student work, and charts of one kind or another. Though to some it may appear cluttered, there are reasons for all of this.

The desks are in groups to encourage and provide the opportunity for conversation between kids. Language is a central component to learning. I see it as a necessity to any program. Students are encouraged to share ideas and to learn from each other. Yes, we do have rules about listening to the teacher or to anyone else who is speaking to the class. And yes, we work on using quiet voices so the noise level is not a distraction for students or teacher. These are life skills necessary within society, but opportunity to talk with each other is essential in striving for a happy medium. Self-discipline rather than teacher control is the goal.

The arrangement also provides quiet, private areas for students to be, whether it's to work independently, with a partner or small group, or to just be alone. Our classroom is very small, so the "get away" corners are very important. Shelves which separate the areas contain all the materials children may need in their daily work.

Very little teacher-prepared and no store-bought material covers the walls. I believe that kids' own work is more meaningful to them and that is most relevant in the doing rather than the displaying of it.


## ORGANIZING THE PROGRAM

A typical day is as follows:

| | |
|---|---|
| 8:15-8:30 | Student Arrival |
| 8:30-9:00 | Journals, Morning Get-Together |
| 9:00-10:30 | Language Arts |
| 10:30-11:15 | Specials (Gym, Art, Music) |
| 11:15-11:55 | Lunch and Recess |
| 11:55-12:20 | Read Aloud by Teacher |
| 12:20-12:50 | Independent Reading |
| 12:50-1:30 | Math |
| 1:30-1:45 | Recess |
| 1:45-2:30 | Social Studies/Science |
| 2:30-3:00 | End-of-Day-Get-Together |
| 3:00 | Dismissal |


### STUDENT ARRIVAL

Before school, students have several responsibilities. As they arrive, they sign up on the "Bus Chart," which shows which bus they'll ride home or what other arrangements they have made. Besides helping both students and me keep track, it shifts the burden of responsibility to the students and shows them one practical purpose for writing.

Students put a hot lunch or milk ticket in a pocket on our "Attendance/Lunch Count Chart." This becomes an automatic lunch graph that shows how many kids are having hot or cold lunch. It also provides an easy attendance check. Using this chart, students themselves are able to do the lunch count and attendance paperwork each day, which I merely have to check. This frees me up for more important tasks and gives students responsibility in the running of our classroom.

JOURNALS

Journals are one of the most worthwhile things I do each day. It gives individual attention, which is difficult to provide for an entire classroom of children. It creates a desire for the kids to read; they really want to know what I will say to them, which will be different from what I write to anyone else because it's "our" conversation. Journal writing provides from five to ten minutes of quiet time, when kids are expected to write. These are dialogue journals between each child and myself (Figure 6-1). It gives us an opportunity to have a one-to-one conversation, which time may not allow for during the rest of the day.

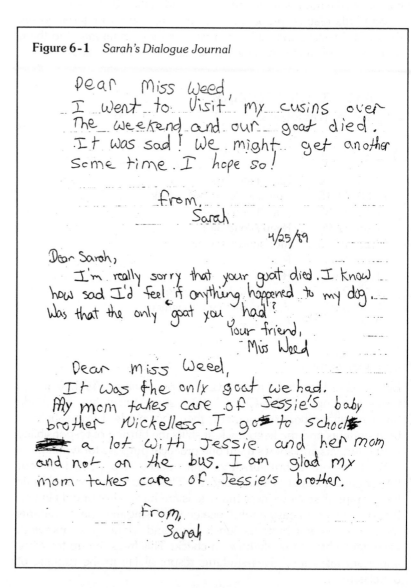

**Figure 6-1** *Sarah's Dialogue Journal*

Dear Miss Weed,
I went to visit my cusins over the weekend and our goat died. It was sad! We might get another some time. I hope so!

from,
Sarah
4/25/89

Dear Sarah,
I'm really sorry that your goat died. I know how sad I'd feel if anything happened to my dog. Was that the only goat you had?
Your friend,
Miss Weed

Dear miss Weed,
It was the only goat we had. My mom takes care of Jessie's baby brother Nickelless. I go to school a lot with Jessie and her mom and not on the bus. I am glad my mom takes care of Jessie's brother.

from,
Sarah

MORNING GET-TOGETHER

Each morning we gather in our group area, sitting on the floor, to go through a daily routine. Early in the year, I run the "Morning Get-Together," modeling the general procedure; after a few weeks, the kids run it themselves. "The Pledge of Allegiance," "Lunch Count," "Lunch Menu," "Days of the Week," "Calendar," "Days-of-School Chart," "Weather Report," and "Things to Do Today" are part of the routine.

CALENDAR

After posting the date and reading it to us, sometimes the student helper will write on the Calendar why the day might be special. This job demonstrates how calendars work; it is also an alternative mode of communicating information or thoughts.

DAYS-OF-SCHOOL CHART

An adding-machine tape encircles the room, counting the days of school that have passed. A number is added daily. We record patterns by underlining even numbers, circling multiples of five, and highlighting multiples of ten. At times we've also recorded the following information:

How many days of school do we have all year? (175)
How many days of school have we had so far? (149)
How many days of school do we have left? (26)

This helps students understand the passage of time, patterns of number, and subtraction.

THINGS TO DO TODAY

Our daily schedule is written on chart paper covered with clear plastic for easy erasing and changing from day to day without totally rewriting it. We read it together daily. First, I take the lead; later in the year, students do. Interestingly enough, when it came time for Ellen, a less confident reader, to read the chart, she asked the rest of the class to "Please read it with me!" This was important, because it demonstrated each student's responsibility to ask for help. This activity allows the kids to take part in the management of our classroom, no matter what their level of comfort is in reading.

As "Things to Do Today" becomes very familiar to the students, I include more and more variation. As we studied about digestion, for example, "Snack and Free Time" became "Down the Esophagus." By "Morning Get-Together," every child could read *esophagus*!

I close "Things to Do Today" by asking for any questions or comments. Once when I had written "3:00 Go Home," David said it sounded like I had said, "GO HOME!!! like you don't want us around anymore!!" The power of print! None of them liked that at all, so I began to use a positive end-of-day message from that point on, something like "Have a super, spectacular day!"

My main purposes for "Things to Do Today" are to use print as a means of communication and to provide a model for organizing time. Children have expressed their need to "know what is going to happen next," so this time allows them to find out for themselves instead of asking me. Many students begin writing their own versions of "Things to Do Today" either for their school day or for their own time at home. The times also serve as a meaningful reason for learning to tell time digitally or on a face clock. We eventually include clock faces with appropriate times for each part of the day.

## ORGANIZING LANGUAGE ARTS

Every year the structural framework of my language arts program varies somewhat, depending mainly on the students' differences and needs. Some work more independently than others; some need more individual attention; some work better in groups than others. During any year, however, I always work with kids in whole groups, small groups, and individually. The small groups are not set up according to ability, because all kids have their own strengths to offer a group and the variation in those strengths allows students to help each other. The mix of abilities helps us all to stimulate and reinforce each other's thinking. We focus approximately one hour and a half on language arts daily, although language (both written and oral) is at the core of everything we do in our classroom.

### READING WORKSHOP

The kids all read different books of their own choice. At the beginning of the year, we simply read during this time and share books with each other. As the year progresses, our conferencing becomes more focused and we get into discussions of how stories work, predictions of outcomes, reasons for our likes and dislikes, and specific strategies for reading and understanding print.

Later in the year, book review sheets are completed as kids finish reading their books (Figure 6-2). I explain to them that I need the review sheets in case I haven't read the book. This gives me a good indication of what they've gotten out of their reading. We work at being concise, yet clear. The review sheets also include a written reaction to the book. I want to get kids thinking about what they read rather than just retelling. I'm interested in building the connections they make as they read. I let the kids know that I value their opinions and that they may not, indeed, like every story they ever read. On the other hand, some of the best writing may be that which makes us cry or feel angry. Written response is difficult for second graders, but it is an area to work on. Rather than expecting perfection, I expect effort and progress from each student.

**Figure 6-2**  *Jennifer's Book Review Sheet*

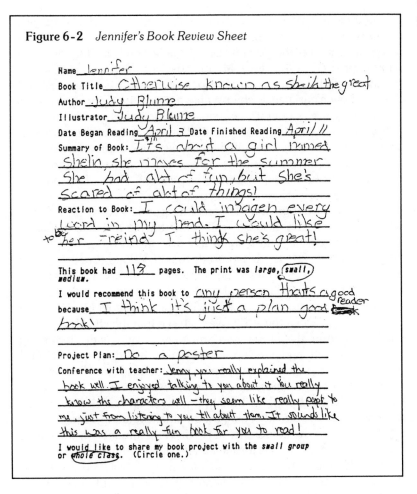

Name ___Jennifer___

Book Title ___Otherwise known as sheila the great___

Author ___Judy Blume___

Illustrator ___Judy Blume___

Date Began Reading ___April 3___ Date Finished Reading ___April 11___

Summary of Book: ___It's about a girl named Shelia, she moves for the summer. She had alot of fun, but she's scared of alot of things!___

Reaction to Book: ___I could imagen every word in my head. I would like to be her friend I think she's great!___

This book had ___113___ pages.  The print was *large,* *(small,)* *medium.*

I would recommend this book to ___any person thats a good reader___ because ___I think it's just a plan good book!___

Project Plan: ___Do a poster___

Conference with teacher: ___Jenny you really explained the book well. I enjoyed talking to you about it You really know the characters well — they seem like really people to me, just from listening to you tell about them. It sounds like this was a really fun book for you to read!___

I would like to share my book project with the *small group* or *(whole class.)*  (Circle one.)

The students decide what project they will do with the book. They record their plan on the review sheet and proceed to carry out the project. This becomes a contract. They may use reading workshop time to do their project whenever they're at that point. We brainstorm a list of ideas for projects, but kids can also come up with their own ideas. Projects have included dioramas (shadowboxes), illustrations, posters, new covers, puppet shows, visits from pets (related to stories), and character "dress-ups." When kids complete their projects, the book review sheets are then submitted to me.

My agenda during reading workshop time is to have at least one formal conference with each child each week. "Formal conference" simply means those times when I record information; actually, I have lots of individual contact with kids every day. First I conference with those students who have turned in review sheets (this lets me know that they are ready to conference on their book). On any given day, I see up to six students either individually or in small groups.

During a conference, the student tells me about the book that he or she has read, and we talk about it. Depending on who it is, I might concentrate on having the student retell the details of the story, give an overview of the story, make inferences or predictions based on the story, or focus on the "connections" made between the child and what happened in the story. My purpose is to find out as much as possible what the child has understood about what was read. Also, I find out how clearly each child is able to retell the story. Does he or she have a sense of how stories work? Does it makes sense to me?

If we're in a small group, we all offer questions and comments, share reactions to stories (often other kids have already read the same book and make comparisons between books and authors). A lot can be gained from sharing perspectives. Kids often provide better models for each other than I can.

Sometimes I design mini-lessons for specific needs, particularly when I notice that a group of children is having a similar problem. Also, I might ask a child to read aloud to me in order to give me insight into the strategies being used. Reading aloud is not the same as reading silently, and I want kids to understand this. Too often kids who have trouble reading aloud think they're not good readers, and this may not be true at all. That is why I always begin by asking the child to tell me about the story. We both see that the child has gotten something from the story, and, thus, we begin with something positive—something I can support. When a child does read aloud, I listen to see what strategies are being used rather than "how many" words are missed. I almost always see the use of at least one effective strategy, so I build on that. I might introduce an additional strategy along with the one already being used to make reading easier.

At the end of the conference, I jot down comments on the child's book review sheet. This is for the benefit of both the student and the parents. Kids can be intimidated by seeing private notes written during conferences. They don't know what's being written and worry whether or not they have "said the right thing." When I write notes right on their paper, they know exactly what I have said and their parents know what kinds of things we're working on and what strengths I'm seeing in their child. I recognize those strengths and include comments about them in what I write.

Once the conference has been completed, the book is ready to be shared. Then the process is repeated. Children do not have to think about doing a book review sheet on another book until they've gone through the entire process on a book.

Before I conference on a second book with any child I make sure I've conferenced with each student in the class. If someone has not completed a book review sheet, we'll investigate the step of the process that he or she is on. Thus, someone cannot "get lost in the shuffle." If need be, I may also put deadlines on completion of book review sheets, but that is usually not necessary.

One of the goals of my reading program is to help strengthen kids' enjoyment of reading. I don't want all of their reading experiences in school to be followed up with a *have-to* like the book review sheet. We have another reading time during the day, usually in the afternoon. We call it "Curl up with a good book" on our "Things to Do Today" chart. We all find a good book and a quiet, comfortable spot in the room and read for twenty to thirty minutes. There is a very quiet, relaxed atmosphere at this time, and we just enjoy books. I read during this time, too—sometimes a children's book (because I really do enjoy them), sometimes an adult book I've chosen, or perhaps a magazine or a newspaper. Sometimes, after ten to fifteen minutes of reading, I may wander around and offer whispered comments or questions to kids about the books they're reading, but with no pencil or paper; only interest and enthusiasm.

Whole group conferences are also part of the language arts program. Group times take advantage of a wide range of student interests, experiences, and abilities and the opportunity to acknowledge the importance of all of those differences. We often share strategies of how people choose books, when they decide if a book is too hard, or what they do when they can't figure out a word sometimes. However, we keep the focus on sharing the enjoyment of good books, and that can be the greatest benefit of all.


WRITING WORKSHOP

For approximately thirty to forty minutes, students all work on pieces of writing, which they keep in writing folders. They write from self-selected topics, styles, and formats, although I occasionally give specific assignments—an invitation or thank-you note, an informational piece about a topic we've been studying or perhaps a particular style we've been discussing.

Students concentrate on content in the first draft of the piece—what they're saying and how it sounds—rather than on what it looks like on paper. When they finish a piece, they begin a new one. But when *at least* three first drafts have been completed, a student will decide which one is the best and may publish that piece, after a bit more work.

When the decision has been made to publish a piece, the student will have a peer conference. The piece will be read to a friend who, hopefully, will let the author know what was liked about the piece and perhaps raise a few questions or comments. It is the author's decision whether or not to do any revising as a result of the conference.

Next, the child will submit the chosen piece to me, which lets me know that a publishing conference is needed. I read over the piece on my own time, noting its strengths and weaknesses but still focusing on content. I used to have the kids read their pieces aloud to me, so that I could hear the authors' intended expression and so that I wouldn't be distracted by mechanical errors. Often I still do, but this year I've found that my students often write long pieces and it takes a long time for me to listen to each piece. So, to save time, I read the piece after school and then spend the conference time discussing it.

In second grade, I am especially concerned that pieces focus on

one topic and have beginnings, middles, and endings. I may retell
the piece to the child, making sure I have understood from it what
was intended and that I have no misconceptions. If the piece is very
sketchy, with little information, I show interest in the topic and
encourage the child to talk about it (rather than the piece, itself).
Then I might say, "You told me (listing several bits of information)
about your topic. Do you think some of that might be important to
add to your piece?" To the child who doesn't want to bother, I might
say, instead, "*Which* bits of information will you add?" I try not to
impose revising on kids; rather, I want them to see that they have
something worthwhile to say and that, by adding or changing what
has been written, they could make the piece clearer or even more
interesting to the reader.

At this point I begin filling out a writing review sheet for the piece
(see Figure 6-3). Following the basic information, I make notes
about our conference, always beginning with positive comments.
This reminds the child of what we talked about and also informs the
parents, since the sheets eventually go home with the piece of

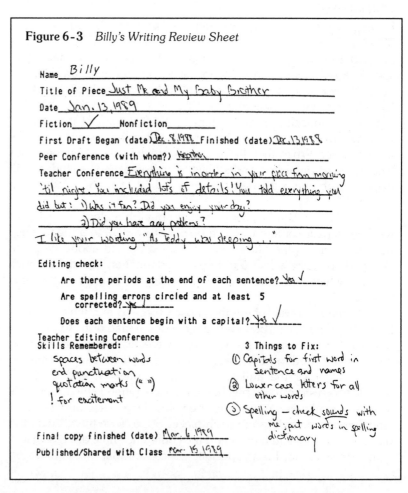

**Figure 6-3**   *Billy's Writing Review Sheet*

Name___*Billy*_____

Title of Piece_Just Me and My Baby Brother_____

Date__Jan. 13, 1989_____

Fiction___✓___Nonfiction_____

First Draft Began (date)_Dec. 8, 1988_Finished (date)_Dec. 13, 1988_

Peer Conference (with whom?)_Heather_____

Teacher Conference_Everything is in order in your piece from morning
'til night. You included lots of details! You told everything you
did but: 1) Was it fun? Did you enjoy your day?
         2) Did you have any problems?
I like your wording "As Teddy was sleeping..."

Editing check:

    Are there periods at the end of each sentence?_Yes ✓____

    Are spelling errors circled and at least 5
      corrected?_yes ✓____

    Does each sentence begin with a capital?_Yes ✓___

Teacher Editing Conference
Skills Remembered:

    Spaces between words
    end punctuation
    quotation marks (" ")
    ! for excitement

3 Things to Fix:

    ① Capitals for first word in
      sentence and names

    ② Lower case letters for all
      other words

    ③ Spelling — check sounds with
      me; put words in spelling
      dictionary

Final copy finished (date) _Mar. 6, 1989_____

Published/Shared with Class _Mar. 15, 1989_

writing. Any revisions to be made are noted so that, when I see the second draft, I can remember what we agreed would be done.

After the content of a piece is set, the child self-edits it. The piece will be proofread for periods, spelling, and capital letters. Again, I don't expect perfection but, rather, effort and progress.

When the piece is again submitted, I carefully look it over and have a final editing conference with the child. I go over all the strengths in the piece and select three growth areas to focus on, considering the particular piece and the abilities of the author. If a piece has lots of conversation in it, for example, I might introduce quotation marks. When Carrie wrote a piece with lots of conversation, and quotation marks in exactly the right places, I taught her about punctuation marks within the quote.

When the final revision is completed, a parent volunteer comes in to type published copies, which are then bound into a book format. When we have at least six newly published books, we hold a "Celebrate Authors Day" in our class. Each of these authors may invite two guests (parents, relatives, or friends) to share the "first public reading" of the published piece.

READ-ALOUD

Perhaps my favorite time of day is read-aloud time, my opportunity to read some of my favorite books to the class. We always discuss the stories I read and share reactions. Certainly everybody will not enjoy the same stories and kids need to know that's okay. Sometimes I let them know when I come to an unfamiliar word (perhaps a name) and what strategy I'll use to figure it out. I also let kids know when something reminds me of an experience I've had. I might even burst into laughter when I come to a funny part. Many of them are beginning readers and are still dealing with figuring out words when they read, so they may miss the "stories" behind the print. I love to share the power behind those words.

## ORGANIZING MATH

We use a textbook in support of manipulative activities in math in a developmental approach very strongly related to the philosophy of whole language. As shown in the lunch graph and calendar time, math, like language arts, is integrated throughout my program. Like language arts, it requires some focus time. Students learn new concepts in a meaningful context by means of discovery. They use what they already know to progress further.

## ORGANIZING SOCIAL STUDIES AND SCIENCE

Social studies and science topics may be suggested by the curriculum guide or recommended by students. We begin by brainstorming what we already know about the topic, resulting in a wealth of information. We share stories, experiences, and so on related to the topic so that we will all have a connection to it somehow. Next, we list the things we'd like to find out about the topic. Student questions always seem to cover any objectives I might have for the topic being studied, but if not I contribute my own questions extending students' thinking.

The next step in our process is to share as many ways as we can think of to learn more about our topic in order to answer our own questions. This encourages student resourcefulness rather than dependence on the teacher to find and to relay all the information. We research our topic to find out as much as possible about it, and discuss ways we can share what we've learned with others. We decide together what we'll do. We may do the same project together or we may work individually or in small groups. However it works out, everyone has a part. We use language, in all its components, for learning about the topic and for sharing our information with each other.

## END-OF-DAY GET-TOGETHER

I try to finish the day with a group time. It's very important for us to reflect on our day and to collect our thoughts. The end of the day in our class seems to be one of the most chaotic, so having an end-of-day get-together allows us to end each day on a reflective, calm note.

## WHERE TO GO FROM HERE

Sometimes I get so caught up in the routines of each day that I lose the opportunity to reflect on why I do what I am doing. I'm fairly comfortable with what I do in language arts at this point. My conferences go well; I am doing fairly well at keeping track of individual kids and what they're doing; and I feel that each one is progressing. I'm seeing an enjoyment of reading and writing, and that is essential to continued progress. Since I am only at one point on my own continuum of development, however, there are some areas of my program which still concern me.

- There is not enough time in the day to get in as much conferencing as I would like with so many students in my class.
- My record-keeping system is too time-consuming and takes me away from working directly with the kids.
- My organizational system, knowledge of my kids, and "plan of action" is primarily in my head, so it's difficult to leave directions for a substitute teacher.
- The rest of my program is not as well integrated as I would like it to be. The day is broken up into subject areas, and I feel that such artificial divisions inhibit learning.
- I still have not developed an effective enough (and again, efficient) means of communicating with parents about my program.

Well, that leaves me with goals to work toward, but isn't lifelong learning what education is truly all about?

# 7

# BECOMING BILITERATE IN
# A WHOLE LANGUAGE CLASSROOM

### Caryl G. Crowell

## PROLOGUE

Maria, who usually does not share in large groups, came to school one day with a plastic dinosaur coin that she had found in a box of cereal. She was anxious for everyone to know where they could get one like it, but she had forgotten the name of the cereal. Her attempts to elicit the name from me were unsuccessful, even with the prompt "Ya-ba-da-ba-doo kind." I could only reply, "If it's not Cheerios, I probably don't know. I don't buy sugared cereals." She walked away disappointed, probably convinced that I was completely ignorant. During the next ten minutes, she moved around the room, talking to some classmates in English and others in Spanish, trying to get help with her problem. She returned to me and triumphantly announced, "Es Fruity Pebbles. Como escribo 'This coin comes in Fruity Pebbles'?" I wrote the sentence she dictated on a scrap of paper and gave her some suggestions for displaying the coin. Sometime later, I found the statement in Figure 7-1 taped to the front chalkboard.

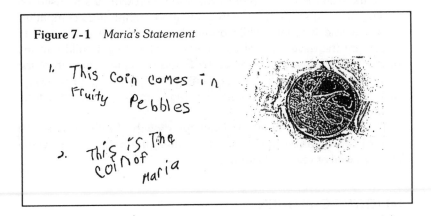

**Figure 7-1** *Maria's Statement*

1. This coin comes in
   Fruity Pebbles

2. This is The
   coin of
        Maria

In my bilingual third-grade classroom, this was a momentous, but not unusual, event. It was momentous because it represented Maria's first attempt at purposeful communication in written English. She had determined that most of her audience would be English speaking and that she would need to write in English to make her message understood. It was not unusual, because the bilingual students in my class make similar decisions about language use all the time.

My classroom at Borton Primary Magnet School is representative of the total school environment. The school provides children with surroundings that are rich in authentic literacy experiences: print drips from the walls, children run a school-wide post office and newspaper, the library offers a research class and a readers' club, and reading and writing take place across the curriculum for many purposes, not the least of which is enjoyment. Within my room, the reading program revolves around a wide variety of literature: small study groups, thematically organized units, and shared and individual reading experiences. The children are urged to write from their own real-life experiences while they are encouraged to explore the stylistic features, patterns, structures, and strategies of the authors they study.

My room also tends to be rather noisy, filled with talk between children and adults. Language learning is not categorized into formal English-as-a-second-language and Spanish-as-a-second-language lessons or time slots. Language choices are dictated by social and academic needs and purposes, just as they would be in the everyday world. To support their interactions, I always group the children heterogeneously and encourage quiet, purposeful talking.

My own discoveries and reflections as a teacher-researcher, as well as my consideration of the research of others, have convinced me that whole language, bilingual classrooms are the most appropriate environments for encouraging and supporting second-language learning. However, since I don't use the adopted basal texts or ESL Program, the instruments designed to test progress through these programs would not be appropriate measures of my students' progress. Still, I am responsible for documenting the growth of my students' biliteracy. My recent professional growth has focused on finding and experimenting with evaluation techniques, compatible with a whole language philosophy, that would give me a way to document the development of biliteracy. Ultimately, I build into my program several ways to look at the English-language growth of the monolingual or Spanish-dominant children in my room: print awareness studies, miscue analysis, writing samples, and anecdotal records.

The more I know about the language growth of my students, the better I can organize my classroom to meet the needs of the whole class, as well as each individual.

## MEET THE CHILDREN

Although Maria was born in Phoenix, she did not speak English when she entered Borton in her kindergarten year. She learned to speak English in the naturally rich language environment that characterizes Borton and from her older sisters, who are bilingual. Although Maria was initially instructed in Spanish reading with Santillana and Economy basal readers in first grade, the majority of her Spanish reading experiences and exposure to English print have been in whole language settings. Since Maria is very quiet and shy, traditional instruments that measure expressive output may not be appropriate for her. Her Language Assessment Screening done six months before the beginning of the school year, showed only a functional level of language use in both Spanish and English. Maria's family speaks mostly Spanish at home, although the older children are more likely to use English among themselves. Both Maria's parents read, usually in Spanish, but they often buy English language magazines and newspapers.

Victor, born in Sonora, Mexico, started kindergarten in California. At that time, he was classified as a monolingual Spanish speaker. He moved to Tucson during his kindergarten year and was enrolled in a bilingual program that provided Spanish basal reader instruction and a traditional ESL format. When Victor transferred to Borton at the beginning of this year, his Language Assessment scores showed a proficient level of ability in English, although he was still predominantly using Spanish. Victor's family speaks Spanish almost exclusively at home, although his parents do speak and read some English. Victor has his own books in both languages.

Victor was highly socially motivated to use English. Most of the boys in my class had been with me last year as second graders, and they formed a tight social circle of predominantly English and English-dominant speakers. To win their attention and the acceptance he wanted, Victor joined the English literature study groups.

## PRINT AWARENESS

Goodman, Goodman, and Flores (1979) found that even children who speak little or no English are reading English print in their environment. To discover what Maria knew about print awareness, I asked her to respond to photographs of signs from the school neighborhood, pictures of signs in Tana Hoban's *I Can Read Signs*, and labels from our classroom (print awareness items). I presented these to her in November with their surrounding contexts and in December without their surrounding contexts. Since Maria was already reading books in English by the spring, I chose not to repeat the print awarness items with her in April.

Maria's long period of residence in an English-print community was evident in her ability to read and to understand almost all of the print awareness items, both with and without contexts, in November and December. Of particular interest to me, as her teacher, was her response on several items from Tana Hoban's book. In response to "NO PARKING FIRE LANE," Maria miscued and read "No parking free line" but immediately corrected it to read "No parking fire line."

Another miscue, "playpol working," was changed to "people working" when Maria realized that her first response did not make sense. Her concern for making meaning with such little print available was an encouraging sign of her growth in dealing with English print.

I chose not to use the print awareness items with Victor, since he was already reading with the English literature study groups.

To extend and build upon Maria's awareness of environmental print, activities such as sign-reading walks were initiated. With her journal in hand, we walked around the school reading and writing down all the environmental print she could read. Newspaper advertisements, department store flyers, and catalogs of Christmas gifts—all printed in English—were used as references for math lessons dealing with estimating, rounding, and mental math. Maria interacted with English print through highly predictable books and big books, song charts, and poetry, read in small- and large-group situations. With the rest of the class, Maria was read to in English at least once a day from a wide variety of literature. Thematically organized center materials, including directions, recording sheets, and reference books in both languages, were available to all the children.

## THE MISCUE STUDIES

Barrera (1981) and Goodman, Goodman, and Flores (1979) believe that bilingual children are not confused by their dual language environment. Even though second-language learning is enhanced by language skills and knowledge about print in the first language, second-language learners will often self-initiate second-language reading simultaneously with the development of literacy in their first language. Barrera (1981) found that English as a Second Language (ESL) learners are able to read English before they have complete oral control of the language. They will miscue, and some miscues will change the meaning of the text, often eliciting self-correction.

Children's ESL reading often reflects the developmental nature of their second-language learning. When ESL children retell in their native language, they often give the teacher a more accurate representation of their comprehension. Moreover, Goodman, Goodman, and Flores (1979) found that as second-language learners become bilingual, their reading reflects their first language as well as the extent to which they control English.

I used miscue analysis in December and in April to understand more about Maria and Victor's reading. By December, Victor had already joined the English literature study groups, and I had observed Maria exploring English books on numerous occasions. I asked the children to read me a story in English, hoping I could get a sense of their developing control of their second language. The children chose stories they wanted to read from books by popular children's authors whose writings deal with friendship and independence.

Over the next several months the children chose books based less on language and more on thematic content. In literature study groups, it was not uncommon for them to read a book in English and to respond to it in Spanish. As of April, Victor was the only one of the bilingual children who had made literature log entries in English.

In April, after having read Rigg and Enright's *Children and ESL: Integrating Perspectives* (1986), I gave more consideration to the text choices I was offering. Hudelson (1986) mentioned that the same genre usually has the same form across languages, and Rigg (1986) recommended using contexts and genres that were familiar to ESL readers in their native language. With this in mind, I selected folktales for the spring miscue analysis sessions in English, since we had read stories of this genre in Spanish during the year.

In December, Maria's English miscue analysis revealed considerable use of Spanish phonology. She miscued frequently and seldom self-corrected. Most of her substitutions had a high level of graphic similarity, indicating that Maria most likely was simply trying to sound out unfamiliar words. In one reading Maria had difficulty with the word *yelling*, pronouncing the "ll" as she would in Spanish. This problem with English phonology had little effect on her understanding of the story; she knew the mother was angry. Despite low miscue scores for syntactic and semantic acceptability, in listening to her retelling, it was obvious that she understood the gist of the story. Maria was even able to build an understanding of new vocabulary items. She was not sure what *blueberries* were, yet she correctly identified them as food, gathered clues from the story, and concluded they were something like *uvas* (grapes).

In her April miscue session, Maria's developing use of English syntax and semantics as a reading strategy became apparent. For the phrase "the goat called out," she read "the goat cried out," a meaningful semantic and syntactic substitution. She chose to retell the story in English, recalling most of the major events and indicating her ability to carry on a conversation in her second language. The one area that seemed to give her the most difficulty concerned the use of pronouns. She frequently substituted *she* for *he*, and vice versa, but only when the pronouns referred to animals. Since the words *goat* and *donkey* don't imply any particular gender, her substitutions were understandable. It may also be that her knowledge of how pronouns work in Spanish (subject pronouns are often not required, and object pronouns are often the same regardless of gender) influenced her miscues.

Maria's miscue analyses indicate that she was depending less on graphophonic cues as an English reading strategy and was becoming more aware of syntactic and semantic predicting and confirming strategies that she already controlled in Spanish and that she would not be able to use in English without a sense of how her second language works.

Victor's November miscue analysis, also showed influence of his Spanish phonology, although he continuously worked at the parts of the text that were giving him difficulty as he read. "Pickled beets" went through several transformations as he attempted to make sense of the phrase. He did conclude that it was something to eat. Throughout his reading, Victor was searching for meaning. He self-corrected regularly and made several high-quality miscues that did not disrupt the meaning of the text. "Nobody in sight yet" became "Nobody is sight yet" and then "Nobody is excited yet."

Victor's syntactic and semantic acceptability scores were quite high. Although many of his word-level substitutions had high or some graphic similarity to the text, most of the inappropriate ones were self-corrected as Victor confirmed his predictions using his language sense. His retelling was in English and fairly complete. He was even able to summarize with an appropriate theme statement: "Always be friends with somebody."

In April, Victor's miscue analysis showed continuous use of his language sense to predict and confirm, integrating the use of grapho-phonic cues efficiently as well. His syntactic and semantic acceptability scores were still high, and, as before, he self-corrected regularly and made high-level miscues that required a knowledge of how English works. "We'll do it tomorrow" became "Well, I'll do it tomorrow." "Soon the cream will turn into butter" became "Soon the cream will be turned into butter," and "As she came near the house" was changed to "As she neared the house." Victor retold in English, capturing most of the details of the story. There was some confusion in his mind about one sequence of events, but it was most likely due to his lack of familiarity with some story concepts.

Both of these children are clearly well along on the road to English literacy. Additionally, their miscues provide information on aspects of English syntax that they are still developing, and vocabulary and concepts they do not know. Their awareness of how stories are constructed is also obvious.

I might add, as a personal note, that the children were delighted with their ability to read in English and understand most of what they were reading. Maria, who was the most hesitant about reading in English, was surprised by her abilities. Miscue analysis resulted in useful information for me to plan more relevant reading experiences for my students, and at the same time it was a highly positive and empowering experience for the children.

## WRITING SAMPLES

Edelsky (1982, 1986), Edelsky and Gilbert (1985), and Hudelson (1984, 1986, 1987) have studied Spanish-speaking children writing in English and have concluded that these children are able to acquire two separate writing systems without any confusion. Moreover, their studies have shown that ESL children can write in English without having full control over the oral language and even without reading it. Hudelson (1986) found that second-language learners can create different kinds of texts for different purposes and that there is variation within their work as they respond to different contexts and purposes.

Throughout the year, I collected English writing samples from the children. Victor consistently wrote in English throughout the school year. Maria's English writing was sporadic and, with the exception of some letters, was usually done at my request.

Even though Maria spontaneously wrote her "Fruity Pebbles" coin label in October (Figure 7-1), she produced only a few, very short pieces of English writing, usually just a few words in answer to questions in her log. Then, toward the end of March, Maria had occasion to write several letters within a week to English-speaking audiences. The first one, on March 23, was to Marie Abbs, a visiting university student, who had brought our class some brownies (Figure 7-2, A, p. 102). The words reflect invented spelling with little or no influence of Spanish phonology. Double-letter endings are a distinctly English feature, as are the letters *k* and *w*. When Maria could not remember the name of the treat we had eaten, she substituted a rebus picture, an ingenious solution to her problem.

Maria wrote another letter the same week thanking the PTO for arranging the Tucson Symphony Program for our schools (Figure 7-2, B). As in the previous letter, the words *thankyou* are chunked together, but this time the spelling is conventional. As a matter of fact, over 60 percent of the words in this letter are spelled conventionally, demonstrating Maria's knowledge of English phonology and spelling patterns. The style of this letter is considerably more formal than the one to Marie Abbs, reflecting the fact that Maria did not know the audience as well.

On April 6, Maria wrote an unassigned letter to Ms. Roche, our student teacher (Figure 7-2, C). Once again, a high proportion of the words are spelled conventionally, and the balance reflect English, rather than Spanish, spelling patterns. Maria's experiment with the punctuation in the contraction *I'm* is seen in most of her English writing toward the end of the year. The direction of a question to Ms. Roche indicates audience awareness and the expectation of a reply.

On April 11, Maria wrote her own version of *Chicken Little* (Figure 7-3, A, p. 103). As in the previous pieces, her use of English spelling for her inventions are characteristic. About 75 percent of the words are spelled conventionally. Once again, Maria has used a comma rather than an apostrophe in the contraction, but it is appropriately placed. In this piece, she uses a variety of links—and, but, then, so—and successfully subordinates clauses. Her awarness of story style is evident in her opening, "onc upon a tem," and in her consistent use of the past tense for the narrative portion of her story. The tense shifts to the present for the dialogues.

Over the next two weeks, Maria did not write anything else in English. I was so excited about her progress that, in my eagerness to see more of what she could do, I resorted to breaking my self-imposed taboo—I requested that Maria write something else for me in English. She returned with a bilingual story (Figure 7-3, B and C),

**Figure 7-2** *Maria's Letters*

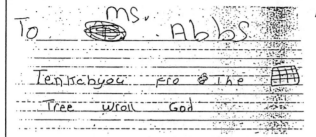

To MS. Ablss
Tenkchyou fro ☺ The 🔲
Tree wroll God

**A.** Maria's thank you
Thank you for the (rebus of brownie).
They were good.

DeAiR _Parents
Thankyou Fros. Helpin as end Fro.
The Maly The you git To me
Worfman and! Fro. Comei To Ar
class

Hers a sicter [M]

**B.** To parents
Thank you for helping us and for
the many things you give to Mr.
Wortman and for coming to our
class.
Here's a sticker.

Dear Mrs. Roche I like ya
So Much ar ya Goin To
Be Hir? Im not 2 I
miss you so Much

You Maria J/6/54
IV 2

**C.** To Mrs. Roche
Dear Mrs. Roche  I like you
so much. Are you going to
be here? I'm not. I
miss you so much.

102

**Figure 7-3** *Maria's Stories*

chicKen Little

Onc opon a Tem I
wen I was walKing I
Sway a chicKen littl and
I Tol hem Come abo
play wich me and he
Tol ma oral I wal play
wich you But don,T Ever

Say ChicKen
litte Say Towme

Oh no chicKen The
sKy is Felling Thene they
went To Tale The King
So they went oh no The
SKey every Fell so They
dicareT To deay

by maria

Yo Soy la reynia
aBia una vez un caballo
que queria una Muchocha
i y la concigio era una Muchacha
Fea pero luego la iso Bonito
E Ella se subio en la Silla
del cabatlo y la llevo al coSTik
y le dió el vesTido y se
Sento en el Sillon y el
Caballo Se Fue y Ella Se quedo
con Todo

ESpañol)

I,T was a Tiam
a hors met ta GrIl he
was figril and The hor Tol
her I woold TeK you To The
Casold and he Tol her hers
dis dres end hers The cher and I
Si bu leTTre and The pricisn
as They Trey

IñglES

A. Chicken Little
Once upon a time
when I was walking I
saw a Chicken Little and
I told him "Come and
play with me," and he
told me "alright, I will play
with you but don't ever
SAY CHICKEN
LITTLE say to me
"oh no, chicken, the
sky is falling." Then they
went to tell the king,
so they went, "oh no, the
sky already fell." So they
decided to die.

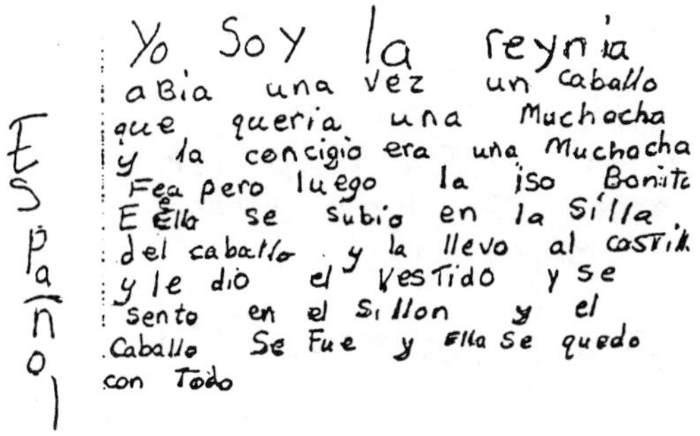

B. *Yo soy la reina*
*Había una vez un caballo*
*que quería una muchacha*
*y la consiguió. Era una muchacha*
*fea, pero luego se hizo bonita.*
*Y ella se subió en la silla*
*del caballo y la llevó al castillo*
*y le dió el vestido y se*
*sentó en el sillón y el*
*caballo se fue y ella se quedó*
*con todo.*
Translation:
I am the Queen
Once there was a horse
who loved a girl
and he won her. She was
ugly but later she became beautiful.
And she got up in the saddle
and he carried her to the castle
and he gave her the dress and she
sat in the throne and the
horse went off and she was left
with everything.

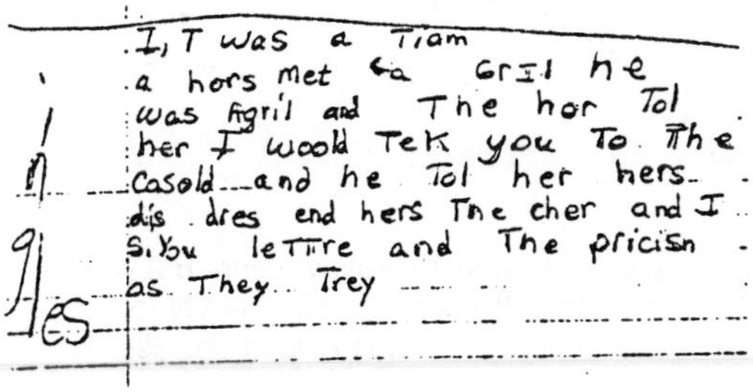

C. It was a time
a horse met a girl. She
was ugly and the horse told
her, "I would take you to the
castle," he told her, "here's
this dress and here's the chair and I
see you later," and the princess
has the treasure.

in which she essentially wrote the same narrative in both languages. It is a powerful statement of her ability to manipulate two languages successfully without creating confusion. The story in English is not a translation of the one in Spanish but, rather, a different version.

In the story in Spanish, the spelling is almost entirely conventional and the Spanish syntax is conventional. Maria appropriately subordinates and consistently uses both preterit and imperfect tenses for narration. The English version includes a number of words where the

**Figure 7-4** *Maria's Goodbye Letter*

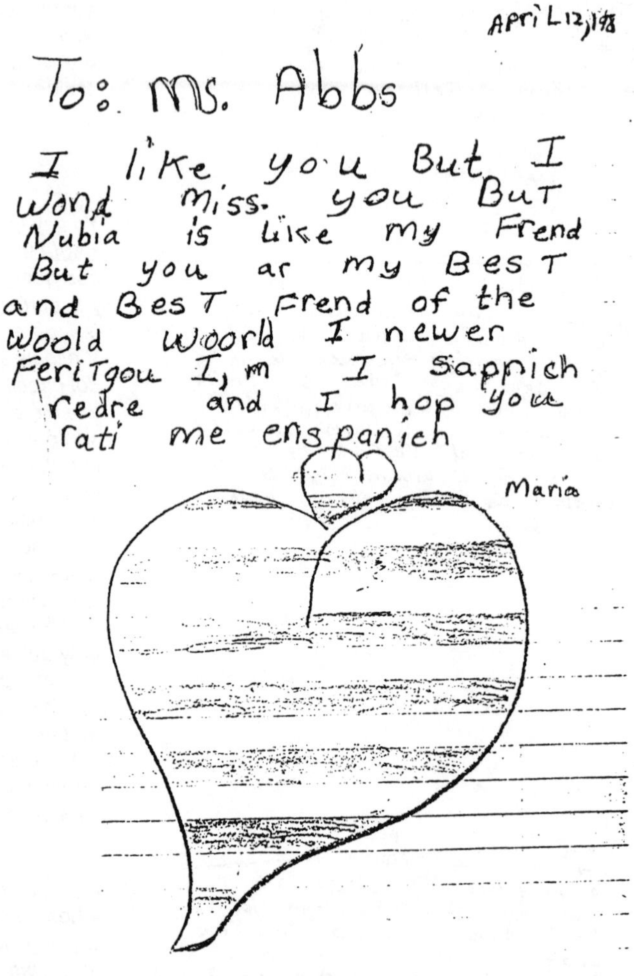

APri L12,198

To: ms. Abbs

I like you But I wond miss. you BuT Nubia is Like my Frend But you ar my BesT and BesT Frend of the woold woorld I newer FeriTgou I, m I Sappich redre and I hop you rati me ensPanich

Maria

I like you but I would miss you. But Nubia is like my friend. But you are my best friend and best friend of the whole world. I never forget you. I'm a Spanish reader and I hope you write to me in Spanish.

spelling is only off by one letter: *hors* (*horse*), *tol* (*told*), *woold* (*would*), *hers* (*here's*), *dres* (*dress*), *as* (*has*), and *the* (*they*). Some words show her awareness of English spelling patterns: *agril* (*ugly*), *casold* (*castle*), and *princisn* (*princess*). A few words reveal use of Spanish orthography for invention: *dis* (*this*), *trey* (*treasure*), *cher* (*chair*). Her English story includes dialogue and consistent use of the past tense for narration.

Maria's latest piece written in English is another letter to Marie Abbs (Figure 7-4). This time there's been a change in the form of her letter. The date has been included, and there's a colon in the greeting. Maria has chunked some pieces of language: *ferityou* (*forget you*) and *enspanich* (*in Spanish*). Her experimentation with the punctuation required for contractions continues, with commas placed in *won't* and *I'm*. Lest anyone doubt that Maria is writing in English, she very deliberately chose to write the name of her native language, *spanich*, in English.

Since Maria rarely speaks English in the classroom and never speaks English to me, I was thrilled to see how well she controls the language in her writing. Her message is always understandable, her syntax is usually appropriate, and her English spelling patterns are phenomenal considering that she is a relative newcomer to English reading and writing.

Victor began writing in English in November, shortly after joining the English literature study groups. The first English book he read in class was *Nate the Great* by M. Sharmat (1972), and his first literature log entry was typical of many of the children at that point (Figure 7-5, A, p. 106).

Victor was observed using the book itself as a resource for writing. The only invented words were *YELLO* and *AN*. *PICTRE* was most likely miscopied. His entry is limited to facts from the story.

The following week Victor wrote another entry about the book, but in Spanish. This time, his own voice is present as he discusses his reaction and thoughts about the main character (Figure 7-5, B).

Within days, Victor used English again in his literature log (Figure 7-5, C). This time he did not copy words from the book. But, once again, his writing is limited to a retelling of the plot. Despite the limitations in terms of content, Victor's entry does provide information about his control of English. His invented spelling reflects both Spanish orthography and English spelling patterns. Although he correctly uses *h* in *His* and *hum*, he uses Spanish orthography to write *he* as *ge*. He has chunked together *foundet* for *found it*. He successfully uses a complex structure and a variety of links (*because*, *when*, *then*, *and*).

At this time, at the risk of not getting any writing in English from him, I encouraged Victor to continue to write in his literature log in Spanish, feeling I would get a much better idea of how well he was reading in English. He did not oblige me for long. By January, he was once again using English in his log. However, this time, I got the personal response I was hoping for (Figure 7-5, D).

**Figure 7-5** *Victor's Literature Log*

---

Victor R.    11-28-88
Nate The Great is a detective
Annes lost a picture of Fang Annis rom,
is yello an the picture was orange.

**A** "Nate the Great" (English)

---

El es vien vueno porque le allo el
retrato de la anne Tambien se canso mucho
nomas porque quiere ala otra jente Tambien
Tubo muchas cosas que ava encontrado pero
el Tuvo que encontrar un retrato luego Tuvo
que allar un Gato me gusta mucho porque lo
leei Tambien parese que es de deveras porque
jente pueda allar cosas y no saben de quien es
meisosentir feliz porque yo lei el libro me
gusto mucho el fin

**B.** "Nate the Great" (Spanish)
*Translation:* He is very good because he found Annie's picture. Also he got very tired, only because he liked people a lot. Also, he had to find a picture. Then he had to find a cat. I liked it a lot because I read it. Also, it seemed real to me because people find things and don't know who owns them. I felt happy because I read this book. I liked it a lot.

---

12-12-88
HuBert HuNTs His Hum

His por an y got sad becas His
Humm got lost an ye cudent founde
Then it was ay na's day uRn ge
lost j's voice an Thats al of The story.

**C.** "Hubert Hunts His Hum"
He's poor and I got sad because his hum got lost and he couldn't find it. Then it was a nice day when he lost his voice and that's all of the story.

---

1-9-89
the pain and the
grett one is so fone but
The first story They like The
brother an in Te nekst story They
like The sister an That is fau it is
i liket The story To mush maybi i
can sheket uot oun day it gav me a
filing like redineT agen the end.

**D.** "The Pain and the Great One"
The Pain and the Great One is so funny. But the first story, they like the brother and in the next story they like the sister and that is how it is. I liked the story too much. Maybe I can check it out one day. It gave me a feeling like reading it again. the end.

Here, Victor uses a high percentage of conventional English spelling and influences from both Spanish orthography and English spelling patterns for his inventions. He was still chunking language: *sheket* (*check it*) and *ridinet* (*reading it*). In Spanish, to express the same idea would require using the infinitive form of the verb with the object pronoun attached: *sacarlo* and *leerlo*. There seemed to be a cohesion problem with the lack of a pronoun referent for the *they* in the third line. But, in order to encourage a personal response to the reading, I had told the children not to recount the plot, "because everyone has read the book." I wonder if Victor just assumed we would all know who *they* was. Syntactically, Victor's entry shows an ability to subordinate clauses and to use several different links (*and, but, maybe,* and prepositional phrases).

Victor did one piece of expository writing in English in March. He read a book about earthworms as part of our preparation for gardening and was asked to prepare a report for the class (Figure 7-6).

Hudelson (1986) reported that young children often have a difficult time removing themselves from expository writing, and Victor is certainly no exception. His personal opinion of earthworms comes through loud and clear. Although more and more of Victor's

**Figure 7-6**   *Victor: "Earthworms," March 10*

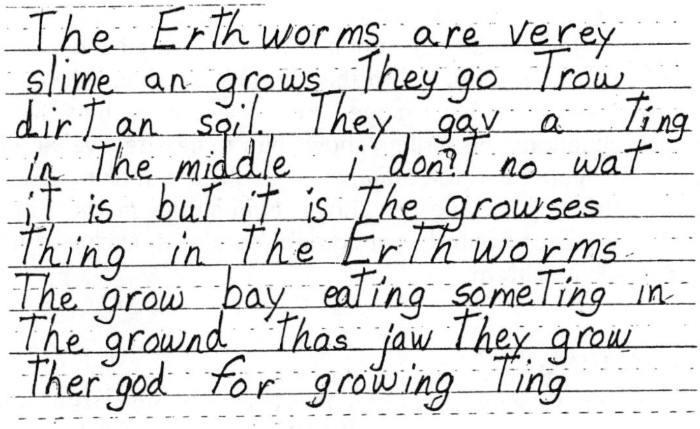

The Erth worms are verey
slime an grows. They go Trow
dir[ an soi[. They gav a Ting
in The middle i don'T no waT
it is but it is The growses
Thing in The ErTh worms.
The grow bay eaTing someTing in
The grownd Thas jaw They grow
Ther god for growing Ting

The earthworms are very slimy and gross. They go through dirt and soil. They have a thing in the middle. I don't know what it is, but it is the grossest thing in the earthworms. They grow by eating something in the ground. That's how they grow. They're good for growing things.

invented spellings reflect his knowledge of English spelling patterns, he is still using Spanish orthography to represent the English *h* sound. Victor, like Maria, experimented with punctuation for contractions, and decided to try using a question mark. Unlike his references to stories in his literature log entries, Victor consistently uses the present tense throughout this piece, an appropriate style for expository writing.

Victor's latest writings in English are letters, all of which were written within one week of each other (Figure 7-7, A, B, C). The first letter (Figure 7-7, A) is a thank-you note to Marie Abbs for the brownies. Here, the initial *h* sound is conventionally represented, and the *w* as well. Both of these had been written using Spanish orthography in Victor's earlier writing. The principal spelling patterns he relies on are English. Victor chunked together *Thankyou*, a form that Maria used, too. Once again, his control over subordination is evident.

The second letter of the week (Figure 7-7, B) was noticeably different in style, being much more informal and personal. It is directed to a classmate who was home recovering from an accident. *Tumoro* is most likely based on Spanish orthography, as is Victor's use of *g* in *your* and *you*. The balance of the letter uses English spelling patterns for inventions and English conventional spelling. His language use is syntactically appropriate for his audience.

Victor's last letter (Figure 7-7, C) was written to the parents of our student teacher who had brought in a honeycomb with honey for the children to see and to sample. Just days earlier, Victor had chunked together *thankyou*, but in this letter it is conventionally segmented.

As mentioned before, Victor was very motivated to use English in order to survive socially. Were it not for the Spanish reading going on in his home, I would be concerned about his losing his biliteracy in favor of English. In addition to the information about Victor's language abilities that I have gained from listening to him talk in a variety of situations, his writing shows him to be effectively controlling English syntax and the pragmatics involved in making language choices. Also, his spelling has shown tremendous growth, moving from heavy use of Spanish orthography to almost exclusive use of English spelling patterns.

## KIDWATCHING

I spend a lot of time watching all of the children in my class whenever I can. I keep records by placing self-sticking labels on notebook pages designated for each child.

Observing Maria, Victor, and the other bilingual students as they communicate in both of their languages enables me to truly appreciate and to delight in their growth. Knowing a good deal about their reading and writing helps me organize for literacy experiences that have real purposes and that take place in authentic contexts. The

**Figure 7-7**  *Victor's Letters*

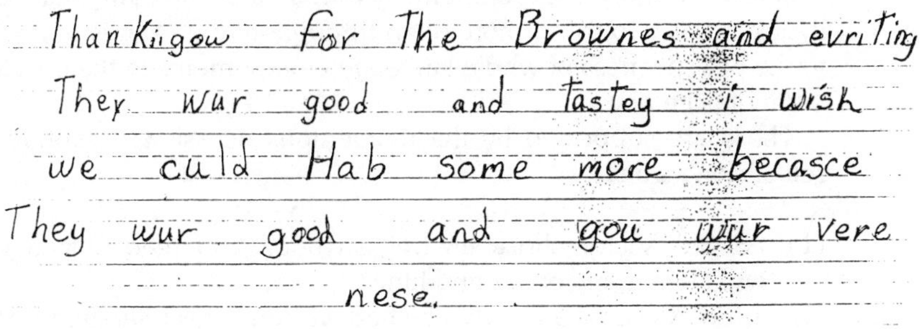

ThanKiigow for The Brownes and evriTing
They wur good and tasTey i wish
we culd Hab some more becasce
They wur good and gou wur vere.
nese.

**A. Letter to Marie**

Thank you for the brownies and everything. They were good and tasty. I
wish we could have some more because they were good and you were
very nice.

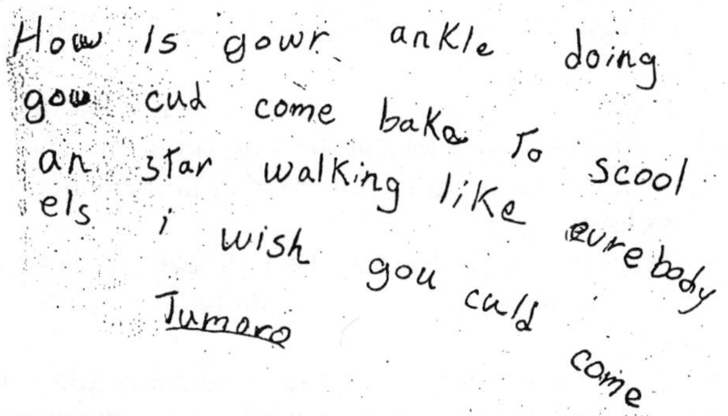

How Is gowr anKle doing i wish
gou cud come baka To scool
an sTar walking like eure body
els i wish gou cu/d
Tumoro come

**B. To a friend**

How is your ankle doing? I wish you could come back to school and start
walking like everybody else. I wish you could come tomorrow.

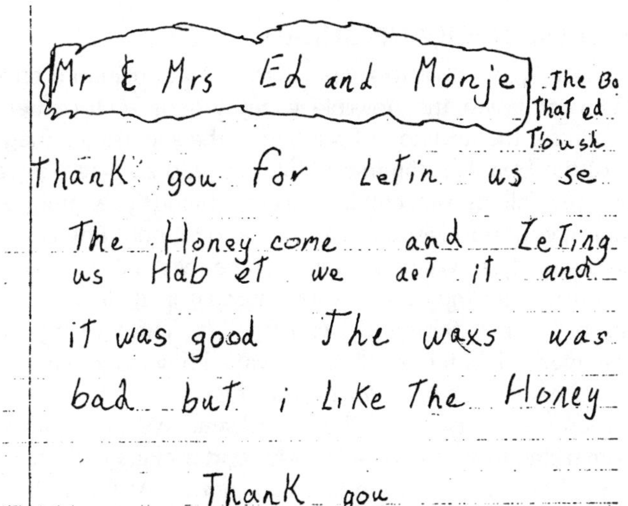

Mr & Mrs Ed and Monje . The Bo
That ed
ToushK
ThanK gou for LeTin us se
The Honey come and LeTing
us Hab et we aoT it and
iT was good The waxs was
bad but i LiKe The Honey

ThanK gou

**C. To Mr. and Mrs. Monje**

Thank you for letting us see the honeycomb and letting us have it. We ate it
and it was good. The wax was bad, but I like the honey. Thank you.

children's comfort in experimenting with their second language, and their tendency to do so more often throughout the year, is testimony to the effectiveness of whole language environments in the development of biliteracy.

These are supported by the momentous occasions I capture on self-sticking labels:

(11/28/88) Victor chose an English book and read oblivious to what was going on around him

(12/1/88) Victor shared what he had written in his Literature Log in English. It was stilted and very superficial. When I looked later, I found his entry had actually been in Spanish in considerably more detail than his shared version. He expressed great satisfaction with himself at having read the book.

(1/5/89) Maria has chosen an English story for SSR, *Pierre*, one that is familiar. She's reading, or rather, singing, quietly to herself.

(3/7/89) Maria has chosen *not* to work with a group of native English speakers on a logical thinking problem. There is a fair amount of discussion going on. Maria's participation is limited, but she's listening.

(3/7/89) How quickly Victor visualizes problems! He's solved the locomotive problem in just a few minutes and is able to explain his strategy.

(4/24/89) Victor was thrilled with the double-entendres of *Amelia Bedelia and the Baby* when another group presented it as a play. He kept saying, "baby food, get it? Baby hamburgers, little tiny food. Get it?" I think he may have just figured it out.

## LOOKING BACK AND AHEAD

At the beginning of this year, none of the bilingual children in my classroom, with the possible exception of Victor, met the district criteria for the addition of reading in the second language, although all of the Spanish-dominant children read sufficiently well in Spanish. Yet, all of the children were obviously acquiring literacy in English continuously, successfully, and without any confusion. Their miscue studies, writing samples, and anecdotal records revealed that they use what they know about literacy in their native language to support their experiments with English. Through my evaluation of their work, I build on their growing knowledge and continuously organize for a rich biliterate classroom.

Today is the last day of the school year. We are running around the room trying to exchange addresses and making sure that nothing will be left behind—except memories, that is. At this point, as I watch Victor and Maria talking excitedly with their peers, I feel both pride and joy at their accomplishment, and sorrow that I will not continue the journey with them. As I move past Maria, she slips a small, folded piece of paper into my hand. As I read her message, my tears come:

to MR.S cRowell

I will miss you
So Much thath
a dot wanto
let go I will
miss you So much
and Remenber me

Maria

# BREAKING AWAY FROM THE BASALS

**Constance J. McCarthy**

Day after day I sat in my classroom very much troubled. What was wrong? Why couldn't I get it all together enough to pull off a nice smooth reading lesson each day and have neat columns of grades to average at the end of the quarter? Why couldn't I do it all as smoothly as the other teachers?

I mused over these questions constantly. Every day I would call each group to the reading table and go through another story, workbook pages, or some related skill sheets. Every day someone from each group had not finished yesterday's work, was absent, or had been absent the previous day. No matter how I planned to conduct the lesson, someone lagged behind with papers undone or a story unread. Finally, I concluded what I could hardly accept as true, yet I knew it was: Reading class was boring. As the teacher, I was bored with the content and frustrated by the lack of purpose and progress. Daily I heard myself saying, "When you finish your work, get a book and read." Yet the reality was that my students perceived the reading table as the only place where they had to read. If I watched closely, I would always notice that any books they got to read were just to fill time. Seldom did a student mark his or her place in a book and put it in his or her desk for later. Consistently, they borrowed books only briefly, returning them to the shelf when I finished instructing at the table. Their reading was meaningless, and it was done with no investment of pride, interest, or curiosity.

The reading table had become a cold, detailed, regimented place. We were reading nothing more than words and the sounds of letters.

I thought back to my own childhood. How had I learned to read? Yes, I had sat through *Dick, Jane, and Sally* in school, but I had read before that. My earliest memories were of the blackboard easel in our kitchen. My mother would write one word on the board. I would then write all the words I could that rhymed with her word. But the strongest memories I have are of her and me snuggled together in a stuffed armchair while she read aloud to me. Those hours spent together were the most valuable ones we ever had together. As she read to me, I learned the sounds and flow of language. I learned to follow a story from beginning to end. I met new places and characters through the books we shared that would stay with me for decades. The reading aloud between us continued long after I started school. Gradually, I learned to follow along as my mother read aloud. One day she was interrupted and could not find her place when she returned to the page.

"You were right here," I said pointing to the words she had last read.

"How did you know that?" she asked in surprise.

"Because I was reading with you," I responded.

Our read-aloud sessions did not stop then. We continued just as we always had, only with me following her as she read, increasing my reading ability daily.

My discovery of reading was aided by hearing the written language, by having lots of books around, and by someone providing me with "times to read." Reading had been presented to me as a pleasure to be shared, something done for fun, and something worth doing.

Yet, in my classroom of third and fourth graders, reading was a chore to be accomplished daily, with books and papers to be completed in order to qualify one as a reader at a certain level. Reading happened only at the reading table, and students read only what I told them to. I could only conclude that I was not teaching my students that reading was fun or worth doing for themselves, not for me.

I had spent a recent year and a half working with the Boothbay Writing Project under the direction of Nancie Atwell. As a result of that project and my keen interest in looking at what it is we actually do as writers, my students had taken charge of their writing. They chose their own topics and made many decisions about each piece they wrote. Time was provided for writing each day.

One area of the room was set up as a permanent writing area containing all the necessary tools for writers. Paper of all colors and sizes (including stationery) sat in a prominent place, along with pens, pencils, markers, paper clips, stapler, white out, glue sticks, and scissors. As soon as I planted the seed that some students might be comfortable writing in places other than their desks, the room suddenly had a number of cozy writing spots that I had never considered. It was not uncommon to see students sitting amidst the coat lockers or lying under tables or desks. One area of the room was left free of furniture so there was always a carpeted spot ready for group conferencing or sharing.

Before long, students who had never written before were turning out stories, biographies, poems, and letters. They saw themselves as writers and felt good about what they wrote. My room was alive with learning at writing time. It was the time of day that I felt best about my classroom.

At that point I had been avidly reading Holdaway's *Independence in Reading* (1980) and Smith's *Reading Without Nonsense* (1978). Smith's comment "We learn to read by reading" (p. 94) kept coming back to me. It sounded so simple and made so much sense. Yet, as I considered all the instructional reading books, teacher's manuals, workbooks, and testing materials on my shelves, I realized how very complicated learning to read had been made within the educational system.

If I could relax and let students take direction of their writing, why not do the same with their reading? Yet, I knew that I could not just tell the class to read books of their own choice, because they'd learned to hate books. Books were hard, and trying to read them only confirmed their perceptions of themselves as poor readers. I saw clearly that first I would have to show the children that books could be fun. I knew how easy it was to say that and how difficult it could be to achieve.

Many of my students had never been read to at home. It seemed impractical and futile to ask children who had not been exposed to picture books suddenly to become interested in long books with no illustrations. I recognized a need to go back and bridge the gaps in their literature experiences.

I collected the basal readers and told the class that we would no longer be coming to the reading table in groups. I began bringing picture books into my classroom by the armload. All books were displayed with their covers showing, set upright on tables and chalk rails, or on bookshelves. I told the children that I wanted to share with them some books that I had enjoyed and many that my own children loved. Initially, I presented the works of H. A. Rey. I chose them, not because they were favorites of mine, but because I knew most young children responded favorably to Rey's books. I needed an attention grabber and I sensed that these books might be it. For three days, I read *Curious George* (1941) and its sequels aloud to my class as we all sat on the floor together. After each reading, we took the time to talk about the book. I did not ask questions to probe how well they had listened. Instead I nudged them for their responses to the books. What did they like? Could they tell what was going to happen at particular points in the story? Were the pictures important to the story?

On the third day, I gave each student a list of Rey's books. I told them that I now expected them to read to themselves all of the books I had read aloud and to record the date they finished each one beside its title. There was no time limit. When they finished, they were to turn their list in to me. There were no papers to do, and no questions would be asked.

Some students were surprised to discover they actually could read the books. Since I had read them aloud, much of the text became predictable. They recalled my voice and associated the story context with the illustrations. These clues helped them feel successful as readers of real books.

As the days and weeks passed, we shared and enjoyed collections of books by Marjorie Flack, Ezra Jack Keats, Robert McCloskey, Virginia Lee Burton, Dr. Seuss, Maurice Sendak, Peggy Parish, Jan and Stan Berenstain, Leo Leonni, Don Freeman, Bill Peet, C. W. Anderson, Elsie Minerak, and others. The students began to look forward to reading time, and so did I. I was anxious to share real books with them and sensed that they were equally anxious to receive my enthusiasm. I told them why I liked certain books and didn't like others. I commented on pictures, language, rhyme, and the effect various books had on me. I told them which books my own children really liked and pointed out the ones I recalled from my childhood. Each time I introduced a new author to the class, we looked in *Junior Authors* to learn as much as we could about the person. Before long the children were commenting on what they liked and disliked in various books, identifying books by their authors, and asking for more books by certain authors.

In time, I no longer asked them to read the books I had read aloud. I still put a list of an author's works on a table, but there was no requirement to read them. Some students continued to read any books I had read aloud, while others began choosing their own. Each child was required to keep a log of all books she or he had read. Some students who had not thought they could read were delighted to see how many books they had read over a period of time.

Billy, a blond ten-year-old, was spending his second year with me in my combination third- and fourth-grade classroom. Books had never been a part of Billy's world, and as a preschooler he had not been read to. He had attended a Head Start program for two years, had been retained in kindergarten, and had received resource room reading instruction for five years.

Shortly after I changed the format of our reading time, Billy came to me with great pride in his voice. "Mrs. McCarthy, I read this word! I didn't know it at first. But then I could hear (in my head) you reading that part out loud, and I looked again and I got it!"

As my students became more accustomed to this new type of reading class, I slowly decreased the time spent on reading aloud. I built in time for silent reading and for individual conferences with students to talk about the books they were reading. The time allotted for silent reading was consistently well used. I had full confidence that my students would read as we all sat down with our books. When I conferenced with students about the books they had read, I purposely did not ask questions with the intent of evaluating their "comprehension." Comprehension no longer meant checking one's memory of the text. After my exposure to Frank Smith, comprehension meant each individual reader's understanding of the text based on the experiences he or she brought to the text. Since the students were all reading and responding to their reading, I could only conclude that they were comprehending the various texts through an understanding of their own experiences. I did not need to ask a list of questions to know this. They did not need to answer questions at the end of the story to understand it. I was free to talk with my students about their books, instead of quizzing them on their reading.

At the end of the year I still opened class by reading a picture book aloud. I also read aloud from a novel every afternoon all year long. My students were feeling very confident and enjoying their reading. They had gone from hating reading class and believing they weren't very good readers to loving reading time and seeing themselves as accomplished readers. They also were aware of the authors behind the books and were beginning to connect the process they themselves were going through as they wrote with that of published authors.

As my students became more confident readers, I began to see significant changes in their writing. Jon had been slow to start writing in my classroom. After several months of having time provided for writing daily, he became more comfortable with expressing himself in print, yet he frequently had difficulty knowing what to write. One of his pieces about fruit was written in segments with a page devoted to each particular fruit.

*Fruit*

APPLES
Applies are fruit. I like applies. Applies are red.

ORANGES
Oranges are fruit. They are juicy. I liked oranges. They are orange.

PEARS
Pears are fruit. I like pears. They are juicy too. Fruit is good for you.

Several months after I had changed my approach to reading time, Jon's writing showed significant changes. In his piece titled "Fishing," he demonstrated his increased confidence in authoring a piece of writing.

*Fishing*

Last summer I went fishing with my Grandpa. We went upcountry in his truck. We camped in his truck. It was fun. We had a good time on that trip.

Jon's writing had changed significantly. As I had changed the focus of reading time to enjoying meaningful texts together with lots of read aloud and silent reading, Jon had gained confidence as a reader. He had struggled a great deal with reading during all of his school years. Now he was listening intently as I read aloud for more than an hour each day. He was totally drawn into the world of children's literature through both illustrations and the sounds of language. As Jon listened to language, his sense of story evolved. He now realized he had stories of his own to tell. His writing developed quickly from factual pieces in which he had little invested to stories based on his experiences. Jon had fond memories of his fishing trip with his grandfather and had gained a sense of language that now gave him the ability to express his own thoughts about that trip in written language.

Finally, I gave up the teaching of skills from reading class and, instead, taught strategies in language lessons with the whole class. A typical reading class consisted of a picture book read-aloud, with all of us sitting on the floor in a circle, followed by response to the text and illustrations and a discussion of other books written by the author. A silent reading time would then follow for at least a thirty minute period.

At another point in the day, I conducted a language lesson with the use of a meaningful text with the whole class. Using either a big book or an easel with chart paper, the whole class read the text aloud. We talked about the meaning of the text. I then chose one or two strategies to focus on. Skills previously taught at reading time, such as singular and plural nouns, initial blends, silent letters, and vowel sounds, took their place in the context of the language lesson. More often these skills would be taught in individual editing conferences at writing time with only those students whose writing showed a particular need for these skills.

By structuring lessons this way I am now teaching the skills of our language in the contexts in which they are used. All four language areas are highly intertwined—writing, reading, listening, and speaking. Now I am able to present reading through literature as a pleasurable activity.

The change in my approach to teaching reading has brought new life and meaning to my reading classes. My discussions with students about books and authors now occur throughout the day, and they come from a sincere love for the literature and a desire to share that love.

# 9

# THE CHICKEN STUDY: THIRD GRADERS PREPARE FOR INDEPENDENT STUDY OF ANIMALS

## Karen Sabers Dalrymple

It was a Friday afternoon in early April 1985. My third graders and I had completed our Space Study a few weeks earlier and had followed that with a short science fiction literature study. We had spent the past week rather "generically," as we had come to call our nonspecific study time. Some children had published books written during writing workshop; others had illustrated books they had read or the book I'd been reading for read-aloud. Several students had been using the math manipulatives in a response or discovery mode.

I called the children together for a meeting about thirty minutes before the close of school that day. We gathered in the discussion area, known as the "large-group area" to us, a spot which allowed us to meet as a group and to share a book, an idea, a problem, and so on. As the children were getting into their favorite spots upon the carpet, Toby asked, "What are we going to study next?" Little did he know that I had pondered the question throughout the day.

I told the children I'd been thinking about the next unit of study but I really hadn't decided on a definite focus for us. I told them we might study fairy tales or specific authors and their literature. I explained that our studies of the year had really allowed us opportunities to think as scientists, social scientists, literary critics, and mathematicians and, therefore, I was comfortable with whatever we might choose as our last topic for study of the year.

"I want to study about lizards," Noah said definitely.

"Yeh, and I want to learn about frogs," said Jim. "I love frogs but I don't know much about them." That seemed to be the cue for others to recall the animal they wanted to learn more about—moths, birds, pandas, and so on.

118

**119**
*The Chicken Study:
Third Graders
Prepare for
Independent Study of
Animals*

I wasn't comfortable with the thought of just beginning a study the following Monday with each third grader pursuing an individual topic. At that moment, I couldn't quickly conjure up any initial activities which might cement these individual studies. I told the children that I was uncomfortable but that, if we were to use two weeks to study one living animal together and write down the steps or the activities we were taking in the study, I could relax and enjoy their individual studies.

"Well we can't take lizards. I want those for my own study," Noah announced. And again, the chorus continued as most of the children stated their opposition to the group studying "their" topic.

Finally, I said, "Well, do any of you want to know about chickens?" The response was a wonderful chorus of disgusted faces, "Yucks," and "No's."

"Great. Then, on Monday, we'll begin a study of the chicken." I smiled as some kids frowned. Others were sighing with relief that I hadn't chosen "their" animal. Shortly thereafter, the children were en route home while I quickly sketched out the web shown in Figure 9-1.

Feeling secure that we could use the chicken study as a model for independent study of any animal, as well as integrate objectives for various curricular areas, I completed three tasks quickly before I left for the weekend. I posted a notice in the teachers' mailroom asking teachers if they were aware of any contemporary stories which used the chicken as a major or a minor character. While I was in the

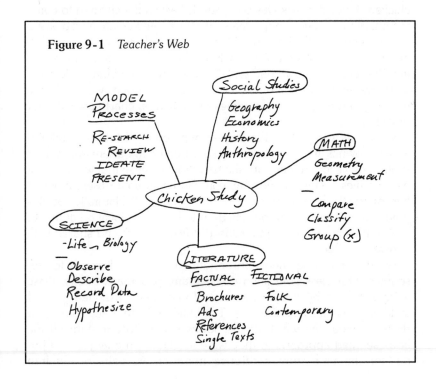

**Figure 9-1**  *Teacher's Web*

mailroom, I made a phone call to the Cooperative Extension Agency in Eagle County, Colorado. I explained to the director that I would be conducting a chicken study with my third graders. He asked for the school's address and promised to mail some pertinent brochures to me. The third task was writing a note to remind myself to check my bookshelves at home for any books which might be helpful to us.

A quick perusal of two books from home—*The Chicken Book* (Smith and Daniel, 1975) and *Eggs* (Sonntag, 1980)—offered me further assurance that the study would be legitimate for the dual purposes I had established. With books in hand, I returned to school on Monday knowing the day would include a focus writing session, a large group webbing session, a read-aloud, and a response time.

Just one-half hour before the start of the school day, a parent was knocking at the door. His daughter had told him we were going to study chickens and he had a chicken named "Brownie" in his truck. Would we like Brownie to visit for two or three days? Already another activity fell into place in my lesson plans. We placed the caged Brownie in the quietest area of the classroom. Within minutes the first of the children began arriving.

Our first activity—the focus writing—was fun for me, though it was perplexing to some of the children. I asked the children to record what they knew about chickens in their learning logs (a spiral notebook). They were given about six minutes for this first focus writing. (It may have been too long a time, because most of the children wrote they knew nothing or very little about the chicken.) Then, I asked the children to write three questions they had about the chicken. Once this task was completed, I asked the children to come together in the large-group area so that we could create a web based on our knowledge about the chicken and ask our questions as a group. The web was quickly concluded because, just a few moments into the session, Shawn had said, "Have you noticed that Julie is the only one who knows about chickens?" At that point, we ended the webbing and focused our energies on making a chart based on our questions.

While we were still in the large-group setting, I told the children about Brownie, who was becoming acclimated to our environment. I suggested we ignore her until she had time to sense that we were not her enemies. "Then, tomorrow, you can begin your observations of her physical characteristics and her behavior." Naturally, at this point, we lost several curious children to Brownie's location at the far end of the classroom in an enclosed office area which I shared with another teacher.

At this time it seemed appropriate to scan our libraries for resources. Our classroom library held many paperback books; these were organized by size for the sake of neatness. I assigned pairs of children to each stack of books. The children were asked to make a decision about the worth of the books related to our study. If the book seemed appropriate, they were to place it in a large box I put out for thematic study reference material. As pairs of children

**121**
*The Chicken Study:*
*Third Graders*
*Prepare for*
*Independent Study of*
*Animals*

worked, I could observe their discussions about the books, notice as children would return to read the charts we had made, and note the obvious knowledge found in our books. "In stack 6, there's a great book on birds," reminded a child not assigned to stack 6. That remark spurred the children to look for books that did not have only *chicken* in the title. Within a twenty- or thirty-minute period, we had perhaps thirty paperbacks in our reference box, which we called "the unit study books." As we were going to P.E. class, one child reminded us that we needed to look through our *National Geographic* magazines and "those other real books."

While the children were at their physical education class, I did a quick first reading of their focus writings. As I mentioned earlier, many of the children were unable to demonstrate a lot of knowledge about the chicken. Emily wrote, "I don't know anything about chickens. I've never even seen a chicken in real life. I only see the chickens mom and dad buy for cooking. But I do hope by the end of this unit I know why chickens run around with their heads cut off."

That remark of Emily's, besides making me smile and remember my early days on the South Dakota prairie where once, yearly, chickens did run around with their heads cut off, reminded me that this would be a perfect opportunity to introduce children to proverbs. Another teaching/learning activity had surfaced. When the children returned from their physical education period, I had selected a book for read-aloud. The book *Chickens Aren't the Only Ones* (Heller, 1981) was fun to share with the children, because the brilliant illustrations and delightful text are so compatible. I had read just a few pages when Toby said, "Hey, this is a fact book, but it is also a poem!"

I read the book twice during that session and told the children that after lunch we would have time for a response to the text. (I thought of an art technique I had learned from a colleague of mine in Wyoming. The technique would be perfect for a first response to this text.)

While the children lunched, I went to my files to pull the material I needed for the art lesson. The exercise asks the artist to use a shape and to force an entire whole within that shape—for example, draw a whole piano within the shape of a triangle. I had used the technique with fifth and sixth graders several years before and was eager to try it with children at an earlier stage of cognitive development. I decided to use the oval (egg-shaped) stencil and quickly made four or five on tagboard. As children entered the classroom from lunch play, I asked several to cut the stencils so we could use them. "Oh, we're going to decorate eggs, huh?" was the comment. At that time, another child came out of the "office" area where I had stashed Brownie announcing, "We got a egg! We got a egg!" We'd been so engrossed in our chicken study in the morning, we'd forgotten all about Brownie. How fortunate for us that she had been able to continue her business of doing what chickens do. After quieting the children for the sake of Brownie, we removed the egg from the cage

and allowed the children to feel its warmth before someone set it aside.

In a large-group setting, I asked the children to remember the information we had found in *Chickens Aren't the Only Ones*. They thought for a minute, and then I asked, "What's the poet really telling us?"

"That lots of animals lay eggs!" said Jim, pleased.

"Yeah, they're o-vi- . . . that big word," Kai contributed.

We took a quick look at the word. I wrote it on the chalkboard as someone spelled it from the text. Then we discussed the way the word looked as well as how it sounded when we spoke it, and we talked about its meaning.

I explained that our next activity would be a science and art activity. "You'll be working with an oviparous creature as you are drawing." I explained the forcing-a-whole-into-a-shape activity. I told the children that some artists use this activity as a warm-up, just as we use free writing sometimes as a warm-up to our writing workshop period. The children were instructed to think of an oviparous creature and then to draw that creature as an adult within the egg shape. This was no easy task for eight-year-old children, but the concentration given to the work was commendable. Some students took some time in deciding their animal, while others chose immediately and began drawing. Robbie went to the reference library and began looking for oviparous creatures not mentioned in Heller's text; others used Heller's text for advice, while still others would sit and think before physically beginning the task of drawing. All but two children found drawings or pictures of the oviparous animal they had chosen to draw. There were a number of false starts: Children had great difficulty using the whole shape; they would leave a border or use the shape for just the face of the animal. I moved about the classroom and talked with the children individually about their work: why they chose the animal, how they planned their work, where they had secured the reference they were using, and so on.

The classroom aide came for her assignment. I showed her Heller's text and asked her to prepare the text as a hand-out for the children so that we might use it for a choral reading. (Still another teaching/learning activity had surfaced.)

As the children completed their drawings, they noted the display board which had been singled out, and they began posting their work on the board. They moved to the box of books which we had located in the morning, and they began to peruse those books. Only a few children finished within the first hour of this activity, and, since the "artists/scientists" were still attentive to their work, I joined the book-perusal group. I read some pages to one or two children, and I listened to others pair up and begin reading. Kate used the time to look through the stacks of *National Geographic* and other scientific periodicals for pertinent resources.

As I left that group, I noticed Mark shaking his head at the display board.

**123**

*The Chicken Study:*
*Third Graders*
*Prepare for*
*Independent Study of*
*Animals*

"Look at this mess, Mrs. Dalrymple. They just put these up and didn't even think." I watched as Mark took the pins out of the work and placed each oviparous creature into a particular pile.

"Tell me about your piles, Mark," I asked.

"These are birds, these amphibians, here's an insect group, this is a reptile, and we have two fish."

I was impressed with his ability to categorize, of course, but I was more impressed with his reluctance to display the art without a classification system.

At some point during the afternoon, we took a break outside and then returned for a mathematics workshop. When the children left for the day, not without bidding farewell to Brownie, of course, I knew we were well on our way to learning about chickens. Already the children were aware of the species to which chickens belonged, and they had a sense of oviparous animals. As independent researchers, they had been introduced to the steps of asking questions, writing down already known facts, and locating multiple resources. And Emily had now seen a real, live chicken!

Planning Tuesday morning's unit study consisted more of choosing what *not* to do rather than what to do. Already there seemed so many activities for us to do. In preparation, I looked through the brochures and materials I had received from the Cooperative Extension Agency that afternoon. I selected diagrams of a rooster and a hen, of which I made several copies. (During our previous space study, the children had learned much about reading and comprehending diagrams, and I know that the actual remaking of a diagram and the labeling of the various sections can be helpful to a student. I think the copying forces attention, which assists comprehension.)

I knew that some children would continue drawing oviparous creatures within the oval shapes, that many would be eager to study Brownie, and that others would still want to look at the books we had found for the unit. It seemed wise to present a few pertinent words for study. Once I selected the activities for the day, I decided their sequence and structure and wrote the schedule on the chalkboard.

Unit Study

*Scientific Observation*
- study Brownie
- peruse books
- copy diagram of rooster or hen (Figure 9-2, p. 124)

*Language Study*
- pretest of spelling words

*Independent Study of Chickens*

*Read Together* Chickens Aren't the Only Ones

*Math Workshop*

I don't write times on the schedule. Rather, I prefer to write the activities and then use time as we need it to accomplish our work.

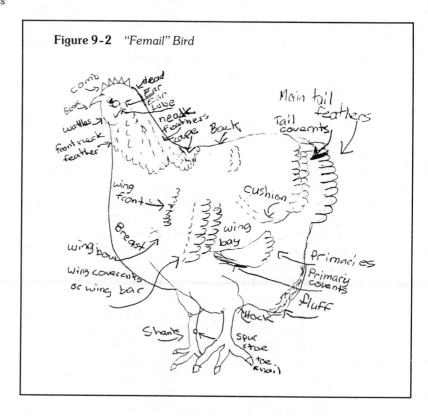

Figure 9-2    *"Femail" Bird*

The children soon learn that these are plans, not necessarily *work orders*, and that some days may end without having completed the plans. Of course, we respect the schedules for special classes, such as physical education, music, and art. Also, we'd never think of not going to lunch during our scheduled block. With this practice, the children acquire a respect for schedules and an appreciation for large blocks of time for concentration.

Tuesday was great! To introduce the scientific observation period, I asked the children how they thought scientists and social scientists collected information about their subjects. At this point in the year, the children knew, and there was a chorus of "Look at books," "Look for yourself at the real subject," and "Study pictures and diagrams." With the limit of three children quietly studying Brownie at one time, the distribution of materials for diagram work, and reiteration of the procedure for logging information, we were set for a long period of study. This work, in fact, lasted about two hours. During that time, I talked to the children about their work, read to some children in the reading area, discussed pictures and ideas with them, and probably reminded them about the need for being quiet around Brownie. The children respected the need for quiet, but whenever Brownie would "poop" in her food, they were obviously unable to remain quiet. Naturally, many of the children's drawings of Brownie included captions about her bad manners with her food.

**125**

*The Chicken Study:
Third Graders
Prepare for
Independent Study of
Animals*

I'm sure the rest of the day continued with the usual breaks from the unit study with math workshop, outside play, lunch, P.E., and an independent period. I don't recall whether we were even able to find time to read together, but I do remember the delight of the children upon returning from lunch to discover that once again Brownie had gifted them with another egg! Elaine mentioned that Brownie's eggs were much bigger than her chickens' eggs. I do remember that, when I called the children together in a large group at the end of the day after an independent period, they were able to list the behaviors of a student who wanted to learn about a living animal. Their work for the day included a cardboard two-dimensional model of Brownie's egg, notes in their logs about the good and "dumb" books in our unit study box, many pictures of Brownie, and several completed diagrams.

Once the children had left for the day, I placed a large sheet of butcher paper on a dividing wall and wrote "Independent Responses to the Chicken Study" on it. Then I read through the children's logs and studied their pictures of Brownie and the diagrams; every child had been involved in some aspect of the study. I checked the spelling of the words and made a ditto for the children to take home with them on Wednesday: *chicken, chick, chicken-hearted, poultry, feather, feathers, feathered, egg, eggs,* and *oviparous.*

At this point, I knew the study was well grounded, and I needed to decide which activities to use for large- and small-group lessons. I sat down at the typewriter with an encyclopedia opened to information on chickens; I typed one fact on about four inches of paper. I typed a variety of facts which I thought would please or puzzle the children. When I had about twenty facts, I made copies for ten sets, and the aide cut and sorted the sets so they'd be ready for class the following day. Because of their age and experience, third graders can become befuddled with the vast amount of information in an encyclopedia. I decided that I could use the information from the encyclopedia in a classification activity which might encourage confidence with the data and excitement about reaching for an encyclopedia for more information. Also, I pulled out a few books which would be good read-aloud material, and I made lists of materials which were coming in from other classroom teachers. I was so impressed with the number of contemporary books which used the chicken as a character that I knew I would plan an activity around them.

One of my students had already made arrangements for us to have fertilized eggs in the classroom, and a high school teacher had volunteered the use of his brooder. Julie's parents had invited us to their home to study the chickens they raised for eggs and meat. I prepared a note to send home with Julie suggesting that we visit their pens on the following Friday. I also prepared a note to send with Sarah for her father to get Brownie on Friday so that she could be returned to her own environment. (One of the children so wanted a chicken that his parent had already called Sarah's home to see if they could buy Brownie.)

Wednesday morning started off with our Math Workshop. During this period, I introduced the idea of square measurement. The children used the geoboards, centimeter squares, and other manipulatives to "play" around with the concept. After we put away our math materials, we gathered in the large-group area for a read-together and a read-aloud session. The children liked reading Heller's poem and were glad they understood the meaning of *oviparous*; they pronounced it with authority. I selected several short readings from *Eggs* (Sonntag, 1980). At that point, I was careful to share only the factual entries from the text. I didn't want to confuse the issue of fact and fiction so early in the study. I preferred to have the children gather a "nest" of factual information about chickens.

After lunch and after applauding Brownie for producing her third egg, the children were instructed to use their time for independent study and come together in about two hours to talk about our new discoveries. Shawn and Toby were interested in "hard-core" facts; I'd overheard their talk earlier about types of chickens and uses of chickens for fighting and for pets. I invited them into the reading area with me and presented them each with a prepared packet of facts from the encyclopedia about chickens. "Sort these into categories" was the instruction. Kate, Erin, and Steven came over to see what was going on, so I gave them packets also. They approached this task with a seriousness that made me smile. I felt comfortable leaving them; I walked about to observe and assist other children in their work. (I carried about my clipboard with pages for noting my observations. The kids were so accustomed to my note taking, so comfortable, in fact, that Noah said, "Write down that I can read this book alone." He held up a book entitled *Chickens and More Chickens*.) Julie was reading books to find answers to the questions on our chart. Kai was reading about how to test the freshness of eggs. Eugene was on a fact-finding and reporting mission; he would read a fact, and then he would go to another child and say, "Did you know that the ostrich lays the largest egg?" "Did you know that some grown-up chickens are smaller than some kid chickens?" Of course, some children would just look at Eugene and continue their work, others would tell him to "prove it," while still others were never approached by Eugene.

Our Space Study and the following Science Fiction Literature Study had given us a good background for talking about fact and fiction. I structured an activity for Thursday which would allow children the opportunity to sort the books in our resource box into fact and fiction categories. After reading from *Eggs*, I asked the children to tell me about the book. Most of the children agreed that it was a little book with short factual stories in it. "Let's test your theory," I said. I read a selection which was folklore. "Oops," we all agreed that the book had both fact and fiction in it. "Read some more," they said. I read two more selections, and the children identified the stories as fact or fiction.

"Just so you can become real experts at this, I'll give each of you a book or two from our resource box. You decide if it's fact or fiction."

**127**

*The Chicken Study:
Third Graders
Prepare for
Independent Study of
Animals*

"Oops," Rachel said. "Another oops?" I asked. Rachel had already sorted the box, partitioned it, and labeled the sides "True" and "Not True." Obviously, it was time to conjure up another activity.

"Let's web what we know already," I suggested. The children agreed, because they were so eager to share (or show off, which is usually the case) their new learnings.

"*Comb* should be on the web."

I looked at the speaker and asked where I should place *comb* on the web. She answered, "In a new place. It doesn't go with anything else we have yet. And *feathers* can go there, too."

"*Wattles* and *spur* go there, too," announced one child.

"Are they the name of a category?" I questioned.

"No," she nearly growled, "but I don't know the name of the box they go under."

The webbing session was well on its way. I had used a purple pen during the first session. During this second session I was using a brown pen. Different-colored ink allows us a good visual about the information we began with, the information learned and reported next, and so on. The dates of our web work are written in the color used during that webbing period. As I wrote quickly to the children's commands, the piece of paper was becoming very full.

"Gosh, look how much we've learned already!"

"Yeah, we almost know everything." I loved that remark; a full paper indicated all of the knowledge, right? (During our Space Study, we had to add several pieces of paper onto our original web because we kept gathering so much more information. Obviously, the child who made this comment hadn't conceptualized the relationship between knowledge and record keeping.)

"Do you have any questions?" I asked as quiet followed the final fact being added to the web.

"Yeah, how do kids know about wattles and lobes?" asked one child.

"It's on the diagrams that we drew," said Sam, as he walked over to the table holding the diagrams. He showed the diagrams to the group.

The webbing session was over, and the kids were off searching for more information. The language study lists were passed out, and children knew they were to submit some work from home which would show that they had used the words. We had a homework word wall, and each week the children would tack up their homework. Homework is a district requirement. Teachers with whom I work attempt to design tasks which encourage family participation in the work. We try to set up situations for dialogue about our work at school among parents, siblings, and our students. The chicken homework varied. Some children brought in notes from their parents that said, "We talked about the words at dinner" or, "We didn't know what *oviparous* meant, but Rachel told us." Figure 9-3, A and B (p. 128), are examples of two homework activities which appeared on the wall on Friday.

At this point, I don't remember the sequence of teaching/learning

**Figure 9-3**  *Homework*

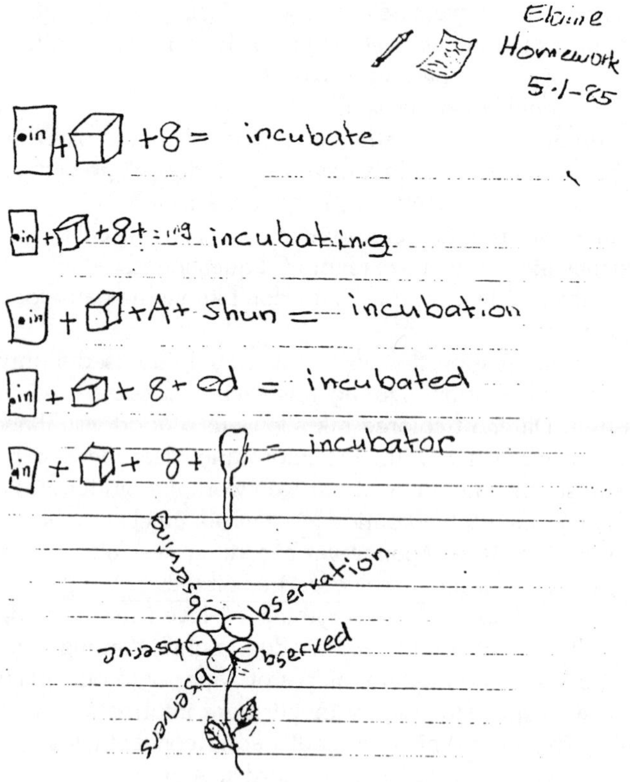

Elaine
Homework
5-1-85

[in] + [cube] + 8 = incubate

[in] + [cube] + 8 + ing incubating

[in] + [cube] + A + shun = incubation

[in] + [cube] + 8 + ed = incubated

[in] + [cube] + 8 + [fork] = incubator

observing
observation
observe
observed

**A.** Elaine's homework

ⓞ composetion

I used to have a chicken when I
was 5. every morning I
wold go coleced eggs. I became
chicken-hearted of my chicken.
because they wold peck at
me. I wonder how a chicken
develops inside an egg? I
lernd that all anamalls that
lay eggs ore oviparous,

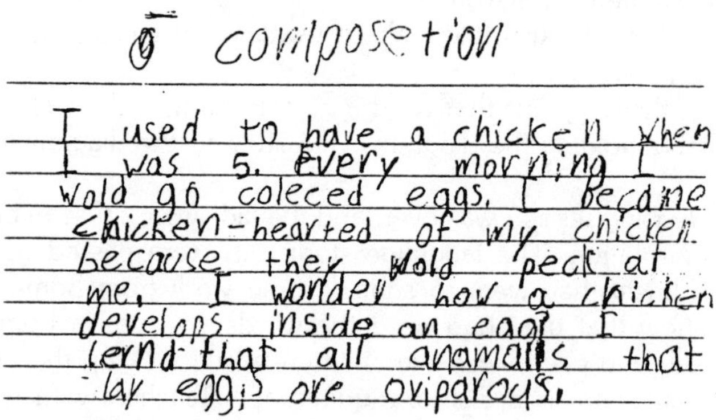

**B.** Matt's homework

**129**
*The Chicken Study:
Third Graders
Prepare for
Independent Study of
Animals*

activities which carried us through that week and the following week. However, I still have my "Chicken Unit" folder, which contains my initial planning web, a list of resources, lists of activities, chicken jokes from magazines, articles about eggs or chickens, or both, brochures from the Cooperative Extension Agency, and a unit evaluation form (Figure 9-4). Many of the pieces trigger images for me; several deserve elaboration.

## PROVERBS

Spurred by Emily's comment during her first focus writing on why chickens run around with their heads cut off, I decided to design a lesson which would introduce the idea of figurative language. *Eggs* and my own prairie background served as valuable resources for a collection of proverbs. I wrote one proverb per card in preparation for the lesson. These were some of our favorites:

Don't count your chickens before they are hatched.
Scarce as hen's teeth.
He who wants eggs must endure the clucking of the hen.

---

**Figure 9-4**  *Unit Evaluation Form*

UNIT EVALUATION FORM
NAME OF UNIT  Chicken Study
DATE TAUGHT  APRIL 22. MAY 14  1985
8.9.10                    K.S. Dalrymple
AGE  /  GRADE  /  TEACHER

| | |
|---|---|
| ENCOURAGED STUDENTS TO BECOME MORE SKILLFUL COMMUNICATORS | · Reading Charts   Poetry (Heller's/Hoban's)   · Natural Sketches<br>· Folklore   · Composition: a story to support characterization<br>· Proverbs<br>· Encyclopedia Info   · Clay Sculptures   "Chicken Fat" Move to Music |
| PROVIDED FOR MATHEMATICAL SKILLS AND CONCEPTS | · Comparisons of egg sizes   · Introduce Square Measurement<br>· Making models of eggs |
| PROVIDED FOR PROCESSES AND CONCEPTS IN LITERATURE | · Criticism: How is the chicken "treated" in literature (folklore + contemporary)<br>· Fables (Chinese/Jewish)  · Introduce the allegory "Green Eggs + Ham" |
| PROVIDED PROCESSES AND CONCEPTS IN SCIENCE | · Observation   · Oviparous Creatures  · Making Hypothesis<br>· Record Data  · Classification   [age of eggs/egg laying] |
| PROVIDED FOR PROCESSES AND CONCEPTS IN SOCIAL STUDIES | · History (anthropology – man + chicken)<br>· Small Group Work (time line, skits, proverb discussion) |
| ALLOWED FOR USE OF SKILLS, KNOWLEDGE, OR MATERIALS TO BECOME BETTER PROBLEM SOLVERS | · Model making<br>· Use math (of chicken facts) to |
| TAPPED AN INTEREST WHICH LEADS TO INDEPENDENCE | · Getting chicks at home   · Several fact Projects<br>· Egg Book of facts   · Wrote Poetry   · If chess were... |
| HELPED IDENTIFY STRENGTHS/ WEAKNESSES OF STUDENT LEARNING | · Pursued answers to questions on chart<br>· Use of encyclopedias |

INTEGRATED CURRICULUM PROGRAM
Prepared by K.S.Dalrymple

One rotten egg spoils the pudding.
Send not for a hatchet to break open an egg.
*and, of course,*
Run around like chickens with their heads cut off.
Don't put all your eggs in one basket. (To which Noah said, "But isn't
    it hard to carry two baskets?!")

How delightful it was to work with proverbs and third graders. I introduced the lesson by asking Emily's permission to share her initial focus writing. She was not only willing but offered to read it aloud to the class. I asked her questions about where and when she'd heard about chickens with their heads cut off, and she gave us instances. I explained that we use descriptive language sometimes to explain a situation and that sometimes our words can be confusing unless we know about metaphoric language. Once we know, we can use the language to better explain situations to people. I told the children about our once-a-year episodes of butchering chickens. The children responded with gasps or giggles. The events seemed so terrible now through the retelling and in the eyes of eight-year-old children. I was somewhat ashamed of the story but not aware of it until I had told them about how my father would take his ax, lay the chicken's head on a stump, and "ax the head off." Then he would toss the chicken into the yard, and the chicken would run around with its head off until . . . . What an awful story!

The children were impressed that I had actually been a part of such history. And, at any rate, the children were catching onto the idea of the proverbs because I had asked them to name situations in their life when it could be said that it was like a "bunch of chickens running around with their heads cut off." It was a good language class as children told of "getting to music class before the teacher arrived and they all *ran around like* . . ." or of "the time in kindergarten when the fire alarm went off and Sheila screamed so loud that everyone got scared and they started *running around like chickens* . . ." or "when the man next door was drunk and came to the wrong house, he walked into our house sort of yelling and we were all watching TV but we saw him and we all went *running around like chickens with our heads cut off.*" By the time the fourth child told a story, the children would join in the chorus to the final line.

The second portion of this activity was to share one proverb card with the children and to have them think about what it meant. Then, together we would think of a real-life situation which would parallel the proverb. Next I gave the children (in triads) a proverb which they were to discuss. I'd move about and talk with them about their ideas about the proverb. Once they could describe the meaning, I would ask them to design a skit which they would present to the class. The skit was to be sans chickens. I'm sure it was a couple of days before each triad had its skit ready. When the time came, I placed all the proverbs on the chalktray, and as each group performed a skit, the audience would select the proberb which provoked the skit.

The work was difficult but fun. I'm not sure the children under-

**131**
*The Chicken Study:*
*Third Graders*
*Prepare for*
*Independent Study of*
*Animals*

stood the genesis of proverbs or even gained the ability to use proverbs, but I think some children came to understand that the printed word isn't always to be taken literally.

## SPECIAL EDUCATOR'S ACTIVITY

One of my students would spend a period a day in a special education classroom. His teacher would use the time to help him become a more capable user of the language that we were using in our unit studies. On several days, the two of them used one of our "fact packets"; the resource teacher would read the content to the student, who would then categorize the information. Later the student composed a web of facts about chickens, which he displayed in our classroom. The poster became a resource for other students.

## MATH WORKSHOP ACTIVITIES

During one math workshop session, I gave each student a copy of "Chicken Facts in Numbers" (Figure 9-5), which I had composed

Figure 9-5   *Chicken Facts in Numbers*

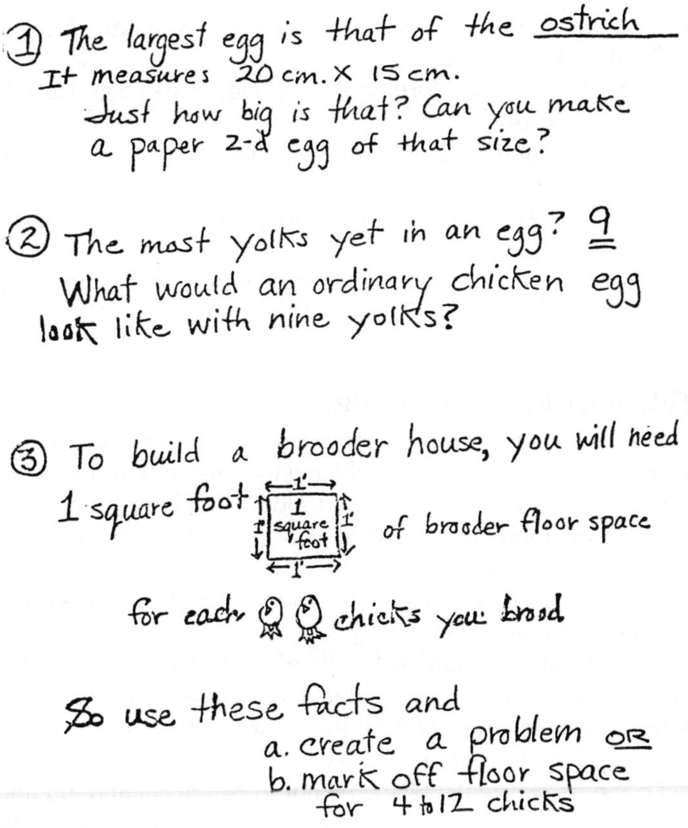

① The largest egg is that of the ostrich.
It measures 20 cm. × 15 cm.
Just how big is that? Can you make a paper 2-d egg of that size?

② The most yolks yet in an egg? 9
What would an ordinary chicken egg look like with nine yolks?

③ To build a brooder house, you will need 1 square foot of brooder floor space for each chicks you brood

So use these facts and
  a. create a problem OR
  b. mark off floor space for 4 to 12 chicks

using the facts that had surfaced during our study. These facts encouraged student thinking and problem solving. I was especially interested in using the workshop time to ask the children how they were approaching the problems. As the students worked, I would move about and question their procedures. The activities from this worksheet progressed over several days. Sandra thought of her solution to the first problem as she was about to fall asleep one night and, in fact, hurried from her bed to find pencil, paper, and scissors so that she could demonstrate her solution.

## LITERATURE STUDY

During one reading class, I read a story to the children and asked them to describe the chicken: "What is this chicken's character?" After we discussed the chicken in the story, I presented the children with an assortment of contemporary books which used the chicken as a character. I asked the children to select a story, read it, and then write their analysis of the chicken. They wrote in their logs the name of the story, the type of character, and the clues that were given in the text. These assumptions were good meat for discussion about characters.

Following are some of the books used for this work:

Berri, Claude. *The Rooster Who Laid Eggs*. Katonah, NY: Young Readers' Press, 1967.

Ginsburg, Mirra. *Good Morning, Chick*. New York: Scholastic Book Services, 1980.

Hartelius, Margaret. *The Chicken's Child*. New York: Scholastic Book Services, 1975.

Lobel, Arnold. *How the Rooster Saved the Day*. Rae Publishing Co., 1977.

Macaulay, David. *Why the Chicken Crossed the Road*. Boston: Houghton Mifflin, 1987.

## INTRODUCING A NEW GENRE

At home one evening, I made smoked eggs and refrigerated them while I thought of a way of introducing the new food to the children. I've always enjoyed offering new foods to children (not so much preparing the food as observing the children's responses to the foods). Smoked eggs are boiled and in a sesame oil and are, in fact, black. Once a group of fifth graders and I had written "gross" poems about foods such as blackened eggs.

At school, I noticed *Green Eggs and Ham* (Dr. Seuss, 1960) was in our reference book box. I decided to use it to introduce the children to smoked eggs and, at the same time, to allegorical literature. It was great fun. I read the text, and the kids and I talked about how Dr. Seuss was really telling us not to be critical and judgmental about something unless we know a lot about it. I told the children

**133**
*The Chicken Study:
Third Graders
Prepare for
Independent Study of
Animals*

they would be reading many allegories as they grew older. Then, we discussed how silly it is to say we don't like the taste of something we haven't even tried to eat. Then I popped up and said, "Oh, by the way, I've prepared a snack for us today." I asked Rachel to get the jar from the sack under my desk. It was wonderful to see her returning, jar in hand, with a most disgusted look on her face. When the kids saw the eggs, there was a cacophony! (Three years later I worked with some of those same children, and *black eggs* was a part of their spoken and written language. It was always associated with disgusting tastes and sights. I love it.)

## THE FINALE

Two weeks after we had begun the study of chickens, we completed the study. We had a wonderful final activity; a local potter brought us clay, and with her assistance each of us sculpted a chicken. She was impressed with the fullness of the figures, and we discussed reasons for this. Perhaps having Brownie to observe and having the diagrams to copy and label contributed to the sculpturing success.

Figure 9-4 is the evaluation form which I completed as we finished the study. It doesn't show the excitement and wonder that accompanied the study, but, even as I read it today, I smile as I remember the competence the learners exhibited as they pursued the study. I can still see the masking tape on the floor of the room marking off brooder space for baby chicks, the *Eggstra GOOD Fact Book* written by Erin and read several times by everyone else in the class, the amazed faces of discovery, the satisfaction of questions answered along with the puzzle of discovering new questions.

Not so "chicken-hearted" was I as we completed the study and began individual studies of animals. The children had a large poster in the room, which listed "Ways to Find Out About Animals." We had written the poster together throughout our two-week Chicken Study, and now the students were prepared for their individual studies. I felt confident about our work.

# growing pains

# 10

# TEACHING IN THE REAL WORLD

## Debra Goodman / Toby Kahn Curry

A plastic milk crate with the bottom punched out has been tied to the high fence surrounding the tiny play lot. This forms a makeshift basketball hoop for school kids during the day. In the evening, young immigrants from Pakistan, India, and the Philippines take over the "court."

This sight always comes to mind when we think of Burton International, where we worked together for six years. It is inner-city teaching at its finest. We often receive sympathetic looks and cryptic remarks when we say we are teaching in Detroit. But the rumors and negative reports have nothing to do with our experience teaching in the city we both love.

No, we do not teach in fear of our lives. The prostitutes and drug dealers we see as we drive to school maintain a respectful distance from the school grounds. We have never been assaulted by our students.

The children we teach are much the same as children anywhere. They laugh, they cry, they work hard, they talk "too much," they get silly, and they want to learn. The teachers that we work with are much the same as teachers anywhere. They work very hard, they care about kids, they complain about kids and parents, and they look forward to vacation. Yet, there are some real differences between teaching in our inner-city schools and teaching in other communities. In a declining industrial area, our school system generates up to $2,000 less per pupil than the surrounding suburbs, despite the high rate of property taxes that city residents pay.

We have rarely taught a class with less than thirty students and frequently teach groups of thirty-three or thirty-four. There is a shortage of substitute teachers, and we often lose planning time filling in for each other during absences. Common supplies such as crayons, scissors, staples, and construction paper are often difficult to come by. At Burton International, we used a "platoon" system in order to provide special-subject classes such as gym, music, and art. At our current school classes are self-contained, and our children have no music, gym, or art specialists.

We are currently teaching at the Dewey Center for Urban Education. It is a new whole language magnet school within the Detroit public school system. The proposal for this school was written by four Detroit teachers (including ourselves) and adopted by an inner-city community that was faced with losing its neighborhood school. It sits across from Detroit's largest federal housing project complex. It's the area that spawned Motown and the Supremes.

We had wanted to interweave our article, just as our teaching and inquiry have been interwoven for the last seven years. In an impersonal city school system, we have clung to our humanism and our beliefs only by clinging to each other. However, our teaching and consulting demands with the new school make this sort of collaboration impossible.

Debi's section will focus on Debi and Toby's experiences designing and organizing social studies and language arts programs at Burton International, where Debi taught two groups of fifth graders and Toby taught two seventh grade groups. Toby's section will discuss the special challenges of organizing self-contained classrooms at the new Dewey Center, where Toby is teaching sixth and seventh graders and Debi is teaching fourth and fifth.

---

## ORGANIZING A CLASSROOM AS A COMMUNITY
### Debra Goodman

Dear Ms. Goodman,

Hello, It's me Amy D. I just thought I'd write to see how you were. I have had a very unproductive summer. All I've really done is make bracelets and read.

I've read quite a lot. I read A little Princess, The Secret Garden, and Pollyanna. Have you heard of them? You probably have. I saw the movies; Pollyanna and the Secret Garden and I loved them and A Little Princess looked interesting so I borrowed it from a friend.

Now I'm reading Rebecca of Sunny Brook Farm. I'm not done yet- or half way done. I went to a used book store and I bought a thick book called Ivanhoe. I got it because in Rebecca of SBF she said she had read it and I like books about medieval times. Specially witches.

I can't believe people are that stupid that they would really kill someone because they thought she was a witch. I

read once there was a man who was in charge of finding
witches and one way to see if someone was a witch was to
put a needle in their birthmark and he made a fake needle
like the knifes they use in Hollywood that go in when you
push down on it. So that way he could say a bunch of inno-
cent people were guilty.

I hope you have fun at your new school. Although I will
miss you and Mrs. Curry, I think that the other school
needs you. (A lot)

Well, I gotta go. You're ex-pupil, soon to be seventh
grader,

Amy Amy Amy

I got this letter from Amy over a year after she completed the fifth
grade in my room. I was her teacher, but more than that, I am
someone who enjoys talking about books. Amy knows that it isn't
just the reading I care about; I care about content, too. In my
classroom, Amy read a lot of historic fiction. Issues and aesthetics
were often discussed in the same conversation. Amy also knows that
I care about her. She cares about me, too.

Amy's letter reflects the three walls that cradle my classroom. The
first wall is *the learning process*. I want students to leave my room
with strategies for becoming independent readers, writers, and
learners. The second wall is *content*. Yes, there are things I want
children to know. For example, I want them to know that history is
the story of people struggling with issues that are similar and different
from those we are struggling with today, and that books have authors
and illustrators and come in many forms and functions.

The third wall is *culture or society*. Schools are cultural institutions, and each child comes to school with the cultural strengths of
their families and communities. These walls are supported by my
own theoretical understandings of language, learning, teaching, and
curriculum. Ken Goodman (1986) has called these theories the four
pillars of whole language.

The fourth wall is open. It represents the endless invitations and
possibilities for learning, content, and social interactions. It is within
these walls that I begin to plan and organize my classroom each year.
None of these walls stand alone. Each wall and each pillar are
present in every learning experience.

The task of organizing a classroom is always new with each group.
My own organization is a dynamic process involving constant observation and refinement of what "works" and "doesn't work" with a
particular group. When I think something "works," I don't mean
everything is going really smoothly. Sometimes a seemingly noisy
and chaotic morning produces a pile of good work. Other times a
quiet and politely attentive group has dismissed and ignored an
entire discussion.

In order to see if things are "working," I have to pay close
attention. During quiet reading, I might look up from my book and

count the number of kids who are reading. Mike and Quentin are talking, but they're sharing a book. Jason is quietly drawing, while Susan stares out the window. Is she thinking about her book? If only seven kids are reading, should I stop? And what if the same seven kids are *not* reading every day, what then? These are the issues I consider when I organize my classroom.

Rather than sit and wonder, I also ask my students what they think "works" and "doesn't work." Over the course of the year, we work together to determine topics, experiences, schedule, and room arrangement. With kids like Amy, this works very well. Amy came to me already a learner, a reader and writer, and a thoughtful and caring young person. She came into the room full of ideas and plans. She was ready to listen and participate, to share and help, and to organize the classroom with me.

But, for most of the students in my classroom, organizing the classroom is a new and sometimes overwhelming process. They have had a long time to lose their curiosity and separate their natural interests from their school learning. The question, "What do you want to learn about?" is often met with blank stares. Some students decide anything goes and run around the room disrupting activities and destroying materials. Other students, successful in a "traditional program," beg for assigned desks and textbook assignments.

Planning *with* the kids is a slow and tentative process. But it is probably the most important thing I do. I don't need a "higher-order thinking skills program." As we organize the classroom, the kids learn to brainstorm, discuss, persuade, outline, chart, schedule, pose problems, find solutions, negotiate, consult, compromise, etc., etc. But, more important, the children take ownership of their own learning, and the classroom becomes unified into a community of learners. It is well worth the trouble.

In this atmosphere, organization and curriculum development can be described as a transaction between students and teacher within a specific classroom context. The "classroom" that grows out of this transaction is much greater than I could create alone and changes the kids and myself as it provides us with a day-to-day schedule of experiences.

## GETTING TO KNOW YOU

I start out each year with many ideas for learning experiences I might enjoy. But I am only one person in a crowded classroom. I have to get to know who the kids are before I can truly get organized. There are four things I do during the first weeks of school to get acquainted with the kids and help them get acquainted with a very new style of classroom organization.

First, I organize the room into centers. These centers aren't elaborate. Physically, they are small areas separated by shelves or files (Figure 10-1). At first, each center contains just one or two activities with file folders telling the kids what to do when they get there and a

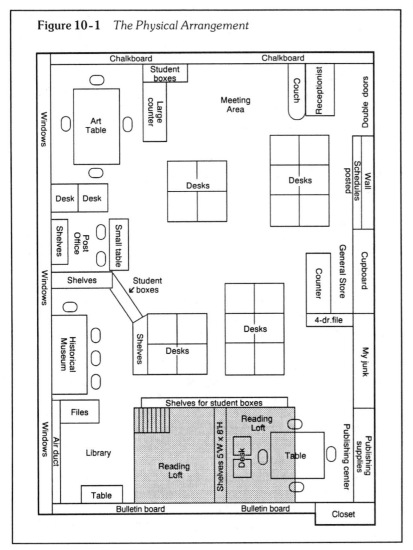

**Figure 10-1**  *The Physical Arrangement*

class list to check off what they've done. The activities are fairly simple. At the Library, they are asked to choose three books to put in their cubby for quiet reading. At the Post Office, they assign themselves a box and write a letter. At the Art Center, they decorate their writing folder or draw a picture. At the Museum, they work on a jigsaw puzzle. A Listening Post provides the tape and book for *Charlie and the Chocolate Factory*.

There are good reasons for starting out with centers. Centers can provide authentic learning experiences that allow children to think and interact. The center activities demonstate to children that in my room they will have choices and learning will be active and enjoyable. Working in small groups encourages the kids to recognize resources in their peers, while fostering social interactions and friendships. Preparing the centers takes up a large chunk of my prestart planning time, but then I am set for the first few weeks of school. After a while, the kids help with the planning and organizing of the centers.

In my first years of teaching, the first week of school always seemed to involve a lot of sitting and lengthy explanations. Now, as much as possible, I let the kids jump in feet first. When they come in, I hand them a folder with a sticker on it. The stickers are different colors and arbitrarily organize the kids into groups. For the first week, the kids follow a set rotation, visiting every center. After the first rotation, the students have a chance to sign up for their choice of centers.

The centers allow the kids to get involved with the classroom right away, but they also provide me with an opportunity to get to know the kids. One of the centers is my Teaching Station, where I sit with no more than five students (even with groups of four or five I end up with seven groups!) and talk with them about personal writing. We talk about "The Real Me": "What are the important things about you that your classmates might not know?" "What are you like on the inside?" I tell about myself, and the children share some things about themselves. I encourage them to describe not just their appearance but also their inner self.

After each child has had a chance to share, we all write. We don't usually finish this writing during the meeting, but the important part—sharing and thinking through what we plan to write—is well grounded. Introducing the writing activity in these small groups is a very special experience for me. I am there by their side as they pick up their pencils to write, and I can detect how they feel about the task and how they approach it.

These pieces of writing are revised, proofread, and rewritten for a class collection. I publish them by placing the loose-leaf pages into plastic shields and collecting them all in a binder. This first class book is popular reading throughout the year. Through these writings, we really get to know each other.

I also use this first writing to evaluate the children's writing when they come into the room. I count the words, determine the percentage of words spelled conventionally, and write out a short evaluation of each child's ability to write clearly and expressively. These evaluations are placed in my "grade book"—another loose-leaf binder with dividers for each child. The actual rough draft that the child has written is also placed in the binder. This gives me a basis for discussion with parents and provides me with "marks" to use for the traditional English and Spelling grades that I am required to give (Figure 10-2, A and B).

I also have a written reading survey, which asks students about their reading interests and tastes. Six or seven questions provide more information than any reading placement test I can imagine. From the students' responses I can tell who likes to read, who is a confident reader, and the specific titles, authors, and genres that my

**Figure 10-2** *Writing Evaluations*

Michael's "grades".

Michael

WRITING · PROGRESS CHECK – 1988-89

| Date | Topic | Clarity/Style | Mechanics | # words | % Spelling | Final Draft |
|---|---|---|---|---|---|---|
| 9/87 | Who am I? | Clear and communicative. | Has basic conventions | 32 | 100% | |
| 11/87 | Missing TV | Sets problem immediately. Good intro/builds plot | Needs work on paragraph divisions. No revision. | ~250 | 96% | |
| 1/6/88 | Rabbit (ABCS test) | Solves problem in direct manner. | Uses all paragraph conventions | 49 | 100% | |
| 4/88 | Childhood Sketch. | Strong voice, very informative. | Uses paragraphs and had outline. | 177 | 99% | |

**A.** Michael

Class "Grades"

English First Card-Marking (Writing Check) / English Second Card

| | Letters | holistic | # words | % spelling | Final Draft | Folder Check | Folder Check | holistic score | # words | % spelling | Final Draft | Spell check | Letters |
|---|---|---|---|---|---|---|---|---|---|---|---|---|---|
| GERALD | ✓ | 2 | 15 | 93% | + | 1 page inc. | | 2½ | 153 | 92% | late | | |
| ✓ MONIQUE | | 3 | 45 | 100% | | 9 pages | 12 pages | 3 | 70 | 99% | ✓ | | |
| ✓ KRISTINA | ✓ | 3 | 22 | 95% | + | 7 pages | 14 pages | 3 | 152 | 99% | | | ✓✓✓ |
| → MICHAEL | ✓ | 3 | 32 | 100% | | 1 story 2 pages | 5 cnmes story 4 pages | 3½ | ~250 | 96% | ✓ little | | ✓ |
| ✓ BRANDON | ✓ | 3 | 39 | 85% | INC | 1 page inc. | 2 pages | | 150 | 87% | | | |
| ✓ JUDE | ✓ | 3 | 29 | 93% | + | 1 story 4 pages | 1 page | 3 | 110 | 92% | ✓ | | |
| KAHLIL | | 3 | 22 | 100% | ✓ | 1½ stories 4 pages | 17 pages w/Phillip | 3½ | 1400 (200) | 98% | + Not finished | | ✓ |
| ✓ ATHENA | ✓+ | 3 | 19 | 100% | + | 1 story 16 pages | | | | | | | ✓✓ |
| PHILLIP | ✓✓ | 3 | 44 | 95% | + | 4 several 8 pages | 17 pages w/Kahlil | 3½ | 1400 (200) | 98% | + Not finished | | ✓ |
| KIWAN | ✓ | 2½ | 25 | 92% | ✓ | 1½ stories 5 pages | 2 pages | 3 | 130 | 92% | Not done | | |
| ✓ JESSE | ✓ | 3 | 31 | 97% | + | ½ story 3 pages | 5 pages | 3 | ~350 | | + | | ✓ |
| ✓ SHARRON | | | | 96% | | 2 stories 4 pages | 5 pages | | | | | | |
| ✓ LATICIA | ✓ | 3 | 23 | 97% | + | 7 pages but 3/4 full | 7 pages double sp. | 3 | 353 | 97% | ✓ little | ? | |
| HILLARY | ✓ | 3½ | 39 | 95% | + | 1 page | 1 each pd 3 short pgs | | | | | | ✓ |

**B.** Class summary

students enjoy. I repeat the surveys from time to time throughout the year.

Finally, I spend a lot of time the first few weeks of school working with my students to think about our goals for the year. The goals of fifth graders express the full range of interests and concerns that fifth graders have (Figure 10-3, A through C). These goals are revised, proofread, and rewritten on a sheet of paper, along with my own goals for the year. The goals are sent home to parents, who are invited to write goals of their own.

By the end of the first month of school, I have gotten to know my kids pretty well. I know some of their interests and hopes. I know how they approach reading and writing, and how they work in independent and small group situations. I have shared my own goals for the rest of the year, too: how the kids are going to help me plan and organize the room, some of the things we might do, my interest in studying things that really matter, and bringing our community and our culture into the school.

**Figure 10-3** *Student and Parent Goals*

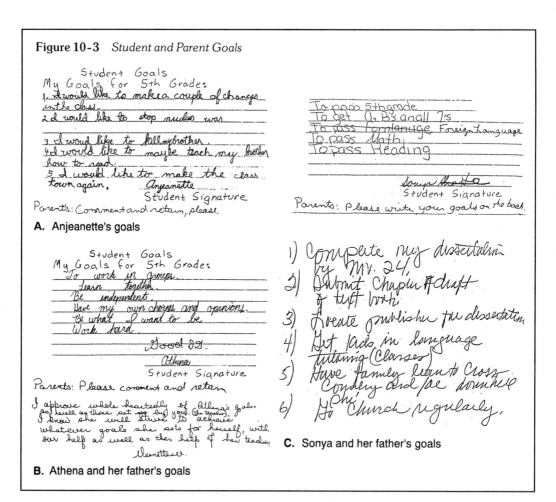

A. Anjeanette's goals

B. Athena and her father's goals

C. Sonya and her father's goals

This description sounds great, but reality has a way of working out differently. After all, not every kid is Amy. I didn't have to teach Amy to be an independent learner, but kids like Amy flourish in my classroom. They read and write more than any other year of their lives. They rise to the challenge of doing great works, and they contribute much more than they take from me and their peers.

But Amy is only one kid in the room. What about Katy, who jumps up after five minutes of quiet reading to announce, "I'm done!" How about Joseph, who *only* reads Garfield books? What about Linda, who's such a "good" student that she's never had to listen to any directions and instructions? And Tom, who manages to spend entire mornings doing nothing at all?

I always feel guilty writing about only the "wonderful" things that happen in my classroom. The day-to-day reality is far from ideal. On any given day, things can fall apart.

## WHEN THINGS FALL APART

It's time for centers, and everyone seems to be yelling at the top of their lungs. My conference with Jason has been interrupted countless times. Brandie complains that Sean is hogging all the Legos. Terry gives me news reports: Don has swiped all the paper, and James has been in the hall for the last fifteen minutes. Tammy is wandering around the room poking kids in the back. Soon Terry is chasing her. James sneaks out of the room once again. Michele wanders over to whine petulantly that she doesn't have anything to do.

When the kids in the library start throwing books, I apologize to Jason and call everything to a halt. Clean-up goes badly. Tammy and Terry scatter the Legos all over the room. The markers and crayons I purchased with my own money are left broken, and all of the paper and pencils have disappeared. At dismissal time, Terry's father stops in to let me know that Terry isn't being challenged enough and asks when I will be sending homework.

What do I do when centers don't work and I can't give ownership away? First, I go home, have a good cry, and wonder why I ever got into teaching. Then I have a good laugh as I recount the day's antics with a friend. After that I rethink, revise, and try again.

## RETHINK—WHAT'S GOING ON?

"Seems like I've got management problems. I spend my evenings racking my brain to provide schedules and systems for kids to make choices and work on their own. I spend my own money to buy nice supplies for the room. And these ingrates can't appreciate it!" But now let's rethink this position.

Of course, I have to stop James from wandering, prevent Tammy's disruptions, redirect Terry's interruptions to tattle or Michele's to ask me what to do. But while management addresses symptoms, curriculum development focuses on these issues on another plane. I address these issues within the context of my three classroom walls.

What has happened to James in five years of school to make the halls more interesting than the room? Is Tammy bored with the classroom, or is something happening at home? How can I help Terry and Michele through their bewilderment at having to develop challenges for themselves? Why do some kids want to throw books and break markers rather than use them for reading and writing?

These questions cannot be answered with management techniques, such as "time on task" and "positive reinforcement." If I notice that Terry's not reading, I don't ask "How can I get Terry to read for five more minutes each day?" Instead I ask, "What book will Terry find so compelling that he won't be able to put it down?" I don't ask, "How can I get James to sit in his seat and work?" Instead, I ask, "What are we doing when James decides to stay in the room and join us?" My own questions have evolved as they are informed by observation and theoretical study.

Last February Joshua came up to me after quiet reading and asked if he could go up to the loft and continue reading. He was reading *Roll of Thunder Hear My Cry* (Taylor, 1976), and he wanted to finish the chapter.

"Of course," I answered. I had deliberately arranged my schedule so that quiet reading precedes work time in order to encourage kids to continue reading. The answer was simple, but the question was complicated. Almost every day since September, I had signaled the end of silent reading with an invitation to continue quiet reading as one of the options for the work time.

It's possible that Joshua never heard me say that he could continue reading. He never heard me because, until that day in February, it never mattered to him. It's also possible that Joshua heard me extend the invitation to continue reading. His question may have been a report to me that he was (for the first time in his life) anxious and able to finish the chapter. Regardless of the reasons behind his question, it was February before he decided to take on an invitation that I had extended in September. Interactions like this have convinced me that it is not enough to offer kids lots of books and writing materials and choices and time. What else can I do to encourage kids to become independent readers and writers? I can have minimal requirements, and I do. I have definite assignments and expectations. Silent reading and personal writing are required. This demonstrates to students that I value these activities, which have always been done during free time before. But that means I have students working for grades and not for learning. I can also offer treats and incentives, and I do. But that means I have students working for rewards and not for learning.

In the long run, the kids have to see that learning experiences matter to them. When there is something important to say, they will say it. When there is something interesting to read, they will read it. In his "Conditions for Learning," Brian Cambourne calls this important ingredient "engagement" (Cambourne, 1989). Cambourne lists three important factors of engagement. First, is the learning experience "do-able" for that learner? Second, is the learning experience relevant to the learner? Finally, as Cambourne says, does the learner feel safe to have a go?

This explains Joshua's question. Until he started reading *Roll of Thunder* and wanted to finish the chapter, the notion that he could continue reading wasn't do-able or relevant. My invitation was simply ignored.

When things fall apart, I think through the situation, posing tough problems for myself to solve. Many of my students have had little experience making decisions or handling interesting materials. They start out viewing me as incompetent for not loading them with paperwork or as a soft touch for letting them play during school time. Without practice in controlling themselves, they are out of control. They depend on me to pull everything back together.

How do I meet their immediate need for guidance and direction and still give them an opportunity to learn to organize learning? I involve the kids overtly in rethinking and reorganization. I may point out to them that I'm not able to complete a conference because of interruptions and work. I may ask a child to observe the clean-up time and describe the observations to the class. Sometimes I stop raising my voice for attention, and ask the kids to raise their hands when they can't hear anyone talking. I am calling their attention to the running of the classroom. At first, they see it as my problem. I ask for ideas about how to handle problems during work time, and they come up with teacher-directed solutions they've experienced in the past: "Ms. Goodman, you should isolate the bad ones and punish them. You should call parents. You should take away center time."

Little by little, one by one, each child begins to see that I can't control and direct everything. I can't read a story and make sure no one's talking or poking someone. The kids start to see that the solution has to come from each of us. I offer them control of their own learning, but they must decide to take on the responsibility— personally and socially—that goes with ownership.

I organize the kids into committees to take charge of each center area. As they try to organize their center, my problems become their problems. They grow concerned that students use material appropriately and follow the procedures that they have established. It's essential that the students be part of the rethinking and revision process.

So far I've asked myself why the kids are responding the way they do. I must also consider what I may be doing wrong. When Toby and I first started to design an integrated social studies and language arts program, we felt the kids needed instruction in how to read for information and how to take notes. I did workshops on brainstorming, posing questions, reading texts, and taking notes. The kids had a difficult time with the entire activity. They didn't know how to ask questions, read for information, or take notes. Assuming we were going too fast for them, we planned more activities. A four-day workshop turned into a weekly ordeal, and many of the students became resistant and turned off (in that way that only seventh graders can!). Finally, we retreated, leaving in our wake a group of "bored" and confused seventh graders.

Throwing up our hands, we dropped the whole idea, but we didn't abandon the idea that our kids could do research. Rethinking the whole experience, we decided to try again. This time we would just jump into content-focused research and deal with research strategies as they came along.

## REVISE AND REORGANIZE

For me, organization isn't static; it's a constant process. This year I'm working on my fourth classroom schedule. When the kids interpreted centers as "free play," I moved center time to the afternoon. During the morning, we had one activity at a time. We'd start with a group meeting, making plans for the day and working on our social studies investigations. I continued to make learning experiences active by dividing the students into small groups and regrouping to share information. We'd have quiet reading and then write in our reading logs. We'd have a writing time and sharing or music. In the afternoon, we worked on math in small groups and then had a more open choice time.

After a while, I grew dissatisfied with the schedule again. I was losing the child by working with the whole group. I needed a structure that would allow me to meet with kids alone or in small groups for extended times. I needed to consolidate those who were working with me and win over those who were not.

I tried centers again. This time the kids signed up when they walked into the room for two half-hour time slots. I also made lists of assignments that had to be completed. The kids were even assigned to accept and complete an invitation each week in order to push them to choose a learning experience for themselves. They had their own weekly records to keep track of assignments and activities. I scheduled myself to see them in small groups to introduce projects and work on ongoing assignments. They would sign up for conferences in open time slots.

Even a classroom filled with self-directed learners would call for rethinking and revision as the teacher and students negotiate their interests and goals.

I don't eliminate choices and options, because kids must have control over their own learning in order to become self-directed learners, but I do limit choices in order to allow the students to adjust to working in my classroom. I have even imposed limitations that I am uncomfortable with, such as having a girls' line and a boys' line in the hallway because the children consider a less restrictive arrangement an invitation for chaos. As soon as I can, I ignore the kids who are noisy or fooling around so that I can focus on a conference or a discussion. I am constantly pushing the balance in favor of a classroom where we can all learn and work freely.

## TRY AGAIN. AND AGAIN. AND AGAIN.

Toby and I learned not to try to get the kids ready to learn but to expect they will learn. We start a social studies unit by brainstorming what we know and what we want to know about the topic we've selected with the kids. Each student comes up with a few questions that he or she wants to investigate.

Most of the students still start out the year not knowing how to ask questions, read for information, or take notes. But they soon find that these strategies are essential in order to do research. They struggle with a question that is too broad or too specific. They eagerly ask me how they can find out information that they need to know. They struggle to organize their notes so that they are easier to understand.

When we culminate a two-month family research project, my students ask each presenter process questions, as well as content questions: "How long did it take you to plan your presentation?" "How did you think of your display?" "Where did you get your information?" They gently ask the less prepared presenters why they didn't write some notes. They want the well-prepared presenters to show them their note cards and other organizers.

Before, when Toby and I set the agenda for learning—focusing on strategies rather than on content—the kids were confused and disinterested. When the kids are focused on an exciting learning experience, they demand strategies and information, and eagerly attend the results. At this point, a short workshop on finding information or on taking notes is appreciated, but the kids learn more from their own experiences and the opportunities to work together.

The usefulness and relevance of the learning activity help kids to become engaged. This makes further learning possible as they actually begin to pay attention, read, write, share, and so forth. But the third aspect of engagement is equally important: The students have to feel safe to "have a go." This is encouraged by accepting any and all learning attempts that a student makes. I am asking a lot when I throw fifth graders into the research arena without much preparation.

All students who do research have the full attention of the class when they are making their presentations. I am there to assure that "critiques" remain positive and are focused on strengths. I praise each child for effort and actual work. I am required to give out grades, so I use them to show that I value the effort that the student has made. Grades on final presentations generally range from B + to A + . Without this acceptance, the students would no longer find the assignment "do-able" and would soon give up. With acceptance, the students go on to "have a go" at the next assignment. Throughout the year, their learning strategies are revised and extended, and their work more closely approximates adult research.

I know that approximation (Cambourne, 1989) occurs as children learn to read and write. As we rethink and revise our classroom organization, I must expect approximations of self-directed learning as well. For example, grouping kids for projects usually involves several meetings before kids even get to work. The first two or three meetings are chaotic and frustrating as I am rushing to get this group quiet and that group focused. Somewhere around the third meeting things start to settle into place, and the room buzzes with productive and busy groups. It's easy to assume that group collaboration doesn't work without giving it a fair try.

This year I tend to meet with students on Fridays to review what they've accomplished. The first week four students had finished all of their work for the week. By December about half of the students had completed their work by Friday. I don't penalize students for not completing their work; I provide more direction and limit choices once again. Offering more choices to students who have become self-directed reemphasizes the value of student ownership.

Seen in this light, fooling around and missing deadlines can be seen as part of the process of getting organized for learning. If children don't have the freedom to mess up, how will they learn to take charge? I look for small signs of progress: I finished three conferences in a morning rather than one; we spent half an hour of work time without stopping for reminders on procedures. And sometimes there is even that magic moment when I look around and see a classroom of students engaged in a myriad of learning experiences.

## WHEN THINGS COME TOGETHER

During the winter, Amanda came up to me during writing time and said, "I can't think of anything to write about. What should I do?" I asked Amanda if she had a piece of writing she would like to have a conference about, and she brought me the story shown in Figure 10-4, A.

"Well," I asked, after Amanda had read me her story, "what do you think of your story?"

"You wrote 'great story,' so it must be a great story."

"What do you think?" I insisted.

"I think it's a great story."

"Is there anything you'd like to change?" I asked.

"No," Amanda replied promptly.

I didn't push Amanda to change her story, nor did I immediately begin to proofread her story for a final draft. Instead, I talked to her about some of the images in the story. I really liked the image of hanging from the cloud, and we discussed what that must have looked like. I asked Amanda where she found the ladder. She said she didn't know. I reminded her that she had made up the story and asked if she could make up where she found the ladder.

**Figure 10-4** *Amanda's Story*

The day I fell from the Sky

taken

I had took a
ladder to the sky. But by
the time I got to the
top. The ladder fell and I was
hanging on to the clouds.
And it started raining it got
real slippery. And I fell, I past
the Imper State Building. I fell
in a garbage can and a garbage
truck came and took me to
the junk yard I was about
to get squashed and then Super
Man came and took me to
my house. And my
mother said where have you
been I said you wouldn't
belive me

By Amanda

Great story –
I especially like the part
about hanging on to a cloud.

**A. First draft**

The day I fell from the sky

One day I wanted to cross
a bridge. I it was cold, I heard
that it would rain, so I was
trying to get home. I got to
the other side the other bridge
is out, but, I found a ladder
on the ground, I picked it up
and it was magic. I climbed
to the top and it stopped
and the ladder was about to
fall I, I hung onto the
clouds. Then it started to rain
It got slippery and I fell. I
passed the Empire State Building.
I fell in the garbage can and
a truck came and took me
to the junk yard, I was about
to get "sqoashed" When super-
man came and took me home.
My mother -asked me where I
was I said it is a long story!

"The
n
d"

By Amanda

**B. Revision**

At the end of our meeting, Amanda hurried off and got a fresh sheet of paper. She put her rough draft aside and began to rewrite her story. After a few minutes, she looked up and asked, "How much time do I have?"

"You have as much time as you need," I answered.

"You mean we'll be here for another two or three hours?"

I explained to Amanda that we had a short time left for *that* day but that she could continue her story during the next writing time or work time. "Just think," I said, "next time you won't have to think of something to write about."

But, in fact, Amanda did not wait until the next day to write. Instead, she came up to me with her writing folder wrapped in her arms and said, "Mrs. Goodman, could I *please* take my writing folder home and finish my story?"

The next day she brought in her revised story (Figure 10-4, B).

I learned a great deal from my conference with Amanda that day. I learned that Amanda (and probably the other students in my room) felt that writing assignments should be completed within a class period. Form (in this case, the actual school scheduling) came before meaning and function in her view of this assignment. Just as Joshua had often heard me invite him to continue reading, Amanda had heard my invitation to write at home as well as at school. When Amanda became engaged with the writing experience my invitation had meaning for her.

I also learned more about writing conferences. I used to be an expert editor, admired by other teachers for my ability to gently guide children to revise by suggesting simple changes that would strengthen the story. But, in this conference, I simply discussed the story without focusing on words or sentences. Focusing at the global story level left ownership of the writing with Amanda and allowed her to decide to do some major revision. In this case, I think she took her story beyond where I might have suggested.

The twenty minutes that I spent with Amanda that day were probably some of the most valuable minutes she spent in my class. Learning doesn't happen because kids work quietly and diligently for most of their school day. Learning happens in spurts and lags. If some kids were "wasting their time" while I met with Amanda, so what? I'll have the time to meet with them another day.

Meanwhile, I'm giving them an opportunity to take charge. They don't have true ownership over their own learning if I step in and take charge every time their minds start to wander. I organize my room in the least restrictive environment possible, giving each student room to grow.

## SCHEDULING

Yan Fang's letters (Figure 10-5, A through D, pp. 153-54) were written in an environment in which students were allowed the time to talk and learn from each other. I had expected that she would

---

**Figure 10-5** *Yan Fang's Letters*

Dear Miss. Goodman,
    Thank you to read the book to us. I like to see you read the book. Next time can you read the book to us? And I very like that book. I can speak English, but it's a little ..
    Next time I will learn the little boy. Now I finish the letter. I'm sorry about I can't write a lot for you Because I can't write a lot English. And I know you are my nice teachea.
                                                    Yan Fang

**A. September**


Dear Mrs Goodman :.
        This is second time I write to you. Rember the first time you wrote to me, you asked me what language do I speak at home? Some times I speak English, and some times I speak Chinese.
        I think you know that I can't speek much English, so I can't write a lot, so this time I can stop here. I really don't know what to say. I hope you can have very good days!

                                    Yan Fang
                                        11/21/86
                                        In Berton School

**B. November 21**

---

participate and learn English but had anticipated that she would join in the various learning invitations at her own pace.

While Yan Fang is writing me a letter, Daniel is anxious to read his latest fantasy book. Michael is composing a new rap song. Camille is working on a novel. Dena is studying the Great Depression. Billie Jo wants to tell her friends about a fight that occurred in her house last night. Steven wants to go work with his kindergarten pen pal. I need to find time to sit down with a child for a conference, meet with the

Figure 10-5   *Continued*

Dear Ms. Goodman:                         12/18/86

How are you?
Since I came dat your classroom, I think
you are very nice to me. And I really like
you very much. I hope I can speak English
like a American, but I don't think I can.
I don't know how to write the
book log. Because I don't know how to write
the sentences. I can write them, but in
fact I can't understand them. My father
always told me read books, sometimes
he ask me to read to him but I
cont. I just don't know why. Maybe
thats why I can't write book log.
          Thank you                    Sincerly Yours
                                            Yanfong

C. December 18

Dear Ms. Goodman:                         1/30/86

How are you?
I do have some books in
chinese, and I think maybe I
can write write a chinese story.
But I lost my self
evealuation, so I can't turn it
in yet, maybe I can find it.
I'm not sure if I can.
Thank you for everything. I
know you are so good to me.
                                            Love
                                         Sincerly Yours
                                            Yanfung

D. January 30

script committee for the end of year program, help the newspaper
staff lay out the latest edition, and sit down with a literature group to
discuss a book they've read.

There is no reason why we can't negotiate a classroom organization and a schedule in which all of these things can happen. By
planning together and creating open work periods, we can have time
to do any number of things in a day. We do have some basic

requirements and assignments, but each student can get these done on his or her own time schedule without disturbing other people. Work records and organizers help them plan their weekly schedule (Figure 10-6, A, p. 156).

My classroom schedule and organization grows more informal and flexible throughout the year. For the last few months of school the students plan their own projects and schedules for large chunks of the day. Our day becomes very busy as students go off to work at the food co-op, plant flowers around the school grounds, or spend an hour in the library. The kids plan their own clubs and schedule meeting times for the "baseball card club," the "chess club," the "comic book club," and so on. I always laugh at the notion that some people have that whole language classrooms are "unstructured" as I help the students to coordinate scheduling for all of these activities (Figure 10-6, B).

## THE CLASSROOM AS A CULTURAL INSTITUTION

Some time in the fall, Amanda wrote me a letter:

> Dear Mrs. Goodman.
> I have a problem. Nobody wants to be my friend. I want to be Terri's friend, but she plays with Monique, Mavala, Ashani, and Cortney. I am really lonely. Felicia just keeps bossing me around. Sometimes I think they talk about me. So I don't know what to do. What do you think? Should I try to play with them, or what?
> PLEASE get all of us together to talk.
> Write back,
> Your lonely student
> Amanda
> p.s. Please Help

Although school writing was artificial and confusing to Amanda, her letter eloquently expresses her concern. She recognizes that writing allows her to share a delicate problem and begins to explore solutions. Karen Smith (1989) recently suggested that finding a voice as a writer involves posing problems, a prerequisite and perhaps more important skill than problem solving. Common folk advice concurs: Once you have recognized the problem, you are halfway to the solution.

There is nothing so important to fifth graders as friends. The ups and downs of ten-year-old friendships are taken as seriously as any love affair. The girls swear devotion to their friends, even dressing the same and doing everything together. And nothing makes a boy more unhappy than a fight with his best friend. The entire class embraces best friend pairs, jealously guarding their ties and angrily confronting any who dare interefere with the friendship. And throughout the year, hearts are broken as friendship circles group and regroup.

Amanda wrote her letter because she knows that her social acceptance and personal well-being are important to me. Social and

**Figure 10-6** *Student Work Schedules*

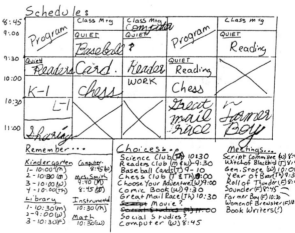

A. Matthew's schedule—February 1989. A working copy

B. Jon's schedule—June 1989. A working copy

cultural interactions are built into the classroom curriculum. Once a week we have "magic circle," a class period devoted to sharing personal triumphs and tragedies and working out problems through discussion. But social interactions are woven into everything we do. From the moment the students walk in the door, they are placed in small groups for class experiences. Eventually, the class is organized into working committees: library staff, math center, games, and more. Decisions are usually made by consensus, which requires that all opinions be valued and that dissenters be convinced rather than alienated. Students get to request who they want to work with, but most recognize that *all* of their classmates are members of the group. No one can be rejected.

After a few years of teaching fifth grade in one school, you get a reputation. The kids in Amanda's class had come into the room expecting a social/cultural curriculum. Billie Jo had enrolled in our school in fourth grade after a ten-year battle to overcome cerebral palsy. She walked with a limp and had a slight speech impediment. On the fourth day of school, she signed up for sharing time.

"I want you to know I don't like being teased," she said. "A lot of people been making fun of me and laughing at me. Last year I used to get upset and fly off the handle about it. But I decided I'm going to let it roll off my back."

When she finished her short speech, she called on students and answered their questions straightforwardly. The conversation continued in the hallway on the way to lunch. Some kids scoffed, but others admired Billie Jo for her bravery. Regardless, Billie Jo felt triumphant for having made her statement to the class.

Billie Jo was able to take this step because my classroom schedule offers a "sharing" time each day. I initiated this time to encourage students to share books and writings, but it has grown into much more. This year many of my students have used the time for science demonstrations or audiotape "news shows." By opening up a half hour of student-run discussion time each day, I allow and invite them to bring their interests and concerns into the classroom.

The cultural wall exists in every classroom, but it is often ignored or even thwarted. Teachers often arrange seating charts to separate friends. Children are expected to be quiet, which prevents them from interacting with others. The teacher's lounge is rife with complaints: "I'm responsible for their education; I don't have time to deal with their problems," is one teacher's gruff refrain, while another puts down his eighth graders, saying, "they all have their minds in their pants."

John Goodlad (1984) discusses the discrepancy between the social interests of high school students and the curriculum of high school classes in his book *A Place Called School*. Friendship, growing up, conflicts with parents and siblings—these are the issues that occupy the minds of students and distract them from focusing on civics or English grammar. When I legitimize the concerns of students by making them a part of the classroom curriculum, I am no longer competing for my fifth graders' attention.

Issues that concern the effective schools movement, such as "setting purpose," "tapping into prior knowledge," "motivation," and "relevance," become nonissues when we allow kids to bring their own world into the classroom. Discussions range wide and far. "Is this a mature audience?" Camille asked one day as she launched us into a discussion of sex and growing up. With this introduction, none dared snicker or scoff.

A few carefully explained and enforced guidelines make such discussion possible. We listen when others talk; we care about each other and don't call one another names or try to hurt other people; we talk to help and to solve problems, not to gossip or probe.

Mostly we share "good news." Without this forum, I might never have known that Amy spends her Saturdays winning gymnastics trophies, that Jason has a new sister, or that Ethan is an electronics whiz. In this safe forum we can also share John's heartbreaking story of a phone call he made to have his father arrested for assaulting his mother.

In this confusing world, I am also offering my students the benefit of adult resources and guidance. Amanda's guarded questions grow into eloquently posed problems. Billie Jo's secret pain turns into public triumph. John's friends have a new understanding about why he's been quick to snap or fight.

By recognizing the role of schools in supporting family and community, we open ourselves to the awesome responsibility of helping young people to grow up as well as to learn. But we have opened the walls to the community, and we are not alone.

## BRINGING THE COMMUNITY INTO THE CLASSROOM

In organizing social studies units that are authentic and relevant, the place I always start is the child's own community. Community study provides students with special strength and inspiration, as they realize the expertise and knowledge that exists all around them.

The fifth graders listen in rare silence as visitors talk of days gone by. They hear the streetcars screeching through the busy neighborhoods where freeways now bypass the empty shells of burned-out houses. They see filled inkwells in rows of bolted desks where their desks and chairs are now scattered about. They taste the candy bought at the friendly corner store, which now greets them with steel bars and Plexiglas shields.

Eagerly they ply guests with questions about values and how children should behave, seeking advice and refining their own (often differing) opinions. Later, they are inspired to write essays, stories, and poems that explore the meaning of these community stories in their lives today (Figures 10–7, A and B).

For three years, we have started out each year researching our own family histories (D. Goodman, 1990). The research has allowed the children to discover the wealth of resources and information that is available within their own family. Often the entire family got involved in the investigations. The presentations have differed in

**Figure 10-7** *Matthew and Terrance Use Notes from Interviews with Grandparents to Write Character Sketches*

Childhood
Interview    Terrence
             May 6, 1988
             Section #6

My Grandmother

She is sixty-eight years old and was born in 1920. Her family lived in Atlanta, Georgia until she came to live in Detroit. She came to live in detroit in 1945. She had two brothers. One of them lives in New Jersey and one stayed in Atlanta. Her mother died. I don't remember what year. My grand mother never knew her father.

I was amazed when she told me how cheap things were back then. A loaf of bread cost five cents. Pepsi and Coca-Cola cost five cents too. Movies cost five cents. Now they cost five dollars.

For fun she went to five cent movies and went to the park and listened to the radio. She played with her friends. She went to the park with her friends on weekends and days she didn't have chores.

I interviewed my grandma at her kitchen table and while she was laying down.

**A.**

Family History

All about grampa Al!

My grampa was born in Italy. When he was about my age there was a war. The war was rough on them because sometimes there was no food. Alot of people had there houses blown up and It happen to my granpa's house too, but luckily my grampa's aunt pulled him out of the house when she saw the bomb coming towards the house. All the men In Town were killed But my grampa's dad because he was a Baker and They needed him to Bake bread so they could have something to eat. My grampa only went to school for four years because when the war started school ended. After four years the war ended. While there was no school during The war my grampa mostly played and looked for food. Once he was playing with a grenade but luckily he did not get hurt, Him and his family would eat leaves off of trees and when the America soldiers were around my grampa would beg for candy bars. My grampa really didn't give a crap who won just as long as he got food.

by matthew

**B.**

content, genre, and style and have been a fascinating learning experience. Lisa (Rousseau-Clark, 1990) told of the French-Canadian lumberjacks, German farmers, and Appalachian copper miners that made their mark on Michigan's history. Kareem shared his visit to historic slave-ports of Africa and his grandmother's stories of Southern segregation. Karin answered questions about India that her classmates had never before thought to ask.

A primary function of schooling has always been to socialize children to the larger culture and society. Lately, there is a disturbing trend to ask parents and society to support "schooling." Homework is stressed, concerned parents are urged to buy school-like work-books, and there is growing discussion of extending the school day and the school year, as if schools were the sole dispensers of learning. Even young elementary school children often have no time for after-school activities and hobbies because they have so much homework, and parents are considered uncaring if they don't super-vise and support these activities. I feel this dominance of schooling over family life is backwards. Schools, classrooms, and teachers should support families and communities.

## THE CLASSROOM AS A COMMUNITY

Last year my first group of fifth graders were in Toby's seventh-grade class. In the spring, they started working on a class literary anthol-ogy. Toby's program focused on social studies units, and she was surprised at how quickly they got organized into groups and started writing. She listened in awe at the stories, essays, and poems that they began to share and wondered where this wealth of ideas and ability had come from. "It comes from the community," I said. "They are a community of writers."

This group was in fifth grade when I brought some "mailboxes" into my classroom so that students would be encouraged to write each other letters. (They were cardboard wine boxes, reinforced with tape and contact paper.) Cassie waved her hand eagerly, "Could we have a *Post Office*," she asked. "And could we pretend to be mail carriers and . . . well, we could have a whole town and play that we were the people that lived there. . . ."

Fifth graders. One day they are in love, the next day they bring their baby dolls in or play with plastic figures in the sandbox. Vygotsky (1978, p. 102) stresses the importance of play in his book *Mind in Society*: "Play creates a zone of proximal development. In play a child always behaves beyond his average age, above his daily behavior; in play it is as though he were a head taller than himself. As in the focus of a magnifying glass, play contains all developmental tendencies in a condensed form and is itself a major source of development."

For the fifth graders, the town was more than just fun. I used the town to allow the students to take over the various aspects of the classroom. There was the post office, a museum, a library, and a publishing center. Cassie's mom made us a storefront, and we had a general store. The next year one of the dads built a loft that provided a quiet reading area above and a bookshelf below, separating the library and the publishing house.

The other areas of the town have varied, depending on the interests of each group. We've had an art center, a recreation center, a maintenance crew, a theater group, a courthouse, and a town hall.

While playing "town," the kids were involved in a great deal of reading and writing. They made charts and signs, wrote out plans and instructions, and participated in a variety of activities, including organizing and reading the library books, and writing, editing, and publishing written works in the publishing house.

But the town also created a strong sense of community and a chance to explore what a community should be like. Toby's seventh graders scoff at playing "town," but get fully involved in electronic mail computer simulations of world problems and historic events. Simulation is to social studies what animals in the classroom are to science. They provide the same hands-on experience.

With encouragement to think of their town as the ideal society, Cassie's class called the town Utopia. After much collaboration and revision, they came up with this sign post for the classroom door:

---

Welcome to Utopia
Pop. 63
Utopia is a town where you can be yourself. You can do what you want as long as it is not insulting, cruel, disobedient to other people.
Utopia is a town where people share with other people.
Utopia is a town where people are allowed to think about what they want.
Utopia is a town where you have the freedom to do what *you* think is right, and make the friends *you* want to make.

---

I want my students to grow as people. I want them to know how to contribute to a democratic world. We start by learning to work together and care for each other. In her final evaluation of her school year, Cassie again reflects on the content, process, and social aspects of our curriculum:

I learned about American History and culture very much. I did town work, joined the publishing house but then quit to help the library. I brought things from Mexico for my family tree. I worked hard on my literature reports and childhood unit. I read interesting books and really enjoyed my research. I loved finding out about Mr. Servetter's childhood. And I really like social studies now. I learned some things about being responsible for myself. I had to do my work on time and get it in by myself. I learned about working with other people when we had to work in group projects on committees. I learned how to organize my time by working on work at school and at home. I learned how to find things out by doing research and asking questions. The most important thing about this year is making friends. School and your schoolwork are very important, but not having friends can have effect on everything.

I teach in a real classroom. It has four walls, a ceiling, and a floor. I teach in a bureaucratic school system with many requirements and restrictions. Yet, within these four walls thirty-three kids and I work to construct another classroom. It is supported by theory and cradled by knowledge and process and culture. It is our utopia.

## EDWIN HAS NO SHOELACES
### Toby Kahn Curry

I was spoiled. For ten years I was spoiled. I had convinced myself that, in the inner-city Detroit school in which I was teaching, I was surrounded by predominantly middle class kids. Whenever I was asked to identify the students at Burton International, I'd say things like, "My kids come from all over the city, they're mostly middle class, 50% of them black. The bilingual kids in my classes who live in the immediate neighborhood are usually from families that have immigrated to the downtown area to attend Wayne State University or work in the Medical Center." Although many of my former students were poor, it didn't cripple them. The middle class majority enveloped the poorer kids, clothed them with their values, wooed them with their birthday parties and sleep-overs, and threw them into the shadows of their Jordache jeans and Adidas sneakers. Conversely, the lower income kids inspired the others with their resourcefulness and determination. Their voices provided a sobering balance to the affluent group. The mixture of economic and cultural groups benefited everyone. The lower class kids were pulled into the mobile world of the middle class. The economically advantaged kids grew to appreciate the realities and practicalities of the inner city. It was in this setting that I developed into a whole language teacher.

This semester has been *the best of times and the worst of times*. The biggest challenge of my teaching career is upon me. How do I organize our new whole language classroom? How do I help my new students become independent readers and writers? In a community where many kids never make it through high school, is there hope that my kids can become productive members in our democratic society? We are struggling together to define our place in the world and to make meaning out of our school life. What is our classroom curriculum?

I've heard Jerome Harste say curriculum is "the learner's mental trip." What about the teacher's? Why do I feel like a novice again? I've set up three centers in our room: a math center; a social studies center; and a computer center (with a borrowed Apple IIe computer). There are games and activities in each center. The kids love the activities and fight for their rotation into the centers. They are actually beginning to collaborate on the different activities. *But Edwin has no shoelaces in his sneakers, no warm coat, and he seems to wear the same clothes, day after day after day.*

## REALITIES

My new school, The Dewey Center, is geographically five blocks away from my former school. Five city blocks, but economically and culturally a million miles. I have a few middle class kids in my new classroom, but most of my students come from a housing project community, one of the most economically depressed areas in Detroit. Many of my kids come from single-parent homes with subsidized incomes. Along with the kids from "stable" homes in the projects, I have two to four students at a time enrolled from a Detroit temporary shelter for the homeless. These kids come for a day, a week, a month, and occasionally for the whole semester. When Tonya moved into her uncle's home on the other side of town, her mom found a way to get her to our school by bus. But, usually, the children disappear as abruptly as they arrive: no forwarding address, no connections or bonds to tie them to our class; just a stack of partially filled log books, empty writing folders, and a vacant slot in our classroom mailbox.

These displaced children arrive scared, disoriented, angry, and anxious. And, of course, with each new arrival, the social dynamics of our classroom goes through a myriad of changes. I have to remind myself that I am also a new arrival to this school and its community.

Several of my students have been retained once; some, twice. Many think they can't read and have never tried to read a book without "lots of pictures." Most of them have never done any real writing, and many think they can't write because they can't spell. My kids have come into our whole language classroom from what I consider to be the horrors of fragmented learning.

Most of my kids have never read a novel, so I began reading *Roll of Thunder, Hear My Cry* by Mildred Taylor (1976) the first week of school. I read *every* day to them after outdoor recess. For most, it's their first experience with powerful historical fiction—a story that focuses on a black family's survival in the racist, rural Mississippi of the 1930s. Together we analyze the plot, discuss the characters' thoughts and actions, make comparisons of the historical setting with 1989 city life, and make predictions about the story based on what the author has already revealed to us, the readers. I love to see literature and history come alive for my students. Their comments show how serious they are, how much they care about the book, and how eager they are to learn.

*But last week, coming in from recess, we found a syringe full of blood on the playground. The kids shouted to me not to touch it and told me that I'd "get AIDS." I explained we couldn't leave it outside because the younger kids were coming out and it had to be disposed of properly. I gingerly picked it up, passed it along to my principal for disposal, washed my hands with hot, soapy water, and ushered my kids into the classroom.*

We spent the next several minutes talking about drug addicts and AIDS. All of a sudden, *the curriculum had changed*. School took on a whole new focus, and, as the "instructional leader," I had no idea it was going to happen. If I had had a lesson plan, an AIDS current events discussion might have been in it, but it definitely wasn't on the day's agenda that the kids and I had planned together that morning.

In an effort to stimulate writing, I asked my students to write a biography for "The Real Me," an idea for a classroom book that I borrowed from Debra Goodman and that she describes in her article. I conferenced with each child. Many of the kids ended up with three and four drafts.

Most of the kids had limited experience with productive writing. Some of my kids had to dictate their stories to me, they just couldn't put pencil to paper yet. These reluctant writers thought writing was spelling instead of their personal ideas and thoughts, and they knew they couldn't spell. One mistake and their "messed up" paper was tossed in the basket. I've had to convince the students that we won't correct any spelling except when we edit for publication. The kids are beginning to learn about writing, and I'm beginning to learn about their lives. Following is an excerpt from David's "The Real Me."

My name is David and I love to eat pizza. I am 5' 6" and I live in Detroit. I love reading books. Today I am writing about myself for a book. This is the first writing that I have published.

I work downtown at the Broadway Market. I like to go places with my grandfather. We go fishing on the weekends. I ride my bike up on the hills in my neighborhood. I like drawing pictures and I like making science projects. I love listening to tapes on my brother's headphones. I like reading comic books.

The thing I hate about my neighborhood is dope dealing and drugs. Everyday I see drug dealings around my house. Everything is straight with me because I go to C.C.Y.A. where I can have fun and not be around dope dealings. My community is great because I can watch cable in my house without my antenna getting broken down and my cord getting pulled out of my house wall.

I have friends around my neighborhoods and we play sports like baseball. Sometimes we go to Belle Isle to play. This summer was bad because of all the violence I had to live through. My friends were always fighting and throwing rocks and busting bottles. I worried about getting hit or hurt.

But I had fun this summer, too. I went swimming with Jamal and Derrick. We took swimming lessons every Thursday at Stone Pool which is run by Detroit's Park Depearment. Then we went to C.C.Y.A. and went on field trips like to The Sweden House Restaurant and the movies. In general, this summer was really great for me. I loved it.

What you don't learn from this excerpt of David's life is that it took me two months to convince him to refrain from calling his classmates "nigger" and that I had to exclude him from my class in order to get his mother to come in for a three-way conference. In anticipation of the questions that experienced whole language teachers may ask, let me say

- Yes, David and I wrote out a contract about our expectations for one another.
- Yes, I counseled David countless times individually.
- Yes, I've written him letters about our interactions and my expectations.
- No, I don't believe excluding a student from class accomplishes a great deal.

What David's brief exclusions did for me was give me some insights into his family, his values, and his past schooling experiences.

My principal suggested exclusion as the most efficient way to get a parent response. I scoffed at first but after numerous missed appointments and a great deal of frustration over David's in-class behavioral displays, I succumbed to the exclusion process. David was out for a day and then reappeared with his mother. Through the three-way conference, I learned that David was having more success in my program than he'd ever had in school, as far as his mother could remember. When I recounted some of David's antics to his mother, she turned to David with an incredulous look on her face and said, "Have you forgotten that this is the best classroom you've ever been in? How could you do this in her class?"

I was thrilled to learn that somehow I was having a positive impact on David's schooling experience, but the real impact of his mother's words for me were: "How could you do this in *her* class?" For herein lies the problem. How can I help David understand that this is *his* class, *his* education, and *his* life, and that I'm just one more stop along the way? In the past, I've been a great one for talking to others about student ownership, but this school year it has been extremely difficult to translate the words of ownership into real student-controlled learning.

I watched and waited for many weeks for my kids to take ownership over their reading selections, organization of their time, topics for their writing, and decisions about where our studies should take us. When I asked my students to help me name our classroom, they drew a blank for days. I finally suggested "2001: A Classroom Odyssey," because I'm interested in futurist studies, especially environmental issues. The kids went along with this idea and proceeded to make a sign for our door, but I worry that I'm the only wanderer on this year's journey because I alone seem able to conjure up the marvelous possibilities that await us.

My kids, victims of years of fragmented learning, failing grades, and systemized, prepackaged programs that devalue them as learners, can't quite see the learning opportunities that await them. They have yet to realize that I value them as readers and writers and that I believe that they can make informed decisions about their own curriculum. Building my students' trust, helping them to revalue themselves as learners, and striving for authenticity in our studies are *my* challenges in our "classroom odyssey." How do I get my kids to come along for the ride?

This has been a highly unusual semester for me as my twenty-five struggling, reluctant learners have taught me some uncomfortable, raw truths about teaching and learning. I sometimes learn as much by watching them during their thirty-minute outdoor recess as I do in our four or five hours together in the classroom (not an easy admittance for a fifteen-year teaching veteran).

I know they understand ownership because of the successful social events they coordinate. Their first party of the year ran so smoothly that I turned the time over to them the second time a holiday came up. The group organized a class basketball game without consulting or including me. Unfortunately I am left out of these events—not yet a member of this group.

They have also taught me that it is neither simple nor easy to transfer what I know from one school and classroom situation easily to another. Each context is a new one. The same kinds of things that worked for me and the students at Burton International are not working in the same way at The Dewey Center. I must take the time to know my students, to learn who they are and what they know.

## IT'S COMING TOGETHER

I've been struggling since the last week of August to promote a classroom atmosphere and program that will create a group negotiation of room organization and the growth of a curriculum with personal meaning for the students. It took three weeks to get students to volunteer to be our classroom comic book librarian, help organize our listening center, and keep our math center in working order. But my patience seems to be paying off. Still, the struggle continues.

Certainly, I've seen some exceptional growth and more than a glimmer of hope as I have watched the kids learn to cooperate while using the computer or tutoring one another in math. Each student has begun an "I-Search" research project. We've conducted community interviews and have taken notes in our log books.

Inviting community members to be interviewed in our room has had unexpected results. Rose Bell, a resident of the Jeffries Projects, told the kids about her volunteer work knitting and crocheting for young mothers, and the students decided to get involved.

After Danton Wilson came to talk to the kids about his work on the *Michigan Chronicle*, Michigan's only black-owned and operated newspaper, the kids were invited to put together a regular column for it. They now collaborate on self-selected topics for this very real writing assignment.

## "BUT SOMETHING IS NOT RIGHT"

(MISS CLAVELL, *MADELINE*, BY LUDWIG BEMELMANS)

We've had successes. To the casual observer, we have a busy, focused whole language classroom. A thematic unit has begun to evolve around environmental issues. We're calling it "WWIII: The Fight to Save the Planet" from an article I found in the December 1989 issue of *LEARS* magazine.

Everyone has a writing folder, and we're almost ready to publish our first book, *The Real Me*. There is something missing, and I think it relates to a basic mistrust the students have of schools and teachers. I haven't been able to convince my kids that I'm genuine, and in return their participation in the program has lacked authenticity. Building their trust in me and my trust in myself to take more risks is key to our continued growth.

There is only our classroom door that separates many of my kids from drug addicts, alcoholism, prostitution, community violence, and poverty. It seems that both my students and I are driven to ignore these harsh realities during our five hours together each day. We discuss the drug tragedy in generalities and violence as an American phenomenon, but we really don't want to tread too deeply outside our immediate classroom door. Should I discuss the homeless with Darryl and Anthony, who are from Detroit's housing shelter? Should I have Angela, whose brother has been jailed, research prison reform? Should I have Andre, who has sickle-cell anemia, write about what it's like growing up poor, black, in the projects, and fighting a fatal disease? Should I have Antoine tell about his foster family or what it's like to be taken away from his mom? If these life stories had been my life story at eleven or twelve years of age, would I have wanted to pour it out for all (or anyone) to read?

Over the past three months I have picked up bits and pieces of the real-life pains of my students. Through conversations, letters, and parent conferences I have learned some hard facts about my students' lives, none of which are revealed in the writing for *The Real Me* which we did at the start of the semester. I finally have had the courage to start dialogue journals with these students. I hope that by responding to one another in private on a regular basis, we will be able to build the dimension of trust that has been missing from our relationship.

Perhaps we'll write another *The Real Me* version in June. Maybe by then my students will trust me enough to reveal some bigger truths about their lives and their goals for the future. By then I will have learned a good deal more about them, myself, and whole language in this new school setting. Maybe by then the real Patricia will be willing to share more than Double Dutch, stickers, and posters:

### THE REAL ME by Patricia

The real me is someone who likes to play and have fun. I love to swing on the playground at school. I like to jump rope. My favorite game is "Double Dutch."

I am starting to like this school; they give you a lot of work—that is the part I like because you get a lot of work at school. I just love work. Sometimes I get in school late, but that's all right, and sometimes I get to school on time too, and that's all right, too. But the best thing I like is my teacher.

### Goals for the Future

When I grow up I will be a store lady and I hope I get a lot of people in my store so I can get a lot of money.

The real me is when I wish I pass the "50 Book Club." That is why sometimes I read a lot of books. And if I only read 50 books I would be so, so happy. I love stickers. I would like to make a sticker collection. And when I have my very own sticker collection I would let everyone see that is the Real Me.

I really love posters of famous people so I could put it on my locker. I just love posters and I hope I have some money so I can go to the store and buy me some posters and I might put it all over my locker. And that is the Real Me.

## POSTSCRIPT
### Debi and Toby

Whole language works with all kids. We know it does. The students at the new Dewey Center respond with more interest, more writing, more reading, and more learning than we saw when they walked through the door of our classrooms four months ago. They are beginning to apply the capabilities they use to organize their own world outside of school to their lives in school. But whole language can't solve society's problems.

And why are all of society's problems shunted into this small corner of the world so that these preadolescents are confronted with them every day? By designating this new school as a magnet school and inviting students from all over the city, we hope to open the world of possibilities beyond the narrow communities that each group lives in.

Yet, more money is spent to keep a prisoner in jail than to keep a child in school each year. What future do any of our kids have? We may need to fight the tough battles together—teachers and students—before we can build an economically integrated community that nourishes young learners and their education.

# 11

# WHEN THE "WRONG" STUDENTS COME THROUGH THE DOOR

**Mary M. Kitagawa**

In 1987-1988 I had a class that purred so smoothly I thought I had arrived as a whole language teacher. Before that I was only striving to become one. Well, the next fall I opened my classroom door to a group that put me right back in the *striving* category. Maybe my experience helps explain why Ken and Yetta Goodman always say we are *becoming* whole language teachers (and they are not just complimenting us on our good looks!).

*Striving* is being unable to predetermine how any particular learning community will be achieved or how it will function. *Striving* is being unable to claim, "I always do it this way." Paraphrasing Earl Kelley, James Moffett points out that "we build the right facilities, organize the best course of study, work out the finest methods, create the appropriate materials, and then, come September, the wrong students walk through the door" (Moffett, 1983, p. 152).

The students of my 1988-1989 class were not really "wrong," of course. It was just that they were distinctive from other classes, especially from the "easy" class of the year before. My husband, in our supper-table conversations, began to call them "authentic" long before I had such a positive attitude. But he was right. I was learning, in September, that "inauthentic, or sham" cooperation was not going to be their gift to me. What they liked, they devoured, but what they rejected, they sabotaged.

As individuals, there were certainly those who applied themselves with unobtrusive diligence, but the overt norm was to not show oneself as a "schoolboy" or "schoolgirl," derisive terms they equated with "geek" or "nerd." And they tended to act as a unit so much so that it was hard to activate them in risk-taking activities, such as voting as individuals, creative movement, drama, and brainstorming.

I was nostalgic for former students who made me feel like a "good teacher." Finally, I had to ask myself if positive educational qualities were not to be found in this class as well, and, if so, how could I promote those factors? I was determined to see if I could utilize the overall personality with which this group presented itself.

The qualities of former students that I particularly wanted to promote in this class were divergent thinking, with its concomitant risk taking and utilization of writing for self-expression. Public risk taking was being thwarted by negative peer pressure, so the more private avenue of self-expressive writing would be a particularly necessary outlet. I needed a mnemonic way to keep central in my planning the need for these qualities of risk taking and self-expressive writing. For reasons that I will describe later, I named them after former students who seemed to epitomize them, Armando and Virginia.

In identifying these, I realized that my "difficult" class was also loaded with factors I valued highly—factors around which a learning community could be built. Some of these I named the Refugio Factor, the Adam Factor, and the Carmela Factor. I will share the factors from this and former classes and some of the organizational decisions that I made because of them. First, the Refugio Factor.

## AUTHENTICITY IN GROUP DYNAMICS

THE REFUGIO FACTOR

The class that gave me this particular slice of humble pie was a group of sixth graders who had almost all been together since prekindergarten. Therefore, their individual identities within the group and their interpersonal relationships were less malleable than might be true with a class that had experienced greater population changes. I had a long-held ideal of sharing decision making as much as possible, but with this class there was simply no alternative to that ideal.

They loved to sing, so music took its place right up there with P.E. When we put on a simplified version of *H. M. S. Pinafore*, however, Refugio decided that there would be no solos. "We all want to sing all of the music," he insisted, even though there were volunteers for solos and there had also been the suggestion made to have girls alone sing "Little Buttercup" and boys alone sing male solos. We tried the latter alternative, and, although I thought it sounded like a possible compromise, Refugio led the successful opposition with "See, we told you it wouldn't work." So, in the performance the boys sang "I'm Called Little Buttercup" right along with the girls!

I am calling the exerting of control by students the Refugio Factor now. It was not the only time he took a stand. Refugio is a burn victim who carries scars and will probably face more surgery someday. My agenda can only be served by merging it with his. The economically poor Native Americans and Mexican-Americans of this school neighborhood have the highest dropout rate in Tucson. Getting them to take ownership is not just an interesting experiment; it is fundamental to their success in school. The alternative of leaving students like Refugio and his classmates out of the power base of the learning community would be more turned-off, turned-out students.

Refugio was one of five boys whose literature study group rebelled after they had read several chapters of *The Celery Stalks at Midnight* (Howe, 1983). They had chosen it for their next literature study book because they had just enjoyed *Bunnicula* (Howe and Howe, 1979), but, unlike *Bunnicula*, its appeal rests heavily on the appreciation of puns. Since English is not their home language, these boys were apparently not enjoying the puns. Refugio agreed with Jaime, who said "It must have been Mrs. Howe who had all the talent for writing. We're not going to go on with it; that's all." I was inwardly grinning over this little power play, even though it meant hastily rounding up five copies of *Ralph S. Mouse* (Cleary, 1982), which they were enthusiastic to read.

One reason I appreciate the Refugio Factor of student decisiveness is that it is akin to another factor that I value highly, the one that I call the Armando Factor, after a student from several years before Refugio.

## CELEBRATING DIVERGENT THINKING AND RISK TAKING

### THE ARMANDO FACTOR

The inside of Armando's desk always resembled the wastebasket. We rightly attributed most no-name papers to him; and he usually seemed surprised that his books had not followed him like puppies to school in the morning, so the Armando Factor is not responsibility. Instead, it is the ability to respond in terms of divergent thinking and personal reception of new ideas. Armando had the self-confidence to publicly share even vague or outlandish notions. He was *creatively response-able*.

I would read aloud that a book character leaned far out of the window, and Armando's body would tilt precariously. He was not upstaging the reading, just absorbing it. As if to solidify them in his memory, he would echo cleverly worded phrases he heard. His chortling was often our first clue that something just said or read could be taken as a pun.

When our hermit crab died, Armando staged an Ancient Egyptian funeral in keeping with our current subject of study. He organized classmates to "mummify" the body, make a crab version of the Book of the Dead, and construct a cardboard pyramid complete with traps and curses. As high priest, he hired most of us as "paid" mourners to process behind him wailing, our faces authentically smeared with mud.

To Armando, everything has multiple connection points into his own scheme of knowledge. He not only finds the obvious linkages but also maps the range for obscure connections. That mapping frequently dominated our mutual agenda. Even when he made us roll our eyes over an absurdity, it gave us a handle to remember the concept under discussion. For example, in describing the averaging of heights, Armando likened it to lopping off the head of the tallest person and attaching it onto the shortest so we would have three average-sized people.

I do believe that every student has at least latent qualities like Refugio's and Armando's. Some present them readily and remind us to promote traits such as decisiveness and risk taking in their classmates as well.

In the challenging class of 1988-1989, Edmundo was my barometer of Armando-like thinking. One day we were having minimal success in trying to prove that cold water is heavier than warm water. Since we could not be sure we saw the location of the red-colored hot water before it blended with the uncolored cold water, we listed possible explanations for the failure. "We should have used blue food coloring instead," Edmundo suggested facetiously. But then it occurred to him that the coloring might have weighed the hot water down, and he suggested redoing the experiment with the cold water being colored instead. (It still did not work, but we had a sense of scientific inquiry, thanks to Edmundo.)

Less self-assured students than Armando and Edmundo need to hear often that "the only mistake you can make in this class is not to try." And its counterpart is, "No idea is as preposterous as it might sound. Don't be afraid of an idea."

Beginning with the first tentative aside I overhear, I laugh at their humor and provide them with cornier jokes of my own. Humor is fundamentally just the making of a divergent response; if we elevate humor, we are promoting higher-order thinking, even when the jokes are sometimes of a "lower order" of sophistication. In an aside during a discussion about phobias, Bobby speculated that triskadekaphobia (aversion to the number 13) was "a fear of crackers, especially Triscuits," and Phil, after getting the 3 + 10 clue, thought maybe it was his fear of math problems. I laughed with them, but I also chortled to myself over evidence that the Armando Factor was coming out.

## RESPONSIVE MANAGEMENT DECISIONS
### BASED ON REFUGIO AND ARMANDO FACTORS

To support the Refugio and Armando factors in all of the students, I qualified the primary rule in my class, "Follow directions," with "*unless* you have a better idea to suggest." With that kind of addendum, there can be no "assertive discipline" and no detention plan. I explained on the first day that they would have to cooperate to make our community function without those familiar controls. One day in November, my student teacher witnessed a substitute teacher dropping his jaw when he started to write a name on the board for disciplinary purposes and Fernando informed him, "You can't do that, because we don't believe in it." It might sound fresh, but I rejoiced to hear that *we* had a belief system Fernando was ready to defend.

We had a space on the board marked "Appointments" where students and I could put our own names and the name of anyone else. The agreement was that the one calling the appointment should be accommodated before the one called went home that day. The appointment was over as soon as possible, often before dismissal time. I made sure that many of my requests were for positive or neutral reasons. Even if I needed to discuss unacceptable behavior, the appointment was brief and not meant to be punitive. Students could write their own names and mine in the box to get extra help or a personal conference after school. Often I never got involved in an appointment between two students, as when Cora, for example, wrote Steve's and her names because he had tripped her in the hall. By dismissal time, she was erasing their names, however; at Steve's request, they worked it out with his apology before the bell rang. I suggested the idea to our fourth-grade teacher when she said that tattling was a major problem in her class; if students have guaranteed access to the redressing of a situation, it is amazing how many issues they resolve themselves and with dispatch once a cooling-off period occurs!

## MAKING SURE THE PRIVATE SELF HAS A VOICE
### THE VIRGINIA FACTOR

Skillful reading and writing are well known as objectives of schooling. But they are more than skills for future utilization. They are the components of the Virginia Factor, named after a student in Armando's class.

We write "incessantly" from the very first day, from learning logs in science and math that no one else reads to compositions we share in some form of publication. Writing flows from and promotes inner speech if it is a comfortable habit. I think of inner speech as that unfocused stew of "almost languaged" thoughts that link perceptions together in our minds. Some of them can be pushed into external speech (including writing), and some of them will surprise us, as if they had not just come from within our own heads!

These opportunities for self-expression are especially valuable for shy students like Virginia, whose response-ability came out privately, although she hardly shared her ideas publicly at all. Virginia and I had dialogues through her journal that gave us a relationship on a level far deeper than we could reach orally. Even if she had not been shy, there would not have been time orally for our in-depth exchanges about family relationships, women's liberation, and the Yaqui Easter ceremonies. When she went on to junior high, it was her writing that alerted her teachers to Virginia's character strength and mental acuity. Gradually, she began to overcome her shyness under the accolades she won for her writing. And Virginia showed strength in reading, too, bolstering her comprehension by writing reading log entries about the thoughts and feelings that texts brought out for her.

Just as Virginia could shed her reserved nature first in writing, sometimes aggressive students are able to shed their public images through writing. A roughneck can cry over Leslie's death in *Bridge to Terabithia* (Paterson, 1977) and tell me about it in his reading log or use a journal entry to admit to a feeling of helplessness over his mother's alcoholism, all without jeopardizing his image of Mr. Cool before his classmates.

Some reading and some writing, therefore, need to be private. I call this the Virginia Factor of response-ability, even though I could as easily have given it many other names. It probably was not mere coincidence that, in the class that resisted public risk taking, the Virginia Factor was prevalent and enabled me to have a feeling of closeness, even though I was not having an easy time getting students to open up orally.

In addition to promoting the Virginia Factor by responding sincerely to their journals, it is important for teachers to leave many of the genre choices open so that writing can serve the writer in form as well as content. Andy was angry over a home incident one day; his classmates were looking up research subjects of their own choosing, but Andy announced to me, "I have to write a poem." He dashed off four angry lines, shoved the poem in his writing folder, pulled out a novel, and began to read.

Another student used writing to memorialize his deceased cousin; when he showed it to me, he said, "It's not for sharing; it's not for showing anyone; it's just for me." It was one of the most beautiful pieces I have ever read, but the Virginia Factor includes the possibility of writing that serves its purpose without any outside audience.

Therefore, even though writing workshop in my classroom probably looks quite similar to others, I do think that I emphasize audience less and writer satisfaction more. I ask students to start writing time "in your private study," by which I mean, without communicating with each other. After everyone is launched, I let up on this, closing in only on distracting noise or on off-task behavior. The rationale for a private time in the beginning is that I believe that personally significant writing comes more from tapping inner sources than from wanting to impress others. In that regard, also, my usual questions in conferences are, "How does it meet your own expectations?" and "Does it accomplish what you set out to do?"

## KIDWATCHING BY A KID, OR HOW WRITING WORKSHOP LOOKS TO AN INSIDER

On January 20, Rosalinda called for a conference to show me how she "just started to write what I saw everyone doing (in writing workshop)." As she read her description to me, I realized that I was not the only kidwatcher in the room. The following is a brief excerpt of her writing:

> Edmundo and Adam are sitting at the round table writing about skateboarding I guess 'cause Edmundo just stopped me how to spell skateboarding.
>
> Robert is at his desk right by Jaime and Jaime is at his own desk. I can hear them talking about their pieces of writing.
>
> Finally I'm at my friendly little group here in our little island Dahlia, Carmela, Velma and I. I am working on this as you can see. Velma is writing with her black squeaky marker and asking Dahlia for some advice, Carmela is writing very quietly as usual, and Dahlia is giving Velma some advice about her writing. . . .

I was pleased with Rosalinda's piece, far beyond the quality of the writing. My satisfaction came from the fact that she self-selected her topic and genre without questioning that she might have to get my okay first.

I typically cycle the class through mini-lessons on various genres, but rarely are more than a couple of students "between pieces" and therefore ripe for tackling something new. Furthermore, genre decisions ideally follow, rather than precede, content choices: "Let *what* you have to say tell you *how* you need to say it."

There are usually three seasons to the freeing up of restraint over genre choice: fall is "Could I write a story instead?"; early winter is "I'm writing a story instead"; and in late winter I discover only by chance that someone like Rosalinda is launching a genre we have not even discussed. The seasons can be counted upon because I answer all genre-permission questions and statements with the same words in the same slightly exaggerated intonation: "Of course!" One of the ways the "authentic class" earned its title was that it went through all three seasons by the first of December!

## CHOICES WITHIN ASSIGNMENTS

In spite of my belief that the ideal is to decide on form after tapping an inner source to find one's commitment to a particular bit of content, I do sometimes introduce and then assign certain genres. Early in the fall we write poetry. I find this necessary because it seems to legitimize poetry as a means of public expression; without a few weeks of sharing poetry by all of us only a few would use this avenue in class. And, in conjunction with various thematic units, we write myths, folktales, reports, and so forth, as "almost mandatory" assignments. ("If you are not going to do this, you have to let me know what you will be doing in its place.") In our Medieval unit, for example, some students seemed to have "sibling" rivalry over using a study guide written by the class of the previous year. By the time I recognized this, they already knew quite a bit about the Middle Ages in Europe; so, I promised them space in the same study guide (a loose-leaf notebook) for writing done in the persona of a man or woman of those times. Bobby produced my favorite in his diary of a jester, from which this is an excerpt:

> The things I have to do to make the king laugh! The king won't laugh any more when I lock a slave up in a stock and throw pies at him. I even tried to get him to laugh by juggling but that wouldn't make him laugh. My dog act won't work either. I think I'm losing my touch. My dad was a jester, and there wasn't one day he didn't make the king laugh. Now I know I'm losing my touch.
>    Oh, the king is yelling for me. I got to go. I'll finish later.
>    Hi, it's me again and I have good news for you, Diary. I made the king laugh again.
>    I thought of something while I was doing my dog act. Here it is. I'm going to tell it to you. Ready? All I had to do was hit myself on the head with two big logs. It's hard on the head but easier to make the king laugh. Now my problems are over. Thanks for listening to what I had to say, Diary. I will be back tomorrow.

To illustrate the interplay between my choices and the students', let me describe our Renaissance Science Fair. The first year it had been my idea to have such a "fair," and in the next year students expected it, just as they expected a medieval feast and other events that they had heard about from previous sixth graders. But the exact nature of the fair components had their own stamp by reason of the choices they made within my insistence that all had to participate and their contributions had to extend our knowledge of the Renaissance in Europe. Some students presented themselves (in writing that they read to us) as if they were Leonardo da Vinci, Galileo, Newton, and others. Probably this was a carry-over from the "medieal persona" writing of the unit before. Others stretched the definition of a "science" fair by making oral presentations about William Shakespeare and Michelangelo. These added significantly to the models and descriptions done by other students of what was invented or discovered by various Renaissance scientists (my original expectation of what a Renaissance science fair would be).

In spite of such negotiated choices, if I were to give an estimate of the assigned versus the unassigned topics and genres, I would hope that at least two-thirds of the writing in my class would be done under the simple mandate: "Engage yourself in the writing process." To say more is to diminish the need all writers have to look inward first before deciding what and how to write. Beyond that I can also build in a small measure of flexibility about how long to engage oneself with writing by mingling art and reading time with writing. That is how the Virginia Factor goes beyond the requiring of journals and reading logs and influences writing workshop and writing-across-the-curriculum as well.

## WRITING WITH PERSONAL CONVICTION
### THE ADAM FACTOR

Students' "voices" seem to clarify themselves as the year goes on. Adam started the year writing in someone else's voice and writing for shock effect about experiences I was pretty sure he was not having. I had several intense conferences in which I praised the realistic art I had seen him create in his characteristic style. I told him that I believed he could do writing with that same creative realism. Little by little he began to drop the persona of a young punk writing about cruising at 1 A.M. and looking for chicks. His journals, stories, and reading logs took on a twelve-year-old's convictions, and I nurtured those convictions by responding as follows in the extra-wide margins I ask students to leave:

| (ADAM'S WRITING) | (MY RESPONSES) |
|---|---|
| *The Magician's nephew* is a good book, but not as good as *The Lion, the Witch and the Wardrobe* the book. I say C. S. Lewis should of written *The Magician's Nephew* first. I think that Digory's uncl acts like a mad scientes not a magician. Digory is stupid for going after Polly. I would of the uncl to do it himself. | You naturally feel like comparing the two books. I see you don't mean the TV movie version (we saw). In terms of time, it *is* first, as you say. You're absolutely right. I agree. Good observation. If only his uncle were not such a coward. . . . |

Adam's reading log was sketchy and unrefined, but it contained just what I look for in a reading log: reactions stated in the reader's own voice. Adam used forceful language, such as "I say," because he put himself on the line with his opinions. He could disagree with both C. S. Lewis and with the main character, yet still say it was a good book. As an author himself, he knew of the decisions about which a writer might seek opinions. In an earlier reading log about *The Lion, the Witch, and the Wardrobe* (Lewis, 1950), Adam wrote, "If I was having a conference with C. S. Lewis, I would tell him not to give characters childish names like Mr. and Mrs. Beaver."

What I was looking for was Adam's experience with the book, not generic literary criticism. I was also interested in his ongoing reactions, so reading logs could be written at any points that he chose in the reading experience. Even when his syntax was shaky, Adam's voice came through with clarity, as in the following entry, in which his last sentence is redundant, since his love affair with C. S. Lewis books is already apparent.

| (ADAM'S WRITING) | (MY RESPONSES) |
|---|---|
| *THE MAGICIAN'S NEPHEW* is getting better. If I was in Narnia when every thing was growing I would of dug my feet in, so I could grow bigger. Did they had guns | This made me laugh, but I have always been short, so I understand. Yes, they had guns. (Uncle Andrew wanted to shoot Aslan.) That *is* strange, I agree. |

(ADAM'S WRITING)

back then? If they did I would of
shot the witch between the eyes.
Why can't the witch hardly
breathe in the wood between the
world? I like how C. S. Lewis
writes.

(MY RESPONSES)

I'm glad. Adam, I recommend
*The Silver Chair* and *The Last
Battle*. Fernando is planning to
read others also. He seems to
want to read them in order.

Writing with personal conviction is a strength I want to remember
as the Adam Factor.

## LAUNCHING STUDENTS IN SELF-CENTERED WRITING

PROMOTING THE ADAM AND VIRGINIA FACTORS

I started the year by giving class time for writing personal narratives
in a journal that I answer on a line-by-line basis, just as I later do with
the reading logs, such as those shown above. It is a time for establish-
ing my interest in their daily lives and in their narrative expression.
Nothing is too mundane for a journal entry; my attention is guaranteed. By their writing daily in journals and by my responding as a
devoted audience, we begin to share one pre- and postwriting
sphere. It helps break down the classroom walls and extend the
school day past dismissal. Half-realized thoughts and sparsely recalled experiences begin to appear with greater clarity on journal
pages, and I become sensitized to more and more fascinating
nuances in both the content and the mechanics of the writing. (I
recently tried offering my own journal entries for students to respond
to. I enjoyed it and intend to make it a practice.)

By late September, journals move into a semioptional category.
Timing is flexible, including doing them at home. I ask that at least
five entries be written each month. In this way class time is opened
up for reading logs that are extensions of the journals: the fodder for
journals is daily experiences over which the writer gasped, laughed,
cried, pondered, and so forth; such vicarious experiences during
reading are to be described in reading logs. These are not to be book
reports. Retelling is discouraged. I tell them: "Assume that I am
reading the same book and let me know, 'How is it going for you?'"

By letting students write at any point in the reading of a book,
sometimes I can help a student abandon a book that is not satisfying
his or her reading hunger. Students have so many attractions for
their out-of-school time that they should take home only books that
are irresistible to read. The more such experiences they have, the
more likely they are to become lifelong readers. And that surely is the
primary goal of reading instruction.

After emphasizing the journals in early September and the reading
logs after the journals are launched, the students decide for themselves when to write one or the other from then on (as long as a
minimum of five each are submitted within each month). They also

may use reading logs to share with me their private reactions to our current read-aloud book.

My interaction with both the journal and the reading log is to respond in the margins and sometimes at the end. I try to be an over-the-shoulder reader, reacting as spontaneously as possible and on an almost line-by-line basis. (When I am tired, I often do a spotty job of this, but most evenings it is my favorite bit of homework.)

I have found that most classes need no other "credit" than my responses. With the class I am basing this chapter on, however, students who worked hard to write well began to express dissatisfaction that there was no grading system. This was especially ironic, because this was a group that seemed unusually unconcerned about grades in general. By March, even though I felt it represented failure on my part to have to do so, I finally started putting a plus, check plus, check, or check minus in the upper-left corner to acknowledge that some entries seemed to contain greater or lesser depths of apparent involvement. These seemed necessary at the time, but I will continue to resist any grading of specific pieces of writing as my norm for future classes.

## MEETING ESL AND BILINGUAL NEEDS

### THE CARMELA FACTOR

Most of my students could be classified as both ESL and bilingual. By sixth grade there were only a few, usually recent, arrivals in this country who were still monolingual in Spanish. I am not fluent in Spanish, but I can read and write it some. I encouraged Carmela and Dahlia to write and speak either Spanish or English. Dahlia felt comfortable trying English early on, but Carmela had to see me struggle with her Spanish to realize that she could communicate with me better in even broken English. She would often choose which language to use according to the introspection the content required of her. A piece she wrote on friendship, comparing and contrasting her two best friends, was written in Spanish. Part of our conference time involved my translating her writing orally into English to be sure I knew what she was saying. She would correct my mistakes and help me with individual words I did not know. (Incidentally, she became a more meticulous speller in Spanish when she realized that even one letter could throw off my comprehension.) By January, Carmela was willing to write all but the most introspective pieces in English. Her choice of a medieval persona was that of a stained-glass maker, because that is her father's occupation. She said it was an easy choice, because she just remembered his complaints when he comes home at night.

> Today I worked a lot like always. I cut more then five hundred pieces of stained glass. I tink I have little pieces of glass in my fingures. Tomorrow I have to get up early in the morning and start workin. With only tinking about it I'm already getting more tired

then I was before. I forgot that I have to finish the stained glass end take it to the Church by next week. I have already done more then half of it. I have to work a lot so I can finish it by next week. I better stop tinking about it. I have already finish for the day and I don't have to tink about it until tomorrow. I'm so tired I tink I have to rest for a few minutes end stop writing because my hands hurt alot.

Carmela's writing had been surprising me even before her spelling problems dropped to the few "fossilized" misspellings she seemed unable to forget (like END for *and*, THEN for *than*, and TINK for *think*). Her voice seemed to come through clearly, and her sentence constructions were richly varied.

For myself, it is the Carmela Factor that leads me to expect even limited speakers and writers of English to transfer their first language strengths into their writing from the beginning attempts.

## FLEXIBILITY
### MAKING TIME FOR THE PLAYING
### OUT OF STUDENT FACTORS

I have experimented with various general schedules. The 8:15- 10:15 block is for reading and writing, including whatever literature study, read-aloud, writing workshop, personal reading, and mini-lessons we do that are not contained within the thematic unit time of 10:15-11:55. As every teacher knows, sometimes thematic units and special events override workshop schedules, but fortunately they usually involve reading and writing. I do believe that it is essential that there be a minimum of forty-five minutes each for reading and writing on a daily basis—sometimes more of one and less of the other for any individual child. Some of that falls into the homework category because I believe these activities are readily done at home and should be seen as bridging into our out-of-school lives.

By blending reading time and writing in class, there is a measure of flexibility for me and for the students. Usually we start with reading, because we do the most group work in our main reading time and at the beginning of writing time. Students know that they can return to silent reading within the time that others in the class may be writing. It may just be my prejudice, but I think it is easier to lay down a good book and come back to it than to shut down and later take up writing on a hot topic. And, since it is the hot topic—the response-able material—that I most worry about closing off, I try to have the writing time drift beyond most students' endurance. They know that when the muse has departed for the day, they should relax with a good book.

Whenever possible, our thematic units incorporate science, social studies, and some tie-in to literature, visual arts, drama, and music. Besides the late morning block of time, there is an hour after math workshop in the afternoon when we can pick up something that did not fit into, or needs to be completed from, the morning. That last hour also includes P.E. several times a week and sometimes is used for music and art that has no connections to our thematic unit.

My own greatest stress in teaching comes from the feeling that time pressures frequently cut short the sort of exploratory freedom a learning community should enjoy. There never seems to be enough time to explore the perimeters of our studies, to play with unlikely alternatives, and to dabble and dawdle without concern for scheduling restraints. At least with four big blocks of time rather than many small ones, I can more often adjust to the emergence of one of the factors I want to promote.

Sometimes, with the "authentic class" (and I have a feeling I might learn to see all classes as "authentic" after the training this class gave me!) the Refugio Factor got played out in a direct contradiction to my plans: "No, we aren't going to work on our Greek mythology project now; we'll get back to that tomorrow, but we haven't talked all week about the opera we're composing, so we'll do that today," or "We don't care what they did last year; we want to have permanent share groups to hear our writing." Sometimes the students used passivity or even silence to maintain their independence as decision makers. I do not relish nonresponse as a response; that is why I found this class to be provoking at times. But I cannot say that their behavior is not as acceptable as any other. And it can, especially in hindsight, be seen as a refreshing quality!

## THE FACTORS BEYOND THESE

The Armando Factor provides divergent responses that enliven a class in unexpected ways; the Virginia Factor provides depth by opening private avenues to supplement the public responses of the learning community; and the Refugio Factor keeps the teacher from dominating with tight hands on the reins. I will continue to look for the Adam Factor as a child begins to write from personal conviction even before he masters many of the intricacies of English, and the Carmela Factor when a bilingual child begins to write complex sentences in English that seem incongruous with her difficulties in English syntax and spelling. Whatever organizational decisions next year or tomorrow will bring, I hope I will always be alert to these factors as well as to those of which I am not yet aware.

# 12

# COMPREHENSION: FRAMEWORK FOR THEMATIC UNIT STUDIES

## Karen Sabers Dalrymple

In many classrooms, what is to be learned is outlined, programmed, and dictated. It's a type of teaching that controls student learning. Some teachers and administrators refer to such classrooms as well structured. I also use the term "structured" for the work I pursue with children in our classroom, but there is no preprogramming or dictation; rather, the structure is at the base of my work and provides a framework for the many educational decisions I must make. That structure is the content of this chapter; a comprehension model guides my planning and gives me confidence as I initiate, sustain, and conclude a unit of study with my children.

I feel prepared for my work with children, even though I do not write step-by-step plans for a particular unit of study. In fact, I need to spend time with students before I decide which activity to pursue. Of course, the work isn't accidental, even though it is spontaneous; neither is it haphazard, even though decisions about many activities aren't made prior to the initiation of those activities. My work is not based on particular day-to-day lesson plans which might confine student learning; rather, the organization stems from a model of comprehension which offers my students variety and stimulation.

While I was participating in a whole language seminar several years ago, I questioned my use of Bloom's taxonomy as a framework for designing classroom learning activities. I had been using the taxonomy, never hierarchically but as a physical reminder of the need for varied types of learning activities. Yetta Goodman suggested that I study a three-phase model of comprehension— perceiving, ideating, and presenting—proposed by Smith, Goodman, and Meredith (1976, Chap. 6). When I returned to teaching that fall (1984), I began using the model as a guide to my unit structuring, observations, assessments, and evaluations. The model is very advantageous, because it allows freedom of thoughtful behavior for me and my students. Comprehension depends on the processes of gathering new information (perceiving), playing around with that information (ideating), and later presenting related ideas (presenting).

Being too prepared was always my problem. As an enthusiastic and creative teacher, I could always think of a million exciting activities. I could walk into a classroom and fire kids up to doing "my" projects. Constantly, I needed to remind myself that I shared the classroom with nearly thirty other learners who also were capable thinkers. The model controls me in the sense that it won't let me interfere with the children's learning process. Figure 12-1 is the basic worksheet that I use for recording unit activities as we pursue a thematic unit. The worksheet is a visual reminder of the necessity for offering time and opportunity for the three phases—that ideating is an important stage in comprehension and cannot be ventured until

**Figure 12-1** *Activity Planning Form*

ACTIVITY PLANNING FORM
–based on Smith, Goodman, and Meredith
Model for Comprehension

Name of UNIT *Time*

Date *9·86 / 1·88 / 3·89*

STUDENTS *6ᵗʰs*

ACTIVITIES FOR:

1. PERCEIVING (gaining new facts, ideas, and impressions)

Independent Reading   *Factual Literature, Fictional Lit, Textbooks*

Read Aloud   *Green Futures of Tycho (Sleator) Momo (Ender)*

Conversation/Discussion   *re: R·Aloud, quotes, essays, ind·reading*

Presentations   *Einstein, T.S.Eliot, S·Hawking, Camus, Chagall*

Films   *Back To The Future, Time Machine*

Photos, Posters, etc.   *Cover of S.J. Gould's Time's Arrow Time's Circle?*

2. IDEATING (responding to new facts, ideas, and impressions)

Oral   *Web, Statement, Questions Charts, Interview Compare/Contrast*

Drawing (Illustrating)   *Time Machine Diagrams, Time Line*

Writing   *Logs, Essays (PRO + CON Statements),*

Experimenting   *Use time statistics, Design project, Calculations*

Drama   *Create a skit w/ Time as an element*

Other   *Predicting future events / Comparing Literature and Films*

3. PRESENTING (sharing facts, ideas, and impressions)

Oral   *Debate the statements,*

Drawing (Illustrating)   *Graphic Posters of Ideas*

Writing   *Poetry, Essays,*

Drama   *Dance with Varying Themes of Text*

Other   *Time Capsule, 2 Science Fare Projects re: Time Travel* kids have a chance to meet new ideas and concepts and that the presentation mode is only repetitious of already known facts if opportunities for ideating have been denied.

Another part of the framework for my teaching is a schema I used for years when I would decide activities for our classroom. Figure 12-2 is a graphic which my teaching friends and I refer to as a "curriculum basics web." I use the web to remind me of the behaviors and processes within each curricular area. The activities I design are aimed at those behaviors. Using the web in commensuration with the perceiving, ideating, and presentation model works very well.

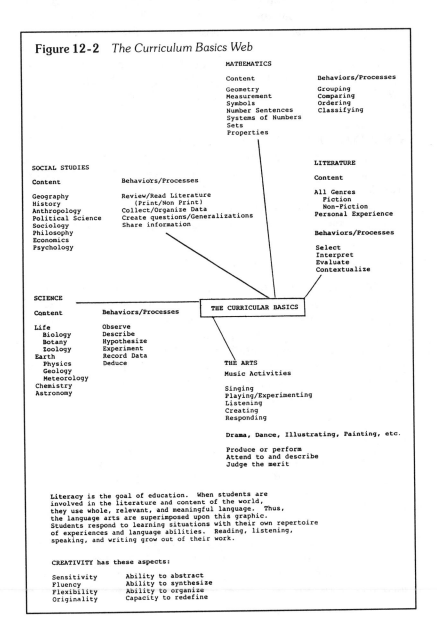

**Figure 12-2**  *The Curriculum Basics Web*

Within each curricular area, there is new content to be perceived; ideation and presentation provide students with opportunities to practice and explore the behaviors and processes which are pertinent to each area.

To explain how these frameworks give me a basis for decision making, I will use a thematic unit study of "Time" that my sixth graders and I pursued. I have used the study with three groups of sixth graders, and I am convinced that it is indeed exciting (even though each year was different from the previous year); the study offers opportunities to analyze and respond to literature, to critique film, to engage in scientific processes, and to propose and play with philosophical and mathematical questions. While it is impossible to list the many activities which took place during the study, I've designed the chapter to feature the activities which will demonstrate the use of the comprehension model—perceiving, ideating, and presenting. The evaluation of this unit study is discussed in *The Whole Language Evaluation Book* (Dalrymple, 1989).

## WEBBING WITH STUDENTS

When I initiate a unit, I call the students together and ask what they know or what questions they have. At the sixth grade, our web work usually becomes tri-graphic. Students offer information already known, pose questions they have, and offer statements which may or may not be true. Figure 12-3 is one example of such work.

### SCHEDULING OUR DAYS

Basically, once the unit of study is initiated and we have our web, questions, and statements, we are spirited and ready to organize the days of study. We spend some of each day reading aloud and discussing the ideas of the texts, conducting independent research, setting up original search projects, and logging responses or observations. On several days of the week, the students read their literature selections, log responses, and join discussion groups to "play" with the ideas of the books.

### LEARNING LOGS

Students are asked to keep accounts of their discoveries in their learning logs. Because the students are logging their thinking as they work, I am free to move about the room during the independent research period and discuss ideas with students, help them locate material, or listen to them explain their ideas about their reading and thinking, observe their strategies for learning, listen to their arguments, and so on. Of course, I collect, read, and respond to the learning log entries. The learning log is a perfect tool for encouraging ideating.

**Figure 12-3**   *The Ongoing Class Web*

QUESTIONS

Are there any real
absolutes?

How did they think
up the measurement of
time?

Does time change
things? Is time on a
wheel or on a line seg-
ment?

Is the 4th dimension
time?

STATEMENTS

Time was before people...but
people could not be without
time. Something has to
exist to have time. Time is
something, but it's nothing.
A museum is a time machine.

Man can move in space but
with time. If time
weren't, we wouldn't be.
If nothing changed, time
wouldn't pass.

CLASS WEB

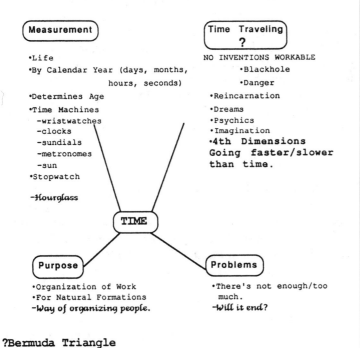

Measurement

•Life
•By Calendar Year (days, months,
                hours, seconds)
•Determines Age
•Time Machines
  -wristwatches
  -clocks
  -sundials
  -metronomes
  -sun
•Stopwatch

-Hourglass

Time Traveling
?

NO INVENTIONS WORKABLE
      •Blackhole
      •Danger
•Reincarnation
•Dreams
•Psychics
•Imagination
•4th Dimensions
Going faster/slower
than time.

TIME

Purpose

•Organization of Work
•For Natural Formations
-Way of organizing people.

Problems

•There's not enough/too
 much.
-Will it end?

?Bermuda Triangle

READING MATERIAL

I began reading aloud *The Green Futures of Tycho* (Sleator, 1981). The text encourages discussion about time. Also, it is a good piece of literature to use to compare the ideas in the films *Back to the Future* and *Time Machine*.

*Momo* (Ende, 1985) and *The Phantom Tollbooth* (Juster, 1961) are also excellent literary pieces related to the theme. I usually find several good pieces of literature to read aloud to the students. These become elemental in offering new ideas to students (perceiving) and for encouraging reader responses (ideating).

During the first week of study, we gathered as many nonfictional reading materials as we could. During the time study, there was a perfect opportunity to introduce our science text: the first chapter dealt with Protista, one-celled organisms found in both plants and animals, and how they behaved in time. Also we looked through our social studies textbook to discover its perspective of time.

Several times a week I would schedule an independent reading period so that students would be able to gather new information about time. We would follow up or proceed these periods with an exploration period wherein the students could extend or contend with ideas they had met in their reading or discussion time. I would also use the texts we had gathered as sources of work for minilessons in reading, writing, or concept development.

I keep a folder for each unit. Besides the planning form, the folder contains specific materials pertinent to the study. The Time Study folder contains the following: a few essays about wormholes, time warps, and physicist Stephan Hawking; a copy of a portion of T. S. Eliot's *The Love Song of J. Alfred Prufrock*, which deals specifically with time; several birthday cards I've received (after forty, birthday cards are very time related); and bibliographies.

LITERATURE STUDY GROUPS

In small groups we studied literary works which dealt with the concept of time: *Tuck Everlasting* by Natalie Babbitt, *A Wrinkle in Time* and others by Madeleine L'Engle, *Time Machine* by H. G. Wells, *Singularity* and *Into the Dream* by William Sleator, and *The Lion, the Witch, and the Wardrobe* by C. S. Lewis.

PICTURE BOOKS

I use picture books with my sixth graders because they are good literature. Also, I think the students need models for their own writing and illustrating. *Annie and the Old One* by Miska Miles, *How Does It Feel to Be Old?* by Norma Farber, and *Wilfred Gordon McDonald Partridge* by Mem Fox are favorites for this work. Another special text by Mitsumasa Anno, *Anno's SUNDIAL*, helps children understand the history of time telling.

RESPONSES TO READING

Scheduling large blocks of time for students to explore, extend, or otherwise "play" around with ideas they've chosen to contend with is paramount. Within these periods, the first year, several students set up experiments with aging or preservation; they used breads, molds, plants, various soils, and a variety of liquids in their work. Patrick and Jeremy experimented with various liquids, testing to see which would preserve apples. Ray's experiments used breads with and without preservatives. Annie and Michelle tried to compose new life-giving soils (enriched with the liquid from the aloe vera plant). The windowsills and counter tops held eight or nine experiments which ran for several weeks; the students charted their observations and discussed their discoveries.

In subsequent years, the experiments varied. While Matthew designed a twenty-eight minute water clock, Colter experimented with the strength of magnets over time. Each year students used plants in their experiments.

Reading and discussing literature led to more reading. Topics pursued were Ponce de Leon, the Fountain of Youth, Rip Van Winkle's story, aloe vera, dinosaurs, time measurement, and mineral waters. Several students studied more than one topic; other students explored a single topic.

Other students became interested in time-traveling devices. They began designing their machines and working with each other, offering advice and criticism. One student decided we needed a design review board—her father was a contractor, and he was simultaneously experiencing work with a design review board. Melissa suggested we find a group who could study the designs and hear the defense of the designers. Two days after the suggestion, the design board (made up of three students) met with individual students who were prepared to present their time-traveling device: they presented their paperwork and answered questions posed by the board. All of these sessions were taped for me so that I could listen to them during my planning periods. The simulation seemed quite exciting for the students who participated and very worthwhile for me to listen to their oral language in such a particular situation.

Elaine and Erin conducted interviews regarding world affairs. They interviewed children and adults, and recorded the trends and patterns of world knowledge and fears according to age groups. From the study, they were able to make some generalizations which they later used as a basis for further reading and researching. Their work showed me the strength of the perceiving, ideating, and presentation model; the students began with text, explored the ideas of the text, created a new text, and then returned to more texts.

I like this "ideating" stage, because it allows me to further encourage creativity of thought and action. Sometimes the work will lead to a presentation, sometimes it will abort itself, and often it will just provide a great chance for students to use their devices for exploration. The fact that we are exploring allows freedom; there are no right or wrong procedures.

## USE OF FILM

Toward the end of the study, we viewed the film *Time Machine* and compared it with the film *Back to the Future*. *Time Machine* was produced thirty years ago, was black and white, and was quite unrealistic physically. I was somewhat concerned that the students would just laugh it off as a farce and use the show time for adolescent play. I did tell them when we were settling into a film-watching mode that neither Steven Spielberg nor present-day film technology was around when H. G. Wells's story was made into a film. I had a sudden fear that I'd made the wrong choice, and I wanted to prepare myself for the rebuttal from the students.

The students were especially impressed with the scientific knowledge in *Time Machine* and were attentive and appreciative of the film. I was impressed with the students' responses and a bit upset with myself for not trusting their intelligence. They were impressed with the work of Spielberg in *Back to the Future*, and several students suggested that Spielberg direct a new edition of *Time Machine*. But the form of the film *Time Machine* did not at all put them off; they dealt with the ideas and the messages of the film with much intelligence.

The changes of the film industry over thirty years is very apparent with this film. Kids immediately picked up on those differences, and we were able to critique the ideas of time as well as the portrayal of those ideas. I was impressed with their acceptance of the film, the story, and the scientific facts presented. They tolerated the technological differences because they were interested in H. G. Wells's theories about time traveling. With all three groups of students, I was somewhat amazed at their maturity in recognizing the relationship between content and form and in accepting the form which so contrasted with their regular film diet.

## WHOLE CLASS SESSIONS FOR PERCEIVING AND IDEATING

I design large group sessions after I have spent time reading and discussing with students, observing them during their independent exploration periods, and reading their log entries. The purposes of the large group sessions (a term we use to describe a teacher-directed whole class session) are varied and dependent upon the needs of the group. While some sessions are used to present new ideas, others may be used to analyze a particular piece of writing or to introduce students to a historical figure. The purpose for these whole class sessions is to introduce, extend, or redirect student thinking or development. To connect it to the three-stage comprehension model, I consider using a presentation to encourage perception and ideation.

Examples of such sessions follow.

## TEXTBOOK READING

I knew I wouldn't be using the social studies textbook in the traditional cover-to-cover sense, yet, I knew the students needed to be aware of the textbook as a possible source of information. Also, I felt responsible to the sixth-grade social studies curriculum, which concentrates on the historical and geographical information of the world. Several of our large group sessions focused on the social studies textbook. In small groups, the students designed time lines, which synthesized the information of a particular chapter. Once the time lines were composed, we organized them onto a huge piece of butcher paper.

## DRAMA

Early in my teaching, I realized the power drama has for encouraging new insights into a topic. I asked the students to come together on several occasions during our time study for the purpose of composing skits which would explore a question or an idea. For example, they were asked to design a skit which would include Sleator's or Eliot's view of time, or both; to design a skit which responds specifically to their literature group study; or to design a skit which uses time as a characteristic.

During the second study of time, I used the later of those cues early in our study. James, Joseph, and Jeremy were very puzzled about the task. They liked drama and wanted a "hit," but they couldn't think of time as a characteristic. Noticing their predicament, I asked, "When is time important?"

James said, "I've got it." Five minutes later, when I called the whole group together, the three boys were grinning and ready to be first to perform. Their skit was a story of a young competitive swimmer who wasn't winning; his two companions were time and practice. With swimmer, time, and practice in concert, a champion was born.

Dramatic play offers students the chance to play with ideas and an opportunity to symbolize thought.

## STATISTICS

During one large group session, I asked the students to review their log entries and to look for any facts using numbers. Once the first students discovered a fact, others retrieved facts from their logs readily. Following are some of those items (I've selected to share these to demonstrate the various curricular areas touched in such an activity):

- 1884 international meeting in Washington, D.C., to talk about clocking time.
- Steven's maternal grandfather died in 1983 (dates related to family genealogy).
- International date line at 180° longitude.
- In a billion seconds, there are twenty-eight years.
- During 1513-1521, Ponce de Leon found the Fountain of Youth in Florida.
- In the 1950s, there were 200,000,000 people in Latin America (1/30 of Earth's population).

Toward the closing of the study, I called the group together and encouraged discussion by asking the implications of these facts. One group of students discovered that, during their senior citizen ages, they would represent the majority of the population in the country. They talked about what that would mean in terms of elections, city planning, housing, and so on. As an observer, I was impressed with the students' interest and intelligent discussion of these issues.

My purpose for conducting Statistics Day was to give purpose to the understanding and application of mathematical concepts; little did I know that the students would advance the study beyond the mathematical to the philosophical implications.

## SMALL GROUP WORK

Sometimes when I want students to work with new content, I use small groups. I vary the number of students in the groups, as well as the composure of the groups, depending upon need and purpose. I've found that the very structured models for cooperative learning are not necessary for students who have been participating in whole language programs. The students are already motivated to learn, share, cooperate, and pursue tasks democratically.

During the Time Study, I used small groups for researching information related to a list of names, places, or events. I wrote the following names on the board: Plato, Buckminster Fuller, Galileo, Descartes, Einstein, and Sir Isaac Newton. The groups of students were asked to gather some basic information about these people in relation to time.

I hand each group a poster board and ask each group to design a graphic which would synthesize their information.

## PRESENTATIONS

Although there is no definite structure outlined for the students, presentations do grow from the students' explorations and begin within a few days after the unit has begun. Some of the presentations are quite short. When Kyle had responded through discussion and drama to the quotes from Einstein, de Chardin, and Camus, he wrote: "If our dreams exceed reality, we are the few, the few who aren't afraid of the future" (Kyle Keyes Egan, 1989).

The cyclical relationship of the three-stage model became apparent to me when I looked at the wall three days later to notice that next to Kyle's quote was Jennifer's quote: "Those of you who live regretting the past are not aware of the power of the present and the future." Jennifer had read Kyle's quote, had played around with her own views of our relationship to time, and then had composed her words to state that view.

Two of the presentations became science fair projects. James and Joseph presented their time-traveling machines based on mathematical calculations and hypothetical types of materials. Their presentations were large free-standing poster displays. Poems surfaced, entered in the students' learning logs (Figure 12-4, A through C). I

---

**Figure 12-4**   *Time Poems*

### TIME
Joshua Rau

Time is a measurement of minutes or so,
but I'll tell you a thing about time that I know.
History is about time a long time ago,
future is about time that we do not yet know.

If you're having lots of fun,
time is really on the run.
But do something boring,
time does not keep going.

Time is something that's to some people a lot.
But others, they appreciate it not.

Now you know what I think about time
and it isn't just any old rhyme.

**A.**

### THE REFLECTION OF TIME
Annie Hill

I ask: Where do you find the reflection of time?
Is it in the heart, the soul, or the mind?
Is it just a silent but meaningful mime?
Does the reflection only exist in the kind?

I answer: You are the reflection of time
because you are time.
It is up to you to decide what time means.
Is it good, is it evil?
You decide which way it leans.

**B.**

---

**Figure 12-4** *Continued*

BOTTLED
Jennifer Mason

Bottled
Bottled in time
Bottled
I was stuck
Stuck in that awful day

It just came out and grabbed me
It wouldn't let me go
There was nothing I could do

C.              Stuck, that's what I was.

---

believe the poetry conveyed some of the thoughts created by Sleator's work but also reflects the power of the poetic form perhaps stirred by T. S. Eliot.

Time, space, or form allows sharing many of the presentations which grew from the thematic study. I share these few to show how the comprehension model gives basis to the productions.

## SUMMARY

Although I have concentrated on only one thematic unit study, my intent was to demonstrate how thematic studies, developed from the framework of a comprehension model, allow students to practice and to learn their literacy skills. The unit helped me to understand the connection between literacy and comprehension and prepared me to allow students to make that connection also. Because the organization for instruction is rooted in a comprehension model, the activities grow from the group and allow students to pursue independent studies. The framework offers me security as an educator, as it provides my students an opportunity to gain new knowledge of their world, explore ideas, and use a variety of forms to present their new ideas to one another.

# 13

# ADOLESCENTS ORGANIZE: WHOLE LANGUAGE IN THE MIDDLE GRADES

**Richard E. Coles**

I recently returned some books to a colleague's whole language grade 8 classroom during the day. I observed the students taking part in a variety of activities. A small group was actively discussing a novel under the direction of one member. Two writers were editing a story draft on a computer. Several others were reading quietly at different locations around the room. A group of students returned from the library and started working on a number of tasks. At two large tables other members of the class were planning and designing a variety of artistic responses to the literature they had read. The teacher circulated around the classroom, observing, asking questions, and responding to the students' inquiries. The classroom was a hum of meaningful conversations that did not impede the progress of each activity. The students knew what they should be doing, and they were actively involved in their learning. This classroom had every appearance of being a well-organized, carefully planned learning environment.

Many middle or junior high school teachers understand the theoretical rationale for a whole language program, but they are not certain about how to organize and implement these notions in their classrooms. Before the beginning of the school year, they decide to take a risk and create a whole language classroom. They read professional literature, attend whole language conferences, and listen with enthusiasm as experienced whole language teachers describe their programs and their students' growth.

As the leaves start to change colour and there is a touch of frost in the morning air, some of these risk-taking teachers experience anxiety, frustration, and doubts about their programs. They are confronted daily with students in transition from the elementary to the junior high or middle school format. Several class members cannot remember their locker combinations, class schedules, or the materials they need. Others are unsure about what they should be doing in class and what to do when they have finished an activity. The teacher fears that the classroom appears noisy, disorganized, and crowded, with students moving from one activity to another without accomplishing anything. When is there time to examine the curriculum guides for each subject area, develop teaching strategies, and locate materials for several topics? The teachers know the students by name but are not acquainted with their personal abilities, areas of interest, apprehensions, or educational experiences. There seems to be so little time to conference with the learners, complete required paperwork, respond to the students' work, change displays, reflect on the day's occurrences, or talk to colleagues about professional concerns.

In frustration, the teacher new to whole language may ask, "How can anyone learn anything in my classroom? How am I ever going to survive this year?" I hope in this chapter to address these concerns.

Givins-Shaw School, located in a multicultural inner-city community in central Toronto, has a model of school organization that enables our students to spend most of the school day with one homeroom teacher. For a portion of the day, our grades 7 and 8 classes are self-contained. As a homeroom grade 7 teacher, my teaching assignment encompasses language arts, math, history, geography, science, and guidance for one class of about thirty-one pupils. My schedule also involves four periods of supervision in the computer lab during a week. The students rotate to specialist teachers for physical education, health, visual arts, music, French, family studies, and industrial arts.

Over a four-year period, the staff has noticed several advantages to this model of school organization. We believe that it assists our diverse school population with the transition into middle school education. Their schooling represents a potpourri of educational experiences. Many have attended schools in Europe, Asia, or the West Indies. Canada has been home to some for only a few years, months, or days. Some have published personal writing, used science equipment to conduct experiments, or manipulated concrete materials to investigate new math concepts. Others have never read complete books or used any hands-on materials.

Many students eagerly look forward to new challenges, friendships, and their new school year; others do not share this enthusiasm for learning or school. A greater amount of class time together helps teachers and students quickly become well acquainted with each other. There are many opportunities to observe and interact with young adolescents as they are engaged in a variety of learning activities. Being cognizant of each learner's personal development, the homeroom teacher provides a classroom atmosphere that encourages risk taking while investigating new ideas and concepts.

When students have developed a rapport with their teachers, they feel more comfortable and secure about asking questions, seeking personal assistance, or talking about anxieties or difficulties related to their learning. They quickly learn the class routine and the teacher's expectations and begin to take responsibility for sharing in the daily life of the classroom.

## WELCOME TO ROOM 58

The first few days of school are important as the students and I establish our class atmosphere. New grade 7 students are excited about finding their classroom and friends. As the teacher, I want all the members of our class to feel comfortable in their new surroundings and to experience success during these first crucial days. We need to interact and get to know each other. Our first two days of school end at noon. In the afternoon, teachers work in their classrooms or attend grade and staff meetings.

I greet my students at the door, and I like to continue this practice throughout the school year. The pupils select a desk for themselves—one stocked with pen, pencil, ruler, and eraser (Figure 13-1). Notebooks, a variety of lined paper, and other materials the

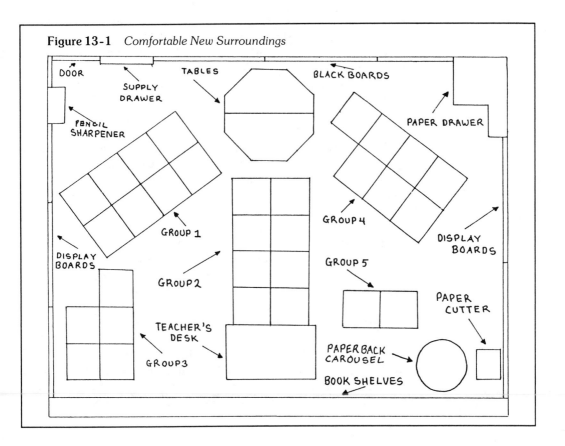

**Figure 13-1** *Comfortable New Surroundings*

pupils require to complete their tasks are available centrally. I introduce myself, welcome the class, and briefly discuss the subjects that comprise the grade 7 program. I minimally outline some routines. We also talk about our expectations regarding academic success and conduct in class.

I use a questionnaire that provides me with insight into students' educational experiences, interests, hobbies, and future goals. After they complete this task, the students may browse and select a book to read from the over 500 titles in my classroom library.

Each year I select an activity that requires the students to interact in pairs or small groups, learning structures we use throughout the year. This is a new experience for some students. Before starting, we discuss the activity and explore ways to work with others. After we work on the activity, the class comments on the parts of the process that worked smoothly. They also suggest ways to improve the process.

Often I choose Human Bingo (Hendrickson, 1986) and interviews. There are several variations of Human Bingo. Each person receives a sheet divided into squares. A statement, such as "Has attended a major league baseball game this year" or "Is wearing something orange," is contained in each space. The middle, free, space is for the player's name. If, for example, you notice that Sonya is wearing something orange, she writes her name in that square on your paper. Students circulate around the room, asking each other questions about the statements, and try to fill in as many squares as possible with the names of their classmates. Next, the students form small groups, each responsible for tabulating the names for one of the squares. The statements and the data from this activity are recorded on larger sheets of paper later displayed with pictures of each member of the class. The students enjoy seeing themselves on the charts and learning about their classmates.

The interview activity involves the whole class generating a list of questions. The students work in pairs, selecting fifteen to twenty questions to ask of each other. Each student introduces and presents to the whole class the subject of the interview. Later in the week, the information is rewritten into a personal booklet. These booklets become popular reading materials.

The class does some free writing about a topic of their choice on the first day, as well. We discuss the nature of free writing and relieve many anxieties by agreeing that they will not be required to read their free writing aloud and that it won't be graded. After answering questions, I join the class as a fellow writer.

Toward the end of the morning, I read a short story to the class. This is part of our daily routine. I invite the students to suggest other materials they'd like me to read. I ask the pupils to bring personal reading material for silent reading time. Finally, in what always appears to be the shortest morning of the year, the bell rings, indicating to all that we have survived the first day of school.

## PLANNING AHEAD

Our model of school organization enables the homeroom teacher to make decisions about the design of the class schedule. It facilitates the development of integrated units. Being familiar with the entire curricula and having a flexible use of class time enables us to plan and implement units that encompass several different subject areas. Teachers receive guidance and assistance to facilitate this endeavor.

As I prepare my class schedule, I consider several important factors. Longer blocks of time—more than a single forty-minute period—are required for students to read and respond to literature or to write about their thoughts and ideas. I plan for small, active learning groups and many individual conferences. During the first half of the year, we usually investigate topics in geography; for the second half, we focus on history.

Since facilities for family studies and industrial arts accommodate only nineteen students, I follow the same procedure with these areas. Half the class is in family studies the first half of the year and industrial arts the second. The other half of the class has the opposite schedule. While half of my class is in family studies or industrial arts, I use the time with the remaining half for small group activities, a class in the computer lab, conferences, or assisting individual students.

Although each subject is allotted a period of time on my schedule, the use of homeroom time is quite flexible. If the students in science class are developing their measuring abilities by estimating and measuring a number of small and large objects, and this activity requires more than a single or double period, I can easily extend the time frame enabling the learners to complete their collection of data. Often during the school year a class may miss several periods of one subject due to special projects, class trips, school assemblies, or holidays. By rearranging classes on the timetable, I can still provide the class with a balanced program.

In September, I separate reading and writing classes. Gradually, as the year progresses, many classes are left open, allowing the students to organize their time and to decide what *they* want to do.

## PLANNING FOR CHANGE

Each year, before school starts, I think over the past year and select several personal goals to consider while planning and organizing my program for the fall term. My goals this year are

- Less teacher talk in class
- More active learning in all content areas
- More integration of the various content areas

Goodlad (1984) and Powell (1985) found that teacher talk or lecturing dominates many middle level and secondary classrooms.

There are occasions throughout the school day when there is information to convey to the whole class. However, my goal is to reduce the amount of teacher talk and have the students initiate meaningful conversation related to their work. Cooperative learning strategies (Slavin, 1987) reduce the need for teacher talk and require the students to be actively involved in their learning. These instructional methods encourage social interaction, one of several developmental needs of young adolescents (Lipsitz, 1984). Clarke, Wideman, and Eadie (1990) suggest a variety of cooperative learning strategies for different content areas. In the grade 7 program, there are many opportunities to integrate or to study related topics at the same time.

During the first few days of school, keeping in mind my personal goals for the year and the district curriculum, I make a flexible outline of the school year. This outline is always subject to change, reflecting the interests of the class and events that occur throughout the year. When the students became concerned about the oil spill in Alaska, they brought many articles and pictures about this environmental tragedy. We decided to investigate this event in more detail. The class divided themselves into several small groups, each probing one of the problems related to oil spills. The students' major focus from all groups was the environmental impact. Although this topic was not on the course of study, it provided the students with an issue and a context for developing and using their research, map reading, and math abilities. Each group recorded their findings, discussed their problem, raised new questions, and expressed their opinions to the whole class.

Many current event issues as well as sporting and cultural events capture the interest of young adolescents and are easily incorporated into the whole curriculum.

I generally follow the same planning and organizing procedures, although implementation may vary, depending on the specific content area, such as motion geometry in math, or an integrated unit involving several subject areas, for example, "Life in New France." Literature study groups, poetry writing workshops, simulations in history, or drama presentations are some components of my program that require special consideration in planning.

Planning a literature reading program involves providing time in class for reading. It is my expectation that the young adolescents are going to spend a significant amount of class time reading literature. There also needs to be time to select reading materials, work on a variety of responses to literature, and participate in discussion groups. It is my experience that those who read in class are more willing to take home a novel and that they view reading as a worthwhile recreational activity. Fielding, Wilson, and Anderson (1986) provide evidence that reading in a nonschool setting contributes to students' reading achievement.

Planning a writing program also involves providing considerable time for the students to be engaged in the writing process in the classroom. My young adolescents' compositions range from six to over one hundred pages. Continuous composing, thinking, revising, talking about their work, rereading their compositions, editing, and publishing require many periods in class.

In content areas, I begin my planning by considering the topic or unit. This means becoming familiar with related concepts or historical periods of time. It may involve thinking about a genre of writing or a theme based on related but varied books for literature study. I select appropriate instructional procedures and strategies based on my knowledge of the students and the topic of study. I usually begin with an introductory activity that familiarizes the students with the topic and provides me with insights into their background knowledge and notions.

Before investigating "Life in Upper Canada in the 1800's," we worked together in small groups, listing, comparing, and contrasting contemporary life in Ontario with what they thought life was like in the 1800s. The ensuing class discussion raised many questions students had, gave me a glimpse of what my students understood, what questions and interests they had, and the kinds of resources I needed to gather to help the students organize for their own learning. The discussion led to areas of interest the students wanted to pursue as well.

The selection of instructional strategies influences the organization of the learning experience. Are the students working alone, in pairs, or in small groups? Do they require additional space to work together on their assignments? After thinking through and resolving those questions, I provide the students with an outline sheet for each unit that guides them through various steps. The guide sheet asks the students to list what they know, what they want to know, how they plan to find out the answers, and what materials they need to continue their study. The guide sheet reduces their reliance on me, assists the learners with their planning, and provides a place for notes and doodles as they study.

Students play an important role and are actively involved throughout the planning and organizing process. They offer suggestions about modifying instructional strategies and making the best use of tables, desks, and floor space throughout the classroom. The class participates in the formation of groups. It is encouraging to observe a small group assist a student new to our country who has little understanding of English and our educational system. They carefully assign tasks to each person and support each other during the activity. Thus, every member of the group experiences personal success and contributes to the success of the group.

## PLANNING FOR EVALUATION

Planning requires the teacher to be sensitive to the needs of the learners. I use a variety of evaluation techniques that indicate the students' developing understanding of a new concept or information (Coles, 1989). As students are working on their activities, there are many occasions to observe their social and academic development. Careful observations inform a teacher when a class or a learner needs assistance or more time to reflect or to work on an assignment. I prefer that students take this time in class rather than rush through their work toward an unrealistic deadline.

I also must think about how the pupils are going to record and share their findings with the class and demonstrate their new understandings. In my class, ideas, opinions, and information may be presented through artistic and written responses to literature, drama, simulations, written reports, learning logs, student-designed activities, oral reports, and published stories or anthologies of poems.

As part of the evaluation process, I assess the lesson, unit, or activity. I record for future reference the successful aspects and those areas that require more thinking or planning. Students help me in this self-reflection. They also participate in their own self-evaluation after working on a topic or activity identifying their strengths and areas that require more attention. When the class works in groups, they evaluate their contribution to the success of the group. Generally, the students are insightful and honest in their self-evaluations. Their ideas and suggestions are most useful when I am revising a lesson or an activity.

Organizing a school and a classroom in this way requires teachers to be knowledgeable and flexible. Teachers are in need of support and help. When teachers work together on a formal or informal basis or when a knowledgeable, experienced teacher acts as a coach, the staff members assist each other in this process. In our school, many of us have informal discussions at lunch and before or after school. We exchange ideas, divide the work load, and consolidate our resources. It is reassuring to know that there are staff members who are willing to listen and share common concerns. In this context, we are all risk takers—not only those new to whole language but also those of us who continuously are developing our whole language teaching.

# 14

## STOP THE TIMETABLE,
## I WANT TO GET OFF

### Jean F. Dunning

A bell rings; your new class surges in. They find places to sit, dump their bags, hang up their coats, get out their books and equipment, continuing all the time the conversation they have been having since they left the last lesson. Whilst waiting for them all to settle, you check your lesson notes and the equipment you will need, answer someone's question, sort out a little dispute that started in the corridor, and finally launch yourself. The lesson takes off. During the lesson, whatever else happens, you must keep your eye on the time so that you are ready to put all these procedures into reverse and finish neatly, with the class ready to leave on the next bell.

In the English high schools, lessons are usually under an hour in length on the timetable, considerably less on the ground. Since there are only three each week in each subject—four if you are very lucky—the loss of time caused by stopping and starting so often is quite noticeable.

The typical "drip-feed" secondary school timetable has other disadvantages, too: new demands are made by each teacher a class meets in the course of a day, demands not necessarily suited to the energy levels of the students but dictated by the teacher's perception of the subject. There are inevitably long gaps between some lessons—maybe four days if you include a weekend. In these gaps, interest can wither, and ideas can be totally forgotten. The constant changes of place and teacher can mean that relationships do not develop as they might, given more time. A teacher, feeling the need to see a tangible outcome from every lesson, may unintentionally block the space that students need to explore ideas or ways of working; students, feeling the need to be ready for their next encounter, may "switch off" as they realize that the bell will ring soon. Furthermore, it can be difficult to develop productive links between classroom and community because the world outside the school does not organize itself on "drip-feed" principles.

I work in Leicestershire Community College, which is a comprehensive high school at present for 400 students aged eleven to fourteen, as well as serving as an educational/cultural/social centre for older and younger members of the community. The college is situated in a "village," which needs the quotation marks because in the last few years housing developments have swollen the population to something like that of a young town. The environment can be described as rural/suburban, and the school population, like the community it serves, as almost entirely monocultural. There are newcomers, but they come mostly from other parts of the British Isles.

Students at the College, which is only eleven miles from Leicester, with its large Asian minority, tend to be insulated from the cultural diversity of Britain and to have insufficient experience generally of people different from themselves. For this reason, a number of teachers have, at different times, built up contacts with other schools, but these have been hard to maintain, for various reasons. Most successful is a long-term relationship with a special school for handicapped students.

## SUSPENDING THE TIMETABLE

In the College, we have been working, over several years, on modifications of the traditionally timetabled school week. To begin with, we instituted an "Activity Week." This happens during the very last week of the school year (end of June for us). Staff offer a series of options, some of which are not available in the curriculum, for example, fishing, camping, visits to places of interest, making and flying model aeroplanes, and so forth. Other options involve intensive extended work on curriculum-based projects—creating, printing, and selling an edition of a community newspaper, painting landscapes in oils, and a practical course on healthy living. Some of these activities involve a charge to parents; others are totally free. "Activity Week" is very popular with students and has been increasingly well supported by parents.

More recently, we have also begun to suspend the timetable for a week at a time during the year as a part of the curriculum. In 1986-1987, there was one such week; in 1987-1988, there were three; and, in 1988-1989, there were six. We call them *Modular Weeks*. During such a week, a class stays with one teacher for a very large part of the time and works on one clearly defined *module* or unit of work. Students are not invited to choose their modules as they choose their activities, since, at this stage of their secondary schooling, there are normally no curriculum options available to them. It is the staff who determine student groupings and the global curriculum content of a module. Over the three years there has been, and will continue to be, an evolution in the content of modules, some of which involve cross-curricular development.

I want to describe one module which Cynthia Martin and I, two English teachers, taught during the first Modular Week, in February 1987.

## PLANNING THE MODULE

November 1986: Planning began in earnest.

Because this was to be the first module, we were anxious. How would we handle fifteen hours in one week with the same class? Could we provide enough different things to do? Wouldn't the students be bored? Wouldn't there be friction, and what would we do with students who behaved badly? What about resources? How would we cope? We knew that there would be parents who would object to Johnny missing a week of math or Jenny missing a week of French. The modular week had to be a success, especially in the eyes of the students; they would be the best ones to convince and reassure their parents.

The staff had decided to work in teams on themes. In the team I worked in there were nine teachers, and our theme was to be "Communication." We first divided the week into morning and afternoon sessions. In the mornings, the students were to stay with one teacher throughout the week in a group which would not number more than fifteen. This group might be scrambled so as to consist of, say, a mixture of first- and second-year students. We would achieve this very favourable student/teacher ratio by dint of foregoing all noncontact time in the mornings and by including in our team one of our vice-principals who normally had a light teaching timetable. In the afternoons the students would go back to their normal classes of between twenty-five and twenty-eight, grouped horizontally, according to year.

In the morning sessions students would work in the following groups:

1. Communication to new students who would be coming to the College the following year (a jackdaw pack of written information and photographs)
2. Science and Communication (looking at the physical basis of communication in animals and humans)
3. Communication through Drama and Music (some items for performance)
4. Making a radio programme
5. Making a wall newspaper
6. Making a video programme about the College for future students (to be linked with item 1 above)

7. Making a slide-tape sequence about career possibilities in the district (including interviews with recent leavers)
8. Making storybooks for younger children

In the afternoon sessions the students would visit a different teacher each day for a self-contained lesson on, for example, "Mime, Masks, and Make-up," "Visual Language," "Taping Poems and Plays," and so on. Because of the larger groups in the afternoons, teachers would be able to have noncontact time to discuss developments and make further preparations as necessary.

## THE STORYBOOK MODULE

Cynthia and I would be working with twenty-eight students in all. It is this experience that I want to write about here, because I found that this way of working, with long stretches of time and with continuity from day to day, was especially conducive to holistic language work with students.

As English teachers we were very much aware of the need for our students to have opportunities to write for people other than themselves, their peers, and their teachers. As the London Institute Writing Research Group wrote in 1975, "One important dimension of development in writing abilities is the growth of a sense of audience . . . the ability to make adjustments and choices which take account of the audience for whom the writing is intended (Britton, et al., pp. 11-18). These adjustments and choices depend upon the degree to which the writer is able to internalize that audience.

We thought that our students would be helped along the path of writing development by our making a new audience visible, actually present, in the classroom. We chose an audience which was different in terms of maturity but also familiar in terms of past experience.

The primary school children at Old Mill Primary School, which is on the same site as the College, seemed a good choice, especially when we discovered that two colleagues there who both taught mixed classes of six- to eight-year-olds had just finished class publishing projects. They would be interested in letting their classes be involved in "audience research" and would be happy to have stories for their children written by ours.

A second piece of luck was that we had just held a Book Fair where one of our guests had been Marion Oughton, a professional storyteller. She had worked with some of our classes and would be happy to come again. We booked her for the first two days of Modular Week.

Cynthia contacted our County Children's Librarian also, and she agreed to come in on the fourth day of the week to talk to some of the students about their experiences as writers of children's books. The plan evolved. We worked out our goals for the week's learning experience:

1. to encourage the students' enjoyment of oral storytelling, both as listeners and as tellers
2. to develop in the students as writers a more sensitive awareness of audience
3. to enable each student to produce an extended piece of narrative writing
4. to highlight the idea of reading as a pleasurable pursuit

Goals are nicely remote and abstract, but student tasks are practical and can be seen to be happening (or not) in the classroom. What would actually be going on from moment to moment? We got down to details.

MODULAR WEEK PROGRAMME

There would have to be a preliminary introductory session, preferably some time before the actual week took place, when we would be able to talk about the whole project and divide the class into two groups, A and B.

- Monday: Group A would go over to Old Mill School with one of us and Marion to listen to her telling traditional stories to one class of six- to eight-year olds. They would also be asked to act as observers of the responses of the younger children to these stories and to talk to them afterwards. Group B would welcome a second class of little ones into our own classroom. These children would be bringing with them the storybooks they had recently produced themselves. Each of our students would be responsible for two of the younger ones and would get them to show, read, and talk about the books they had brought with them. We would already have in the room a collection of library books suitable for six- to eight-year-olds borrowed from County Library, and these could also be read jointly by the trios. We hoped that, by the end of this session, our students would have got to know their prospective readers and might even have collected "orders" for stories to write.
      Finally, groups A and B would meet in our classroom, the younger ones having gone back to theirs. Our students would pair up so that those who had heard a new story from Marion would be able to tell it to someone who had not heard it.
- Tuesday: The same process, with groups reversed. (Marion would tell different stories on the two days so that everyone could learn two or four new stories.) During the last hour, students could begin brainstorming ideas for their writing, working alone, in pairs, or in small groups, as they chose.
- Wednesday: A writing day. First drafts would be written, followed by revision, redrafting, and editing—really intensive work all morning, with teachers on hand for consultation when necessary.
- Thursday: An input from us on illustration, calligraphy, and the making of mock-up versions of the finished products to aid plan-

ning. Students start to hand write or to type their books and to illustrate them. Librarian's visit.

- Friday: Completing and binding own books. These to be displayed and then, at some later date, taken over to the Primary School and read to the children there and finally handed over to them to keep.

## THE CLASSROOM SETTING

The space we used was a large open area big enough for two classes and furnished with plenty of tables grouped in pairs with four chairs round them. There was also a reading alcove with four easy chairs and the collection of library books. This room was next to the School Library, where we had free access to reference books at any time. Around the walls were power points for tape recorders.

Resources such as paper, coloured pens and pencils, and bookbinding materials, as well as tape recorders, dictionaries, and our two typewriters, were all available on a central bench. At this time, we did not have access to any microcomputers for this project as we have now, two years later.

## THE MESHING OF LANGUAGE ACTIVITIES

When all our plans had been laid we reviewed the processes that we hoped would be going on in our classroom during the Modular Week.

Reading would involve a variety of texts:

- Library books for six- to eight-year-olds
- Duplicated stories written by the younger children
- A worksheet by Cynthia: "Hints on Doing Audience Research at a Storytelling Session"
- Their own writings and those of their classmates

It would take place in the following modes:

- Student reading silently
- Student reading aloud to younger pair
- Student listening to younger child read aloud whilst following the shared text
- Student involved in "paired" reading with a younger one

Talking and listening would involve:

- Acting as audience at the storytelling
- Acting as storyteller when relating the story which had been heard to a third party
- Incidental talk in the courses of the reading activities outlined above

- Participating in class discussions
- All the ways of negotiating required when undertaking drafting, redrafting, and collaborative work generally, including art work and bookbinding
- In addition, students would have to talk to both known and unknown adults (ourselves, Primary School teachers, Librarian), as well as to their peers

Writing would take various forms:

- Quick note taking to record impressions after the storytelling and meeting with six- to eight-year-olds
- Recording and reflecting in a personal diary (i.e., some writing to aid thinking)
- The several drafts of the story to go in their book
- Final editing processes
- Presentation of the text in its final, published form (handwritten or typed)

## PRELIMINARY SESSION

The whole school was allowed time for a preliminary meeting about modules a few days before they took place. We were glad to have some time when our group members, who did not usually work together, could get to know each other.

I should make it clear that, although the students were from different classes, Cynthia and I knew all of them well, since we had been teaching them for one or two years already.

We had arranged for the boxes of library books to be delivered early, and, with those around us, we opened up a discussion about reading. We were aiming to help the students make connections between the books in front of them, themselves as they had been at six, seven, and eight, and the children they were going to be writing for.

Our young adolescent students were unwilling, at first, to admit to having liked Mr. Bump or *Little Grey Rabbit* themselves, in case anyone should think they were still attached to such childish stories. However, several of them were able to talk about their younger brothers and sisters, the stories *they* liked, and *their* problems in learning to read. Then, the class relaxed. In no time, they were dipping into the boxes and were either deeply absorbed in reading or buzzing about saying, "Look at this . . . , I remember this . . . ," really enjoying themselves.

## THE STUDENTS THEMSELVES AND
## HOW IT WORKED OUT FOR THEM

Besides being a vertical group of eleven- to thirteen-year-olds, the class was a multiability grouping, and there was a wide range of academic achievement among its members.

**Paul and Colin.** Paul was bilingual, his first language being German. He had been living in the U.K. for about eighteen months only. He was a friendly, outgoing boy; his spoken English was developing well, but he found reading and writing English very difficult.

Colin, on the other hand, very much an indigenous English speaker, was rather quiet and withdrawn and inclined to be a loner. He had missed a lot of early schooling because of illness and an accident. Reading and writing were also laborious for him.

These two boys were absolutely absorbed in listening to the stories Marion told at Old Mill Primary School. Afterwards, Paul talked animatedly to his two partners, whereas Colin had little to say to his. When they got to the point of writing, Paul began a written version of Marion's Haitian story, but, although he could tell me the story quite well, he could not develop a flow because he kept stopping to ask for spellings. He was not sufficiently self-confident to leave correction until later. Colin, meanwhile, wrote the following story, with very few conventional spellings (standardized by me).

### The Space Ship Book

There was two a small boy and their names was Wayne and Steve. They were the best star fighters in the universe. At the time they had a scrap about the prettiest daughter in the universe. The king didn't want anyone to marry her because she was rich. The king went in contact with the two best star fighters. People of the other planet was about to attack the other planet in a day or two. The next day when they were about to attack them, all of a sudden they shoot out and attack them and there was a big scrap and some of the ships transformed into bigger ships.

This took Colin all of the writing time available on the first day. When it came to the second day, he could not continue; it seemed as though the act of writing the story down was in itself too daunting. He just sat there, looking defeated.

I then suggested that the two boys might try reading *The Space Ship Book* onto a tape and see if they could carry on, just telling the story, not doing any writing. They spent all the time available to them over the second and third days on this activity, even staying in the classroom at breaks in order to carry on.

Their joint oral story consists of a series of adventures, which they call *chapters*, relating the heroic deeds of Wayne and Steve. The collaboration involves their alternating between two roles: that of narrator and that of narrator's support. The narrator is mainly responsible for a chapter in terms of its story content and its direction. The supporter provides whispered advice and supplies sound effects.

To illustrate, here is a passage from my transcript of Chapter Three, where Wayne and Steve decide to come to the king's aid.

PAUL: . . . they change their minds and help the king 'cause they always get rich that way, 'cause the king gives them loads of money. So they . . .

COLIN: (*whispers*) . . . but they sometimes refuse . . .

PAUL: . . . but they sometimes refuse. Then it happens again. They wanted to. Today, they thought, really good today. So, they did it. They went to the king and told . . . refused . . . took his offer.

Here, it seems as though Colin, in his whispered phrase, is thinking of changing the way the story seems to be going or is trying to add some complexity. Paul first parrots the words offered, appears to ponder over alternatives, and then plumps for "took his offer," thus making his own decision about the way the chapter will go. He is keeping possession of the chapter through oral redrafting.

PAUL: . . . six thousand pounds.

COLIN: (*whispers*) in gold bullion.

PAUL: . . . of course in gold bullion.

Here Colin is just offering an appropriate lexical item which Paul accepts readily; it does not challenge his concept of the story.

They continue for a while, with Colin playing the delicate supporting role and Paul becoming more and more confident, including scenes from TV commercials in his tale. Then, Paul swings from the role of narrator-as-storyteller into that of narrator-as-commentator-on-the-action-within-the-story-world, as if he were there.

PAUL: . . . Oh, no, oh no. Really here. The monster's trying to attack the castle but I think the two best star fighters are going to make it. Wayne and Steve. Oh no . . . the dragon's throwing fireballs at the space ship. But—wow—you should be here—iniffi . . . inifficence. Oh no! The star fighters are going to hit back to him. . . . (*Noises of battle, explosions, and Colin making sounds of the dragon being hit and groaning*)

PAUL: And the final hit. Is it going to work?

COLIN: (*Dying noises*)

PAUL: It work inifficenking! It work! The last star fighters have done it again. Wayne and Steve. Of course the prince thanks him and the king and the queen for saving all their lives. So, that's the end of that.

COLIN: (*Trumpet noise*)

A transcript alone cannot convey the complete absorption in their task that both boys showed in creating this story or the positively triumphant sound of the words, "It work!" It was, I think, important for Paul's development as a user of English to be able to reach three times for a superlative (magnificent?) without actually finding it and yet not be laughed at by Colin.

When it is Colin's turn to take over in Chapter Four, he is, as a native speaker, much more fluent than Paul and much more fluent than he was himself in writing.

COLIN: Chapter Four. The princess was going for a walk in the village when, all of a sudden, she got kidnapped by two strange men who, when she got to her destination, with them two men, she got thrown into a dungeon and the dungeon was dark and deep.

The long tape which the boys made took them about six hours in all. It was their way of fulfilling our goal of producing an extended narrative and, as such, was the right thing for them at that time, I think.

Once they got really into the story, it became evident that what they were engaged in was a form of dramatic play without action.

In composing it, they completely ignored any audience but themselves and possibly their teachers. Still, Colin did, with a lot of help from Cynthia, make a small illustrated book of the written fragment I quoted earlier. When he came to read this eventually to the young children some weeks later, he filled out the story which was on the page by telling more of the part which he and Paul had made up together. This time he was engaged with his audience.

**Ellie and Zoe.** Ellie and Zoe also worked collaboratively, but their strategies were rather different. Ellie was a capable and imaginative writer who disliked redrafting and editing her work, whereas Zoe, who was much more patient, had many difficulties with the conventions of written English and lacked confidence in her own ideas. They already knew each other quite well, as they were in the same class normally, although they were not close friends.

At the beginning of the week, Ellie produced a string of ideas, each of which she discussed with the admiring Zoe. Although Zoe felt that she could never have thought of whole story outlines herself, she was able to be critical of suggestions put before her and to add a lot of detail.

Their book was called *Harry's Wonderful Red Submarine*. It begins: "In the beginning, God said to Harry, 'Harry, you must build a submarine because there shall be a flood. . . .'" The submarine, once filled with the creatures to be saved, suffers a series of crises—failures of the lighting, heating, and ventilation systems. Each disaster is overcome by the ingenuity of a different animal. The story ends: "The animals all grew to love Harry and each other and when the long voyage was over they loved each other and the submarine so much that they planted the submarine in concrete and made it their home on dry land."

On the Thursday, both girls were interviewed by our visiting librarian. They gave, in response to her tactful questions, a thorough account of the process they had gone through and confessed that there had been "a lot of arguing at first," until they settled on their theme. Then, commitment had developed.

LIBRARIAN: Has it been harder than you thought it would be?

ZOE: Well, I'm getting into the story, you see. I thought, Oh God, I just wish I could go through this dead quick. I can't really care about it.

ELLIE: (*Interrupting*) . . . but you do. When you get into it you really want to make it good.

ZOE: When you get into the story, I'm cracking up. I think, "This story's dead good" and she goes, "Don't be modest, Zoe!"

They made it clear that they were really proud of what they had achieved and that they knew that neither could have done it alone.

Unlike Paul and Colin, they were very concerned about their audience and revealed in the interview that they had made sensitive observations of the Juniors at the storytelling. For example, in discussing the value of the repetition of words and phrases in a story, to encourage children to join in, they were also concerned about the fine line between enjoyment and boredom.

ELLIE: Marion repeated herself all over again and the kids didn't like it much, but she thought they would you see, but they didn't. They got bored of that . . .

ZOE: . . . 'cause they're quite clever really. They're not . . .

ELLIE: They've got good imaginations but they can't read that well.

ZOE: They like to think that they're grown up.

They were anxious not to appear to patronise their audience by offering them fare that would seem too "babyish." In their wish to create an appropriate story, they turned to the safe ground of television. The animals they filled the submarine with were based on TV cartoon characters that they knew their readers would like, as were the jokes.

In their interview with the librarian, the girls reveal that, besides having developed a commitment which seemed to surprise them and a real concern for their audience, they were concerned about matters of literary genre, the children's story genre. They discuss the balance between pictures and text, the need for pictures to match text and to be equally funny. They discuss the difference between a long story and a book of short stories about the same characters.

Ellie and Zoe were extremely vocal, both in their interview and on other occasions, about the constraints of the time allowed. They did not want to go to other lessons in the afternoons. They said they had to cut down their original plan for their story because of shortage of time, even though they did some work at home as well. They saw the work as theirs and the school timetable as getting in their way.

**Simon.** My third and last example is Simon, who, at twelve years old, was already a confident writer who enjoyed writing and did a lot at home. He worked entirely alone all week, once the Juniors had gone. His diary gives a good indication of the way he used his time.

Feb. 23rd. First day.
. . . I was introduced to Chris and Steven who, I believe, were maybe the most well behaved pair that morning!
They chose a book called *The Night of the Paper Bag Monsters!* It was generally about two pigs\*, I forget their names, who fall out over trying to make fancy dress costumes for a party. They were made out of paper bags (Elephant size, not the type you carry your average bunch of bananas in) Of course they win and make friends once more. And they all lived happily . . . well never mind.
Anyway, the two boys likes and dislikes are jotted down on pages 1 & 2. . . . So, the general idea is to write a book with lots of ghosts, monsters, etc., trapdoors and a funny ending.

\*No, it isn't an insult! They're pigs!

Feb. 24th (at Old Mill School) . . .
The last story was a "Jump" story. The teller went very quiet when telling the tale, almost a whisper. Then the last word seemed to jump to a million decibels and the whole room must have jumped to the moon and back. You can't fail as a storyteller when you have a voice as well controlled as that. The Taipingi story used a lot of repetition and in no time the children were joining in.

Feb. 25th
Today is a working day. After writing my first draft of the story I started to produce a quick mock-up of the book itself. The story itself proved too long and too many pictures involved, so I cut it short when I started work on the Jumbo typewriter. I think art work will have to be rather basic. . . .

Feb. 26th
. . . In the evening I worked for four hours to update the book so I had less to worry about tomorrow. . . .

Feb. 27th
Well, after another working-flat-out sort of day, the work really did never stop, and I thoroughly enjoyed myself.
The book itself has turned out fine and much better than I ever expected. Another modular week would be a good idea as this week has given a fresh start to this term. I have learnt more than again I expected. I hope that there are more weeks as this one. The book is made well and I hope the two boys and everyone else enjoys ıt.

## THINKING IT OVER

It seems now that the success of this module depended on a combination of fixed structure, flexibility, and support.

The fixed structure arose from the fact that a number of arrangements were made with people outside the College, and these had necessarily to be agreed upon well in advance, including the commitment to write and publish the storybooks. We teachers were able to present these arrangements to the students as a contract we had agreed on for them, expecting that everyone would fulfill it. (Of course we knew the students well enough to be reasonably certain they would like the proposals!)

Flexibility was apparent and necessary in the freedom students had to decide who they would work with and the manner of their collaboration. The story they created, the illustrations they used for it, and the way of presenting it were all their own choices. They also determined the pace at which they worked within the parameters set. It was their responsibility to be finished on time.

Because the students were at different stages of language development, they needed very different sorts of support from teachers. For example, when Paul and Colin were floundering, getting nowhere with their writing, they needed me to suggest that they should switch to the tape recorder and give up writing for a time. Ellie and Zoe needed to discuss with Cynthia the three ideas they had for stories, because they could not make up their minds which to use. Simon, on the other hand, only needed to be shown how to bind the cover on his book. He was completely independent in all other respects.

The atmosphere in our classroom that week was that of a workshop, with everyone busy on their own projects. Those are the significant words: *their own projects*. There were times when they lost track, felt frustrated, angry but they didn't give up, because they had achieved a sense of ownership of their books and they felt they couldn't disappoint the Juniors. In the event it was some weeks before we could take the finished books over and read them to the children, but, when we did, it was a very rewarding experience for our writers.

The behaviour problems we had imagined might arise because the class were spending fifteen hours together with us simply did not materialize. The same report came from other teachers taking different modules. Discipline was not a problem. No doubt this was partly due to the very favourable ratio of staff to students, but I think it was also brought about by the purposefulness of the modules. (The students understood the aims and the objectives of the week before they began.) Finally, the absence of bells and constant changing of place helped to create a more relaxed atmosphere for everyone.

## RECENT DEVELOPMENTS

As I mentioned at the beginning of this article, Modular Weeks have gone on evolving and increasing in number at the College. They are now accepted as a regular and welcome variation in the work pattern. It has not been possible to maintain the staff/student ratio as it was that first year nor to invest the same amount of extra cash and time in the planning. There are economy models around, as well as some that now use word processors as basic equipment, but we continue to try to find new audiences for our students and to go out into the wider community.

# 15

# NO ROOM FOR MADELINE HUNTER IN MY WHOLE LANGUAGE CLASSROOM

## Deborah Nash Dodd

In her article, "Madeline Hunter in the English Classroom" (1989), Madeline Hunter discusses her teaching model being used in the English classroom. She claims that the model is one that can be applied to any type of classroom: "Our model is a teacher decision-making model that is applicable to any mode or style of teaching, to any learner for any objective, convergent or divergent, grammar or poetry" (p. 16). Her model is not applicable to my whole language middle school English classroom, where instruction is student centered and my students and I make learning decisions based on their needs and requests.

The emphasis of the Hunter model is the planning of the lesson, during which time the teacher addresses "planning questions." These planning questions dictate what the teacher will teach to the students and how the teacher's plan will fit the Hunter model. The model is based on Hunter's theory of learning: "Once skill, process or knowledge has been acquired, students should apply it to many new and different situations through independent practice in problem solving, creativity, and decision making" (p. 18). As a whole language teacher, I also use planning questions. My planning questions ask what the students know and how I, as the teacher, can best help the students learn from authentic experiences. As the whole language teacher, I build upon authentic experiences, because I believe that language learning is a process that cannot be segmented into skills, or bits of knowledge, or subskill objectives.

Hunter's first planning question to be addressed is: "What will these students be able to do as a result of their time today, or at the end of several days (not daze) in this class?" (p. 16). She then gives possible answers to the question for the English classroom. "Answers can range from 'write a persuasive essay,' 'express their feelings in poetry,' 'elect to read more Shakespeare,' 'speak or write in standard English,' 'identify the thesis of a passage,' or 'present an idea cogently'" (p. 16). Whether one day or several, the question sets a time limitation on the learning, the learner, and the teacher. The question puts a time limitation on the learner and the teacher. The question and the suggested answers segment learning and the subject, English, into timed, teacher-designed activities. The students are to fit the plan's time element and content. The whole language teacher's first planning question to be addressed is: "What discoveries, insights, relationships will my students make in their transactions with the reading and writing they do in this class?" The answers to the question take shape and then are reshaped as I watch, read, and listen to what my students are saying and doing. The learning is not limited by time but viewed as continuous, and the subject, language, remains whole—reading, writing, and speaking. The plan is to fit the learners' time demands, needs, and purposes.

Hunter's next planning question is: "What information or skills will students need to achieve that goal?" (p. 16). The answer is found by doing a "task analysis," which "enables the teacher to identify knowledge, skills, and processes that can accelerate or if not present, inhibit learning."

The emphasis is placed on the teacher's goal, not a learner's goal, and on what the teacher thinks the student must know before achieving it. The content to be learned is teacher determined, and the learning is segmented into teachable parts. Yet, Hunter claims, "It does not mean molecularizing learning" (p. 16). As a whole language teacher, I'm concerned with where students are in their learning. My next planning question is "What knowledge and experiences do the students possess to build new learning?" Again, the answer is found in the learners, who are respected for having their own backgrounds and who share themselves in the classroom, where they read, write, and speak. I respect my learner's goals and their purposes for learning.

Next in Hunter's planning, "the teacher determines the learning behavior, based on that student and on research, which has the highest probability of being satisfying and successful, or delegates the decisions to the learner" (p. 16). Even when the decision is delegated, student learning behavior is determined by the plan made by the teacher, which demands specific responses based on the objective. Focus is on observable, measurable behavior and not on the less tangible but more significant goals, such as self-appreciation. Hunter asserts: "There is no one best way to learn, it varies with content, situation, and learner." As a whole language teacher, I use the learning behavior as evidence of growth in my students. I plan strategies and content with them, around their interests and questions. We can't determine in advance what we will learn. I expect students to learn in many ways, because their learning styles naturally vary. Hunter says: "There's no one best way to learn"; yet, what she means is that learning must fit the narrow limits of her model. My students' learning doesn't fit there; neither does my teaching.

Planning, in Hunter's model, then involves evidence that students have learned so the teacher can make a decision in continuing with the plan: "Eventually, there must be perceivable evidence which validates that students have learned so the teacher knows whether to move on, give more practice, go back and reteach, or forget it for today." Again, learning is segmented into step-by-step, measurable increments of knowledge, which are practiced to satisfy the specific learning behavioral objective for a specific time allotment. As a whole language teacher, I view language, reading, and writing as recursive processes that cannot be segmented. Content is valid, and learning is from authentic experiences. The students "move on" and get more practice as they continue to read and write. I'm a *kid-watcher*. My involvement is continuous, and I teach and reteach as needed. Teaching is supporting learning, not controlling it. The students learn from the reading and writing experiences they have each day. There is no "forget it for today."

The last planning question is: "How will the teacher artistically use research and intuition to make students' satisfying achievement more probable?" The answers involve "principles that a teacher can utilize to increase motivation (students' efforts to learn), factors which accelerate the rate and degree of that learning, and factors that promote retention and transfer of that learning to future situations requiring creativity, problem solving, and productive and satisfying decisions."

She suggests "a pharmacy of alternatives from which a teacher selects in relation to particular students and specific learning situations." Language instruction, in this sense, is merely a subject area taught in prescriptive doses of patent medicines from a "pharmacy of alternatives." The whole language teacher's planning question is: "How will I, the teacher, artistically use research and my professional knowledge to make decisions to support my students' needs and interests as they experience and learn during their authentic reading and writing experiences?" Students' motivation is real in authentic speech acts and literary events. It comes from within as they pursue their own goals and make choices in their reading and writing. Rate and degree of learning in my class comes from the students' involvement in real language experiences. In my class, there is time to read and time to write. Students who engage actively in the creative process of reading and writing must consistently activate prior knowledge as they interact with text to make meaning. There is no need to be concerned for "transfer of learning," since the school experience is real experience, and learners have no problem retaining what is useful and functional. Language instruction, in this sense, is learning reading and writing while also learning many subjects.

Hunter presented examples of lessons that showed in the English classroom "artistic implementation" of the model. The first example lesson's "affective objective" was: "The learners will demonstrate increased eagerness to read Shakespeare." The teacher begins the lesson with a modernized situation of the conflict in *Romeo and Juliet*, by presenting the parental disapproval of a teenager's desire to date a particular student. The lesson continues with discussion of the situation and leads the students inevitably into reading the play. This certainly beats simply telling them to just read, but Hunter claims that the "result" is the following: "Shakespeare becomes meaningful, and students are eager to 'read on.' What if, in fact, the students are not eager? Do the students demonstrate the "eagerness" because they read the play? This is still an assignment determined by the teacher, not a task that students have eagerly chosen to do. Does Shakespeare become "meaningful" just from one analogy to modern teen interest and from the act of reading the play? What makes reading this play a meaningful experience depends on each student. In her model, the student has no choice but to read on, and that is interpreted as "eagerness" to read on and "meaningful" to the student. Where is the "science" of learning evident? Why are these students (all) reading this play at this time? Hunter reduces the study of Shakespeare to fulfillment of a reading requirement imposed (however nicely) by the teacher.

In my seventh-grade language arts class, where students make their own purposeful reading choices, Elaine chose to read Shakespeare. She chose to begin her reading with *Romeo and Juliet*. She shared her responses to the play in her response journal:

> This book is written in play form, which I like. It also has footnotes which is good because even using context clues you'd never figure out what the word means. I'm on the second act now. I like this act better because Romeo and Juliet meet now. I have come to the balcony scene. I think this is one of the greatest love scenes of all time. It even passes up Casablanca.* This is supposed to be a tragedy but so far nothing bad has happened. I know these people die, but this is quite humorous in some scenes.
>
> This is the first time I've read Shakespeare and I like it. I plan on reading MACBETH, HAMLET, and JULIUS CAESAR.
>
> *I think it's a great love scene because even though no actual kissing goes on, the words are so true.

Elaine has determined her own objectives and purposes for reading Shakespeare. She expresses her "eagerness" for reading the story, but the meaningfulness goes beyond the story. She is exploring a genre, Shakespeare's play, and learning how to deal with the language with context clues and with footnotes. She questions her concept of "tragedy" as she recognizes the humor in the play. She states her appreciation for the language of the text when she discusses the love scene and its words, not actions. The learning experience is authentic for Elaine, who will continue to read Shakespeare and to build upon what she learns from each reading. As her teacher, a professional who has a scientific view of reading and writing and who possesses her individual teaching style, I work with Elaine as she responds to the text. I see learning in many directions, and I do not limit the learning to predetermined objectives that may limit the learning experiences. I don't say to the seventh grader, "Stop, that's only to be read in high school."

Another "artistic" lesson example is the teaching of prepositional phrases: "The teacher is working on prepositional phrases (and you know how fascinating that is to high-school students)" (p. 17). The lesson is saved by the teacher presenting a subject of interest to the students to frame the teaching of prepositional phrases. The teacher, Hunter claims, "is making material more meaningful for both Tom and the class, and massing practice on prepositional phrases." Again, language is segmented, in this example, into obscure aspects of grammar. As a result, students are uninterested and "bored," as described by Hunter. But what is the purpose for this lesson in prepositional phrases? Is the content valid for these students? As a whole language teacher, I am concerned with the content and context of language experiences from which students learn about the structure of language. Such structure is not taught in isolation or in cute, isolated, inane sentences about another subject. If given a purposeful opportunity to write about a subject or an event of interest, students would certainly use prepositional phrases in their writing and read prepositional phrases in their reading, because the structure is part of their natural language. The learning experience is authentic. If learners want to learn a label for prepositions, they can do so incidental to reading and writing, with no need for "massing practice." I have never met a seventh grader who does not use prepositions.

My classroom is a safe learning environment, where my students and I interact. What makes it so is the most important element—the human element—not "elements of effective instruction" and "principles of learning." "Anticipatory set," a technique used at the beginning to help the students focus on what is to be taught, is an element of Hunter's model. The students depend upon the teacher to begin their learning activity. In my whole language classroom, we read together, write together, and plan together. My students know what is expected and anticipate the activities of the class.

Ken Goodman recently asked me: "If you were not in your classroom, would your students know what to do?" As a whole language teacher, I answered, "Yes." On any given day, if I were not in the room, my students would walk in the door, read silently, write in their journals, or work on their writing projects. Their classroom is a literate environment of reading and writing, where they make decisions about their learning.

"Cooperative learning" is a group activity Hunter described in a lesson to teach more isolated bits of language—the use of the colon and semicolon. In such an activity, students are given input and practice the skill. Cooperation is a vital part of my whole language classroom; students work together to share their writing, their questions, their ideas, their reading, themselves. Cooperative learning is a way of life, not a planned activity used for specific reasons. It is a sense of community, where students feel safe to express themselves and take responsibility for their learning. It cannot be reduced to defined roles of group members, since each individual, active in the reading and writing process, may have a different need from the group. Alone or together, we learn such conventions as colons or semicolons through our reading and writing and not by practice in silly sentence sets.

"Modeling," another important aspect of the classroom environment, is also isolated as an element in the Hunter model: "Modeling is helpful in most situations so that students can see, hear, or experience an artistic, enabling example. There are times, however, when a model can stifle creativity, so it should not be used" (p. 18). In the whole language classroom, the teacher is always a model, for the teacher is a reader, a writer, a speaker, and a learner, along with the students. Students view the teacher as someone who helps them learn. Real literature, student writing, and teacher writing provide models of language which do not stifle creativity but provide text with which students transact and learn at all times.

I believe teaching is an art—an art that comes from the teacher's heart and knowledge of language and from an understanding of children. As a whole language teacher, I view myself as a knowledgeable professional. I know about language, the reading and writing process, language learning, and kids. A *true professional* is one who assumes the power to make teaching decisions to help students learn, not one who routinely follows one model. For this reason, as much as any reason, the Hunter model is not applicable to the whole language classroom. I am a whole language teacher who feels in my heart the pain from staff development being limited to the Hunter model and teachers being professionally and financially rewarded for following that model. I also feel the joy from students learning and sharing in my classroom, where I strive to be a *true professional*, a teacher.

# 16

## GETTING DRESSED TO GO OUT: A WHOLE LANGUAGE APPROACH TO EXPOSITORY WRITING

### Dana Fox

*. . . no individuals learn by giving back to authorities the accepted word the authorities have given them. The two must meet, bringing with them their own experiences and searches, their own effort and commitment.*

Ken Macrorie

During a recent discussion with colleagues, I sat at the table in disbelief, listening as one of the teachers commented on an expository writing course and her requirements:

> There are certain topics which I forbid my students to write about. Abortion and gun control, for example. Why? Because they don't know enough. They don't read the newspaper or news magazines. I've been reading the paper and watching the news for eight years, and there's nothing they can tell me that I don't already know. There's no way they can surprise me.

Her comment continues to trouble me. After listening to her reasoning, I began to think about the message implicit in this remark: students "don't know enough"; teachers "know it all." I wonder how often I have sent this message to students. As Brazilian educator Freire (1970) suggests, this sort of traditional view of education sees the teacher as the bank clerk—one who makes deposits to fill up students' accounts. Like Freire, I believe we should not view students as the "empty accounts" of this banking metaphor but as arriving in our classrooms with tremendous potential for thinking and learning and with genuine experiences upon which they can build. Kenneth

Goodman believes that teachers who apply the principles of whole language share this view of students:

> Whole language programs respect the learners: who they are, where they come from, how they talk, what they read, and what experiences they already had before coming to school (1986, p. 10).

How do we help students believe in their potential, to take themselves and their ideas seriously in writing expository essays? I would like to discuss one approach to expository writing which involves what Goodman, Watson, and Burke (1987) call experiences in whole language: reading familiar written language, talking about their reading, sharing their life and language, and writing a real composition.

In the secondary English classroom, we often make an arbitrary distinction between personal (or even "creative") writing and writing about more "serious issues," using various forms of exposition. Many high school writers I have encountered see expository essays as nothing more than exercises in "skill" or "formula." Often they don't care about their subjects (which have usually been assigned to them), and they don't believe their readers are interested in what they have to say. Why is expository writing often boring and mechanical? Here's what students have to say:

> Exposition has always seemed boring to me because it includes facts. I could never get in touch with that, and maybe other students have that problem as well. I can't get close to my essay because I'm not allowed to put any of "me" into it.

> I've written tedious essays before and gotten good grades, but it wasn't because I was interested in my topic.

> Expository writing is boring and mechanical because students are led to believe that is what teachers are looking for.

> It often seems to me while doing expository essays in school that the forms and techniques required are extremely rigid and immovable. It's as if the teacher is more interested in *how* you say something than in *what* you say.

I think the reason so much expository writing is boring and mechanical is that most of us have been brought up believing and being taught that when we are writing an essay, we have to take the detached view and formal perspective. We are told never to use the personal *I* and are henceforth immediately removed from what we are writing. It becomes dry and dull.

Many educators and theorists believe we should reconsider and even eliminate this distinction we've drawn between personal writing and expository writing. Britton (1975) maintains that all writing begins in the personal or expressive mode. Suggesting "there is no essential difference between writing a poem and writing an essay," Ponsot and Deen believe "all writers we teach in school are creative," and "[expository] writing cannot be learned as something specialized" (1982, p. 65). Kirby and Liner suggest that "this artificial distinction has contributed to the dearth of lucid and exciting student papers and a proliferation of *English* in all school writing" (1981, p. 173). What are some principles for inviting students to produce good expository prose? Martin (1976) believes expository writing activities should build on student experience:

> Much effective writing seems to be on a continuum somewhere between the expressive and the transactional. This applies to adult as well as children's writing. . . . The [effective] expository writing task asks the student to reconcile what he/she already knows with new knowledge or experience. As a student develops as a writer, he/she should be more able to bring appropriate inner resources to bear on knowledge of the outside world (p. 26).

The ideas of Britton and Ponsot, Deen, Kirby, and Liner, and Martin seem to me to be directly related to the principles of whole language theory. Goodman, Watson, and Burke stress the importance of our acknowledging students' own experiences:

> In a whole language program, students are encouraged to bring their experiences and their language into the classroom. A great deal of talk takes place about ideas, events, and people that are already of interest to students or have the potential of stimulating their interests and imaginations (p. 142).

Building upon these ideas, particularly those suggested by Kirby and Liner, teachers of expository writing should keep the following principles in mind when designing expository writing tasks for their students.

1. Good expository writing builds on student experience.
2. Organization for exposition is often implicit in students' ideas.
3. Students should be encouraged to use their own best language for expository writing.
4. Students should be encouraged to become "experts" on their topics.
5. Students should read and talk about contemporary exposition, which is written in familiar language.

One method which I have found useful involves a sequence of activities using *Newsweek*'s "My Turn" column. This one-page column is usually written by nonprofessional writers. Students identify with the voices of what they call "real" writers. We work on the project over several days. First, I distribute several different issues of the magazine to students, asking them to turn to the "My Turn" column and read it silently. After they have read the column, I ask them to write a brief response to the column—something they found interesting or something they questioned. I read a column and write along with students. When we have written for about five to ten minutes, we all share something about the columns we have just read. This sharing is crucial, because each student gets to hear about all sorts of real-life reasons for writing expository prose. Because the writers of the columns often feel compelled to write on their topics for personal reasons, their voices are loud and clear. Bobby responds to a minority writer who longs to receive a job on the basis of her ability instead of filling an affirmative action quota:

> I have never thought much about Chinea-Varela's question: "Am I being picked for my ability or to fulfill a quota?" I always thought that affirmative action programs were beneficial for everyone. I've never looked at it from her point of view.

Louise writes about a woman who chooses to become a homemaker in spite of the persecution she feels from the media or the feminist movement:

> Angela Ward tries to convey the point that a homemaker is not ob- solete, but society pushes us toward an increasing trend of women working outside the home. From watching my mother, I cannot understand how people have the audacity to say that women at home do not work. Women should be able to freely select how they wish to live their lives and no one should interfere.

Reading a column which suggests that different groups of Americans form barriers around themselves and unnecessarily view outsiders as threats, Roger responds:

> I firmly back up Retsinas' point of view. I am a person who believes in the general good character of mankind. The attitude of thinking the outside world is hostile hampers our development because it limits our horizons. We will learn more if we tear down barriers.

During our discussion of the different columns, we talk about the writers' language and style, what we notice about the writing, how we read the columns, and so on. Someone in the class is sure to point out that the writers have personal experiences to share, and that they tend to use personal pronouns in their writing. Someone else remarks that she can't believe the variety of topics which are represented by the various columns: some are funny and light- hearted, while others take a more serious approach.

The next stage involves students selecting a "My Turn" column which they would like to work with a bit more closely in class. Students may select a column which someone else has talked about or may browse through other *Newsweek* magazines in the library or in the back of the classroom. The key here is ownership: they are invited to choose a column for the next activity. Following their selection, students write what I call a summary and a personal response to the column of their choice. Lots of time is built into this assignment for group discussions, reading, and writing. Student writers in my classroom are encouraged to form a community—the kind Australian educator R. D. Walshe describes so well:

> The classroom, in order to become its own interested "discourse community," assumes a workshop form, in the sense of generating and discussing problems, feeling challenged to explore some of them deeply, working out answers with the collecting-and-clarifying help of writing, and then submitting to the critical appraisal of colleagues. Everyone here is a writer, a reader, a talker, a thinker (1987, p. 26).

We talk about how we read and why we choose to remember certain points from the articles. In analyzing the columns, students begin to underline key points and to mark effective passages they will quote. To fully explore the writer's position, Bean and Ramage suggest questions to use as part of prewriting strategies: "What are the strengths and weaknesses of this writer's argument?" "What are the implications of the author's argument?" "How do the author's ideas compare with my ideas or X's ideas?" "How can I believe and doubt the writer's argument?" "Do the author's ideas make sense in terms of my own experience?" "Why is this article important?" (1986, p. 254).

Essentials for expository writing, such as summarizing and questioning, are integrated into the process. Because they have an interest in the subject matter of the column and a goal in mind, students learn that these concepts are more than just an exercise. Even though the summary-response paper is fairly brief, students are surprised to find themselves committed to a topic—one which often has close personal connections for them. I enjoy watching them grow during this process. David reads a column which a father writes about his "culturally biased children," and he recognizes himself:

> I find myself agreeing with Fleishaker. I come from a very prejudiced family because my father was raised in a small town and had never dealt with blacks until he moved to the city. I'd like to think of myself as cool or enlightened, but I know I have picked up some of my father's prejudice. I feel the best point made in this article is that a lot of people look down on blacks as a whole, but they exclude the ones they know. This is a key factor in my experience with blacks. I sometimes find myself calling blacks "niggers," yet I would *never* call one of my black friends a "nigger." I never really thought about this problem until I read this article.

Fleishaker really made me think. I feel that I should work on my problem of being culturally biased.

Sometimes two students will choose the same column and react quite differently to the writer's position. Their reactions create interesting dialogue in class. Mark and Lisa respond to a doctor who explains the many actions he must go through to make his patients more relaxed, cooperative, and healthy. Mark's comments show that he disagrees with the writer:

> I can see how some doctors treat their patients and deal with those who aren't really sick. I can see the problems doctors face with malpractice and losing their clients, but should doctors cater to their patients' "illnesses" just to make them both happy? I believe they shouldn't. Dr. Hoffman mentions how he has to prepare himself every time he is about to enter an examination room, like an actor preparing for a scene. I understand he's saying that each situation is different, but I also think he's saying he needs to put on a facade just to show concern for another patient. If that's the case, he'd better find himself another profession.

On the other hand, Lisa sees some value in the writer's position because, like David, she sees *herself* in the column:

> To find something that I related to on a professional level was surprising to me. I worked every day last summer in a nursing home. I found it hard to play up to a patient, but it was something I had to learn in order to make my patients happy and keep myself sane. I felt like I was deceiving them just to please them. Everyone did it, even the doctors and the families. It took me a while to learn this theatrical part of my job, but I did. I agree totally with Dr. Hoffman. I guess for as long as I am going to work with patients this is something I am going to have to deal with. I'm glad to know someone else finds it just as frustrating.

My ultimate goal in this process is to have students write a "My Turn" column of their own. Reading, summarizing, and responding to the columns prepares students well for this assignment. They aren't forced to fit their ideas into a five-paragraph formula, yet they have discovered the importance of structure and organization. Students begin to see the importance of employing their own experience in writing, using their own best language. In order to generate ideas for this last writing, I have borrowed an idea from a colleague: I ask students to make a list of things that really bother them or that upset them or that they worry about. We narrow those lists down to items which seem manageable, which might be interesting to other readers, or which might be items over which they have at least some control. Our approach to writing this essay follows a process orientation, and we produce essays which might even be sent to *Newsweek*. My students have written their own "My Turn" columns on various topics: one student proudly defends her Ozarks dialect, another explains why she plans never to have children, another discusses the discrepancies he believes exist in laws concerning marijuana and alcohol abuse, another describes an experience in which he and a friend purchase an automatic rifle with unbelievable, frightening ease, and yet another thoughtfully explains her feelings and personal associations with the complex issues surrounding the decision to have an abortion. If I had forbidden them to write about certain topics, I would have eliminated the very subjects which my students think about and struggle with every day.

This sequence of activities has proven valuable for me and my students. Their papers have voice and purpose. They have stories to tell, feelings to express, positions to defend. They enjoy the "My Turn" column, and some of them continue to read it throughout the year. Some even begin to subscribe to a new magazine. When I ask them to reflect on this entire experience, their responses help me validate the process:

> When we are forced to make our ideas fit pre-conceived forms, where is the room for expansion, inventiveness, or delight? [This assignment helps me see] that no two pieces of real writing are exactly alike. All writing is creative!

> I was under the impression that expository writing called for conveying knowledge without personal voice or experience. This is *so* wrong! In my mind, I don't see a distinction between "creative" writing and "expository" writing. While I see the need to be able to communicate knowledge of a subject to an appropriate audience, I don't see why things we associate with "creativity" can't make expository writing better.

> To me the distinction between "creative" writing and "expository" writing is the situation that each addresses. Writing expository papers is like getting dressed up to go out—maybe you wouldn't want to do it all the time, but the change is kind of fun sometimes. When you get dressed up, you usually try to be on your "best behavior," but that shouldn't mean that you're suddenly not *you* anymore.

Macrorie has said:

> The principal reason education doesn't "take" better than it does is that it's a closed loop, with knowledge and experience of experts on one side and no way for it to flow into or over to the other side, where in darkness—unarticulated, unreflected upon, unused—lie the knowledge and experience of students. The discipline of real learning consists of The Self and The Others flowing into each other (1988, p. 13).

I certainly know students who have felt this hopeless, this out-of-touch with school and with our assignments for them. Through their involvement in this series of activities, I hope students can become intimate participants in expository writing. As they read about real issues and as they examine the language and style of the published writers in *Newsweek*'s "My Turn" columns, they begin to connect their own experiences as they write about issues which are important to them. They will share their stories, and they *will* surprise us, if only we will allow them opportunities to do so.

# 17

# A WHOLE LANGUAGE APPROACH
# TO THE TEACHING OF
# BILINGUAL LEARNERS

### Alex Moore

In the autumn of 1987, I found myself privileged to work with the two people whom this chapter is really about: a London school-teacher called Susan and a fifteen-year-old Bangladeshi boy called Mashud.

Mashud had been in England for eighteen months. His first language was Sylheti, for which there exists no standard written form, but he was also able to speak and write fluently in Bengali, which had been the language of instruction of his Bangladeshi schools. His English secondary school, where he was now in the fourth year, had large numbers of bilingual pupils, of whom Sylhetis made up the largest single group: as many as 50 percent in some classes.

During his time so far at the school, Mashud had made unspectacular progress in English, despite having received a good deal of "pull-out" language tutoring, as well as some in-class language support, in both cases by qualified and capable ESL teachers. His handwriting still bore strong traces of the Bengali script, which made it difficult to read. He still attempted to spell many words and combinations of words through a particularly successful strategy related to phonetics. His attempts at replicating English grammatical structures were developing rather slowly, and he had showed little sense of the functions of English punctuation. (These were the aspects of his writing that teachers tended to wring their hands over.) He did, however, write copiously and enthusiastically, if, as we shall see, not yet with any variety, and in this respect his written work was more impressive than his oral work.

Mashud seemed confident enough; indeed he displayed *leadership qualities* in conversation with his Sylheti-speaking peers.

However, he appeared reluctant to expose himself to possible embarrassment and public correction by using spoken English with his teachers or his non-Sylheti-speaking classmates. In his English class, there were twenty-six other students, of whom nine were also Sylheti speakers with less than two years' experience of living in England.

Susan was one of Mashud's two English teachers. I was the other. Two teachers—one an ESL specialist, the other a "regular" English teacher—had been assigned to each fourth-year English class on account of the large numbers of bilingual pupils at the school. However, there had been insufficient ESL teachers to go round, and therefore one class had been obliged to share two English specialists: Susan and myself. But both of us had a great deal of experience working with bilingual children in the same part of England.

This particular kind of collaborative teaching was new to the school and replaced an earlier system whereby fourth- and fifth-year pupils were given "decontextualised" language work by ESL teachers through having their elective subjects (only Maths, English, and Games were at that time compulsory) reduced from five per week to four per week. The dozen teachers involved in the project had been carefully selected according to two broad sets of criteria by the heads of the school's English and ESL Departments. First, they had to believe in and enjoy collaborative teaching. Second, they needed to be on common philosophical and theoretical ground. Eschewing the kind of English teaching many of them had cut their teeth on in the 'sixties and early 'seventies, with its emphases on comprehension exercises, essay titles, spelling tests, class readers, and whole class lessons in grammar and punctuation, their focus would now be on the form and content of various written and spoken genres, on language awareness, and on working with what children brought into the classroom with them: in particular, accepting the responsibility to provide instruction that was both appropriate and challenging, without slavishly following preordained schemes of work.

Their methodology would owe much to the work of Barnes (1976), their theory to the work of Vygotsky (1987), in respect of the relationship between development and instruction, and of Foucault (1977), Bakhtin (1986), and Volosinov (1986), in respect of the philosophy of language and particularly the nature and functions of discourse. They would, in consequence of this, be advocators and practitioners of whole language teaching: that is to say, they would seek, to borrow from Kenneth Goodman's definition, to "create opportunities for pupils to use language in authentic, richly contextualized, functional ways" (K. Goodman, 1989, p. xi).

As far as the teaching of bilingual pupils was concerned, this would be essentially no different from the teaching of monolingual pupils in most respects. It would, however, highlight certain attitudes and strategies. In particular, it would entail a rejection of oversimplified divisions of language into the "social" and the "academic"—divisions which had been used to support the argument for providing bilingual learners with decontextualised language work under the previous system, in favour of models based on a perceived need for such pupils to acquire expertise in a wide range of Western discursive practices, both written and oral, some of which might be at odds with alternative practices already learnt in previous (usually Bangladeshi) schools. While initiating pupils into these new discursive practices, it would be essential to oppose any downgrading or devaluing of alternative practices that might in turn lead to pupils' abandoning or rejecting their own home culture, either in part or in whole.

In short, those same underlying views that underpinned their work with native English-speaking children, with its emphases on contextualisation, on collaboration, and on a resistance to language differentiation, in particular to the teaching of "discrete" language skills, would also be brought to bear on the teaching of their bilingual pupils. The intriguing question was: how would this actually work in practice? And what specific pedagogical skills would be needed to make sure that it *did* happen?

Before the start of the academic year, Susan and I had sat down and agreed on our respective roles vis à vis Mashud's class. For time-tabling purposes, I had been designated subject-teacher and Susan, support-teacher. We had also be invited to work together with another fourth-year class containing far fewer bilingual pupils, where our roles would be reversed. In practice, we decided that we would not take these labels too seriously: we would share on as equitable a basis as possible all lesson planning, marking, and preparation, and we agreed that both of us would help all pupils, both bilingual and monolingual. A timetabling problem, however, had meant that Susan would be able to attend only three out of every four of our weekly lessons with this class; therefore, it was agreed that I would assume ultimate overall responsibility for one major area of organisation—that of classroom discipline.

During the first week, we had observed and attempted to alter some rigid, self-imposed seating arrangements within the class. These were essentially culture based: a group of three Sylheti-born girls in one corner of the room, a group of four Moroccan-born girls in another, four reluctant boys at the rear of the room, the six Sylheti-born boys in a group at the front, and so on. Attempts to break up these groups on anything like a permanent basis had not proved successful: all pupils were resistant to teacher-imposed moves that lasted in excess of one period for one specific task, and we were forced to defer our efforts in this area until later in the year, when we were to achieve some measure of success, chiefly in order to be able to direct our energies to introducing and initiating the course.

We had both quickly picked out Mashud as a particularly interesting and promising pupil. In addition to his oral reticence in English and copious flaws at the surface level of his written work—characteristics shared by most of the other Sylheti children in the class—Mashud's work had a particular idiosyncrasy in that, whenever he was set creative writing—or even discursive writing—assignments, he would come up with heavily formulaic fairy-story-style moral tales which were clearly translations of stories he had learned, almost by rote, in his native tongue. Other assignments, such as responses to works of literature, he would never attempt. This was not a unique phenomenon—many of the Sylheti children at the school sometimes produced similar work in response to similar assignments—but the fact that Mashud was such a productive student and that he never varied his approach had thrown it into particularly sharp focus.

It was a habit that had already been noted by Mashud's English teacher of the previous year, but it was Susan who formulated a first attempt to *account* for it at one of our weekly meetings about halfway into the autumn term:

Mashud seems to have a background where making up stories is not so highly valued . . . not nearly as much as learning moral tales. I suppose that could have something to do with his culture . . . you know, if it's more strongly oral-based than our own . . . or even with the sorts of dangers in Bangladesh, which are maybe more predictable, and located more in the natural environment than they are here: you know, a lot of his stories are to do with snakes and flooding rivers and poisoning . . . and maybe certain social issues are more clear-cut. I don't know. . . . I don't know enough about it, really. . . . Here, on the other hand, making up your own stories and writing them down is a very highly valued activity. I don't think Mashud has quite made that transition yet. . . . You know, he's still operating mentally in one culture and sometimes linguistically in another.

Susan did know enough not to dismiss Mashud's habit as a "problem" of cognitive-linguistic origin or to attribute it, as many teachers would have done, to a vague, deficit-model-inspired notion of "unsureness" or "insecurity." She had asked herself questions about Mashud's cultural-linguistic background—questions which nobody had invited her to ask—and had come to a perfectly tenable hypothesis on which she and I could structure future pedagogy. That pedagogy itself would offer us every opportunity to test out Susan's hypothesis.

In effect, Susan had sought to explain a phenomenon rather than merely describe it. This, I now realised, was a necessary first step towards the kind of understanding we would subsequently need if we were to develop and improve our teaching, not just of Mashud but of all the pupils in all our classes: an obvious point, perhaps, but one that gets all too easily lost in the hurly-burly of coping and survival strategies that carries many teachers through the working day.

Susan's attempt at a rational, nondeficit explanation of Mashud's written work was to prove important in all sorts of ways: chiefly, in that it created a questioning, sympathetic discourse which enabled other, related issues to be recognised, discussed, and approached in a manner far more planned and informed than we had hitherto attempted.

At a subsequent weekly meeting, the question of Mashud's essentially oral Bangladeshi culture resurfaced, this time finding its focus in the *structure* of his narrative work. I had been rereading Ong's *Orality and Literacy* (1982), and I told Susan that I'd been reminded of her comments at our earlier meeting.

AM: I wonder, you know, if you're remembering stories for repetition, if you're likely to *order* them in a particular way: also to cut out . . . not adjectives per se; they could have an important function . . . but a lot of what we would call "background detail."

s: All that description, and characterisation and stuff . . . Yes . . . I suppose you could be right. It would in a sense be irrelevant, wouldn't it? I mean, the moral would be the important thing . . . not what kind of day it was, less still what mood people were in, what was going on inside their heads. . . . None of that so-called realism or naturalism that we're so into. . . . That could all just be so much clutter. . . .

AM: Yes . . . Yes, I think so. . . . So perhaps the things we value in our culture in respect of writing—like, as you say, so-called realism—could be thought of . . . well, as bad, actually, in a culture that was less literacy-orientated. . . . And things like "style." . . .

s: Yes. . . . You'd tell the story or whatever chronologically: that would be the tendency.

AM: Right . . . and it might involve fewer characters. . . .

s: It's fascinating. When you think about it, there could be the most enormous gap between what Mashud has been brought up to value in narratives and what we're telling him he should be valuing.

AM: That's right. Always assuming, of course, that our basic hypothesis is correct!

This particular session was to prove every bit as useful as the earlier one. During the course of our next lesson with Mashud, Susan and I started to look very carefully at the structure of his stories to see if they actually did have the essentially additive structure one might associate with a more oral culture, rather than the subordinate style favoured by our own society. We decided they did. At the same time, we began to reidentify our task and strategy with Mashud and the other Bangladeshi children in the class, away from working mainly on surface features and fine tuning towards initiating them into the kinds of spoken and written discourse that they would need expertise in if they were to do well, that is, be perceived as doing well, in English society: a change of perspective, in fact, but with the same educational goal in mind.

This initiation—or, rather, these initiations—would have to be effected without any devaluation of the kinds of discourse these pupils were already proficient in (for instance, the retelling of moral tales) and without suggesting that ours was the right way of doing things and theirs, the wrong way.

With these new strategies in mind, we decided to effect a slight restructuring of our teaching programme for the middle section of the autumn term. Two weeks into the term, we had already introduced an autobiography project. Our reason for introducing this project at this stage was that our fourth-year class was participating in a writing exchange with a school in the United States. The project, which entailed our pupils exchanging samples of their writing with a parallel class of American pupils and which had an important impact on Mashud's writing, will be returned to later. It seemed safe to assume that our pupils would want to begin this exchange by sending off data about themselves and receiving similar data from their American counterparts. Autobiography writing seemed an obvious and appealing way of doing this, just as the situation—being able to write for a *real* audience of unseen peers—suggested our pupils might be inspired to write fuller, more entertaining pieces than if they had been undertaking the exercise only as another component of their examination course (albeit one that would receive an audience within the school itself).

We had initiated the project by introducing the class to extracts of autobiographies and pseudo-autobiographies written in a variety of styles: Richard Wright's *Black Boy*, Charles Dickens' *David Copperfield*, James Joyce's *Portrait of the Artist*, and so on—essentially to indicate the importance of voice and to remind our pupils that they could work within a range of available styles. A sheet of suggested but not prescriptive chapter headings had then been handed out—Babyhood, Primary School Days, Accidents, and so forth—which could be selected from on a chronological or any other basis or passed over in favour of any alternative structure.

During two subsequent class discussions, memories had been exchanged and discussed to get pupils in the mood. The Bangladeshi children had not joined in these discussions formally, though there had been much informal discussion, in Sylheti, amongst themselves. The whole class discussions, like the guide sheets (there being neither the time nor the expertise for translations), had been in English. Though the project had been carefully introduced, it had not replaced other projects. Unlike other projects, which normally had a production limit of two to three weeks and took up all the pupils' time, the autobiographical work would be spread over two or three months and would be undertaken concurrently with other work. Much of the responsibility for organising this project would therefore be devolved on to the pupils.

Both Susan and I had noted that the Bangladeshi pupils had been particularly slow to get the project started—partly, we thought, because letters to parents explaining the writing exchange itself had not been available in Bengali and because we had not explained carefully enough how their work would be disseminated. An additional problem was that they had clearly been confused by our sheet of suggested chapter headings. Our new strategy would be to focus on the autobiography with these pupils, releasing them from other projects, emphasising the potential audience of American peers, and initiating work through oral discussion of their own and their families' life histories. We were helped in this by having now developed a concept and a plan of our own. We felt that, by introducing an autobiography project to Mashud and the other Sylheti pupils, we would be providing a gentle introduction into one particular set of Western European ways of writing: expressive writing.

Our broad strategy would, we hoped, enable a pupil like Mashud to write from his own experience while at the same time incorporating elements of moral tales into his writing in ways that seemed appropriate to him. These elements would be selective in character: that is to say, true episodes would be chosen on the basis of their capacity to make a moral point. Being invited to write about his life in Bangladesh, in whatever way came most easily to him, would enable Mashud to combine freedom and originality (to choose from a range of possible experiences and details) with conformity and restriction (in this case, whatever he wrote about must be true): the basic paradigm, we felt, within which all Western expressive and creative writing was located. He would not be expected to become an inventive storyteller overnight, but, while not being denied those storytelling abilities he already possessed, he would be given every opportunity of extending existing skills and incorporating them with new ones in an area that was not quite fiction but that had many of the qualities of fiction.

The new skills we expected from Mashud included subordination and drafting—previously, he had produced second drafts of stories at his teachers' request, but these had amounted to no more than neat copyings out of teacher-corrected originals—the description of unique events; the reporting of conversations; and the introduction of characters, feelings, and motives into his writing. If responded to appropriately by us, Mashud would, we hoped, come to learn something of what was valued in expressive writing in his new school and how that was different from what he may have learned to value in previous ones.

Since Susan had shown a particular interest in Mashud and had developed a closer working relationship with him at this stage, she spent more time with him on the project than I did. This was not something we discussed or set up formally: it was just the way things fell out. I did not ignore Mashud, of course, and regularly went over to see what he was doing, both on his own and in his discussions with Susan.

Some examples of his initial approach to the task and of Susan's responses to it are reproduced in the following extracts, taken from transcripts of discussions between Mashud and Susan after he had come up with a rough first draft of his project, which he had entitled "My Life Story."

Susan had decided to use these sessions both to correct surface and vocabulary errors in Mashud's work and to discuss its content with him. In particular, she wanted to encourage him to extend the length of his assignment, which was longer than anything he had previously written—a little under 1,000 words—but still on the short side, considering the nature of the project and the wealth of experience he had to draw on. During the course of these early sessions, Mashud at least twice thought of new material for subsequent inclusion: something he had never been obliged to do in the transcription of his moral tales.

*Discussion between Susan and Mashud about part of Mashud's first draft, which describes his birth at the time of the Bangladeshi War.*

SUSAN: So who was the War between?
MASHUD: Miss, Bangladesh War.
S: Yes . . . but . . . who was fighting? Were Bangladeshi people fighting other Bangladeshi people?
M: No . . . No Bangladesh people . . . Er . . . No Bangladesh . . . Er . . . Pakistan . . . Pakistan people fight . . . And . . . Bangladesh East Pakistan.
S: Oh yes. Bangladesh was East Pakistan.
M: Yes, Miss.
S: Now it's Bangladesh.
M: Miss.

*Discussion between Susan and Mashud about part of Mashud's first draft, which describes him being chased by a "cow."*

S: Tell me about this cow.
M: Miss (*Laughing*) cow hit me.
S: It hit you?
M: Yes, Miss.
S: Like this? (*Raising hand and aiming an imaginary swipe*)
M: (*Laughing*) Miss! Like this. (*Putting fingers to head like horns and using them to "butt" the boy next to him, who, listening, also laughs*) In the lands . . .
S: The lands? What are the lands?
M: Where is cow, Miss. Four cows in our lands my family.
S: Lands . . . I think we would say "fields." So you had four cows in your field?
M: Field?
S: (*Writing it down on Mashud's paper*) Field.
M: Four cows, Miss. (*Laughing*) One cow . . . bad; very, very bad.
S: It chased you . . .
M: (*Excited*) Chase! Yes, Miss. I very scared . . .

s: And it hit you?

M: Yes, Miss. Bad . . . very, very bad.

*Discussion between Susan and Mashud about part of Mashud's first
draft, which describes an injury sustained in a wrestling contest with
another boy.*

s: You *broke* your leg, you say?

M: Yes, Miss.

s: Or did you *hurt* it?

M: Hurt, yes.

s: I see. So you did not actually *break* it.

M: Yes, *break* Miss. (*Gestures breaking with two fists*)

s: Wow! That must have hurt!

M: Yes, Miss.

s: Which bit of your leg was it you broke?

M: Miss?

s: (*Pointing to Mashud's leg*) Where? Here? (*Indicating his shin*)
   Here? (*Indicating his ankle*)

M: Yes, here.

s: On your *ankle*.

M: Uncle . . .

s: A (*Writing*) Ankle.

M: Ankle. Break my ankle, Miss?

s: Right.

Clearly, these conversations were not ideal from a learning view-
point. Partly because of tradition and partly because of Mashud's
lack of confidence and expertise in spoken English, they fell broadly
into the discursive pattern of Teacher Initiates (in this case, Questions)—Pupil Responds. However, there were other characteristics
that impressed me and that had plainly not happened just by
chance. To begin with, Susan had not fallen into the trap, described
by Morgan Dalphini (1988), of questioning her pupil's reality ("This
doesn't sound true? . . . Would it really have happened like this?
. . ."); rather, her aim had been to discover more of what that reality
was and to teach new vocabulary at the same time which would be
of use to Mashud when he wished or needed to express that same
reality in the future.

It is interesting that Mashud never needed to be "taught" the word
*ankle* again and never subsequently confused it with *uncle*. I am
tempted to draw a comparison with Parts of the Body sessions I have
observed in other classes, where bilingual pupils are presented with
labelled diagrams of people and must practise drills in order to
acquire basic vocabulary of the human anatomy. At the end of such
lessons, many pupils find themselves more confused than when they
began.

Susan had also asked *genuine* questions, designed to elicit information, not disguised statements or judgments, as is so often the

case in these situations. She had focused Mashud's attention on what he was writing and had led him to consider further, related material. While Susan had made some surface corrections to Mashud's work, she had made no effort yet to get him to add or delete anything; she merely made a suggestion: "Ramadan sounds very interesting. You must tell me about that some time."

When Mashud had finished his second draft, using the work corrected by Susan, along with some more he had added (including a section on Ramadan), he showed it again to Susan, who first made surface-feature corrections of the added material and then offered her opinion of the work as a whole:

s: Good. That's very good work, Mashud.
m: No, Miss. Short—too short.
s: Well . . . Perhaps you can add a bit? What else do you think you could write about? Let's have a look at what you've got so far.

Together, Susan and Mashud reexamined Mashud's project so far, Susan sitting beside Mashud reading while he followed:

s: (*Reading*) "My Life Story," by Mashud.

I was born in Bangladesh in war-time. The war started in 1971, the year of my birth. Before that, Bangladesh was East Pakistan. Then they had a big war and Pakistan spread into three parts. One is India, another Bangladesh and Pakistan—I don't really know much about it because I was just born at that time. My mum told me about it.

Sometimes I think I can remember things I did, things I saw from the age of eleven, but I don't think I can remember things before that.

My mum and dad told me they had a small house in a small village between the jungles. When the war began, everybody went to the jungle to save their lives. People took food with them and a map and a torch for light, because in those days we didn't have electricity in Bangladesh. People who used to live at the top of a hill or between the fields had to dig a hole that they could hide inside and save their own and their children's lives. My parents said they used to live on the hillside and they dug a hole and hid in it, covering it over with some branches and leaves. My grandfather heard that we were in trouble. He used to live in another village, quite far away. He was so worried that he came looking for my parents, but he never saw anybody. He was shouting and looking for them. The Military were not far away. They heard him calling, and they came and one of them shot him. After about an hour my parents came out and someone told my dad that his dad was dead. He was shocked. It was that night that I was born.

My dad told me they had gone to look for a doctor. Also, I was lucky to be born that night because the Military had gone on to another village.

When I was about ten years old we had some farms, and every family who had a farm if they couldn't look after it by themselves they got another person as a paid help, usually someone very poor.

We had four cows. One day school was closed and I was looking after the cows, suddenly, someone came up behind me and showed a piece of red cloth to the cow. The cow started chasing me. I was running. The cow pushed me with its horns and I went rolling down the hill. I was shocked and hurt in my chest. It took me months to get well.

But in Bangladesh it's lots of fun with your friends. Every morning, we go to the swimming pool with a lot of friends. Then we go to school. School starts at ten o'clock and we have a half hour break at 12 o'clock and finish at 4. Also we have a half-day every Friday because all Muslim people go to the Mosque to pray.

Sometimes after school everyone goes home for dinner and after, when the sun goes down, all the boys come out into the fields to play football and other games. It's nice fun every afternoon, except Saturday—because every Saturday we have a market just beside our house. It's our own market, and we also have our own chemist and a small sweet-shop.

I have two uncles, one in Bangladesh and one in England, and I also have two brothers and a sister in Bangladesh.

Once in my primary school, we held a competition like a wrestling match, and I was in it. I had a big guy against me. I couldn't handle him at all. He was too strong for me and so big. There were a lot of people around and I didn't know what to do, I was so shy and scared. Suddenly he jumped on my ankle and broke it! I was at home about three months. I can still remember how my ankle hurt.

In the winter time we had a big fruit garden. We grew bananas and mangoes and jackfruit, apples and lemons. Some seasons we sold them if we had a lot, or else we'd just eat them.

At Ramadan my parents used to fast until 2:30 P.M. to 9:00 A.M. I used to fast some time if I could, but I couldn't very much. I got too hungry. My parents slept most of the time to use the time up. I used to get some mangoes and jackfruit for them and wash it for them. Ramadan lasts one month. After Ramadan we celebrate. The day we celebrate is called EID. On that day we get new clothes and extra food and we go to our cousins' and friends' houses and have nice fun. On that day we can do anything we want to do.

Also every year we have a big market and we call it "Mala." Everybody goes. They have nice toys and music and a magic show. We enjoyed Mala a lot.

Another day, before the summer holiday, we had a sports day.

We played badminton, volleyball, cricket and throwing heavy stones. There was so many people in the field. I was playing badminton. We had great fun.

This was the "corrected" version of Mashud's work, but basically the words were Mashud's: that is to say, he had essentially put down these words in this order. Susan's corrections had been almost exclusively cosmetic, focusing on spelling, grammar, and odd points of vocabulary, though there had been some impact on what we might call style in small, localised changes of word order. A flavour of Mashud's original draft is given, for the sake of comparison, in the following extracts:

> I was bon in Bangladesh and ther was a war the war strat in 1971 that year I was bon. before Bangladesh was East Pakistan then ther had big war and Pakistan sprede in three parte. one is India an alther is Bangladesh and Pakistan, I do'nt really no much about it becase i was just born that time. my mum told me.
> We had four cows. one day school close and I looking after the cows suddenle, someone come up after me and should a peece of red clouth to the cow. the cow strated chaseing me I was run the cow push me with it's horn and I when roling down the hill. I shokt and hurt pane in my chest. it tolke month to be better.

When Susan had finished reading Mashud's new draft through with him, she returned immediately to his doubts about its length:

s: Well, what else could you say?
m: (*Shrugs*)
s: How about something more about the things you did with your friends? The wrestling match was interesting. What other things did you do?
m: Yes, Miss.
s: Also, you haven't said anything about your life in England. You could write a bit about that: what it's like here for you.
m: Cold, Miss.
s: (*Laughs*) Yes, . . . Cold. . . . Well, you could say that. What else could you say?
m: (*Shrugs*)
s: Well, you think about it. Write down some more bits on a separate sheet of paper and then show it to me.

Mashud seemed happy with Susan's advice. He took a sheet of paper from the teachers' desk and spent the rest of the lesson writing busily. During the next lesson, he presented Susan with two more sections—her edited versions of which follow.

**(1)** One time, our Sunday school was closed, and I called for some friends. We decided to go hunting, for a fox or for birds.

So each one of us got a spear and we went through the jungle shouting, screaming, and running. Our noise scared away all the foxes. If there was one, it would run. But suddenly one small fox just jumped out of a hole and ran away, and we all ran after it. We couldn't kill it, but it was good fun.

In the winter-time in our country, it's not very cold like in England. If we have to wear a jumper, that's winter! And in winter we do a lot of fishing in the canals. Sometimes the water is pushed into our nearest field by the canals, and we can fish in it. But it's far too dangerous to go into the water and pull nets because there are too many snakes in the water. The water is too dirty as well. But we still have a good time and enjoy ourselves in the water.

(2) When I was about 13 years old my dad was in England. He wrote a letter to us saying that he would try to get us to England. We were so happy to come here. After about six months he came back to Bangladesh to get us.

When we came to London we felt so cold! We went to the hotel in Bayswater. Next day my dad went to the council office to apply for a house. We stayed in the hotel for two months then we had a flat in Harrow Road. We stayed in Harrow Road for about two and a half years. Then we bought a house with a nice garden in Kilburn.

Susan's task now was to discuss the two new sections with Mashud and to get him thinking about how to incorporate them into the original text. The rest of the class were busily involved with their own writing at this point, and I was once again able to sit in on Susan and Mashud's conversation:

s: That's really excellent, Mashud. Very good. Do you think this is long enough now?
m: Miss . . . (*tone implies* "Yes")
s: So all you've got to do now is add these bits . . . But . . . Don't just put them on the end. In this kind of writing, it's best to put things together . . .
m: Miss?
s: Mmm . . . It's so hard to explain . . . Look . . . (*pointing to Mashud's work*) here . . . the war . . . Here . . . your home . . . Here, you and your friends playing . . . Here, Ramadan . . . Now . . . these new bits . . . You and your friends playing . . . Put that in here. (*Draws arrows on Mashud's second draft, indicating this section should go after* "a small sweet-shop")
m: (*Pointing to the second new piece*) This, Miss?
s: Er . . .
m: Here, Miss! (*pointing to the end of the original version*)
s: Yes. Good. Put that bit at the end. It actually goes there quite nicely, doesn't it. Good. Well done.

Mashud returned to his work. A few days later, he had finished it. Susan happened to be off school that day, and Mashud asked me to go over his completed third draft with him. This I gladly agreed to do.

The new section (labelled 1, above), on playing with his friends (hunting for animals and birds and fishing) appeared, as Susan had suggested, with the other references to play, tucked in between the paragraph about playing in the fields and the paragraph about the wrestling match. The other new material (labelled 2, above), about life in England, also appeared where Mashud himself had suggested: at the end of his completed script. But Mashud had independently made two further organisational alterations entirely on his own. First, he had removed the short paragraph "I have two uncles. . . . Bangladesh" from its original location (that is, surrounded by paragraphs dealing with recreational activities with his peers) and had placed it at the end of the script after "Then we bought a house with a nice garden in Kilburn." Neither Susan nor I had commented on or, I suspect, had even noticed the inappropriate placing of this paragraph when the suggestion was made to insert part of Mashud's new material here. Second, he had shifted the short paragraph that appeared at the end of his second draft "Another day. . . . We had great fun" to a new position just after the paragraph about the wrestling match.

Most of my next meeting with Susan was spent discussing Mashud's finished autobiography, a remarkable piece of writing made to appear even more remarkable by the halting, embarrassed English of his oral exchanges, to see what we might learn from it to take with us into subsequent lessons. In addition to observing a number of techniques transferred and developed from his moral stories (for instance, the ability to recount a narrative in a very vivid way), we also found what seemed to us to be new techniques. These included the evaluation of experience, the adoption of a conversational voice, and the use of redrafting skills of a far more complex nature than Mashud had ever shown us before.

The appearance of these new redrafting skills we found particularly exciting, not least because we felt they would have a cross-curricular impact. Originally, we had been concerned with initiating Mashud into certain favoured Western European forms of expressive writing, but clearly there were aspects of these forms that occurred also in other forms of writing that he might expect to encounter elsewhere in the curriculum. Essentially, these redrafting skills were to do with the organisation of written material in ways that related to perceptions of *similarity*, an essential ingredient of the subordinative mode of representation, rather than to their location in real time, an essential ingredient of the aggregative model of representation. It may well have been that Mashud's playing of badminton, volleyball, and cricket and his throwing of heavy stones had occurred at the end of his period in Bangladesh (subsequent questioning revealed that indeed they did); however, in his newest draft, the account was located with other recreational activities, now all gathered together in a single section of the composition. Similarly, Mashud's reference to uncles and siblings may originally have seemed more appropriate adjacent to talk of "our house" and "our own market," but, on second thought, it clearly seemed to him to go better with the mention of his father's coming to England and returning for some of his family a little later.

This is not to suggest, of course, that Mashud had no previous grasp at all of these important skills (important matters, that is, of variable representational etiquette) or that many monolingual anglophones do not also reveal a tendency to write sometimes in additive rather than in subordinative ways. All the evidence of Mashud's previous writing, however, suggested that the subordinative style of writing "own" stories, so favoured in Western European schools and cultures, was one in which he had not previously received extensive instruction and also that, through suitable relationships and discourse with his English teachers, he was now beginning to understand and to acquire those styles within a teaching and learning framework that did not question or undermine any previously or concurrently held notions of appropriateness of either content or representation.

It was this kind of sensitivity, we felt, and this awareness and interest in linguistic diversity that stretched far beyond matters of grammar, vocabulary, punctuation, and calligraphy that were still all too lacking in the education of many bilingual learners and that notions of dichotomies between academic and social language, leading to the decontextualised instruction of the former, had done little to encourage.

This is not to say that our teaching of Mashud was a model of excellence, of course, and certainly neither of us perceived it as such then or subsequently. Nor had we come up with any startling, new answers to a perceived problem. All we had done was to exercise our care and judgement, first in selecting an appropriate task and then in handling it in ways that were sensitive to our pupil's personal history.

If we had worries about the handling—and we certainly did—they were to do with the amount and kind of teacher intervention that had remained even after our decision to devolve greater responsibility for the project on to Mashud. Susan, benefiting from hindsight, became critical of her copious surface corrections of Mashud's early drafts, considering herself "lucky not to have put the poor lad off altogether. . . . Thinking about it now, it might easily have destroyed his confidence utterly." I was also concerned about our imposition of length limits on the piece of work. Though Mashud himself had said the original version was "too short," it had been Susan and myself who had first broached this idea, effectively preventing him from deciding for himself and setting up a discourse in which length was *our* concern rather than his.

Finally, because of the communication problems that existed between ourselves and Mashud, no real *explanation* had been given as to why his original piece ought to be rejigged. His subsequent redrafting suggested he had understood what Susan wanted him to do, but there had been no explicit assurance that his original version had not been "wrong" or that the changes he was being asked to make would not somehow render his work universally right.

Having said that, there was no doubt in either of our minds that clear gains had been made by Mashud in the course of the project and that, in some not always clearly definable ways, our change of pedagogical style had been partly instrumental in bringing these about.

What were those gains? And how had they come about? In order to answer these questions, it is necessary briefly to consider two others: What happened to the final draft of Mashud's autobiography? And how did this affect his subsequent writing?

As soon as Mashud's final draft had been completed, it was disseminated in a number of ways: first, it was typed up and a copy pinned to the classroom wall as part of a larger display of the class's autobiographical writings.

Second, it was included in a collection of the class's autobiographies, itself used as a reading resource for the class.

Third, Mashud's final handwritten draft, along with a typed copy, was placed in a folder of his work, on which, at the end of the following year, his English abilities would be assessed on a national basis.

Fourth, it happened that Mashud's Head of Year came into the class one day (as she often did, at our invitation), saw Mashud's autobiography, and asked him if she might read it out, along with one or two others, at a fourth-year assembly. Mashud was happy to agree to this and gained much kudos from the event when it happened.

Fifth, and finally, a copy of Mashud's autobiography was sent (along with copies of all the other pupils' autobiographies) to the school in the United States with whom we had been undertaking our writing exchange. Though there has been little room in this present essay to give anything like a full account of this macroproject, its impact was an important factor in the development of Mashud's writing, which I would not want to appear to underestimate. Having an audience of unseen peers—students who would not necessarily share his English peers' preconceptions either about his background or about his capabilities—undoubtedly acted as a spur and an inspiration. He was keen to impress these unseen students, and his keenness certainly sharpened his appetite for seeking out, and acting upon, his teachers' expert advice. Without this particular variable, his progress may well have been slower or less striking than it was, though I believe it still would have been eminently observable.

I do not, finally, want to appear to make excessive claims for Mashud's development or, for that matter, on behalf of Susan and myself. Our approach to working with Mashud and our other bilingual pupils had not, as I have indicated, thrown up any "secret formula" or really required anything more than a shift of perspective and a corresponding heightened sensitivity towards Mashud as a person with a history. Nor were all the bilingual pupils in the class as receptive as Mashud to our tactics. Two outcomes, however, are indisputable: first, even with less receptive pupils, the same kinds of strategies proved very effective (I have plenty of less spectacular examples of pupils making significant gains in confidence and fluency through variations of these same approaches); second, Mashud's completion of the autobiography project represented something of a watershed in his writing development in English. We noticed in subsequent work a number of significant changes in his approach to his work, of which the following were probably the most striking:

1. Attempting the form, as well as the content, of every written assignment, instead of trying to "squeeze" it into an existing model (that is, the moral tale)
2. Allowing and inviting monolingual English peers to read early and subsequent drafts of his work, and accepting and working on their comments and "corrections" (previously, he had shown his work only to other Sylheti-speaking pupils in the class)
3. Substantially altering early drafts, both by reshaping and by making significant additions and removals

We felt that these changes were all vitally important in Mashud's development as an English-literate writer and that they had their roots in what had happened in the autobiography project, both in the nature of the project itself and in our—and particularly Susan's—mediation of it.

Having some knowledge of Mashud's previous language work in the school, where the emphasis had been on grammar, vocabulary, handwriting, and spelling, we had adopted an approach which saw our task as initiating Mashud into certain discursive practices, some of which would be less familiar to him than others. We helped him look at projects in terms of whole discourses and utterances rather than of discrete collections of aspects and selected appropriate pedagogical techniques of discussion, suggestion, and encouragement to experimentation. We believe that the final draft of Mashud's "My Life Story" offers sufficient proof that the ingredients of our admittedly ad hoc pudding were good.

# 18

## DIFFERENT POSSIBILITIES: POETRY, COMMUNITY, AND LEARNING IN A LONDON CLASSROOM

### John Hardcastle

> You were not born, here
>     my child,
>         not here.
>
> You saw daylight
> among our islands;
> the sun was always there.
>
> John La Rose (Trinidad), "Not from Here"

> *In the English lesson a climate is needed where pupils can express their thoughts and feelings openly, and this means ensuring that the curriculum is such that all pupils within a multicultural classroom can relate to it and can feel that they have a contribution to make. Where this happens pupils write with commitment and this demands a more precise (and often more complex and subtle) use of language.*
>
> J. Goody

> *Simply speaking, the disadvantage of the divergent speaker, Black or White, comes from linguistic discrimination. Instruction based on rejection of linguistic difference is the core of the problem.*
>
> Ken Goodman

> *The oral tradition . . . demands not only the grist, but the audience to complete the community; the noise and the sounds that the maker makes are returned to him. Hence we have the creation of a continuum where meaning truly resides.*
>
> E. Brathwaite

An avenue of tall London plane trees divides the front of the school from the park opposite. Beyond this rise three concrete towers marking the beginning of a public housing complex. At the rear of the school the suburban railway arcs through East London towards the city's commercial centre. The spaces beneath railway arches are leased to a Maltese who owns a car bodywork and paint repair business. Most of the mechanics and paint sprayers are black. Some of them are former students. The small factory opposite the arches employs Asian and Turkish women making garments.

Driving reggae thuds from parked cars. Power tools whine. The air is laden with fine dust blasted from sanding disks, diesel fumes, burning rubber, and the insipid ripe-pear scent of acetate from the paint shop.

Andrew and Kenneth were fourth-year students. There were twenty-five boys in their class, though not all of them attended school regularly. They entered the all-boys comprehensive school at age eleven: now, fourteen, rising fifteen, they knew each other well. This was a mixed-ability class, among whom there were a fair number of inexperienced readers and writers. It was an ethnically mixed group, with students coming from a variety of backgrounds, reflecting the diversity of the neighbourhood. The majority of boys came from Afro-Caribbean families, although they themselves were born in London. The majority of their parents came from the eastern Caribbean: St. Lucia, Dominica, Grenada, Antigua, Montserrat, Trinidad, and Guyana. Elsewhere in London it is more usual to find families from Jamaican backgrounds. Also there were students from Asian and Cypriot families, as well as from the white working class long resident in London.

Andrew was a quiet boy. His rather slow, painstaking approach occasionally made him a target for classmates' teasing. Yet he was popular and made friends easily. He worked with anxious concentration, well aware that he would make mistakes. He would check frequently to make sure that he had understood the task in hand, and usually, if there was uncertainty, he would ask the teacher for clarification; otherwise, he would seek help from a classmate. Kenneth sometimes offered spurious advice before giving genuine help. Such teasing was not malicious, but no doubt Andrew resented it. Occasionally, he would flash back angrily at Kenneth in a way that took us all by surprise! His family was from Guyana, and like Kenneth's (from Antigua), they maintained strong links with "back home."

Outside school Kenneth and Andrew were unlikely to visit clubs or to go to parties. Andrew told me that he spent most weekends at home with his mother and his sister. He liked to watch sports on TV. Kenneth's social life was centred around his church. Early in the mornings, before registration, the two boys would argue over cricket scores and batting averages. Like most of their friends, they collected records, made tapes, and built hi-fi systems. No doubt they had other interests besides. A powerful emergent black London youth culture was available to them, and with it, possible allegiances and identities, but Kenneth and Andrew kept closer contact with the lives of an older generation, drawing upon their values and meanings. In significant ways, they were in touch with ways of life more closely associated with rural Guyana and Antigua than urban London Caribbean culture.

Kenneth had a repertoire of stories and anecdotes from Antigua, and he had the confidence and skill to tell traditional folktales to the whole class when invited to do so. Like his brothers Walter and Philip, who also attended the school, he was respected by his peers, and he was at ease, though reserved, with his teachers. He had a reputation for quick-fire wit and a passion for argument and debate.

Now, Andrew had little of Kenneth's confidence and did not share his status; nevertheless, they had a good deal in common, and they were friends—except, that is, for the teasing. Whereas Kenneth sometimes shifted into Creole to emphasise a point or to dismiss an opponent in an argument ("Move yo' back foot!" was a favourite expression), Andrew was less likely to do so. His speech most of the time remained closer to a white London vernacular. There were hints that parents held highly ambivalent attitudes towards Creole, but this was never made explicit.

These boys were at the start of a two-year examination course. The following year they were to present their course work folders (assessment portfolios) with ten completed assignments. The English Department belonged to a consortium of local schools which had devised its own syllabus within a framework set down by the London Regional Examination Board. English teachers retained a large measure of control, both over the design of units of work and over the assessment process. Local teacher representatives were elected to a panel, where specific issues were discussed at length. It remains to be seen how much teacher autonomy will survive the introduction of a National Curriculum, where specified attainment targets and levels, tied to programmes of study, will be on the statute books. We took an integrative approach to reading, writing, speaking, and listening, and Language and Literature were combined in a unitary fashion which cut across traditional separations. Units of work were planned as a common enterprise within which students, of all abilities and from different starting points, could find access and progress according to their interests and capacities. For assessment purposes, differentiation occurred by outcome.

English was taught in two extended blocks of time (eighty-five minutes in each block—half of a morning and a whole afternoon per week). English teachers found that this allowed them space to establish routines of working in which students could find continuity and enjoy a substantial degree of control over the choice and pace of their work.

In classrooms where there were inexperienced readers, we were constantly reminded that there was a shortage of appropriate reading materials. We recognised an urgent need to provide texts, which engaged students' real interests, which could be read rapidly for pleasure, and which helped to build their confidence.

We also realised that new settings for learning were potentially as important as new materials. On one occasion when the class visited a community bookship which specialised in African and Caribbean literature (our intention was to replenish our dwindling class book box), Tony, a fourteen-year-old whose family came from Jamaica and who was at the earliest stages of acquiring literacy, came along. Not surprisingly, he was ill at ease, facing densely packed shelves of poetry books. Then John La Rose, the bookshop owner, and a Trinidadian poet and publisher, took down an anthology and began to read softly from Edward Brathwaite's *Arrivants Trilogy, Wings of a Dove* (1967):

> Brother Man the Rasta
> man, beard full of lichens
> brain full of lice
> watched the mice
> come up through the floor —
> boards of his down —
> town, shanty-town kitchen,
> and smiled . . .

Back in school Tony memorised sections of the poem, and at a later stage he began to improvise his own version, which a teacher transcribed for him.

This episode was intriguing, suggesting as it did the importance of social and cultural settings for literacy. It would be an exaggeration to claim that a history of reading failure was reversed, but surely it moved Tony forward.

It was not that Tony was particularly interested in the Rastafarian movement. Rather, it was something to do with a curious tension or paradox. The bookshop was part of the black community which it served, yet Tony, up to that point, was unaware of its existence. The owner, like Tony, was black. Differences of education, class, and age separated them, but there were points of contact. Perhaps John La Rose had guessed that Tony was an inexperienced reader; perhaps he assumed that he would read well and that his evident unease stemmed from an unfamiliarity with poetry. Whatever he had in mind, his approach was sensitively judged. Tony was left to decide whether to take up or to decline the invitation. The initiative remained with him.

Such moments are rare. They throw much needed light on the social practices of literacy, which have at their core issues of culture, community, and power.

"Domino" is a poem by Rose Porter, a black woman from South London. She was around the same age as Kenneth and Andrew (fifteen) when she wrote it. It was published in an anthology produced by Black Ink Collective, whose aim is to provide young black writers with the opportunity of seeing their work in print. The experiences Rose Porter writes about (here it is a domino game set in a youth club) were immediately recognisable for Andrew, Kenneth, and their classmates. Her main characters—Ellis, Brown, Porter, and Findley—were familiar figures, though not, perhaps, ones with whom Kenneth and Andrew wholly identified.

### Domino

*Mi enta de club, it waz quiet;*
*Mi start fe mek me way up de stears*
*Mi ear noize*
*Ellis, Brown, Porter an Findley play domino.*

*Ellis atel Findley fi rub it up*
*Findley atel im fe shut up;*
*Brown atel Findley fe play*
*Porter noh sae noting.*

*Brown warn look cool,*
*So im tun up im jacket collar:*
*Ellis tink im dread*
*Findley look dead*
*Porter shave im'ed*
*Im tun barl'ed.*

*Dem clap dun de domino*
*Ana mek up noize*
*Dem arsk one anader if dem play yet,*
*iz pass dem pass*

*Dema run up dem mout'*
*Ana shout*
*Six up six up*
*One a dem shout*

*De game dun now.*
*Soh Ellis dread, Brown cool*
*Findley dead an' Porter barl'ed*
*Dem arl garn 'ome, garn 'ome to bed.*

(Rose Porter, 1978)

"Domino" was only one of a number of poems made available to the class for a sequence of work on poetry. There was a broad range of styles, themes, and levels of difficulty. And poems were deliberately chosen from many ethnic and cultural sources. The students were asked to make a selection of poems which they found interesting and then to go on to write a short piece in response, saying briefly what their chosen poems were about and what in particular had caught their attention. Andrew chose "Domino," and he wrote the following:

### Domino

Domino is about a man walking into a club, he said it was all quiet, then he went up the stairs and heard noises. It was his frends

Brown, Porter finally they desided to play dominos. After Ellis told
them to shut up, him actully. Brown told them to play Porter didn't
see nothing. Brown wanted to look cool, so he turned up his
jacket collar; Ellis thought he was look "dread" because he
dressed up flashy. Dred means you look smart. They looked dead
Porter shave his head he turn balled head. They all clap down the
dominos, that ment they all lashed it down when the were about to
play and also made noise. They ask one another if they'er played
yet "I pass", said the man down they passed it down. They started
to gosip and shout "six up"! "six up"! one of them shout. The
game was finish now so Ellis was good, Brown cool, and Porter
had a dead hand so he started to barl'ed that ment cry out loud.
Then they all went home to bed.

At first glance it may appear that Andrew merely paraphrases the
poem. Closer inspection, however, reveals that he also interprets
"Domino," transposing the London Jamaican Creole into forms
closer to standard English. So, "Brown *warn* look cool/so *im turn*
up *im* jacket collar" becomes Brown *wanted* to look cool, *he turned*
up *his* jacket collar. Here Andrew pays attention to standard verb
tenses and personal pronouns, but elsewhere Creole forms persist.
For example, they remain in his use of unmarked verbs: "Porter
*shave* his head"; "they all *clap* down their dominos," and "the game
was *finish* now." In each of these instances, however, Andrew has
made some additional local changes, (*im* becomes *his*, *dun* becomes
*down*, and later *dun* becomes *finish*). This raises interesting questions about the number and the kinds of features which Andrew was
able to attend to at one time. There are one or two occasions when
he had evidently had difficulty recognising the Creole as it appeared
on the printed page. "Porter noh *sae* noting" is rendered "Porter
didn't *see* nothing," where "didn't *say* anything" seems closer to
Rose Porter's intentions. The point here, surely, is that Andrew was
meeting unfamiliar written forms of Creole speech. So, for example,
Andrew confused "barl'ed" (baldhead), which is consistent with the
earlier line, "Porter shave im 'ed," with "bawled" ("cried out loud").

These are specific difficulties and confusions which Andrew encountered as he worked to make the poem's meanings available to a
wider audience—wider, that is, than a London Jamaican Creole
speaking one. And it is this broad intention which moves him from
paraphrase towards interpretation. It is a highly selective business.
Some phrases are singled out for fuller explanation, for instance,
where he writes, "Ellis thought he was look dread because he
dressed up flashy. Dread means you look smart."

*Dread* is a highly charged religious and political concept laden
with significance, as Roger Hewitt (1982) has made clear by tracing
the changing meaning of the word through its passage from the
Rastafarians of Jamaica to white adolescent Creole users in London.
Weak and strong definitions of *dread*, however, need not detain us
here; what is most significant is that Andrew, at the moment when he

came to explain the meaning in the context of the poem, was faced with a number of alternatives about which he certainly knew more than his teacher. At such moments, Andrew was oriented towards different systems, each with its capacity to symbolise values and meanings, each making different claims on his allegiances and each shaping his identity. He knew a good deal also about contexts, where differences matter, and implicitly about ways in which language expresses different social realities, cultures, and histories.

At the point where the class was asked to write poems of their own, Andrew asked whether he could write a poem similar to "Domino" using London Creole. The outcome was "Record Shop in Birmingham," printed here in full.

### Record Shop in Birmingham
### (Skanking is a dance what Rasters do)

*Mi enta de recard shop, fi er som dub.*
*But dema play ol' time chune*
*Mi sight mi spar Glyn wid two recard in im han'.*
*Mi ask im fi coils, but im sae im brok.*
*So finally me atel de man fi play som lovers rock.*
*Den I start te chat to mi spar im sae imer gwan dong Ferrick*
*Tonight fe' ear som dub.*
*Finally de Rasterman a play some heavy dub*
*Den mi start fe skanck*
*Laiter cole sweat a run dong mi faice.*
*Sooner or laiter mi sight a man who enta di shop*
*I'm sight mi skanck den im faice tun bad*
*De Rasterman atel mi dat im is de dreadest skanker*
*But I sae im waz, because Iz de dreadest skanker*
*Arong tong. dem sae iner de shap dat me*
*An im mus 'ave a competition to sight*
*Who's de dreadest skanker.*
*De Raster DJ a stap de music an atel oonoo fe digs*
*Mi atel im fe hush im noize. Everybody a enta*
*De shap now, even de likkle yout man fe buy Im record*
*Garg is I and I spa who mi a talk bout everytime*
*Everyone atel de DJ dem wan' see a skanking competition*
*So dem a mek space fe mi an de man*
*The DJ turn up de music*
*Den de record a dun*
*Everybody sae Iz de 'ardes' skanker arong tong*
*Mi a lef dem dry wid no money*
*So mi gwan home to sight tele wid Birmingham*
*and Tottenham a play football.*

Encouraging Andrew to write "Record Shop in Birmingham" did not represent a systematic attempt to replace approaches to writing where standard English was the target. Andrew's poem was written within a sequence of lessons where students were presented with a wide range of reading materials and possible writing assignments. I do not wish to mislead the reader into thinking that the English curriculum had abandoned its responsibility towards Standard English. So much has been written about the place of nonstandard language in educational settings that it becomes difficult to describe a particular instance of what actually went on in the classroom without implying that this constituted an entire programme of study. My argument is that room can be made for students to follow their interests (in this instance, writing in Creole) within the larger sequences of work. As will soon become clear, opportunities for looking at standard and nonstandard forms were to arise in ways that were unforseen.

Andrew was pleased with his poem. Shortly after he completed it, he showed it to Junior, who straight away began to read it aloud with great verve. As he read it, however, he began to make minor changes. The interaction between the two boys was taped. There were points where Junior paused to clarify the meaning:

JUNIOR: Wha' dis? What's this word?
ANDREW: *fe buy Im record . . . ?*
JUNIOR: What *is* this? "Garg?"
ANDREW: Eh? "George" . . . you know . . .
JUNIOR: Oh! Yeah! "*Gaarg*" (*laughs*).
   (*And then, suddenly looping back to a line near the beginning*)
JUNIOR: 'A check!'
ANDREW: Wha'?
JUNIOR: *A check out* Ferrick. Not, "*gwan dong Ferrick!*" 'cos most
   people, you know, aint gonna talk like that . . .
   (*Andrew blinks*)

After a moment's reflection Andrew took up Junior's suggestion and incorporated it into a subsequent draft. He recognised, after all, that Junior's knowledge of London Jamaican Creole (and, possibly, record shops) was more assured than his own. Importantly though, Junior had reminded him of a possible reader: one, that is, who may have preferred "check out" (the current idiom) to "gwan dong" ("go on down"). It was a fine distinction to an outsider, perhaps, but for these two black students, working together with seriousness and concentration, it was one that was worthwhile making.

We need to consider, before moving on, what kind of poem it was that Andrew had written. Perhaps we might see this more clearly by looking first at a poem by Christopher Laird, a Trinidadian writer. At the start of "12.30 Is Life," a youth steps from the darkness of a mid-day film show into the dazzling sunlight, heat, and traffic of Port of Spain. His world is transformed.

> *When I come out of a 12.30 brother,*
> *the whole world is a main street in China*
> *and I is Wang Yu.*

*When you see I come out of that 12.30 baby,*
*I feel like dying*
*in a warm way, . . .*

*. . . As I cross the road, the lights hit amber,*
*is a signal to get me and I leap into action,*
*with mih peepers on*
*and mih running shoes*
*running*
*I movin' smooth*
*looking for a meaningful death*

*12.30 ain't cinema*
*is life!*

(Christopher Laird, from *Kairi*)

The impulse to act out fantasies after a film show is probably universal. The youth becomes Wang Yu, and the whole world is a main street in China. No doubt, at one level, Christopher Laird is asking questions about the function of Kung Fu movies in Trinidadian youth culture, but my interest here lies in the way that he is able to make use of recognisable elements from the tall tale as it has been developed within Caribbean oral traditions of storytelling; the Creole flavour of the poem's voice; the "robber-talk" (extravagant language); the boasting; and the deadpan lies.

"Record Shop in Birmingham" includes similar generic elements. Both poems turn on claims to exceptional prowess: outdistancing the midday traffic at a street crossing in Port of Spain or out-skanking a Rasterman in a record shop in Birmingham. The outcome of the skanking contest, of course, is never in doubt, and the storyteller's final boast is that he wins all the money: "mi a lef dem dry wid no money."

By drawing on the tall-tale genre, Andrew showed that larger features of Caribbean language than sentence grammar were available to him as a resource for writing. Over and above this, I want to suggest that there are important links between this kind of storytelling and the ordinary language that communities use to talk about the incidents of daily life and to generally make sense of things. This shared, living resource is part of what binds them together as a community and gives them their identity. But inner-city classrooms are places where communities intersect and sometimes collide, and this in relation to broader patterns in the wider society. A climate is needed where tensions and confusions can be recognised and examined in ways that do not threaten or disable.

Andrew and Junior finally arrived at a version of "Record Shop in Birmingham" with which they were tolerably satisfied. Along the way they managed to involve Peter, whose parents, like Junior's, were from Jamaica. With Andrew's piece on "Domino" still fresh in mind, I discussed with the three of them possible difficulties which a reader, coming from outside the black community, might encounter. Following on from this, Andrew decided to attempt to write a "standard" version as an experiment.

### Record Shop in Birmingham

I went to the record shop in Birmingham to hear some music but it was a bit out of date. then I saw my frend Glyn. he had a couple records in hand so I asked him for some money and he said that he never had none. So finally I told the shop owner if he has any lovers rock. Then he played some. Then I started to chat to my frend. He says that he's going down Ferrich tonight, Ferrich is a club for rosters. they usually go their every weekend to have a good time. Finally the roster started, to play records with a lot of bass in it. Then I started to skanck, skanck is a dance what rosters do. Later on all sweat was pouring down my face. Then suddenly a roster man walked in and started skank. When he saw me skancking his face changed completely. He got a little jealus of me, so afterwards everone came up to me and said that he is the best skanker round town, then "I said he was," because I'm the best round town now. So everyone gathered around and said wha want a skancking compition between me and my apownent so they made space. I gave everybody a pound bet that I was going to win. Then the D.J. turned the music up and I started to dance. After the record finished I was sweating then they all said I was the best skanker round town. I won 18 pound off them and left them. So finally I went to watch tele with Birmingham V. Tottenham.

Andrew and Junior worked hard on their experimental "standard version." It was not an easy task. At one stage, Kenneth was invited to join them, and together they hit upon the idea of getting him to read their current draft aloud.

KENNETH: I went into a record shop in Birmingham to hear some music . . . but the records they had were out of date. . . . I looked round, then I saw my friend Glyn. He had a couple of records in his hand so I asked him for some money. He said he never had none—ah that sound wrong . . .

TEACHER: . . . you were just going to say something, go on finish.

KENNETH: So finally . . .

TEACHER: Just a second . . . that's where you left off . . . right, so I asked him for some money. . . .

KENNETH: So I asked him for some money . . . mm . . . an he said that he never had none. Nah, that don't really go in proper English does it? What do you think Junior?

JUNIOR: I never thought there was nothing wrong with it—and he said he never had none!

KENNETH: But it doesn't say that, it says—I asked him for some money and he—and he said that he never had none. Sorry, look, wait . . . couple of records so I asked him for some money and he said that he never had none so . . . oh yeah! that's right . . . so finally the shop . . . so finally the shop owner. . . .

TEACHER: Look! where did it go wrong . . . did it go . . . you stopped for something there . . . something you wanted to change . . . now what's the bit you wanted to change . . .?

KENNETH: . . . want to change and I've overlooked it . . .

TEACHER: . . . er

KENNETH: I know where I . . . I told the shopkeeper if he had any lovers rock . . . (alright) then he started to play some. . . . Then I started to chat to my friend . . .

Kenneth was aware, at an intuitive level, that "he said he never had none" was not standard English, but then, he could not pin down exactly where it went wrong. He asked Junior's advice, but he was unable to help: "I never thought there was nothing wrong with it." The teacher had a clear responsibility to ensure that the students had access to standard English, but at the same time he was aware that jumping in too quickly might be less likely to produce the desired outcome. The students knew that they could ask for the standard form, but on this occasion they preferred to work it out for themselves. The teacher therefore attempted to hold the focus without taking away the initiative. Now it was Peter's turn to interject.

PETER: Lover's Rock!—that shouldn't be there!

TEACHER: What shouldn't be there? What shouldn't be where?

PETER: Lover's Rock!

KENNETH: Why?

PETER: Music . . . music you got any music?

KENNETH: Nah! There must be something else, man!

JUNIOR: Rock! Steppers!—Nah! NO!

ANDREW: Lover's rock then, innit! That's what they call the music!

PETER: Yeah, but I mean, we puttin' it in English innit!

JUNIOR: GRIND music!

KENNETH: Pop!

ANDREW: That's what it is though, innit? (*Lover's Rock*) Ain't got no other possibilities. . . .

Kenneth, Andrew, and Junior had been concentrating on grammar. Now Peter shifted the focus. He wanted to substitute "music" for "lover's rock" (a form of reggae). Not unreasonably, in the context of rewriting for a "general" reader, he saw their task as an attempt to eliminate all the Caribbean cultural references and to find their equivalents from within white mainstream culture. Junior suggested "rock" as an alternative but then undercut his own suggestion by offering another style of reggae, "steppers." Andrew insisted that "lover's rock" was fine. However, Peter insisted: "but, I mean, we puttin' it in ENGLISH innit!" Junior (teasing Peter) made an outrageous suggestion: "Grind music," and immediately Kenneth countered this with a move in the opposite direction: "pop" (bland, mainstream music). But Andrew stood firm, and it was agreed that "lover's rock" should remain. As Andrew put it: "Ain't got no other possibilities!"

Now Junior suggested that Kenneth should read the piece again from the beginning, using a posh (white, middle-class) voice.

KENNETH: . . . yeah. That's true you know. This is the only way. If I started to read . . . I went to the record shop . . .
TEACHER: Read it like that . . . just like that . . . try reading it posh . . . and see where it goes wrong . . .
KENNETH: Alright. I went into a record shop in Birmingham to hear some music, but it was a bit out of date. Then I saw my friend Glyn. He had a couple of records in his hand, so I asked him for some money. He said he had none so I asked him if he had any lovers' rock. Then he played some. I started to chat to my friend. He said that he was going (*begins to laugh*) down Ferrick's tonight. Ferrick's is a club for Rastas. They usually go there (*collapses*) . . . I can't take no more . . . no man!

By assuming an exaggerated voice, Kenneth was able to produce a hyperstandard negative: "he said he had none," but the mismatch between the standard-speaking first-person narrator and the voice which this kind of story demanded was too extreme. The whole group simply burst out laughing. John, a white student, had joined them by this stage, and Andrew asked him for his opinion:

JOHN: . . . had none.
KENNETH: 'im na 'ave none!
TEACHER: Is it never had none or . . .
JOHN: . . . didn't have any, it should be . . .
JUNIOR: Didn't have any!
KENNETH: 'Im dinna 'ave any coils on 'im.
JUNIOR: Didn't have any . . .
PETER: Didn't have any . . .
JUNIOR: Didn't have none . . .
PETER: Didn't have any . . .
JUNIOR: Didn't have any money at all.

Surprisingly, perhaps, Kenneth and Junior both reverted to non-standard variants. This, however, should not be taken to indicate confusion or uncertainty. Earlier they both had difficulty with An-drew's original sentence, but now they were using a strategy for learning (voicing alternative forms) and playing verbal games by attempting to wrong-foot the others. It is worth noting, too, that the language the students use to discuss the points at issue is their own nonstandard variety, which is closer to London working-class speech than to Creole, although some Creole features are evident. Given that the languages spoken at home vary (sometimes quite markedly), there seemed to be considerable convergence in the classroom.

The group continued working together for a while, reading and discussing the versions of "Record Shop in Birmingham." Kenneth took a prominent role, though Andrew was determined not to be marginalised. He was pleased to see his work taken seriously by his peers. Early on, he had found his point of entry. He had been able to follow through his interest in a way which had involved him collaboratively with his classmates, and together they had moved the project forward. He had seen that he had a definite contribution to make and, consequently, he had begun to be involved with a deepening commitment. The old hesitancy began to be dispelled.

I have attempted to describe something of the life of a Northeast London Classroom. Andrew, Kenneth, Junior, and Peter, over the years, spent a good deal of time in one another's company. They lived in the same neighbourhood, and, as children of Afro-Caribbean families now residing in Britain, they shared similar lives and prospects. As members of the black community, they faced the same material hardships, housing shortages, limited employment opportunities, and racism. But there were differences, too. Their families traced their own particular histories within the wider pattern—each with its own resources, commitments, and aspirations. Over time relationships grew: friendships, rivalries, conflicts, and partnerships within and beyond the classroom. And shared history of experiences accumulated, providing common points of reference for a joint enterprise.

Within this classroom culture, learning took place. Over time a discourse was being built, not by Andrew alone, though he made his own distinctive contribution, but by the group as a whole. The students actively made their own meanings and took their own understandings (each slightly different), according to their initial starting points. The kind of classroom discourse to which I am referring here extends across talking, reading, and writing. It is one which is constructed by students, along with their teachers, within tacit and tangible social relationships. Such a view of discourse as a component of classroom culture aims to connect language with social and historical realities.

This group of students was taking early steps towards an exploration of key questions about language and literature. They were looking at the differences between spoken and written forms; between nonstandard and standard; and between Creole and other language varieties. They were learning, too, about alternative traditions of literature, which have a legitimate place in English classrooms alongside familiar texts: poetry that students might read and write for themselves and works produced by writers from the Caribbean and from the London black community.

Yet, for their English teacher, a tension existed: on the one hand, learning must be organised, and knowledge about language must be presented in a systematic and coherent fashion; on the other hand, students are most likely to learn language effectively when it serves their own real purposes and felt needs. We could not have identified in advance which bits of linguistic knowledge Andrew would need. As it was, the learning that occurred was generated not just through his engagement with cool print but also through his active involvement in heated conversation with his classmates. It was from the busy traffic of classroom interaction that Andrew began to see different possibilities.

# empowering teachers
# and learners

# 19

## ORGANIZING FOR EMPOWERMENT: CLARIFYING A FOCUS TO PLAN PROGRAMS FOR TROUBLED LEARNERS

**Susan W. Haynes**

### THREE TROUBLED LEARNERS

Christopher sat beside me at my dining room (transformed to school room) table. We drew together, and he chatted exuberantly about his picture. His creatures showed unusual form, line, and imagination (Figure 19-1, p. 266). When he completed the drawing, I calmly suggested that he might want to write about it. Trying to comply, he began a tentative process of representing the sounds he heard in the words he wished to write. He worried a lot about how to form the letters and spell the words "correctly." "You tell me if it's not right," he said. "I don't want to make a mistake."

When we read together on the couch in the adjoining living room for the second part of this initial tutoring session, I invited Christopher to read from a selection of predictable books. As he attempted to process the texts, he often rendered linguistic nonsense like, "One upon time stairs was. . . ." It was obvious to me from talking with Christopher, however, that his oral language was extremely sophisticated for a six-year-old.

Christopher had come to me for literacy tutoring through the recommendation of his transitional first-grade teacher. Both in kindergarten and the first half of first grade, Christopher resisted engaging with traditional reading readiness skills. He seemed unsure about letter sounds and letter construction and already hated the decoding process required in his linguistics reading program. His teacher recognized his bright, creative mind, and she was frankly puzzled about his slow progress.

Elizabeth, a woman in her late forties, enrolled in my adult basic education class to seek help for her self-defined severe reading

265

**Figure 19-1** *Chris's Creatures*

problem, which interfered with a needed job change. She was
uncomfortable with all kinds of reading, both narrative and informational. She had a passionate interest, however, in books about
minority cultures (at that time, Indian and Amish) and slowly but
persistently processed these, often falling asleep after reading just a
few pages.

During our first session, we read aloud together from an Indian
myth, "Gluskabe Tames the Wind" (O'Neill, 1983). Elizabeth read
cautiously and was upset when she couldn't figure out a word. All of
her miscues, however, kept the meaning, and her sense of the story
was marvelous.

As we discussed the history of her reading instruction, it became
clear to me that Elizabeth's intimidation with print stemmed from
years of placement in remedial groups in which the students were not
expected to make much progress. As an adult reader, she read
painfully slowly, repeating every word to herself, stopping when she
couldn't get a word in order to attempt to sound it out.

Richard looked belligerent when I asked my senior English class of three boys (special education track) to choose a class theme.

"What are you interested in learning about?" I inquired.

"I ain't interested in nothing," retorted Richard, a large seventeen-year-old who worked afternoons repairing cars through the school's co-op program. His posture told me, "And you can't make me!"

Richard was particularly negative about writing. His PET (Pupil Evaluation Team) report listed writing as his "major handicap." When I asked the students to write about their research and the literature we read together, he wrote tersely, often in a huff.

## THE GOAL: LEARNING EMPOWERMENT

As a whole language practitioner, my first and all succeeding phases in program planning are grounded in a goal of learning empowerment, the growing orientation of the learner toward self-direction, followed by self-determination in relation to chosen personal purpose. Maxine Greene, a professor of philosophy and education at Teachers College, Columbia University, warned in a recent *Language Arts* article:

> There is a growing tendency to describe children as "resources" rather than persons, with all the implications of "use value" and even "exchange value." Proposed improvements in their education are argued in the name of the nation's economic competitiveness, not for the sake of the growth of persons viewed as centers of choice, agents of their own becoming (Greene, 1988).

While I noted the literacy skills and strategies my students learned as they became more meaningfully involved in literacy processes, I particularly valued signs of the students' self-initiative.

I am convinced that, before troubled students can redirect an orientation toward personal empowerment, they must first come to terms with the obstacles that have intimidated and disabled them. The teacher, through valuing the students' intrinsic strengths, can act as a catalyst to encourage students to become self-affirming.

> Buber, an existential philosopher, described the ideal teacher-student relationship in this manner: Genuine dialogue, like genuine fulfillment of relation, involves acceptance of otherness. Influencing the other is not injecting one's own "rightness" into him but is using one's influence to let what is recognized as right, just, and true take seed and grow in the substance of the other and in the form suited to his individuation (Morris, 1966).

Any interaction on the part of the teacher which diminishes rather than enhances the valuing of intrinsic strengths could undermine in the long run support for student empowerment.

Troubled learners develop an orientation of avoiding learning tasks due to past failure and an ongoing sense of deficiency. Even when they assert strong goals (like Elizabeth's intense interest in her reading), they cannot seem to break through a pervasive learning intimidation. By recognizing a student's need for a healthy reorientation toward learning (a revaluing), I can begin to plan activities within a personally affirmative context in which I nudge the learner toward risk taking.

## ORGANIZING FOR EMPOWERMENT

PHASE 1—DISPELLING THE OBSTACLES TO LEARNING

**Christopher.** Christopher is a highly creative child who had become frozen in literacy development. His kindergarten and first-grade literacy program focused on skills in isolation within a right/wrong paradigm. Christopher's sense of failure with these tasks had stymied his personal initiative in generating his own understanding of the principles of written language. I identified specific obstacles to his literacy growth in three areas:

Concern over perfection in letter formation
Concern over perfection in spelling
A mistaken view of reading as word identification unrelated to
    language sense and meaning

These three obstacles had become a barrier to personally purposeful literacy growth. Until he dispelled these adopted rigid standards, Christopher would not be able to initiate his own active literacy exploration based on his competent, if not gifted, strengths in language and in creative thinking.

Over the next few sessions, I nudged Christopher toward self-exploration. During one drawing/writing period, I shared a scary story my son had written in first grade, in which he had transformed his letters into monstrous forms compatible with his theme. This model seemed to encourage Christopher's own experimentation with letter forms, releasing his fear of meeting specific standards (see Figure 19-2). I also praised Christopher's competent sound/symbol knowledge evident in his invented spellings. I conveyed genuine enthusiasm over his delightful drawings.

For our reading sessions, I gathered a collection of predictable books to support his excellent language sense. I encouraged Christopher to retell the stories, after I read them to him, relying on his own reconstruction without confronting the print. I also engaged Christopher in Cloze activities, periodically pointing out a predictable word for him to "guess" as I read the story.

Breakthroughs came quickly in reading; more slowly in writing. Christopher loved the fluency captured by retelling stories and filling in predictable words. He keyed in easily to predictable language structures, tapping his expressive language strengths and excellent

**269**

*Organizing for
Empowerment:
Clarifying a Focus to
Plan Programs for
Troubled Learners*

**Figure 19-2**   *Chris's Scary Story*

Ghosts and goblins are a pest. But all kinds of monsters can be a pest.

sense of story. He delighted in reading without confronting the print within his old right/wrong paradigm. When ready on his own terms, Christopher began to integrate print information in the early predictable books, this time using all three cueing systems (semantic, syntactic, and grapho-phonic), self-correcting when necessary within consistent self-monitoring for sense.

When writing, Christopher's experimentation with letters helped somewhat to release his concern over "correct" form. He began to trust his own spelling to convey meaning but remained tentative about composing. At school his teacher began a writing program, and she observed that, while Christopher seemed eager to help other students figure out spelling, he rarely wrote himself.

Then a breakthrough occurred at school. The teacher assigned a project for Groundhog Day, consisting of writing the words a groundhog might say when it emerged from its hole. The children cut out and colored a groundhog figure and wrote their message in the bubble attached to its mouth. Christopher couldn't wait to share his project at our tutoring session. He had written

No mo wedr I wus lest gedin red to sedl dan (No more weather. I was just getting ready to settle down.)

"It's perfect," he said. "No mistakes. I did it all myself."
"Fantastic!" I said.
"Will you write that here on my paper?" he asked.
Unlike many of his school papers, this one contained no red marks. Uncritical support for self-exploration at school significantly fueled Christopher's risk taking.

**Elizabeth.** I organized my sessions with Elizabeth in the following manner. We began with a discussion of her independent reading. I had gathered a repertoire of books which I felt would personally interest her from which she could choose. The first set included: *North to Freedom* (Holm, 1965), *Mama's Bank Account* (Forbes, 1943), *Island of the Blue Dolphins* (O'Dell, 1960), and *A Day No Pigs Would Die* (Peck, 1972). I felt that these books would nourish Elizabeth's intense interest in the elements of simpler patterns of living. It became clear from our literature discussions that Elizabeth had rich sensitivity to key facets of literature and made many connections between her own experiences and ideas and those described and explored in the books. She lent me some favorite books from her own collection, and our conversations became collaborative, with delicious teasing over each other's predictions within books we had already read.

The second part of our sessions consisted of shared reading. At first I selected short stories from *Cricket* magazine, which related to Elizabeth's interest in Indian cultures and animals (I had recently recorded stories from a large personal collection of *Cricket* magazine under themes). We could complete the short stories in one session. I then suggested reading the marvelous read aloud *Stone Fox* (Gardiner, 1980). Whenever possible, we made dramatic readings from the dialogue, which encouraged Elizabeth's fluency in relation to her affinity for characterization. I noticed that she unconsciously made more miscues (all keeping semantic, syntactic integrity) when reading dialogue, releasing her strict attention to each word. I shared this observation with her, and Elizabeth began to recognize her growing abilities to process texts more easily and enjoyably.

As Elizabeth loosened up, she seemed to enjoy our shared reading more and more. A key breakthrough came in a session in which we were reading *Stone Fox*. She came upon the word *forged* in the context of a dogsled moving rapidly ahead. At first puzzled, she thought a minute and then said, "Oh well, it means 'raced' anyway," and blithely continued. At home she began devouring books. When I asked her about her silent reading progress, she reflected that she no longer seemed to need to repeat every word to herself. She rarely fell asleep while reading, except when the print size and quality of paper

**271**

*Organizing for*
*Empowerment:*
*Clarifying a Focus to*
*Plan Programs for*
*Troubled Learners*

made processing particularly tedious. Even under these circumstances, she remained persistent with self-selected books like *Jane Eyre* (Bronte, 1848), and *To Kill a Mockingbird* (Lee, 1960). Her animation during our literature discussion revealed an increasingly sturdy self-concept as an empowered reader.

**Richard.** Richard had felt like a failure in school for so many years that he had developed numerous strategies for avoiding learning activities as a safeguard against negative feedback. I understood and respected his defense system while concurrently nudging him toward risk taking within personally relevant reading and writing activities.

Within our class theme of "oceans," I planned activities like shared reading of relevant novels and articles, individual research on sea creatures, and writing in a response journal about the ideas we explored. Richard often rejected the day's agenda and suggested alternative activities, often word games like "Hangman." If we played games one class period, he would acknowledge my agenda the following class period.

As Richard and I bargained about each class's plan, we walked a thin line together. Although he was desperate to avoid risk-taking activities, he valued my respect for him and knew he couldn't push too far. Although I was eager to introduce literacy activities which would encourage his reorientation toward reading and writing in the context of personal purpose, I wouldn't challenge Richard's carefully constructed safety net until he showed signs of no longer needing it.

Trust among us evolved slowly in this class, as I respected the bargaining process and was increasingly able to confirm the students' development of strategic skills. Using computer word processing in writing also enticed these students into further risk taking.

By the second semester, our class was becoming more collaborative in developing curriculum. First semester, I offered the theme, "Oceans," because it related to shared circumstances: we all live on Mt. Desert Island, Maine. I gathered, however, that one theme was as good as any other, according to the students, if any had to be chosen at all. When I asked the class during the second semester what they might be interested in studying, one student suggested "food" (the class met the period just before lunch, and the boys were always hungry).

We launched a unit on survival food. We watched documentaries like *Will the World Survive?* and *Nomads of the Rain Forest* and films like *Never Cry Wolf* (1983). We shared the reading of Steven Callahan's *Adrift* (1987). The students really took over, however, during a once-a-week cooking class when, using an electric frying pan and toaster oven and a budget of fifty dollars, they planned, cooked, and served a lunch. "After all," one student said, "after this year, we will be out on our own; that's survival."

The nature of negotiation in our class during the second semester changed as well. If Richard did not want to participate in the group activity for the day, he would initiate another literacy activity which

> **Figure 19-3**  *Richard's Story, "Just a Story"*
>
> ```
>                  JUST A STOR
>
> THE ONLY THING THAT I LIKE ABOUT THE SCHOOL IS THAT I GET TO
> LEAVE AT 11:00.THERE IS ONE MORE THING A DO LIKE,THAT IS ENGLISH
> CLASS.THE SCHOOL IS SO DIFFERNT.WE HAVE TO DO WHAT EVERY BODYN
> TELLS USE TO DO .PEOPLE I HAVE NEVER TALK TO BEFORE TELL ME THAT
> I BETTER GO TO MY CLASS.THEY SHOULD GO AFTER THE PEOPLE THAT DO
> THAT STUFF.I HAVE BEEN I ALOT OF TROUBLE IN THIS SCHOOL.THE ONLY
> THING ABOUT IT IS THAT PEOPLE NEVER FORGET.THE TEACHERS LOOK AT
> ME LIKE I SHOULD BE SOME WHERE ,NOT HERE.I GET SICK OF PEOPLE
> SAYING STUFF ABOUT ME AND LOOKING AT ME FUNNY.THE TEACHER IS ONE
> OF THE THINGS THAT MAKE THING HARD FOR ME .THEY ALLWAYS NO THE
> BEST.THEY ARE NEVER WRONG.THE PRISCIPLE NEVER BELEAVES THE
> STUDENT THEY ALLWAYS SAY THAT THEY BELEAVE THE TEACHER.I WOULD
> SOME DAY LIKE TO BE IN THE HIGH SEAT FOR ONE DAY.LET THE TEACHERS
> BE THE STUDENT.THEY WILL THINK ABOUT WHAT I HAVE SAID.
> ```

affirmed his growing risk taking, often writing on the computer. On one of these occasions, Richard claimed that this story was not about himself, and he risked considerable exposure by allowing me to read it to the class (Figure 19-3). His text, "Just a Story," is evidence, I think, for the whole language practitioner's belief that every student has a story to tell and a way to tell it. However tentative Richard's self-concept as a learner remained, he had successfully tapped his voice.

## ORGANIZING FOR WHOLE LANGUAGE

### PHASES OF EMPOWERMENT

As I plan programs for my troubled students, I keep in mind evolving phases of empowerment. Initially, I assess the obstacles to growth that have disempowered the learner. In recognition of these obstacles, I create a program which honors and supports the learner's intrinsic strengths. Don Holdaway describes the relationship between teacher and student that encourages empowerment as a client-teacher relationship. In his book *The Foundations of Literacy* (1979), Holdaway draws an analogy between the client-therapist and client-teacher relationship.

> In a professional setting the client does in a sense put himself into the hands of the professional—he delimits his own rights in a proper act of trust and in the expectation that the special knowledge of the expert will be used always to his, the client's benefit. . . .

Holdaway goes on to say,

> Difficulties in learning to become literate are as important and as personal to the child as the difficulties which drive us as adults to

professionals of every kind. The child who has trouble in learning phonics or gets similar words confused, or is so fatigued with conscious trying that he can't make sense of what he is doing has a personal and private problem equal in its importance for him to the symptoms of a neurotic phobia. He needs expert guidance and protection of a highly professional kind, and he needs to be able to make use of that guidance without fear and without a growing sense of guilt and despair (pp. 186, 187).

The whole language practitioner believes in the natural learning ability of every student when it is built upon a foundation of personal strength. Holdaway describes this belief and the supporting role of the teacher in this manner:

The first responsibility of any professional is to set those conditions under which the remarkable complexities of the human system restore healthy functioning autonomously. Literacy should be seen as a necessary part of self-actualizing and the most important responsibility of the professional towards child clients is to help them incorporate the challenge of becoming literate into their own self-improving system (p. 187).

My planning for learning empowerment thus begins with the initial recognition of the obstacles to growth which helps me organize activities to reorient the learner toward his or her self-improving system. As the learner begins to take personal risks, my planning focuses on organizing a learning environment which recognizes and supports the increasingly self-directed and finally self-determined orientation of my students.

Figure 19-4 (p. 274) represents my present thinking involving these phases of empowerment. Each phase includes four components: the teacher's role, the curriculum, a description of the learner, and the underlying philosophy which informs my planning, organization, and evaluation.

## LEARNERS TAKE CONTROL

Christopher activated his self-improving system as he took creative initiative in writing tasks and brought to bear his considerable language strengths in reading. Elizabeth overcame her self-concept as a disabled reader as she refocused on meaning and delighted in an opportunity to develop and discuss the ideas explored in literature. Richard redirected energy from avoiding learning tasks to choosing among literacy tasks, seeking freedom to explore on his own, instead of freedom from risking potential failure. He became free to risk, I feel, because first his needed defenses and then his competent abilities were honored.

For all three learners, the second phase of my program became more selective as they became more self-directed. I increasingly

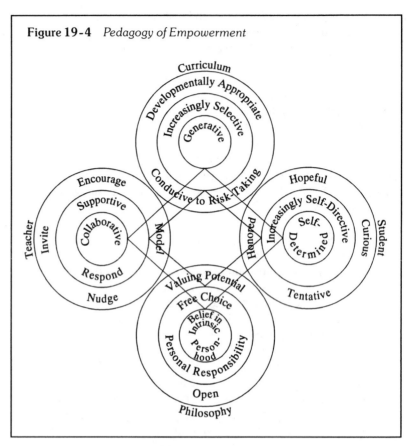

**Figure 19-4** *Pedagogy of Empowerment*

supported and responded to their learning initiative as they exercised free choice with committed responsibility.

All three troubled learners became self-determined, the final phase of empowerment, to some degree in particular learning contexts. Christopher became capable of utilizing writing to support and to enhance his artwork according to defined personal purpose. Elizabeth increasingly selected literature according to personal interest, regardless of potential text difficulties. Richard showed increasing responsibility for his need to negotiate our class curriculum in choosing literacy tasks within which he explored personal meaning. "Just a Story" reveals the determination of a learner to reclaim his student rights in the face of years of intimidation.

At the level of student self-determination, the curriculum becomes generative, and the teacher's role becomes collaborative. The philosophy which supports this level of empowerment is the valuing and celebration of individual uniqueness in conjunction with the belief in intrinsic personhood. This philosophy is at the heart of trusting the learner to grow, in Buber's term, "in his own form of individuation." This philosophy underlines both the first phase of "openness" to creating an individualized curriculum and the second phase of offering selective choice to the evolving self-directed, then self-determined, learner.

As I organize programs tailored for individualized empowerment, I continually attempt to come to a sense of clearness about the evolving needs of my learners. My focus on coming to clearness about the learning needs and abilities of my students parallels my faith in their coming to clearness about their intrinsic, self-growth needs. Their success in recognizing and exploring their personal needs and interests confirms the realizable goal of learning empowerment for even very troubled learners.

## EPILOGUE: ANOTHER BEGINNING

Two weeks ago, a high school student began literacy tutoring with me to fulfill a half-credit English requirement. He has been put on a home-school program due to behavior difficulties at school and an increasingly uncooperative attitude toward his teachers. He has been a troubled reader for years, and the PET meeting recommended a remedial English program.

Brian works with me for a two-hour session, two days a week. The session is divided into a writing component, using my word processor, and a shared reading component, related to a mutually agreed upon theme. His homework consists of self-selected personal reading for two hours in between sessions.

Brian told me during the first session that he had never finished a book. The first books I steered him toward were a selection of *Choose Your Own Adventures* with a wide variety of themes and easily achievable mini-stories within each book. He selected two to take home. We read together from a book of short, short stories. He was aware of meaning-oriented strategies but asked for my help when stuck on a word because he was unaware of which ones to use. He also asked me for confirmation. We shared the reading paragraph by paragraph. He sighed over the longer ones that came his way. His writing piece that day was a rather impersonal account of a puppy he hoped to get that summer.

By our second session, I had gathered a collection of books with survival themes because I sensed that both the action and theme might appeal to him. He chose *Hatchet* (Paulsen, 1987), a story of a young teenager who must survive on his own for months in the Canadian wilderness after a plane crash. Although his reading was plodding, he seemed more willing to try strategies on his own and to self-monitor their success. We conversed comfortably about the book, and he asked a number of questions about matters which interested him. He requested permission to take the book home as his personal reading. His writing was another impersonal piece about a new motorcycle he was buying.

Two sessions later I noted a significant generative energy taking over. Brian had read a number of chapters of *Hatchet* on his own and showed a great deal of interest in the book. We spun off on other survival books we had heard of, and he related the theme to a risky experience of his own on Maine's Mt. Katahdin. He was still reluctant to explore his feelings about his own experiences in either writing or reading discussions, but he was showing genuine curiosity about others' experiences. He asked permission to look through the survival books I had set aside for him and to examine my map of Maine hanging on the dining room (school room) wall. He selected a piece to edit in writing, and, despite his self-defined severe spelling handicap and confusion over where to start, he displayed a competent repertoire of spelling, punctuation, capitalization, and paragraphing ability after I provided some "scaffolding" assistance.

I told Brian that we could celebrate finishing *Hatchet* by watching the video of *Never Cry Wolf* (based on Farley Mowatt's book about a solo expedition into the Arctic to study wolves suspected by some as being responsible for the endangerment of the caribou population), which had come up in our discussion.

"Would you be able to finish the last five chapters of *Hatchet* on your own over the weekend, so that we could watch the film during our Monday session?"

"No problem," he said.

We're both looking forward to Monday!

# 20

# HERDMANS, DUCKS, AND ROBOTS: SPECIAL EDUCATION STUDENTS AND TEACHER NEGOTIATE THE CURRICULUM

**Lynne Griffiths**

"So, Mrs. Griffiths, can we read *The Best Christmas Pageant Ever* (Robinson, 1979) for Literature Studies?" (Edelsky and Smith, 1986) Robert's sincere young face looks beseechingly in my direction.

I hesitate, knowing that Robert, although a sixth grader, is reading at about a fourth-grade level. *The Best Christmas Pageant Ever* is a difficult sixth-grade book; the going will be tough. "I don't know," I answer. "Maybe we should pick out something a bit less involved." I'm searching for the right words as I try to let him down gently. Robert is not to be persuaded.

"I know I'll like it," he volunteers. "One of my friends told me how funny the book is and there is going to be a special about it on TV." The three other students decide that Robert is right—this is the book for them. I should know better than to go up against Robert, whom I had first met in his (then permanent) residence, the hallway outside his classroom. This is the kid who described in detail how he purposely set out to make a teacher furious just to watch the expression on her face. He emerged the victor in that round, just as he will here.

"OK," I shrug. "You guys are really going to have to concentrate on this book, because you might find it a bit difficult." "Right," I think to myself—a real bit difficult, since it's about two grade levels above where they're reading. I'm usually not overly concerned with grade levels. (Who ever heard of a 14.3 grade level?) Robert also stumbles considerably when he reads aloud. How will he be able to understand what he's reading when he'll probably miss every fourth or fifth word? In spite of all these problems, it's agreed that we will meet in two weeks to discuss the book.

277

Two weeks later, I find myself sitting down to the literature study session with some trepidation. I probably should have taken more of a leadership role and told the students that the book was too hard for them (since, of course, it is). I'm wondering what they'll get from a book that is nowhere near their *functional level* and light years from their *independent level*. I needn't have worried.

"Well?" (My standard opener for literature studies is not hard to remember.) Robert dives in.

"I really liked the way the author introduces the Herdmans," he starts. Picking up his copy, he flips open to page 1 and illustrates his point by reading the first paragraph aloud. He then continues: "The author paints a great picture for us." (Hadn't I used similar words at one time?) "She shows us how bad they were, not tells us." As we continue through the study, we talk about the importance of character, plot, and action. We touch on a perceived impression versus the real image, and we discuss what you think of yourself and how it reflects how you act. All of these topics are introduced by the students, as I am an equal member of this group—no more and no less. We are unable to agree on the sex of the narrator; we split three to two. It's an interesting question that had not occurred to me before and remains unresolved.

How fortunate that I didn't allow what I thought I knew about Robert's reading *level* to interfere with the learning process. My mistake was assuming that his reading aloud was a reflection of his overall reading ability, and I underestimated his focus on meaning. I also didn't take into account how much he *wanted* to read the book. Robert's desire to understand the book far outweighed the fact that he probably didn't catch *every* word. This suspicion was confirmed a few days later when I asked him about the TV special made from the story. "The book was better," he said simply. Live and learn, I thought to myself.

Ken Goodman has stated (Berkeley course, 1987) that all kids are whole language learners; they just don't have whole language teachers. He said that most problems in school come from the learning environment and the curriculum, not learning problems. Since our brains operate in similar ways, problems are caused when the natural learning process is disrupted and learning is made too abstract. I couldn't agree more. Special education too often concerns itself with identifying deficits and remediating through isolated skill worksheets. Language rarely remains whole as students are drilled on their weakness in medial vowels or terminal consonants. Instead of building on their strengths, we reinforce their weakness. Whole language teachers, whether regular or special education, focus on strength.

The foundation of my educational philosophy rests on the belief that my students are capable and creative learners. When visitors come to see whole language in a special education setting, I direct them to our *Visitor's Guide*, which explains what they will see and why. The *Visitor's Guide* is a small envelope with a large message:

## Visitors—Beware

Don't be fooled by the children of room 16! These youngsters are true students continually concentrating on the serious business of learning. Whether it's creating their special books, assisting other writers, listening to a taped story or just enjoying the company of a good book, these kids are learners. They know what it means to be a student.

They learn by doing, not watching. They read to learn, not learn to read. A book is chosen for what it has to offer or because the author is a familiar friend. In literature studies they talk about "whys" not "whats." Sincere comprehension is assumed, elements of literature are discussed at a new level. These kids know about voice, similes and metaphors. Not bad for an elementary "learning disabled" resource room. They read because they want to, not because they have to. They choose their own books.

Sometimes they select student work to read. These kids write their own books! They go through a five step process to achieve this and the results speak for themselves. Check the back shelf for the latest in student authors. They conference with the teacher or each other to work on content, style and grammar. Spelling and punctuation are not issues until the author is satisfied with the content.

Journal writing is another element of their experience. This is written conversaton where meaning is the driving force. Students strive to be heard, share their experiences. No corrections are made because communication is the key, not correctness.

Students learn to be readers and writers by following the natural progression of oral language. They learn to read and write the same way they learned to speak, by experimenting and making mistakes. They are encouraged to take chances with learning and by risking, internalize their insights. These kids not only accept this challenge—they surpass it. They are supportive of each other and share their expertise. Together they are a force to be reckoned with.

The students of room 16 are also learning about themselves as they explore the world. They are beginning to see that while education is enjoyable, it requires work and effort on their part. They are striving for self discipline, a force far more effective than external constraints. They are thoughtful of each other and are encouraged to be supportive of the group.

In short, students are learning the skills that will help them become successful and integral members of society. They are students of life. Watch them in action. . . .

Thus, a visitor is introduced to my learning disabled resource room. I am the resource specialist at Fair Oaks School in Redwood City, California. We are a district designated Bilingual (Spanish/English) whole language school, serving approximately 560 students, grades kindergarten through sixth. The school is located in one of the poorest socioeconomic areas of the city. My job is to provide appropriate intervention for twenty-eight plus identified learning disabled students on a pull-out basis, one to two hours, four days a week. The fifth day is used for observation, assessment, and Child Study Team meetings. I work on language arts and math primarily, although I am expected to ameliorate visual motor integration, general information, auditory and visual sequencing, and other areas. I have a very capable and talented aide who shares my whole language perspective five hours a day. The groups average from six to twelve students. Many of my students are emerging readers, even at the higher grade levels, and most of them speak Spanish as their first language, so I also teach Spanish reading. Though I'm not a proficient Spanish speaker, my students are patient and, through our combined efforts, we succeed.

Since I have been collecting books for a while, I have a large library of sets of books and individual copies spanning all ability levels and appealing to varied tastes. The school buys some books for me, but mostly I purchase them through book clubs. I don't use basals and am not required to do so. Like the other classes, my language arts program uses literature exclusively and revolves around writer's workshop, literature studies, and individual reading strategy instruction. I read aloud daily so students can familiarize themselves with book language. During this time I point out the devices the authors use, and the kids then put this knowledge to use in their own writing. To maintain continuity, I read at least ten or fifteen minutes a day to each group.

Because we learn to read by reading, sustained silent reading is an integral part of the program. Each group spends about ten to fifteen minutes with SSR. Students read aloud to me at least twice a week, as we strengthen individual reading strategies. Although reading out loud is not the same as reading silently, this activity allows me to help the reader build both efficient and effective strategies. Writer's workshop is twice a week for about an hour or an hour and a half. The other two days are spent in interactive journal writing, as described in the *Visitor's Guide*.

The kids have free access to paper, markers, scissors, rulers, and other items that are on top of a rolling cart I have in one corner. This cart is also home to our collection of nonfiction books and magazines. The students use these references for their own interests or for any research project they may be doing. All the nonfiction books are in one place so I can easily answer such pressing questions as "What do we have on dogs?" This section is not meant to replace the library; it's merely a starting point. Binder paper and draft paper are readily available on the back shelf for the blossoming writer.

How do I actually implement my whole language philosophy in our special education classroom? Ken Goodman speaks of the zone of proximal development, a point in learning where the learner

**281**
*Herdmans, Ducks,
and Robots: Special
Education Students
and Teacher
Negotiate the
Curriculum*

would progress if there were some help present (Vygotsky, 1978). Teachers must recognize when help will or won't make a difference. We don't create these "teachable moments"; we just take advantage of them. We can't control the learning process, because there is not a direct correlation between teaching and learning. If we become too anxious to direct learning, we fail to utilize the student's total abilities. I think this is just as true for a learning disabled student as any other. Whole language in special education means being flexible and utilizing existing learning energy, drawing from the children's agenda. Let me give you an example.

The bell has rung, and I'm waiting for the kids to troop in. As I peer over my book from my desk, I notice that it is taking them a bit longer than usual to arrive. What can be keeping them, and why are they all together? Normally, they would straggle in by twos and threes. Suddenly there is a small commotion outside and the gang arrives. They come en masse through the door, blown in with an air of expectation I don't quite understand. Experience has taught me to sit back and learn before making any sudden moves or speeches (I expect the Old West inspired similar sentiments), so I do nothing. Although I am extremely curious about what's going on, I figure they will tell me if they want me to know. I read my silent reading book. The students do the same. I notice that, although it is probably 78 degrees out, Lalo has his heavy bomber jacket on and seems to be holding it rather close to him. I doubt that he is protecting himself from imminent chill, but one never knows. I continue reading.

"Mrs. Griffiths, ducks like to swim, don't they?" The conversation starts innocently enough. Not being a duck expert but feeling fairly safe with this aspect, I respond, "Why sure; I guess they do."

"They're probably happier swimming than not, wouldn't you say?" the voice continues. Sensing a trap but having no proof, I answer that a duck is probably more content in the water than out of it. I am beginning to suspect that this is more than a casual generic interest in waterfowl and that there may be a specific request coming. I am not disappointed.

"So, if we had a duck, you would want him to be happy, wouldn't you?" Lalo moves in for the kill.

"Yes, Lalo, *IF* we had a duck, I would want him to be happy." I am a goner. From under his coat, Lalo carefully pulls out a tiny yellow fluff of feathers with webbed feet. Cradling the little duck in his hands, Lalo walks confidently to our sink and begins to fill it with water. He adjusts the temperature of the water so the little fellow will be comfy and we all stand back to admire the swimming skills of the new arrival. Boy, that little guy can paddle! Knowing I need to go with the flow, we talk about how his feet are adapted for swimming, why his feathers shed water, how he feels being stared at by students and teacher alike, and other pressing issues. More importantly to me, we talk about why Room 16's sink is probably not the best habitat for him for any extended length of time. Fortunately, Lalo concurs, and the duck goes home that afternoon, but not before I have seized the moment to fill in my agenda about living things, and so on.

The children's interest and considerable learning energies were focused on ducks at that moment, so it was my task to utilize the opportunity. Had I not gone with ducks at that point, I would have been swimming upstream (so to speak). What I am saying is that, even though I start with a general plan or outline, what actually ends up happening may be different. My plans on paper look quite similar from week to week. I block out chunks of time for writer's workshop, literature studies, math, SSR, reading out loud, and other basic activities. We follow those time slots, unless some current event or school activity alters the focus for the day. That box of time that Lalo used to teach us about ducks was writer's workshop. If the duck had not made his appearance, we would have continued the stories and books already in progress. But, because something more gripping and immediate popped (floated?) up, we changed the agenda. I have an overall plan in mind, based on where the children are now and where I want them to be at the end of the year, but the kids pretty much choose how we get there on a daily basis.

How do you discover this agenda of your students? First, you must be a *kidwatcher*, and second you must *share yourself*. You are a unique individual; just be yourself. You're one of the members of the group; if you're expecting them to open up to you, you must reciprocate. I find myself saying, "You can draw that better than I can; you do it" or "You know much more about wrestling than I do; teach me." The children offer suggestions, knowing that their ideas will be taken seriously and that they can affect the direction the class will take. This does not mean that they always do what they want. I have my agenda, and they have theirs, so we usually meet in the middle. Sometimes they utilize activities differently than my preconceived notion, and their ideas may turn out to be more viable than mine. I need to remain responsive and flexible enough to take advantage of their learning energy.

I have a number of books that I think of as "jumping off" books, that come with fascinating titles like "Magic Tricks You Can Do," "How to Make a Robot," or "Creative Ideas with Paper." The kids are forever finding things to make or do in these books. Many are able to extend the ideas and create all sorts of exciting gadgets. I am continually surprised and pleased with the students' inventiveness. When they have completed the work that I expect from them, they have time for themselves. It is in this time frame that many unusual projects get started and I can kidwatch. I learn a lot by studying how they interact with materials and each other. Since I save all sorts of things (there's a bit of pack rat in every teacher), the students know that their project won't be limited by items on hand.

Sometimes these projects turn into something I can utilize in my sneaky *teachable moment* thinking, but at other times they remain in the total domain of the children, not needing or desiring adult intervention. I once had an entire life-size robot built on my back table by an industrious lad who was a science fiction buff. He even had a walky talky installed in the mouth of the gigantic one so it could "communicate." I would have hated to miss that adventure because I had a *better* learning task in mind.

I like the freedom a whole language classroom affords me. It seems to me that when I'm interested and involved, the students are, too. I feel free to try out new activities and ideas based on what I know about how children learn. I am continually changing and modifying plans as I go, not bound by skill and drill worksheets. I stay open and flexible in order to focus the considerable learning energies of the students. I keep reading and talking with other whole language teachers so I'll recognize and utilize the "teachable moment" to its fullest. Whole language makes my job interesting and exciting, but, more importantly, whole language in special education is effective.

Our resource room becomes somewhat of a haven, a place to be yourself, to be accepted, and a place to learn. All of us contribute to this process—students and teacher alike. We are members of the same team, pulling together toward a common goal. Since we are all learners, we can be tolerant of each other's failings. We are learning that expertise requires risk and commitment. Since I know this more surely than ten-year-olds, I lead the way. But it is the students who should and do own the major voice in their own education. They are capable learners with an insatiable curiosity. If they possess the power to shape and alter the direction their learning will take, they will seize the opportunity and take responsibility for their own education. Given the choice, combined with the expectation, students choose to learn quickly and well. Regardless of educational labels, all children are powerful learners. I know; I see it on a daily basis.

# 21

## PARENTS SUPPORTING WHOLE LANGUAGE

### Sari Windsor et al.

*Debbie Manning participates in a community of learners.*

Through the following personal responses, we, the parents of Dailey Elementary School in Fresno, California, want to share our experiences in a whole language classroom. It has been difficult to decide on a format for this writing. You will read the reactions of different parents. You will hear individual voices. We hope you will find some common message in these varied attempts to share what it means to be involved in our children's learning. Our children have been deeply affected by this experience. They have grown in their knowledge of language, and they use it to listen and speak, read and write to each other and to the community they live in. They have grown in their ability to respect themselves and others. They have become self-directed learners who are free to pursue their interests and develop their own style of learning and sharing. They have learned to love school. They have learned to love language, seeing it as a tool to express themselves and to understand the world they inhabit. Here you will meet us and learn about our children.

---

# RYAN
## Kathleen O'Connor

First, I must express the feelings I experienced when my son first entered Debbie Manning's kindergarten classroom, an entirely holistic developmental literature-rich classroom environment, three years ago. We enrolled two weeks late, and the organization was in place and in progress. My son was not outgoing or particularly confident about beginning his educational career; however, he had good pre-school experiences and until then had been read to continually, but never taught letters, sounds, or words.

From the day he walked into the classroom, he was asked to do a daily journal, where the students could write or express in pictures their thoughts and ideas. At first, he cried out of frustration or some imagined fear that he should already know how to read and write.

By the second week, he was writing easily, often using squiggles for letters or forming his words with a lively variety of letters grouped haphazardly over the page. But he wasn't crying anymore. He was discussing his work, owning his writing, becoming confident about his ability to produce something meaningful. By January his writing was readable to anyone who took the time to decipher his inventive spelling. He could write stories and discuss topics easily. He could stand in front of the class and read his writing aloud and have conversations on multitudes of topics. My fear over his risk taking was replaced by confidence and an extreme sense of contentment. I felt that this was right and good. This was the way children should learn. My child was not alone. We parents saw growth daily in verbal and written expression, ability, and eagerness to learn.

I became involved in the class on a weekly basis, reading journals, assisting in activities, and playing guitar. I couldn't stay away. I was wanted and appreciated by both teacher and students, and I began to realize that my contribution was valuable and respected. Every week we would meet and sing together. We began to brainstorm ideas around certain themes, such as snow, spring, saying goodbye, holidays, things we are thankful for, or playing. I would take their ideas, organize them into rhymes, add a simple tune, and be off. We wrote at least ten songs together that year. They could read, sing, and sign them all, and they still remember them now three years later.

Yes, I see a great difference in my son when he is involved in a classroom such as this one. He is now a second grader, and Mrs. Manning is again his teacher. I see the wheels turning. I hear the pride in his voice when he talks about their plans, the books he has read, the radio station they are building. He is learning authentic, valuable information about life and how life applies to him. But no one has to tell him that this is valid and real learning. Believe me; he knows the difference.

I see already a difference in the way I treat my three-year-old son. We talk, read, and write together often. He writes me messages, cards, and lists, and I write back. I never knew to take his behavior so seriously. But I now know this is serious business—the stuff learning is made of.

---

## MEGHAN AND CHRISTOPHER
### Michael Quinn

My children like to read. They read for information. They read for fun. They love a good story. They love a good joke. They expect all of this to be waiting for them when they open the covers of the books they choose to read. The whole language classrooms that they have been involved in have nurtured this expectation. This love for reading I understand. My wife and I both expect these things to happen when we open books. What I find truly amazing about the whole language approach is the attitude that my children bring to writing.

My daughter, Meghan, writes like she reads. She expects to communicate. In many ways, she is more qualified to write this than I. Whereas I approach this task with a mixture of fear and dread, she approaches writing as a natural communication process. For her, writing is little more than talking carefully. She uses writing to communicate with her grandparents. She writes notes to friends. She writes letters to politicians and other people from whom she wants information. Writing itself is a friend to her.

For me writing has always been something that I had to be forced to do. I needed an assignment. I would call home before I would write. I doubt I ever wrote my grandparents. Don't you hate confessions? The point is, my children have not learned their ease with writing in the home. We have the whole language classroom and the whole language teachers to thank for this.

## THOMAS
### Kim Micek

The greatest difference between this year's classroom situation and the classroom situation of the past is the individual attention and concern shown each child. The children learn the basics of reading, writing, and math by pursuing areas of interest to them. Thomas' attitude toward school has changed in that he now feels a purpose for being there—to learn that which interests him, not to perform repetitive assignments for which he sees no future application. While Thomas still may not be a model student or always excited to see each new school day come, he does have a renewed desire to learn—a desire that all but died out in his first years.

As a working mother, I appreciate the increased opportunity to be involved. When I have the chance to visit the classroom unexpectedly, I am welcomed and allowed to participate. In the traditional classroom, unscheduled visits were viewed as disruptions.

Most of all, Thomas' self-esteem has returned. He no longer feels a need to always compete or to compare himself to the other students. While disruptive behavior is addressed and disciplined, each child's special gifts and positive efforts are recognized.

My greatest concern is where to go from here. How will he handle the transition back to the traditional classroom?

## SETH
### Marilyn Williams

One of the best parts of a whole language classroom is that children read "real" books rather than "canned" literature from basals. This year, Seth's exposure to books has been vast. He has read so many books that he has developed preferences for specific authors and is very comfortable talking about literary elements, such as character, plot, and symbolism. I'm continually amazed at his perceptive analyses of literature and am delighted that he enjoys reading so much.

A whole language classroom has also afforded Seth lots of opportunities to write. He has explored a variety of kinds of writing, including journalism! I love the fact that the children in Mrs. Manning's class write out math problems and their observations and hypotheses regarding science experiments, as well as write within the "language arts and social studies" areas. One thing I've noticed is that Seth has confidence in his writing to take risks and through this to discover his own style. I can actually hear his voice in his writing. At the same time, Seth seems to have a sense of audience and how that audience varies with various kinds of writing. As a parent who values effective writing skills, I'm thrilled to see how comfortable and fluent Seth is in his writing.

From visiting Mrs. Manning's classroom weekly, I have observed how the children are quick to use writing as a vehicle to express themselves. Recently, on one of my weekly visits, I had come directly from my job and was more dressed up than usual. Keisha handed me a note which said, "Dear Seth's Mom, You look nice today. Thank you for going to the assembly with us." I appreciated the compliment, but I was particularly struck with her ease in writing and her use of writing as functional communication rather than as something to be done to fulfill a teacher's writing assignment.

---

# ANDREW
## Lynn Rutledge

Our family was introduced to the whole language concept when our seven-year-old son, Andrew, entered the second grade. Although we thought that the idea of whole language was fascinating, we were skeptical of its value for Andrew. He had not been an "honor" student in the first grade, and his conduct was even less desirable. Homework was a constant power struggle in our home, not the learning process that it was meant to be. Andrew's greatest accomplishment was his cherished A's which he received on the weekly

*The whole language philosophy builds self-confidence.*

spelling test, although he could not recall his memorized words when he needed to use them in different contexts.

Our first fear about the whole language process was that Andrew needed a more structured and orderly environment so that he might learn about self-control and start to feel seriously committed to his academic studies. Our second fear was that he might have difficulty readjusting to a traditional classroom when it came time for him to enter the third grade. These readjustment fears and the implications for Andrew were discussed with his teacher. Her response convinced us that the whole language idea was worth a chance. The response? "It's better to have been to Europe once than to never have gone at all." This way of thinking has proven its merit throughout the school year.

Andrew started the second grade with difficult behavior, but, by his second report card, his behavior and grades were turned around. He had become proud of his abilities in school and had begun to take responsibility for his homework. After reading how parents should respond to a child's writing, we no longer corrected Andrew's spelling but learned to ask if he wanted us to edit his work. When he reads to us now, we are amazed at how well he does, and we can actually read his essays. He has learned to conceptualize in a way that was not taught to his mother until college.

Andrew's teacher has been supportive and caring, which has caused our family to react to school as a positive process, not something that tested our family's and our son's abilities. And, because Andrew feels that he is doing well in school, he feels better about himself as a person. What better way could a new little human be prepared for being a responsible, productive, and giving member of our society?

---

## AVERY
### Sari Windsor

When my eldest son, Ethan, was about eighteen months old, I began teaching him phonics. At the ripe age of three, I introduced him to workbooks, and I, of course, would correct them. When he started kindergarten, he was placed in a kindergarten-first grade combination class. His teacher was strong on academics, and my son worked very hard all day. In first grade, he had his first taste of spelling tests. Being a good mother, I drilled him on his spelling words twice a week: once for the practice test, once for the final test. Every time he misspelled a word, I felt I had failed him. I did this for him *every* week for three years. Why did I stop doing this for him? Because that was the year my second child entered kindergarten and we were introduced to the whole language philosophy.

The teacher explained to us what we would see in her class during the year. It was no ordinary kindergarten orientation. What came to my mind after her speech was, "This is a teacher who loves kids and loves to teach." I came away that night very happy that my son was in that class. I have to admit, I had absolutely no idea what whole language was. I bit my tongue every time my son cried to have me spell words for him. I felt I was letting him down. I thought he couldn't possibly learn to spell this way.

The teacher kept a parents' library open, with numerous books on whole language. She always had time to explain things to me and to answer my concerns. What really helped were the monthly parent meetings. Once a month all parents were invited to come to a meeting where we discussed classroom projects, upcoming events, for example, field trips, parties, class visitors, and so on. She would also let us know what things our children were doing.

I learned that my son had started writing—nothing legible at that point, but really taking a risk and putting something down on paper. I noticed a change in his personality, too. He was becoming more self-confident and independent. I still hadn't quite figured out what whole language was, but I liked what I saw.

*Parents are encouraged and welcomed into the classroom.*

On Valentine's Day, one of the projects the kids did was a giant Valentine card for the teacher. One of the moms called me over and said, "Look, Avery's got it." I looked at what he wrote, and a tear came to my eye when I saw "Hpy Vlntns Da" written in a big heart. Yes, he had become a writer.

It just kept getting better. At the end of the year, the kids had a pet show. Avery wrote an entire page of facts about his turtle and read it aloud to everyone. He had become a happy, independent writer and reader, and he hadn't colored one ditto sheet—not one "A is for apple." He just had a lot of good literature.

Now, in second grade, he's reading several books a day. He writes stories that are pages long. I see whole language as giving kids opportunity for unlimited growth. It teaches them reading for the sake of enjoying a good book. It teaches them writing for communication and information. It teaches them that they can put something in writing and it will be accepted as their individual style and not broken down into spelling and handwriting corrections. They learn the editing process from first draft to final product. Math in a whole language class puts things in a meaningful context so that it can be used in real-life situations.

In watching my younger son grow in a whole language class, I'm learning how to encourage my kids to keep up their love for reading and writing, even when they are not involved in a whole language class. I've learned that all those years I drilled my oldest son for his spelling tests, he wasn't learning to write. Children learn to write by writing. They learn to read by looking at books, being read to by parents and teachers, and by having a good self-image.

In summary, the whole language philosophy builds self-confidence, and reading, writing, and social skills that will follow them into their adulthood.

---

# ALICIA
### Mary and Cary Davidian

We, the parents of Alicia Grace O'Neill, are very excited about our daughter's growth in a whole language program.

Her first grade was a tough one for her and us. She rejected doing her homework, feeling she was being tested on a nightly basis. She lacked confidence in her own abilities.

When she began the second grade in Mrs. Manning's whole language class, she chose the last table, back-corner seat. Two weeks after her first report card, she requested to be moved. Her self-esteem was just beginning to grow.

Alicia's reading and writing skills have improved dramatically. She has learned that making mistakes is OK and part of the natural learning process. The whole language format has taught her respect for other people and their property and has taught us to respect her and the way she thinks and learns. Our only regret is that there aren't more classes being taught with the whole language approach.

---

# MAX
## Jill Fisher and Keith Seaman

Inspiring a child's love of reading and writing may be the most obvious benefits of a whole language classroom, but they are certainly not the only ones.

In a whole language environment, children are encouraged to cooperate with one another and to appreciate each other's uniqueness and special abilities. In our son's classroom, children are not grouped according to ability but, rather, according to which book they *prefer* of those offered. It is amazing to see the give and take that occurs within these groups. Children are suggesting, critiquing, discussing, helping, and enjoying one another's contributions. The self-esteem that springs from this setup is remarkable. Contrast this against a more traditional grouping of high, middle, and low where children learn only to rank order their ability against their classmates, and it's easy to see why so many children *never* learn to love reading or even how to read.

In addressing these issues, we speak with assurance, not only about our son but about many of the kids in his classroom. During the year, we have seen children who initially wouldn't even attempt writing a sentence *voluntarily* stay in through recess to finish the story they were writing because they "didn't want to break my thoughts." We have seen children who, at first, said they *hated* reading rush up proudly to show us their written and illustrated review of "the best book I've ever read."

How is it that we have seen this in so many children in our son's class? Because we have spent so much more time in the classroom than *ever* before. This is yet another benefit of the whole language classroom. Parents are encouraged and welcomed into the classroom. They are made to feel valuable and knowledgeable. And, because the classroom is so interesting and so much fun, parents actually want to be there. Gone are the rows of desks with students quietly working (or not working) in their workbooks. Instead, one is surrounded by enthusiastic, bright kids who want your attention and who want to show you a project or a story or a book they're reading or a book they want *you* to read. In our son's classroom, many *different* kinds of parents have participated this year, and we have enjoyed one another outside of the classroom at potlucks, parent meetings, and field trips, as well. We love what Mrs. Manning's whole language classroom has done for our son and for us.

---

# SAM
## Dan and Kathy Spears

Sam and Peter, our nine-year-old twins, were born prematurely. We have grown to understand learning delays and frustrations. Reading and writing have been especially difficult. We kept the twins in preschool an extra year to allow maturing to take place. Still, kindergarten was full of peril, and first grade was little better. It has been slow going, especially for Sam.

In second grade, Sam has really blossomed in his reading and writing. We think much of his success this year has to do with the lack of pressure, coupled with the sense of responsibility he has learned. Sam has almost singlehandedly kept many classroom animals fed and watered. The children have learned what care each type of animal requires, and Sam has played the role of "Science Expert."

This nurturing environment has helped Sam to avoid becoming self-conscious about his "reading level." He still does read far short of his verbal capabilities, but whole language has helped to avoid unpleasant comparisons. We are grateful to Mrs. Manning for meeting his learning needs.

---

# TERESA
## Mark Rivera

After witnessing a substantial improvement in my daughter's learning process and her social behavior, I felt compelled to write about some of these observations and what whole language teaching has done for my daughter, Teresa. I can only imagine the change in my life if there had been a method like whole language and more teachers like Mrs. Manning when I was in grade school.

I must take a quick moment to applaud Teresa's teacher for her successes; her successes are her students. I know, because my daughter is one of them. I have sat in on her classes, and I have seen the progress and change within the students. They have grown from a bunch of rambunctious ragamuffins to a bunch of studious children who are developing a love for learning.

When Teresa first entered Mrs. Manning's classroom, she was a rebellious student. Teresa had a very difficult time dealing with other children, as well as with adults. In fact, Teresa was moved several times in the hope that she would get along with some classmates. No such luck, but, thanks to Mrs. Manning's consistency in her practice of whole language, Teresa's behavior has changed. Teresa's relationships with others have dramatically improved. From my observations, I have attributed a large part of the change to Teresa's teacher and the teacher's implementation of whole language.

Teresa really relates to the practical aspects of whole language teachings. Teresa and her classmates have checking accounts at a local bank. I'm certainly not talking large dollar amounts. But Teresa can really see the practicality of mathematics in having a checking account.

Teresa and her classmates have pen pals at one of our local colleges. Teresa loves to write now. She didn't before.

Teresa and her classmates read sections of our local newspaper every day. Please keep in mind this is a second-grade class. Teresa loves to read now. She didn't before.

Before, I couldn't get Teresa to read with me, short of tying her up and reading to her. Today, things are very different. She is constantly taking her stepmother and me by the hand and reading to us. Needless to say, I am pleased with Teresa's progress academically and socially. I'm forced to admit that a significant part of Teresa's change for the better is due to Teresa's teacher and whole language instruction.

However, I do have a very deep concern that Teresa may not receive whole language instruction next year. As a parent who has witnessed an entire change in my child, I do not want to risk the betterment my daughter has achieved by going to a traditional basal class next year.

I may sound a bit biased, but I know something great when I see it. Whole language works. Maybe, if I'd had whole language instruction, I would have developed a whole different attitude toward learning and maybe I would have graduated from high school.

---

# JAMIE
## Zena Stelzenmueller

Good reading is the foundation of good speaking and writing. At the age of forty-four, after functioning well as a businesswoman and homemaker in a very social environment, this information came as a great revelation to me. I didn't realize how vital reading was to communication.

It takes the gift of a magical teacher to stimulate and involve her pupils' imagination by using whole language. Whole language is drawn from our daily lives through not only spoken words but also written words.

A person who is familiar with the language of reputable writers and speakers will use good language without conscious effort. The child brought up among refined people generally has good manners without knowing it. Whole language comes naturally to those who read.

I have seen without a doubt the child who has an expressive vocabulary become filled with expounded expression through literature. My daughter comes home so delighted as she discovers the exciting opportunities for reading her teacher introduces to her in books, periodicals, and newspapers. Jamie ran in waving the newspaper, "Look, look Mommy! Our class is in the paper. We wrote the President of the United States. Our letters are being heard. We're on the front page. Look. There it is! All about gun control!"

As we read the article together, I asked her where her class is mentioned. She responded, "Well Mother! We were just one of many to make a whole."

Yes, and such is whole language. I only wish I was given the choice as a child to learn to read from the wealth of the written word rather than forced to struggle through boring, repetitive Dick and Jane nonadventure.

Today, through the enlightenment of my daughter, I too have an insatiable thirst for literary knowledge.

---

# ALANA
### Debbie and Al Shapazian

One of the things I like most about whole language learning is the self-esteem that is gained while in the class. A good sense of self-esteem leaves the children open to absorb the subject matter that is being taught. A good whole language learning teacher will make sure that each child is given that extra boost that will help each achieve.

For this reason, we say that a wonderful thing happened for our daughter Alana as she entered kindergarten. She was assigned to Room 4, with Debbie Manning as her instructor. Room 4, we heard, was either loved or dreaded by parents, because Debbie taught "whole language," a way of teaching that was very controversial in our school. As parents of a daughter going into this classroom, my husband and I were very curious as to the controversy about this method. We decided to go in with an open mind.

Any misgivings were certainly put to rest at the parents' meeting that took place the first day back to school. That evening I remember Debbie saying that she loved each of her students already and, if the parents wanted a child in her class transferred out, to do so immediately before that love deepened, making it very hard to part. She explained how the classroom worked and what the children would be doing during the day.

We noticed the classroom environment was different. Tables and chairs were set up so the children could explore and socialize. There was visual stimulation everywhere. Nothing was rigid. There was a flow in the classroom. It was a wonderful environment, one where I would have loved to have been in kindergarten—not anything like the strict parochial schooling I had.

Alana has always been a creative child, and her creativity was nurtured in this class. Her self-esteem has been built up so much that she is not afraid to take risks in her schoolwork or to make a mistake. She continues to take the initiative to try things, even if they don't work out the first or the second time. Today, in second grade, she still has not lost that drive that was instilled in her in kindergarten. She writes, illustrates, and constructs with the same appetite that she had then.

Recently, I stumbled across Alana talking to a friend on the phone, sketching out plans to write a full-length play. They were discussing what action should take place in each act. It excites me to know that someday Alana *will* write that play, edit it, and rewrite it, and possibly present it. I attribute this to the great beginnings she had with whole language.

---

## STEPHANIE
### Brenda Graves

Our daughter, Stephanie, entered whole language as a kindergartner. From the first day of school, we experienced a warm and welcoming atmosphere.

Stephanie had very few skills when she began school. We were prepared to struggle through the year. But we were soon to realize the encouragement and devotion from the teacher helped Stephanie develop many of her abilities without the struggle. The techniques used are reinforced in such a way that my child can advance at her own pace and not be compared to the others. The teacher shows it's OK to take chances rather than not to try at all. This encourages the child to continue and to be more eager to learn.

There is such a positive attitude in the whole language class. The creative activities available to the children are by their choice, not by assignment. Stephanie was reluctant to stand up front for sharing until she understood it was OK to do it on her own time and not be pushed. This enabled her to be more relaxed and willing to express herself better.

The children were exposed to so many good books. The literature studies involved the class in sharing ideas and gave them an eagerness to read more and more. This has helped Stephanie develop an interest in books and authors, too. In turn, her interest in reading has expanded her interest in writing.

Putting ideas on paper has always been hard for us to accomplish. I believe it has to start at an early age and be positively reinforced. Stephanie has continued her journal writing, showing greater interest in numerous subjects with encouragement behind her. Whole language was her beginning.

We developed many friendships in a whole language class. Our involvement with the parents and kids was very rewarding. Many friendships continue to this day, even though we have moved out of the area.

Stephanie is now in a second-grade classroom with total language: a mixture of traditional and whole language. We are happy with her progress and know whole language set her foundation to learn and to love it.

---

# SARA
## Cathie Fernandez

I would like to share some of my feelings and experiences about what I've observed as a parent in a total whole language classroom.

My daughter, Sara, was fortunate enough to be in a kindergarten classroom that had an intelligent, sensitive, and devoted teacher who encouraged and nurtured the love and willingness to read and to write. In this total whole language classroom environment, she never experienced any feelings of failure. Starting with her first day of school and from that day forward, she was told by her teacher what a brilliant person she was and what a wonderful writer and reader she was.

Instead of the basal readers, my daughter was introduced to outstanding and varied literature books every day. She and her classmates were able to respond freely to these books, share their ideas, learn from these books, and just experience these books. I strongly feel that this early literary exposure has increased her awareness and interest. I also credit her willingness to write and illustrate her own stories either by collaborating with another student or on her own to this early exposure to fine literature.

By seeing written language everywhere in the room, by being able to write her ideas on paper without the worry of failure, she became a strong, self-confident reader and writer. In this type of noncompetitive learning environment, my daughter was free to be Sara. She never had to be like anyone else, nor was she compared to anyone else. Sara's creativity blossomed with the many hands-on projects that the children were able to pick at their own discretion.

I applaud the teacher who has the willingness and dedication to teach this child-centered whole language class. I wish more children could be as fortunate as these children are to benefit from this class.

---

# IVAN
## Peter B. Porter

Whole language is using every activity and learning experience to improve language. Instead of breaking language into meaningless semantic parts, a more pragmatic approach is used to encourage children to use and enjoy language. Language is practiced, used, and improved every minute in Debbie Manning's class.

In class, language is first taught and shown by example. The teacher aides and parents use books, songs, and poems to demonstrate correct use of language. Plays are used to give the students a chance to recite examples of good language. Every day the students are given examples of language that are interesting and exciting, helping the children realize that, if you master the language, the whole world is at your fingertips.

The most constructive activity to developing whole language is writing. The students write about everything, from personal everyday experiences to hands-on experiments in class. The writings are kept in different literature logs to keep things organized and show progress. The students write to pen pals, expressing ideas, feelings, and thoughts, as well as asking questions. The letters back to the students give good examples of language as the pen pals answer the students' questions and ask their own.

The most important aspect about the writing is that the students are encouraged to write and feel good about writing. They enjoy writing which allows for language development, not critical analysis of grammar. Instead of becoming nervous about making mistakes, the students are encouraged to write, regardless of spelling or grammatical errors. Given this supportive atmosphere for expression, the students' language develops to complex, lengthy expressions of observations, ideas, and feelings.

The other part of language development occurs when the students are allowed to share certain projects, as well as teach specific concepts in which they have become knowledgeable. Being able to speak and express ideas and thoughts helps the students sort and develop what needs to be said.

The students invent math problems as well as stories. Inventing helps the students to create their own language, developing the structure to fit what needs to be said. Invention also encourages upper-level critical thinking, which allows the students to apply the learning directly to themselves.

Books are read daily, with reports being given on certain selections. Being allowed to choose the books that are interesting to them helps motivate the students to read. The students discover that reading is fun and provides information about subjects that interest them.

The students coming out of this atmosphere are more comfortable writing and speaking in front of others, and enjoy reading as the learning adventure it should be. The students are comfortable with language and are ready for continued improvement. The grammar will develop later and will come easily as long as the students are confident in language use. The atmosphere in class gives the students the confidence they need in language use and development.

## CONCLUSION

The whole language classroom has benefited our children. Their experience of the joy of learning has become ours. We have learned with our children that school can be fun. Being parents of children in a whole language classroom has opened our eyes to a number of things. We have learned that ability grouping is not necessary. Children can be challenged at all levels. Because our kids are not competing with each other, they have become a learning team, helping each other to understand and articulate their ideas. Our children have learned to care about each other and the language they encounter in the books they read and in the books they write. Our children have taught us to care about the language they read and write. We have learned to work with the teacher and with each other to help enrich the classroom. In the whole language classroom, our kids have increased their self-esteem. They have maintained their curiosity about the world and trust themselves to generate questions without fear of failure. They learn through mistakes, regarding them as opportunities. We as parents have learned these same lessons. We support and encourage whole language in all grades.

# 22

# MATHING: A WHOLE LANGUAGE PROCESS

## Deborah Landwehr Bosnos

Math today just isn't what it used to be. Thank goodness! For in the United States we had allowed everyone but ourselves as educators to dictate a curriculum which was dominated in the elementary years by an emphasis on computational speed in arithmetic, rather than on a depth of understanding of the larger field of mathematics.

Shirley Hill, past president of the National Council of Teachers of Mathematics (NCTM), points out that it is "ironic that at the very time we are on the threshold of 'teaching machines to reason,' we are spending an inordinate amount of our educational energy teaching our children mechanistic skills" (1979).

There is an urgent need in the United States to redesign our math teaching to reflect our world today and our students' world tomorrow. The NCTM has created a set of curriculum and evaluation standards in order "to establish a broad framework to guide reform in school mathematics in the next decade":

> Educational goals for students must reflect the importance of mathematical literacy. Toward this end, the K-12 standards articulate five general goals for all students: (1) that they learn to value mathematics. (2) that they become confident in their ability to do mathematics. (3) that they become mathematical problem solvers. (4) that they learn to communicate mathematically, and (5) that they learn to reason mathematically. These goals imply that students should be exposed to numerous and varied interrelated experiences that encourage them to value the mathematical enterprise, to develop mathematical habits of mind, and to understand and appreciate the role of mathematics in human affairs;

that they should be encouraged to explore, to guess, and even to make and correct errors so that they gain confidence in their ability to solve complex problems; that they should conjecture, test, and build arguments about a conjecture's validity. (1989, p. 5)

How do we plan and organize a comprehensive mathematics program for our students? One way is to think of three components:

The Ongoing Component
The Integrated Component
The Make-Math-Last-All-Day Component

All three components are necessary to every math program. This approach assures that math will not be fractured—for no matter how wonderful individual activities are, they often remain separate pieces of a jigsaw puzzle. The power (ownership) of mathematics comes only when we see for ourselves the larger picture—the pattern, purpose, beauty, and usefulness of math. The larger picture comes together only when these math jigsaw pieces are related and integrated to each other and to life. Essential to this process is language development. Mathematics always makes use of language—reading, writing, speaking, and listening—and adds a new symbol system, thereby expanding language itself. Mathematical language development is tied to firsthand experiences and connects and extends understandings. Through language, mathematics knowledge becomes usable, whether in the realm of theory or of application.

## THE ONGOING COMPONENT

The Ongoing Component is the mainstay—the core, the heart—of the math learning. This is an organized and planned pathway, an overall plan continually modified to be appropriate for the students. This is the spiral curriculum, a revisiting of concepts to extend understanding, reaching back to connect previous experiences. Each time the child sees something familiar and something new. When activities are rich enough to engage students at different levels, children at an initial stage of understanding can sense from those around them that there is even more to know; therefore, an awareness is created that, even though they may have played this game or used those blocks previously, there is even more to learn each time.

I begin by looking at the year, keeping in mind the different strands of math:

Pattern
Logical thinking
Measurement
Geometry
Number (arithmetic)
Probability and statistics (including graphing)

I put these topic titles across a blank school year calendar to block off time to focus on a particular strand. Usually, each two- to four-week block would have one arithmetic emphasis and one other-than-arithmetic emphasis. A sample calendar of focus areas might look like Figure 22-1.

This calendar is written in pencil and changes easily to adapt to shifting needs or interests. What it accomplishes for me is that it keeps my attention on the larger picture of the year—what have the children experienced and where can that lead? What gaps need to be considered? While time is hurrying onward, has geometry been overlooked? or probability? The calendar is the structure for the On-Going Math Program and ensures that we do not spend two months on division only to smush fractions, decimals, or percent into the last days of May.

CONCEPT IMMERSION

Another purpose the oft-erased calendar serves is to encourage immersion into a concept or a topic. For a hands-on, problem-solving approach to mathematics, students need time to be immersed in an environment of ideas, doings, and language. The central purpose of concept immersion is that, in spite of the fact that students may use different materials and strategies, they are surrounded by a cluster of common concepts. There is common ground

---

**Figure 22-1**  *Sample Calendars*

| For older students | | For younger students | |
|---|---|---|---|
| **SEPTEMBER** | **OCTOBER** | **SEPTEMBER** | **OCTOBER** |
| Add./Sub. Estimation Logical Thinking Pattern | Begin. Mult./Division Geometry, Pattern and Function | Number – Beginning Pattern | Number Concepts 0-9 Sorting, Classifying |
| **NOVEMBER** | **DECEMBER** | **NOVEMBER** | **DECEMBER** |
| Place Value/Large #'s Estimation Measurement | Mult./Division Geometry/Meas. | Number Concepts 0-9 Comparison | Number Concepts 0-9 Geometry |
| **JANUARY** | **FEBRUARY** | **JANUARY** | **FEBRUARY** |
| Fractions Geometry | Fractions/Decimals Measurement | Number Concepts 0-9 Geometry | Beginning Add./Sub. Non-Standard Meas. |
| **MARCH** | **APRIL** | **MARCH** | **APRIL** |
| Percent Probability | Ratio, Proportion Measurement/Geom. | Place Value Pattern | Beginning Mult./Div. Non-Standard Meas. |

May is left open for review and extension.
Throughout the year: problem solving, graphing, pattern and function, mental computation, estimation, calculators.

Number Beginnings: counting, 1-1 correspondence, numeral recognition.
Throughout the year: problem solving, graphing, estimation, number sense, story problems, sorting and classifying.

for discussion, sharing, and peer teaching—a base for broader understanding. This common ground is built upon firsthand experience
and language that is tied to experience. For example, for K-2,
*Mathematics Their Way* (Baratta-Lorton, 1976) has about ten stations (like centers), all of which deal with the idea of pattern,
although each offers a different material or activity. These stations
might include hooking together plastic cubes in a red-yellow-red-
yellow pattern, placing pattern blocks in a line of triangle-trapezoid,
or continuing a zigzag line by connecting a row of dots. Children
choose a station and decide how long they will work with a particular
activity. They need not do every station, because they all deal with
the concept of pattern, and, while some may learn best by repeating
the same activity over and over, each time seeing it a little differently,
another child might better develop the concept by working with a
variety of materials and seeing pattern represented in many different
ways.

A similar immersion in the area of pattern and function for older
students can be organized with a listing of problems which all involve
pattern and function. This is sometimes called a menu. As with
the stations, the students can select all of the problems or a few, for,
in either case, they will be learning something about pattern and
function.

Activities and problems must be 'meaty' enough so that students
with different experiential backgrounds can all learn at different
levels.

A cooperative group of three or four children may choose the
following problem:

> The recycling center gives us 50 cents for each pound of alumi-
> num cans. How much will we get for 10, 50, 100, or more pounds
> of cans? The following table is one way to attack the problem.

| Pounds | Money |
|:------:|:------:|
| 1 | $ .50 |
| 2 | 1.00 |
| 3 | 1.50 |
| 4 | 2.00 |
| ⋮ | |
| 10 | ? |
| ⋮ | |
| 50 | ? |
| ⋮ | |
| 100 | ? |

One child fills in and continues the table for 5, then 6, then 7, and
so on. Another child sees that you multiply by 50 cents each time, so
you can skip to the number of pounds that you are interested in: 7
times 50 would be $3.50 for 7 pounds. A third child may produce a

formula: $m = p \times .50$ (money = pounds times $.50). A formula is a special name for a pattern that is consistent! (For beginning hands-on activities with pattern and functions, see the *Pattern Factory* (Holden and Roper, 1989).

Teachers adapt problems to different levels by the questions they ask. For example (during a probability immersion), students take turns pulling a crayon from a bag which secretly holds four yellow crayons and eight blue ones. Simpler questions would include: "Do you think there are more blue or more yellow?" If a response is *blue*, follow up with questions: "Do you *think* there are *many more* blue or *a few more* blue? How many blue? yellow? Do you think that there is a *better chance* that the next person will pull out a blue or a yellow? Is it *more likely* that the next person will pull a blue or *more likely* that the person will pull a yellow?"

Harder questions would be: "Do you think more than half the crayons are blue? More than three-quarters? More than 50 percent? More than 75 percent? What percentage do you think will be blue? What probability fraction would you guess?"

I find that thinking of appropriate questions comes easiest when children are involved in their stations or cooperative groups and I am free for a while to walk around and observe how they are approaching the problem, what kind of discussion they are having, and how they might be recording their findings. I can then use these questions later when we come together as a total group to share, discuss, and compare what we did and what we found out.

For recording and reporting work, it is beneficial for the students to decide how to organize their paper rather than filling in dittoed sheets. (It happens also to be easier for the teacher.) I point out various forms of recording from time to time. These include making graphs, tallying results, drawing pictures, narrative writing, having one person as a recorder for all, or each person in the group doing part of the final report. With cooperative grouping, usually only one paper is turned in for the group or partner-pair, and this also cuts down the teacher's work load. Furthermore, a lot of paperwork can be thrown away if the class understands that such work served to *help their brains* and is no longer important because the *learning* is now carried internally.

When I ask groups to report on a single paper, it is important for me to make task goals specific and group accountability clear. Such methods of recording and reporting work are a rich source of language development, and, in themselves, these methods foster concept development.

ORGANIZING MATERIALS

When I plan for concept immersion using the yearly calendar, I use math strand titles (such as Pattern, Probability) and Arithmetic concept-cluster titles (such as Fractions, Place Value). I put each of these titles on an index card and list ideas, activities, and materials I know and have on file (Figure 22-2). I pool resources and brain-storm ideas with other teachers. The cards provide a quick reference for planning and are easily updated as new ideas come along.

For each index card title, I make a file folder with the same title. Here I keep activity direction sheets, sample math problems, and any materials which are flat. "Lumpy" things go into a box and can be further separated if necessary by using ziplock plastic bags labeled with a permanent ink pen. The box is marked on both ends with the same title that is on the card. I list the contents of the box on the inside of the lid so that I know when something is missing. Boxes are the same size (letter-legal size) and have punched out holes for easier carrying. These things are gathered and organized gradually over time.

If an area is new, I start with a few problem-solving activities. Later in the year, I repeat these and add a few more. Next year, ideas and materials will build from there. General supplies and manipulatives are kept on a supply shelf in a convenient location so that students can get these for themselves as needed. With cooperative grouping, one child in each group may be designated the supply person and is the only one to take or return things to the shelf. This cuts down on congestion around the supply location.

The more students are involved, the more ownership they have. In addition to involving them in planning and giving them some choice of activities/problems, I include them in the preparation of materials. If blocks need to be separated by color or containers gathered for measurement, students can do this. They need to know that their help is needed and appreciated. This has a secondary effect of

---

**Figure 22-2**  *Sample Card — Probability*

| PROBABILITY |
| --- |
| word collections — common language terms |
| coin flipping |
| crayons in a bag |
| spinners |
| design a spinner / diseñar un girador |
| drop a cup / cae la taza |
| odd and even / par o impar |
|  |

easing the demand on teachers' time while creating a sense of ownership within the child.

MAKING CONNECTIONS

The Ongoing Component also allows for the greatest amount of time in the daily and weekly schedule to ensure sufficient experience for students at a concept-concrete level of learning. I believe a *minimum* of 60 percent of a child's math learning time needs to be spent at the concept level with hands-on activities and opportunity for language to be *hooked* to experience. The connecting level which connects math symbols to concepts need be only a short time (about 10 percent) when concepts are well developed. This symbol-experience connection made by the teacher is vital; otherwise, students develop two separate systems and say to themselves, "When I have blocks, I do this, and when I do the textbook pages, I do this." Learners must become aware that the symbols represent what they already know.

The next level, the symbolic level, is when the child can use the symbols in a meaningful way. The student mentally supplies meaning by recalling past experiences. Practice at the symbolic level is what most textbooks provide, and, unfortunately, that often makes up the entire math program. I believe that practice at the symbolic level should *never be more than* 25 percent of the total amount of learning time for a particular topic. If students need more practice than this, I take it as a signal that more time should have been spent at the concept level; if students succeed in this much practice time, why have them practice further?

The concept, connecting, and symbolic learning levels help me to assess student learning and plan appropriate activities, but they are a guide, not a rigid set of hurdles to be mastered before moving forward. Learning is a fluid process of moving forward to the unknown while connecting back to established *knowns*. Children who can function at a symbolic level for particular concepts (let's say naming fractions), still need concrete materials to progress further. The more hands-on experiences there are over time, the greater the opportunity for seeing more complex relationships and patterns (Figure 22-3).

SUMMARY OF THE ONGOING COMPONENT

The Ongoing Component provides the structure and an overall view to ensure that

- All the strands of the math curriculum are included.
- There is sufficient time allotted for concept immersion.
- There is sufficient time allotted for students to progress through concrete, connecting, and symbolic levels of learning.
- There is a spiraling of the curriculum in which students revisit previous concepts in order to broaden understanding and maintain skills.

**Figure 22-3**  *Understanding Complex Relationships and Patterns*

**Concept Level**
When we share our graham cracker with the group, we each get one out of the four equal pieces.

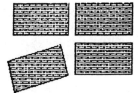

**Connecting Level**
The math writing that shows how much we each get to eat looks like this: $\dfrac{1}{4}$

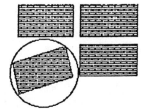

If some creature popped up and snatched all of the pieces and ate them, we could use math writing to show how much it ate. $\dfrac{1}{4} + \dfrac{1}{4} + \dfrac{1}{4} + \dfrac{1}{4} = \dfrac{4}{4} = 1$

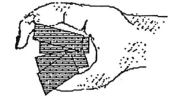

**Symbolic Level**
$$\dfrac{1}{4} + \dfrac{1}{4} + \dfrac{1}{4} + \dfrac{1}{4} = \dfrac{4}{4} = 1$$

## THE INTEGRATED MATH COMPONENT

The Integrated Math Component refers to the math-related applications within each theme or unit taken up by students. The importance of integrating math with other curriculum areas is that the child can see the impact and usefulness of learning math. Math becomes a way of describing and recording our *happenings* and a tool for solving real and right-now problems.

With each new thematic unit of study, look for math applications when brainstorming ideas with students. Any theme can usually include sorting and classifying, comparison, measuring, cyclical or sequential or geometric patterning, pattern and function, estimation of measurement, estimation of quantity, and graphing.

When I plan a particular unit, it is often possible to emphasize whichever topics are currently the subject of the ongoing program.

For instance, if place value is the current arithmetic focus and geometry is the current nonarithmetic focus, I would see in which ways I could relate these to the thematic unit, which, let's say, is China. So, depending on appropriateness for my students, we could compare our place value system to the Chinese abacus and compare our numeral notation system with Chinese numerals. I would look on my geometry index cards for tangram ideas, and we may notice line and shape and symmetry as we tried our hand at the art of Chinese paper folding and cutting. Should the current topics on the yearly calendar seem difficult to mesh with the thematic unit, other topics can be substituted for a while in the Ongoing Component, because the integration of math with other curriculum areas needs to be natural and appropriate, rather than forced. Further math applications during a study of China could be:

Developing a concept of one mile (or kilometer) by comparing it to the number of times around the playground perimeter and then using a scale of miles (or kilometers) to estimate map distances

Using ratio when cooking; for example, for every bunch of bok choy, add one can of bamboo shoots, and, for every four eaters, use one cup of uncooked rice

Graphing the number of bicycles and cars in China and the United States (What are the implications for pollution?)

Sorting books about China into categories of stories, recipes, art, history, and so on

Playing the logical thinking game of NIM

SUMMARY OF THE INTEGRATED COMPONENT

Merely integrating math activities into units of study can be limiting. For, as we tend to integrate in ways most familiar to us, some ideas or strands of mathematics could be left out completely from the overall program. Conversely, to have an isolated Ongoing Component and omit integration would be limiting as well. Integrating math in abundant and various ways is of major importance. If the Ongoing Component is the heart of the child's learning of mathematics, then the Integrated Component is the spirit—it is where and how math lives in our world—its usefulness and its beauty.

## THE MAKE-MATH-LAST-ALL-DAY COMPONENT

To make math last all day long, math needs to be viewed as a way of thinking and communicating rather than as a body of knowledge. We need to capitalize on seeing the world and our "happenings" in ways that are math related. We need to use math eyes, math language, and math thinking all the time. I take advantage of *mathable* moments in the course of each day.

- Alicia is our third new student since school began this month. If we continue to get three new students a month, how many more will we have by May?
- What percentage of the class do you think will return the parent notes by tomorrow?
- How many paces do you estimate it will take to walk to the cafeteria?
- Who has "math clothes" on today? (geometric shapes, color patterns of red and yellow, symmetrical designs, stripes are parallel lines, plaids have both parallel and perpendicular lines, etc.)

The more teachers can carry the math curriculum in their heads, the more able we are to seize math opportunities in the context of the day's events. Opportunities can also be created for special days, such as the Hundredth Day of school or a How Many Day. During a How Many Day, we do a regular kind of schedule but take every chance to estimate how many books, pages, floor tiles, or steps there might be.

## THE THREE MATH COMPONENTS AT WORK

Throughout the school year, the three math components work this way. Looking at one block of time, from the yearly calendar the area of focus for arithmetic is fractions and the other than arithmetic area is geometry. A few geometry activities (perhaps polygons, tangrams, and tessellations) are introduced one at a time to the whole group or cooperative groups within the class. These activities or related ones then become independent activities, and this is the beginning of a menu. Each day one new related activity (such as finding the area of geoboard polygons) is introduced and added to the others as a choice. Menu/choices can be every day for a number of days, for example, three or five or eight days until most of the children have done most of the tasks. If the menu incorporates the focus area of geometry, time set aside for an arithmetic topic would precede and follow the menu block of time (see Figure 22-4, p. 310).

Menu can also be one or two days a week, ongoing. In this case, the greater part of the week would be given to daily lessons which can still be worked in cooperative groups; the difference is that all groups would work on the same problem/activity rather than choosing. On menu day, groups would choose from activities which review or extend the week's learning. Total group discussion would take place when most students have had a chance to become familiar with the activity/problem being summarized (see Figure 22-5, p. 311).

With either scheduling system, the Integrated Component is scheduled into another part of each day during time allotted for thematic unit study. This math integration may take the form of a center activity if learning centers are used, be within group discussion, and/or part of individual research and reporting projects. On some days, the "regular lesson" time can be given to the Integrated

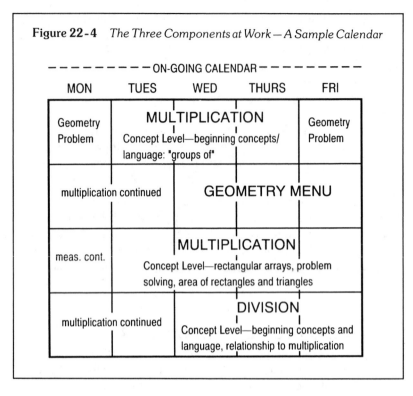

**Figure 22-4** *The Three Components at Work — A Sample Calendar*

```
– – – – – – – – ON-GOING CALENDAR – – – – – – – –
    MON        TUES       WED       THURS       FRI
```

| Geometry Problem | MULTIPLICATION<br>Concept Level—beginning concepts/<br>language: "groups of" | | | Geometry Problem |
| multiplication continued | | GEOMETRY MENU | | |
| meas. cont. | | MULTIPLICATION<br>Concept Level—rectangular arrays, problem<br>solving, area of rectangles and triangles | | |
| multiplication continued | | DIVISION<br>Concept Level—beginning concepts and<br>language, relationship to multiplication | | |

time to allow for more extensive projects. Meanwhile, the Math-All-Day-Long Component (Figure 22-6) is an ever present part of what we do.

## ORGANIZING FOR ASSESSMENT AND EVALUATION

The National Council of Teachers of Mathematics (NCTM) calls for a shift of emphasis in the evaluation of students and math programs. NCTM (1989, p. 191) advocates the following:

**Increased Attention**
- Assessing what students know and how they think about mathematics
- Having assessment be an integral part of teaching

- Focusing on a broad range of mathematical tasks and taking a holistic view of mathematics
- Developing problem situations that require the applications of a number of mathematical ideas

**Decreased Attention**
- Assessing what students do not know
- Having assessment be simply counting correct answers on tests for the sole purpose of assigning grades

- Focusing on a large number of specific and isolated skills organized by a content-behavior matrix
- Using exercises or word problems requiring only one or two skills

**Figure 22-5** *The Three Components at Work — Sample Calendars*

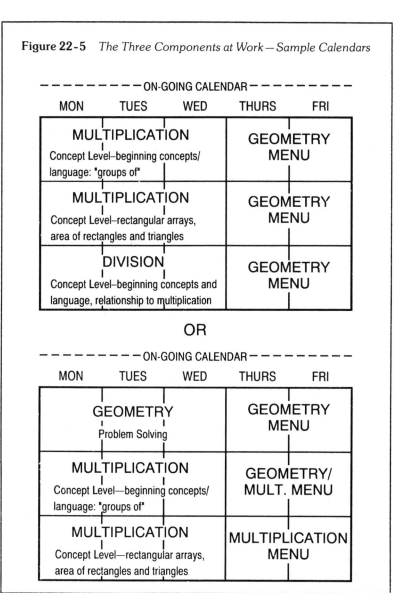

– – – – – – – – – ON-GOING CALENDAR – – – – – – – – –

| MON | TUES | WED | THURS | FRI |
|---|---|---|---|---|

| MULTIPLICATION<br>Concept Level–beginning concepts/<br>language: "groups of" | GEOMETRY<br>MENU |
|---|---|
| MULTIPLICATION<br>Concept Level–rectangular arrays,<br>area of rectangles and triangles | GEOMETRY<br>MENU |
| DIVISION<br>Concept Level–beginning concepts and<br>language, relationship to multiplication | GEOMETRY<br>MENU |

OR

– – – – – – – – – ON-GOING CALENDAR – – – – – – – – –

| MON | TUES | WED | THURS | FRI |
|---|---|---|---|---|

| GEOMETRY<br>Problem Solving | GEOMETRY<br>MENU |
|---|---|
| MULTIPLICATION<br>Concept Level—beginning concepts/<br>language: "groups of" | GEOMETRY/<br>MULT. MENU |
| MULTIPLICATION<br>Concept Level—rectangular arrays,<br>area of rectangles and triangles | MULTIPLICATION<br>MENU |

**Figure 22-6** *The Three Components at Work — A Daily Schedule*

DAILY SCHEDULE

| MATH INTEGRATED with whole language block |
|---|
| LUNCH |
| 1:00 to 2:00  ON-GOING MATH |

| Increased Attention | Decreased Attention |
|---|---|
| • Using multiple assessment techniques, including written, oral, and demonstration formats | • Using only written tests |
| • Using calculators, computers, and manipulatives in assessment | • Excluding calculators, computers, and manipulatives from the assessment process |
| • Evaluating the program by systematically collecting information on outcomes, curriculum, and instruction | • Evaluating the program only on the basis of test scores |
| • Using standardized achievement tests as only one of many indicators of program outcomes | • Using standardized achievement tests as the only indicator of program outcomes |

One of the most valuable uses of continuous assessment is to enable teachers to adapt and readapt questions, problems, and activities as they interact with and observe students. The Ongoing Component addresses the continuous development of concepts and abilities, many of which are not sequential. A child need not master addition and subtraction in order to begin learning about multiplication by developing concepts which deal with identifying equal groups of things. Other concepts are sequential. For example, it would be nonproductive to ask children to recognize equal groups if they cannot count with one-to-one correspondence or have not yet developed conservation of number.

Teachers need a mental curriculum, including the knowledge of what is sequential and what is not, and this may take time to develop for an individual teacher. Beginning teachers need not worry about getting "it" all perfectly sorted out, if they are observant kidwatchers. Whereas some confusion is a companion to the learning process, children will always show those who look for it when confusion is insurmountable and unbridgeable gaps call for other kinds of experiences. Some specific ways I carry out informal diagnostic/planning procedures include kidwatching, math journals/writing, and individual record sheets.

KIDWATCHING

Kidwatching is most easily done while cooperative groups are engaged in their activities or problem solving. I make an anecdotal notebook by adding alphabetical tabs to a spiral notebook or to a narrow three-ring binder. Student names are written at the upper-right and lower-right corners; one or two pages are left between individuals. The notebook is kept in a convenient place (a small one can be kept in an apron pocket), so that I can get to it quickly as I observe the groups at work. I make notes concerning how a child acts within the group: as a leader, with full or limited participation, as a watcher but not participating, if disruptive or constantly off-task. Another category for kidwatching would be how creatively children approach a problem: Do they have more than one problem-solving strategy? Do they generalize past learning to new situations? Other assessment categories include ability to communicate and math understanding and abilities.

MATH JOURNALS

Assessment also must be sensitive to students' language development. As in any language, communication in mathematics means that one is able to use its vocabulary, notation, and structure to express and understand ideas and relationships. In this sense, communicating mathematics is integral to knowing and doing mathematics (NCTM, 1989, p. 214).

One means of language assessment can be math journals (Figure 22-7, A–C, p. 314). Students are asked to record what they did to solve a problem and/or what they found out by doing the task. A child may have demonstrated understanding by using concrete materials but may lack the language or symbols needed in order to communicate that understanding. Likewise, it may be assumed that some children, because of an advanced verbal level, have understanding, but this may be only "jargon-parroting." Whether in journal form or not, writing about math tells us a lot about the child's level of understanding and ability to communicate mathematically.

RECORD KEEPING AND SCORING

Individual record sheets are checklists of skills and understandings. These can also be kept in an alphabetized binder (and the anecdotal notes can be written on the back of each student's sheet). A student is never assessed with the total sheet at any one time. Assessment should be used only to give information which is helpful to teaching, learning, and reporting to parents. I pick and choose those items which are most useful and create my own individual record.

A recording sheet for the arithmetic strand for younger children may include:

Rote Counting
1:1 Correspondence
Conservation of Number
Counting On
Instant Recognition
Numeral Recognition
Number at the Concept Level
Stories
Oral Math Stories

**Figure 22-7** *Math Journals from Marcia Thayer's Class*

March 30. 1988

**A.**

What we did
First we got 3 Crackers
and we had to divid them
in 4. We got three
out of Four
and I dicoverd that
the cookie's were good
and I said that
it was specil For
Ms. B to Bring the cookie's
to Our class.

**B.**

March 31,1988
First we got grancrackers,
three whole grancrackers.
We had to talk about how
to dwvide them.

Then each of us got 3/4.

And we got 1/4 less of crackers.

**C.**

March 31 1988
Ve lookd at them
for a wil and then
monica merde; had
a good I dia from tha
hot cracer we wod get
haf and from the other
oun we wodget haf or
the other haf it's
like this.

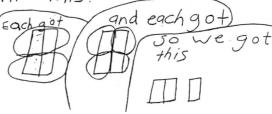

Each got   and each got
so we got
this

**C.** We looked at them
for a while and then
Monica Martha had a good idea. From the
whole cracker we would get
half and from the other
one we would get half or
the other half. It's like this.

I use the NCTM Evaluation Standards method for documenting students' problem-solving efforts:

> Scoring schemes include giving two scores (one for the answer and one for the strategies used); rating the student's work on a scale (e.g., 4—perfect, 3—nearly all correct with some computational errors, 2—right idea but poor execution, 1—tried the problem, 0—nothing was done); or giving points for such primary features as computation, pictures, tables, strategies, and verification. One way of reporting progress in problem solving is with a problem-solving profile. The profile can include ratings on a student's willingness to engage in problem solving, the use of a variety of strategies, facility in finding the solution to problems, and consistency in verifying the solution. The report to parents should include a sample of the student's problem-solving work (NCTM, 1989, p. 209).

## PROGRAM EVALUATION

As I organize my mathematics program, I let the NCTM Standards guide my evaluation by considering "what mathematics students know; how they learn mathematics; and the curriculum, means of instruction, and expectations of those who influence the program. In addition, an evaluation should consider any barriers that prevent students from attaining the full benefits of the program and what can be done to eliminate such barriers" (NCTM, 1989, p. 238).

We must evaluate and constantly restructure and improve the mathematics program we offer our students by examining the balance of the three components: *the Ongoing Component, the Integrated Component,* and *the Make-Math-Last-All-Day Component.* And, as we look to the impact on the child's learning, we must also be gentle and patient with ourselves as lifelong learners who slowly but continuously improve our own abilities and understandings, not only to improve our teaching, but also because learning more is what it's all about!

# 23

# THE CHAPTER I READING TEACHER ENTERS THE CLASSROOM

**Debra Jacobson**

At 9:45 every school day I walk out of my first class of the day, where I just spent forty-five minutes, and go right next door. Usually Judy and her twenty-nine second graders are finishing up a read-aloud and they're ready for the work we will do together. Currently, we're focusing on the author, Arnold Lobel. Judy and I model with two of her students how groups can read together, stopping to discuss whenever something comes up that an individual wants to talk about with the group. As these second graders read *Frog and Toad* and other Lobel books in small groups, Judy and I meander from group to group as participant observers. The students are considering which part of the book might make a good readers' theater. They just saw the class next door perform a readers' theater based on an Arnold Lobel book and are eager to create one themselves.

When the 10:15 bell rings, students mark their places in their book so they can continue reading after recess. I walk upstairs to the third grade and enter Cathy's class where everyone is writing and beginning to conference with each other. Cathy has already involved her students in a mini-lesson which Cathy and I discussed the day before. I go over to one of my targeted Chapter I students to see how he is doing. After about ten minutes of mini-conferencing, mostly with my Chapter I students, I meet with a literature study group in the small conference room adjoining the classroom. The group is comprised of some of my Chapter I students, as well as other students.

Cathy keeps writing with the rest of her class, and after a while they make the transition into reading. She checks in with individuals, recording pertinent information on students' reading conference cards. When the discussion with the group I'm working with in the conference room is over, we join the rest of the class and decide to either continue to read the literature study book or another book.

During my four years as a Chapter I reading teacher at this school, I've made and implemented organizational decisions anchored by my understanding of whole language. My major goals for my fifty targeted students are for them to engage in meaningful reading/ writing/learning activities while enhancing their self-concept as learners. Therefore, rather than have a pull-out program, I decided to work in classrooms.

When I started this job I was told how to select my students, and I began as the teacher before me did and as many others in similar roles around the country have done: I organized my time into half-hour blocks and pulled from six to eight students at a time out of their classrooms each school day. I began to question whether this was the best plan of action. In some ways it was good for me and my students. I got to work with small groups, and my students seemed to be enjoying and profiting from our time together. I was concerned, though, about my students' self-concepts. Did they perceive them-selves as the low ones needing special help? Also, I wondered how missing class time affected them.

My Chapter I administrator was encouraging us to facilitate coordi-nated curriculum, which meant to me that, in the best interest of the children, it would be helpful for specialists to work in conjunction with the classroom teachers so that the messages we give kids aren't contradictory. I attempted to work toward this goal by holding monthly meetings with individual teachers to share what we were doing in the language arts. I began to realize that, by working in classrooms rather than pulling kids out, I'd come as close to curricu-lum congruence as possible and that it would be in the best interest of everyone involved. I also knew that I didn't want to work in a corner of the room with my Chapter I students but in the context of the whole class.

So, during my third year, Cathy and I organized a pilot program for her third graders. The year before I had invited Karen Dalrymple, an experienced teacher from Colorado (now from Oregon), to in-service our school staff on Don Graves' model of writing workshop. Cathy, who had not been satisfied with her writing program, imple-mented it into her classroom right away. Now that writing was in place, she said she wanted to move on to working on her reading program. So, in addition to thinking that my working in her class-room would be good for her students because they wouldn't be pulled out, we shared the agenda of teaming within the classroom context in hopes of learning more about how to implement a whole language philosophy in her language arts program.

I had heard about literature study in the classroom from Phoenix teachers at language arts conferences, and, during the summer before that third year, I had read *When Writers Read* by Jane Hansen (1987), so I was interested in trying these new ways to study reading in the classroom. I was unsuccessful in getting Hansen's book to Cathy over the summer, so, when the school year started, Cathy felt compelled to start her reading program as she knew it—with the basal and reading groups.

I scheduled myself into Cathy's room for a half hour a day. We did writing workshop for two of those days; I presented a reading strategy lesson on the third day, and the fourth and fifth days were organized to either follow up on the strategy lesson or to experiment with literature study. At the beginning of the school year, this entailed reading to kids in either the large or small groups and asking them for responses. This was to prepare all of us for discussions without any predetermined right answers. Cathy was interested in the lessons I shared with her students but was not yet ready to embark fully on her own with a similar program when I wasn't present. It was frustrating for me because it left such a short time in which to implement literature study.

Then, in October, Karen did a second in-service on integrated curriculum. She mentioned her "reading workshop" that she uses in her classroom, and Cathy and other teachers in the school wanted to hear more. Karen spoke to us about this over lunch, and, from that time on, Cathy was ready to drop her basal program and move toward defining her own reading program with me. I think that Cathy welcomed me in this team situation because she saw it partly as professional development for herself. She saw me as having some knowledge about whole language, and she wanted to know about it herself.

Our literature study/reading workshop evolved through many trials for the rest of the school year; frequently, we conferred about successes and problems and considered where we ought to go. One thing that remained constant was that I was to team with her and work with her whole class while targeting, but not isolating, my Chapter I students. I never actually said to them that they were Chapter I students. I discussed this experiment with their parents, and we worked together to help their kids. It was definitely a year for exploration of possibilities. We spent a lot of time planning and refining.

We tried literature study groups, with students choosing their group by the book they wanted to read, not by ability. We grappled with having students keep literature logs. We had kids choose a basal book by browsing through several and considering which had the most interesting group of stories for them. (We did this when we still didn't have enough multiple copies of novels.) They got into groups in which each individual had a chance to choose a story and to lead a discussion after everyone read it silently.

We had a whole class folktale unit. Then we went through a period in which kids signed up for informal book-sharing groups where kids shared whatever individual book they happened to be reading at the time.

Cathy's students were reading a lot and knew a lot about books and authors. Enthusiasm was high. When I asked kids on a posttest to list books and authors they knew, they couldn't stop listing.

As I conducted my monthly coordinated curriculum meetings with the other teachers, I described what was happening in Cathy's room. Many more teachers were interested in having me work in their classrooms the next year. During the last three weeks of school, I went into two more classrooms to give the teachers and kids a taste of what it could be like. At the end of that third year, all six of the teachers that I'd be working with the following year wanted me to come into their classrooms.

During the summer, I had telephone conversations with the teachers, talking about a model of how language arts could look in their classrooms. This developing model would be an overall language arts plan which would encompass more time than the actual half-hour of time I could be there each day.

There would be a whole group meeting at the beginning of the language arts block where we'd sing songs from charts, read big books, introduce new books that would be available in the classroom, celebrate newly published classroom authors, make announcements of options or deadlines, and any other relevant information for that day.

Then we would break up into individual choice time or small groups as appropriate. Kids usually would start by browsing through their reading/writing portfolio, a six-pocketed, spiral-bound folder kept in their desks. The portfolio had pieces they were working on and papers on which teachers would note what they were involved in. Then they would make a decision to read or write. At the end of this block, we would get together as a whole group to share insights from the day, performances, revisions made on a story, or other relevant things. I would be in most classes during the individual or small group work time, although in some I'd plan to be there when things were introduced if the teacher wanted my support or wanted to watch me do the initial introductions. In this model, my role also would include times of my nonpresent support, as we planned in detail together.

When the school year got started, it was interesting how this overall model took shape in the different rooms. Each classroom teacher took ownership. Depending on their comfort level with whole language, some used the model only while I was there, while others implemented it as their total program and planned with me how my time could be used most productively.

In one second-grade classroom, I worked with Louisa for the first forty-five minutes every morning. I added fifteen minutes to my usual time slot because she had a high number of Chapter I students in her class. Although interested in whole language, she seemed to prefer our working together as the way to find out more about it. We slowly introduced choices to her students so that on any day they could choose from several standard reading or writing choices as well as things that came up periodically, such as a contest or an opportunity to make a thank-you card.

At the beginning of the year, on the first day, we introduced a song from a chart, sang it together, and read a few predictable books. We showed the kids where these books would be housed, in case they wanted to read them on their own when we broke up to make choices later. Then we went on to begin to introduce writing workshop to the whole group. Everyone received a portfolio and listed possible ideas they could write about. Everyone started their first written piece, and, when they wrote all they wanted to, they decided to read, individually or in pairs, the song or the books.

On the next day, we continued introducing more elements of writing workshop, while adding a few new easy books to the growing collection and singing the song. As the days went on, we introduced something new every few days. Especially when we introduced something that was quite different, we would all do it together before it became one of a growing list of choices. For instance, when we introduced letter writing and the whole school post office, we asked that everyone write a letter to someone in the school and learn to address it properly so that the letter would be received.

We listed the choices on a large chart as we introduced them so that, when we were ready for the children to make their own choices, we reviewed the options from the chart. Our time together developed a very regular structure, and we soon did not refer to the chart, because everyone had internalized the choices and the level of involvement was very high.

A usual day found Louisa taking the attendance (silently) and doing other morning housekeeping routines, while I sang songs or read poems or big books with the kids. Here is a partial snapshot of some of what was happening in her classroom on one typical day when the whole group time was over and students began making their own choices:

Sarah and Taruna were writing a readers' theater script for one of the chapters in an Arnold Lobel *Frog and Toad* book. Louisa was meeting and discussing with a small group who had all read the same Arnold Lobel book. Betsy was illustrating a book that someone else wrote. Tommy and Scott were grappling over an ending for their cowboy story. They couldn't agree, so they eventually decided to write their own endings. Cindy was copying a book, changing some of the color words. Mark was starting a new story, and Gina was writing a letter to be sent through the school post office. Thuy Mai was looking through her folder for a poem she started last week that she wanted to expand. I had reminded everyone that we would be having a small writing sharing group the next day, so she wanted to get it ready for that. Jermaine was on the floor with a big song book, quietly singing "Miss Lucy Had a Baby" and pointing to the words with a ruler.

I was walking around conferring with individuals and noting what they were doing on the reading or writing conference cards that students keep in their writing folders and put out on their desks as they're working. I paid special attention to the ten students I knew were my Chapter I kids. I also looked for opportunities to invite kids to work together. For instance, as I started to read a book with one child, I noticed another had been browsing through some *Ranger Rick* magazines, mostly looking at the pictures for quite some time. I invited that child to come and join us. Then, after we'd all gotten started on the book, I slipped away, saying that I'd be back a little later so they could tell me what I'd missed.

After forty-five minutes, I quietly moved next door to the next second-grade classroom where I work. It was different in all the classrooms. In some, I participated in small writing groups where individuals wanted feedback on a piece they were working on or I met with a literature study group. Other times, I would work with individuals as they were reading or writing while the classroom teacher met with a small group. Sometimes the two of us would model something the students would be getting into groups to do.

How did I organize to work so individually in each class? At first, it was very time consuming meeting with six different people each Friday afternoon after the kids left to evaluate what had happened that week, make specific daily lesson plans for the following week, and discuss long-range plans. Then, as the year went on, things fell into place and planning got easier. We found time for planning during the week and saved some stuff for weekend phone calls. In some classes, such as Louisa's, things were going so well and we felt the kids were responding so well to the established routine that we didn't want to change much, and planning was minimized.

As inconspicuously as possible, I try to make sure my Chapter I students are bringing books home to read and recycling these frequently. If any of my students need some special attention, it's easy to do individual conferencing. In the pull-out situation, there were always six or seven others to consider, and there was rarely time to confer individually.

If a class schedule isn't going according to plan and they're not ready for me when I arrive, I have it worked out with the teacher that I take one of my students for some individual work. Meanwhile, I keep an ear on what's happening with the rest of the class so the child and I can easily move back into the big group. I organize my schedule so that I have an hour free one afternoon each week. This is proving useful for classrooms where we need some extra time together or to work with individuals.

It's presently the end of my first year of trying this in-class work. Reflecting back on the year, I think that finding more planning time within the school day would be helpful. There are many benefits of working in classrooms. Second to continuing to feel that it's better for the students is that it brings teachers together on a regular basis to discuss the developing curriculum.

I'll be moving on to a new school where I'll be a half time Chapter I teacher. Instead of my fifty students being spread among six classrooms, my twenty-five students will be spread among twelve classrooms. This will present a challenge as far as trying to continue my in-class work. It's unrealistic to think I could get into everyone's classroom. I plan to determine who my targeted students are and then to plan creatively. One tentative plan is to team teach with a fourth-grade teacher, opening the wall between our two rooms and integrating my students from all the grade levels into her daily schedule. I might also go into a second-grade classroom, as I did last year, where I know the teacher is philosophically consistent with me. As a new teacher in the school, nothing will be determined until the school year begins and I see who my students are and whose classrooms they're in.

It's an interesting role I've taken on for myself in that it takes some juggling to work out scheduling and everyone's needs. There's always reevaluating and reorganizing, and at one time this would have made me nervous, but a whole language point of view of learning and living as a dynamic process helps me see the value in being open to vulnerability and continued inquiry.

# 24

## PROFESSIONAL DEVELOPMENT AT FAIR OAKS

### Lois Bridges Bird

## IN THE BEGINNING

> I spent the morning visiting Fair Oaks classrooms; what a warm
> and bright environment! I felt overwhelmed by the life and energy I
> felt in those rooms. These teachers are on the front lines. I'm not at
> all sure what I can do for them. I'm surely the one who needs to
> learn what they are doing.

So begins the reflective journal that I initiated when I started working
as a whole language consultant at Fair Oaks School in Redwood
City, California. Seven years had passed since I myself had faced a
roomful of eager youngsters. During that time, I had completed a
doctorate with Ken and Yetta Goodman at the University of Arizona,
become a mother, and moved with my husband and our children to
the San Francisco Bay Area. That first journal note not only marked
my entry into Fair Oaks classrooms but also my reentry into professional life. And noting that I felt overwhelmed was putting it mildly. I
well knew how much I didn't know, including how best to guide the
professional development of nineteen teachers, who staffed classes
from kindergarten through the sixth grade and brought to whole
language various degrees of experience, commitment, and understanding. I eased my worries by reminding myself that Fair Oaks was
officially committed to whole language.

In 1980, after a visit from two officials from the California State
Department of Education who wanted to know why Fair Oaks
students were, according to standardized test results, three to four
years below grade level, the Fair Oaks staff began taking a long, hard
look at their educational program. First to go were basal readers. A

psycholinguistic reading lab was opened and, initially, a small experimental group of sixty fourth, fifth, and sixth graders were invited
in to read and respond to children's literature books. Test scores and
student attitudes toward reading improved dramatically, buoying the
school's commitment to a literature-centered reading program.

Largely through the efforts of Gloria Norton, the school resource
teacher, and supported by a three-year grant from Raychem, a
neighborhood corporation, Fair Oaks gradually moved from a commitment to literature into school-wide whole language. By the time I
arrived in the spring of 1986, the teachers already had two years of
in-service with such prominent whole language educators and researchers as Jayne DeLawter, Carole Edelsky, Barbara Flores, and
Yetta Goodman. My task, as outlined by Gloria Norton and Norm
Smith, the principal at that time, was deceptively simple: help
teachers move into whole language. I was on campus two days a
week, for a total of about ten hours. Simple arithmetic (10 hours
divided by 19 teachers equals .52 times 60 minutes equals ½ hour)
reveals the seeming impossibility of the task. If we had absolutely
optimum working time with absolutely no interruptions, I would
have approximately 30 minutes with each teacher. Of course, a
school day with no interruptions exists only in teacher paradise, so
even half an hour was an overly optimistic calculation.

The result was something I soon came to refer to wryly as the "gas
station model of professional development." It worked like this: I ran
from class to class, seldom stopping even for a bite of lunch, "filling
up" the teachers with demonstration teaching, feedback on their
teaching, outlines of holistic instructional strategies, professional articles, and anything else I thought might keep them going until my
next service stop the following week. By June, I was thoroughly
frustrated, as this journal entry reveals:

> The lack of time is killing me. Today I launched a writer's work-
> shop in Diane's room. I had just barely introduced my writing
> topics and suddenly it was recess and I was scheduled to go into
> Beth's room so I had to leave. I felt like I was leaving Diane high
> and dry. I've got to find a way to spend more time in each room!

I shared my concerns with Gloria and Norm during the weekly
meetings we set up but weren't always able to keep, again because of
a myriad of interruptions. I had to spend more time in each classroom. A week would be ideal. Given reality, I'd have to settle for a
day. They agreed, and in the fall semester of 1986 I began scheduling one teacher per day. The change for the better was immediately
apparent: I was able to see the progression of a whole day and
develop a feel for each teacher's philosophy and instructional strategies; I came to know the students; and perhaps, most importantly, I
was able to be a real participant in the classroom, working side by
side with the teacher. Sometimes I would teach, enabling him or her
to step back and to observe and reflect on what I was doing and how

the students were responding. Other times, I observed the teacher at work and then shared what I had learned from his or her interaction.

In 1986, I was invited to give the keynote address at a whole language conference in Lethbridge, Canada. I organized my slide show presentation, "What Is Whole Language?" around five themes: trust, ownership, time, meaning, and interaction. Two and a half years later I can see that these same themes also apply to effective professional development.

## TRUST

It is parents' absolute faith that their children will learn to talk that makes them perfect language-learning partners. The same trust that parents bring to their relationship with their children, whole language teachers bring to their classrooms, and all who are involved in professional development must bring to their job as well. I tried hard to bring a basic kindness, sensitivity, and respect to all my interactions with Fair Oaks teachers. I tried to convey what I believed: that teachers are professional educators who know what is best for their kids. I was there to learn with them, not to dictate one right way of teaching.

Learning entails a willingness to risk. When we feel respected and valued, we are more likely to take those necessary risks. It can be very threatening to have someone come into your classroom and observe you at work with your students. Teaching, like writing, is intensely personal. Reflected in every aspect of teaching—from the way we organize our classrooms to the ways in which we interact with our students—is our innermost personality. Therefore, my first order of business was to establish myself as a co-learner in the professional development process. The hallmark of a true professional is a commitment to continual learning. If I could somehow convey to the teachers with whom I worked that we were in this together—that I had every bit as much to learn as they did—then we could begin to work at it together.

## OWNERSHIP

Accordingly, I never imposed an agenda of change but rather invited each teacher to set his or her own goals. "How can I help you? What are your needs?" I would ask. I asked each to identify a goal or goals that we could work on together. It seemed to work best when teachers identified one specific goal, such as launching a writers' workshop or designing their curriculum around themes.

Not only did teachers need to own their professional goals but they also had to define how they wanted to achieve those goals. Once they had identified a goal, my next question would be, "How can I best help you achieve it?" Some teachers simply wanted to talk outside of class—over lunch, after school, or sometimes over the phone in the evenings or on the weekends—and discuss their prob-

lems and concerns with a sympathetic listener. Others invited me
into their classrooms to demonstrate with their students a particular
instructional strategy, like shared reading or an editing conference.
Still others, often those who felt most confident as teachers, invited
me to participate in classroom activities and to observe them at work
with their students.

Eventually, as my relationships with the teachers grew and real
friendships formed, I was invited to all the classrooms to observe
teachers at work. The important thing was to follow the teacher's
lead. I tried never to push but to let each teacher set the pace and
move ahead in a way that was most comfortable for him or her.

## TIME

Patricia Brown, a Redwood City school board member wrote recently, "Time is the greatest enemy of change in public schools"
(Brown, 1989). How right she is! I was constantly chasing the clock,
and I never once won the race. Because my limited schedule allowed
for so little time to talk with teachers, I often followed up our
meetings by writing a letter to the teacher and saying on paper
everything I would have liked to talk about. For example, a lunchtime
meeting with kindergarten teacher Carol Cross, in which we discussed her program, came to an end when Carol's afternoon students arrived; I sat at the back of the classroom and wrote her this
letter:

April 16, 1986

Dear Carol,

Thank you for sharing with me this afternoon. I very much enjoyed meeting with you and learning from you.

The way you are involving the students' families in your room
is wonderful, Carol. As we discussed, education should be a
shared endeavor between home and school. We need to find
ways—as you certainly have—to reach out to the homes and
the communities of our students. By inviting the families into
our rooms to share their unique and rich culture and experiences, you are validating them and enriching the lives of all
participants. I do hope that you will be able to share what you
are doing with our colleagues.

You mentioned that the children respond verbally to whatever the "child of the week" brings in to share with his or her
classmates. What do you think about hanging a sheet of paper
near what the child has shared and invite the children to respond in writing as well? They could sign their names next to
their comments. It would be a fun way to stimulate more writing, especially since the children already enjoy the whole sharing experience so much.

Carol, I've enclosed a chapter on kindergarten writing from Lucy Calkins' fine book, *The Art of Teaching Writing* (1986). I think you'll find it most helpful. I know that you want documentation of the benefits of kindergarten writing. I have some additional articles at home that I'll bring for you next time.

Thanks again for a stimulating visit.

Sincerely,

I found that, when the time to talk had run out, written communication was a reasonable substitute but never as desirable as face-to-face communication. I xeroxed all the letters and added them to my reflective journal so that I had a record of everything I'd shared with the teacher. Just as a whole language teacher's anecdotal classroom records inform his or her instruction, so my reflective journal, a loose-leaf notebook with a separate section for each teacher, was my constant companion and source of guidance and inspiration.

The first year, my written communications often included typewritten handouts of possible instructional strategies the teachers might try. Sometimes I jotted down lists of ideas off the top of my head; at other times, I condensed the main points of articles or books that I knew they would find helpful but did not have time to read. The teachers understood that these handouts were best used as points of departure and not as blueprints for teaching; that ultimately each teacher had to find his or her own way. Nevertheless, the handouts did provide helpful guidelines. I also xeroxed articles for teachers, brought in books from my personal professional library, and, in general, tried to share anything and everything I had at my disposal that might be helpful.

I also tried hard to reassure teachers that the same time they afforded their students to grow they also needed to give themselves. Change takes time. Most of us have infinite patience when it comes to working with our students; we need to be equally patient with ourselves.

MEANING

Just as effective teachers respect, listen, and respond to each child's creation of meaning, so I always tried to be sensitive to each teacher's personal response to whole language. Since each teacher brought to the learning experience different levels of understanding and commitment to whole language, I always tried to begin where the teacher was. For some, this meant helping them to rearrange their classroom, pushing together desks to create a physical environment that would better support active, cooperative learning. For others, it meant engaging in lengthy philosophical discussions and exploring together the meaning of curriculum and the need to respond to student needs and interests while meeting the demands of state and district curricular guidelines.

In other words, whole language meant something different to each teacher. I tried my best to respond to that meaning in a nonjudgmental way. I felt reassured when I read the comments of a second-grade teacher, Beth Anselmi, who wrote, "Lois helps you to think things through, until you figure out what you can do. She takes us through it personally, so I am working with her on how to start this thing in my classroom, with my kids, and my personality."

INTERACTION

Teachers occasionally feel isolated—depressingly alone with classroom problems that can be demanding, exhausting, and emotionally wrenching. They may have to spend the whole day without exchanging a word with another adult. Sometimes just being there for the teacher as a sympathetic listener was the most important role I could play. Listening, in fact, was my most important strategy. After I had demonstrated a particular lesson or had watched them teach, we would sit down and talk: "How had it felt to them? Had it gone the way they had wanted? What seemed to work? What didn't work as well?" I wanted to serve as a sounding board and help them engage in self-evaluation and reflection. Together, we would discuss alternative strategies that they might try next time. At the same time, I shared my observations and suggestions for new directions they might consider exploring. Then, together, we would negotiate the next step: would they like me to come in and demonstrate, or should I observe them at work and respond? Did I know articles that might help? Again, I trusted the lead of the teacher; he or she knew which direction to move in and how best to get there.

**STRATEGIES THAT WORKED**

I was just one part of a whole school-wide context that was designed to support change. As I worked with teachers, helping them to develop and refine their whole language teaching, some strategies worked better than others. I will share those that worked.

DIALOGUE JOURNALS

As part of a ten-week "Language and Literacy" course I taught for the school, I asked teachers to keep dialogue journals. These were open-ended and could include a response to the articles they were reading for the class or could serve as an opportunity to write and reflect about things that were happening in their classrooms. I responded in writing to their journals; their colleagues responded as well. The first ten minutes of each class session were devoted to a journal exchange: they exchanged their journals with at least one colleague and then responded in writing to the journal entry they had read. In this way, teachers had an opportunity to see what their colleagues were grappling with in the classroom or what their reaction was to a particular article.

Sometimes, a teacher wrote about a concern that he or she wished to keep private. Teachers always had the option of not sharing their writing. While it's hard for busy classroom teachers to find time to write, most of the faculty seemed to agree that this was a helpful experience. In fact, some teachers confessed that they had never felt good about themselves as writers. Writing every week (and more frequently in some cases) helped them to overcome years of negative feelings about writing. It also helped them to experience what they were asking their students to do—to write and to share their writing. More than one teacher remarked, "Now I know how my kids feel during writers' workshop!" Here is an excerpt from Leslie's journal that is typical of the written conversations that occurred between the teacher, a colleague, and me:

Things don't feel so good. I can tell the kids are not all with me. It's sort of like I'm starting all over again.

In writing, for example, I've conferenced with kids and they've talked about their piece. We (maybe just I) talked about focus. They are writing bed-to-bed stories, primarily and they've chosen a part to write about. We have a good conference, we make good plans and then they leave their story and wander off! I don't know if I'm too dominant or they are not committed to changing or revising. Anyway, I'm frustrated! I tried a lesson today designed to slow down their writing and help them to concentrate on adding detail and it flopped!

Tomorrow's another—and I hope—better day!
Colleague responds: I think always, that you are too hard on yourself. We've all noticed how good things are going in your room. If I wrote this to you, you would tell me: "Remember, it's a process!" Right?! Maybe more peer conferencing would help? I know that's a process, too, and takes time.
I respond: My hunch is that if they are not wanting to revise at all it's because they are not engaged with their topics. Bed-to-bed stories tend to be boring for all concerned, including the writer. Can you do a new topic launch? I'll be glad to tackle one for you. When children have found what Graves calls a "best topic," they are more likely to spend time on their writing and revise. This has to be coupled with lots and lots of opportunities to share. Kids will revise when they care about their topic and when they care what others think who read it.

I sympathize with your frustration! Let's talk more.

Two years later, second-grade teacher Beth Anselmi says that she still refers to her journal for inspiration and guidance. These journals were so helpful for many teachers, in fact, that I've often wished we had extended their use beyond the class and made them a routine part of the professional development process.

VISITOR'S GUIDES

As a final project for the class, I asked the teachers to create a "Visitor Guide" to their classrooms. As one of the few bilingual, whole language schools in the country, Fair Oaks receives almost daily visitors. Since it is not possible or desirable for teachers to chat with visitors during class time, visitors can instead read the Visitor's Guide, conveniently stored in a pocket near the front door of the classroom, and, at a glance, get a sense of the teacher's educational philosophy, as well as an explanation of the activities they are likely to observe in the classroom. In addition, some teachers include a daily schedule and classroom map along with photographs of the kids at work on different projects. These Guides have proved helpful for visitors, but their real value lies in the incentive they have given each teacher to think about, reflect upon, and examine through writing what they really believe about teaching and learning.

Whole language teaching demands that teachers engage in a conscious examination of their educational philosophy; "for trying to teach without a philosophy . . . is like trying to sail without a compass. You will inevitably sail somewhere but you may not reach your destination" (Bird, 1989, p. 22).

GRADE LEVEL MEETINGS

In the original proposal to make Fair Oaks a whole language school, time for talking and reflection was built into the monthly schedule. Every Thursday is a minimum day. Regular staff meetings, held twice a month, are alternated with grade level meetings. For the grade level meetings, the staff splits into two groups, kindergarten through third and fourth through sixth, and spends approximately two hours talking and sharing their concerns, questions, breakthroughs, and triumphs.

Those who are moving into whole language teaching understand well its experimental nature. There is no one right way to do whole language. While specific theoretical knowledge about language and learning unite all whole language teachers (children are active learners; they learn language while they use language to learn about the world around them), each whole language classroom also reflects the unique personalities, needs, and interests of the teacher, the students, and the social-cultural community of which the school is a part. Unlike traditional skill approaches, in which teachers simply plug into a step-by-step program or kit or textbook, whole language teachers must rely primarily on their own knowledge base and understanding. It's an understanding that is continually evolving.

The grade level meetings have been structured in several ways. Last year, I used this time to give a brief presentation of a particular issue and then invited the teachers to discuss it. In some ways these meetings were not as successful as the ones in which I played a more participatory role. I have since learned that this open time for sharing and reflection is so necessary that it's important not to impose too much structure. The meetings seem to work best when teachers bring in samples of student work to share and to evaluate, or simply talk about their most pressing issues. "Go with the flow" has become our motto for these meetings.

## OBSERVATION IN EACH OTHER'S CLASSROOMS

We have used our grant money to hire substitutes to free teachers to observe in each other's classrooms. For many reasons, Fair Oaks tends to have a high teacher turnover. This means that every year we have teachers who are brand new to whole language. One of the most effective ways of helping them is to provide them with time to observe whole language in action in their colleagues' classrooms. This strategy has proved equally helpful for veteran Fair Oaks teachers. The opportunity to see alternative ways of organizing the learning environment and relating to students helps to expand their options. Whole language is all about options. The more aware one is of the alternatives, the easier it becomes to design a classroom that works best for you and your students.

## VIDEO AND AUDIO TAPING

With the understanding that "the camera never lies," some teachers have asked me or others to videotape them teaching and have then viewed the tapes privately or have allowed the tapes to be used in a grade level meeting, so that their colleagues could observe them and comment. To varying degrees, teachers have also audio taped their literature study sessions or writer's workshop conferences. Again, the idea is to step outside the rush of classroom activity, to examine and reflect on what seems to work and what doesn't, and then to revise instructional strategies accordingly.

Last year sixth-grade teacher Pat Yencho audio taped most of her literature study sessions and, through careful analysis, was able to identify the ways in which she could influence an effective session. She eliminated responses that inhibited student talk and increased the strategies that encouraged student talk.

## PROFESSIONAL LIBRARY

Over the years, Gloria has worked hard to develop a professional library that will support teachers on their odyssey into whole language. Books such as Ken Goodman's *What's Whole in Whole Language* (1986), Don Graves's *Writing: Teachers and Children at Work* (1983), and Lucy Calkins' *The Art of Teaching Writing* (1986) have proved to be invaluable guides. Fair Oaks teachers routinely borrow and read these. Gloria has also collected an impressive file of professional articles. Together, we organized these by topic and put them in a loose-leaf binder so that teachers could easily remove and xerox the ones that looked most useful. Teachers are also encouraged to add articles that they have found themselves.

As Dorothy Watson says, "Whole language teachers share their best." Fair Oaks teachers make copies of helpful instructional strategies they've discovered and thematic units they've designed with their kids. These are kept in a file in the teachers' room and are available for all to borrow and use.

### MY PERSONAL JOURNAL

At all times I carried a loose-leaf notebook. In it I kept a copy of every techer's classroom schedule and a list of their students' names. I also kept a fairly detailed record of my work with each teacher: everything we had done, everything we still wanted to do, and notes about how best to accomplish our goals. This notebook served the same purpose anecdotal records serve whole language teachers. It enabled me to monitor and evaluate what I was doing. Writing is discovery. I often discovered, through writing, answers that had eluded me. I could not have functioned without this notebook.

### WRITERS' WORKSHOP

Believing that Fair Oaks teachers had important stories to tell, I encouraged them to write a book for other classroom teachers who were interested in learning about whole language. While it was exciting to contemplate publication, what really counted was the opportunity to write, to share our writing, and to experience first-hand what we were demanding of our students in writers' workshop. We started meeting and sharing our writing during the summer of 1987. As it turned out, we were able to publish. *Becoming a Whole Language School: The Fair Oaks Story* (Bird, 1989) was the fruit of our efforts. What we learned about ourselves as writers along the way will go far in helping our students become writers.

### STRATEGIES THAT DIDN'T WORK VERY WELL

Since starting at Fair Oaks as a whole language consultant, I have become more aware than ever that learning necessarily entails risk taking, and taking risks often leads to failure. I have surely made my share of mistakes, but, instead of berating myself, I have tried to step back, look at them objectively, and learn from them. Here are some strategies I tried that didn't work very well.

### TRADITIONAL IN-SERVICE SESSIONS

Whole language is built on a solid foundation of research and theory; a strong grasp of this theory is essential for whole language teaching. One of the most difficult aspects of my job was how to share this knowledge base with teachers without resorting to a lecture format. While some teachers stated outright that they didn't mind lectures and, at times, even preferred this format, others were vocal about disliking it. The first two years, especially in the "Language and Literacy" course I taught, I resorted to lecture far more than I would have liked, and I lost teachers because of it. At the risk of stating the obvious, here are some pointers from my experience.

1. There is no substitute for firsthand experience. Our introduction to literature study with Carole Edelsky was successful because she had us participate in one. While it is not always easy to figure out how to make a concept experiential, the more often it can be done, the better. Fair Oaks teachers have participated in writers' workshop, literature studies, hands-on math and science activities, and holistic approaches to research and thematic units. In each case, they left the sessions feeling invigorated and more confident about how to share what they had learned with their students because they had been through the process themselves.

2. Just as whole language teachers validate their students by asking them to share their knowledge in class, so we need to validate teachers by inviting them to share their expertise in in-service sessions. Teachers who are on the "front lines"—in classrooms day in and day out—possess the sort of firsthand knowledge about children and teaching that those of us who have left the classroom may have lost. Our in-service sessions were most successful when time was built in for teachers to share with each other in small groups; asking individual teachers to present to the whole group was also effective.

3. This year, in our whole language in-service sessions, we have moved completely away from an authority who stands up and presents. We have simply shared meaty articles, such as "What Do We Find in Whole Language Classrooms?" by Dorothy Watson and Paul Crowley; we've given teachers time to read them during the in-service; we've broken into small groups and discussed what we learned, what we liked, what we question, and how we might utilize the information in our classrooms. Eventually, the small groups come together again and share with the whole group. We end the session with fifteen minutes for written reflection. Teachers write answers to such questions as "What did I learn today, and how will it influence my teaching?"

## COMMUNITY BOARD

In the school office, I put up a whole language/bilingual bulletin board. My idea was that teachers could post wonderful samples of their students' writing, great quotes by kids, teachers, and researchers, announcements of classroom presentations—anything that other teachers, parents, and visitors to the school might enjoy reading or knowing about. Unfortunately, it never evolved into the community board I had hoped for. Some teachers utilized it, but I was the primary "keeper of the board." I suspect this was the case because it was my idea and didn't fulfill any real need for the teachers.

## WHERE WE ARE NOW

In August 1988, when the Whole Language Advisory Committee, comprising the Fair Oaks principal and resource teacher, district administrators, and school board members, met to discuss the upcoming school year, Gloria suggested that the Fair Oaks faculty would benefit from a "Whole Language Course" taught on campus after school. But who would teach it? The answer suddenly was obvious—Fair Oaks teachers. And so it is that every other Thursday the Fair Oaks faculty and other interested district teachers gather in the teacher's room for sessions on whole language theory and philosophy, writer's workshop, literature studies, thematic units, and holistic evaluation. The class will culminate with a Literacy Fair run very much like a professional conference. We'll invite teachers from the district to listen to a keynote address, "What Is Whole Language?" and then disperse to individual classrooms for presentations and demonstrations by the Fair Oaks faculty and students on various aspects of whole language.

It's easy to get discouraged at times. Sometimes it seems that, for every step we move forward, we slip two behind. But at such times I need only think back on my experiences as a classroom teacher. When we had one of our infrequent in-services, it was organized by the principal or district personnel without our knowledge or input, often on some program or topic or which we had very little, if any, interest. I can't remember an in-service ever making a difference in the way I interacted with my own students—at least not until 1978 when I taught on the Tohono O'odham Reservation in Arizona and reaped the benefits of a full year of in-service with Ken and Yetta Goodman. At Fair Oaks, not only are the teachers organizing their own in-service, they are also giving it. Now, that's progress.

## CONCLUSION

Donald Murray has written, "The job of a good writing teacher is to put him/herself out of a job." Likewise, the job of anyone involved in professional development is gradually to become unnecessary. Fair Oaks teachers have written professional articles in professional journals and chapters in their own book. They have presented at local, state, and national conferences. They have worked as mentor teachers in our district and as consultants in other districts.

There is an old adage that states "The best way to learn is to teach." It is equally true that the best way to teach is to learn. From the very first day I stepped into Fair Oaks, I was very much aware of all that I had to learn. At that time, I viewed it as professional insecurity. Now, with the gift of hindsight, I can see that it served me well. It made me open to what the teachers knew, forced me to recognize their expertise, and made me just exactly what I needed to be to function best in my role as an outside consultant: a co-learner. I am most grateful to the Fair Oaks faculty for allowing me to learn from them and with them. Truly, we all learned together.

# 25

# REFLECTIVE TEACHING
# IN AN INTERDISCIPLINARY
# METHODS COURSE

**Phyllis E. Brazee** / **Warren C. Tomkiewicz**

A combination of fate and free choice often seems to bring people together. Phyllis Brazee and Warren Tomkiewicz, the voices heard in this chapter, shared one floor of the University of Maine (UM) Education Building with just one other science education faculty member. Within this very fragile connection, coming from different disciplines, with no built-in common planning time or even any particular reason to begin collaboration, we exchanged pleasantries and, eventually, a few academic ideas over three semesters' worth of time. In those exchanges, we began to recognize in the other some very similar philosophical views about teaching and learning. Phyllis was hired in the fall of 1984 to teach reading and language arts methods courses in a two-day-a-week, four-hours-a-day block of time. Warren joined the UM staff as the elementary science methods instructor in the fall of 1985. He was given seventy-five minutes twice a week to teach his science methods class.

Over time, our shared beliefs led us to collaborate and to build an integrated, interdisciplinary elementary undergraduate methods block combining reading, language arts, and science. With little preplanning but a very real commitment to process education (including our own!), we launched into our first semester during the spring of 1987. What follows is a description of how we structured our own classroom, examples of specific experiences devised for students, and a brief rationale for such collaboration.

## BRIEF OVERVIEW OF THE STRUCTURE OF THE COURSE

Whole language teachers have learned that real process education cannot be replicated. That is what makes its articulation elusive on the one hand and dynamic on the other. This is also the case with good science education, where students are actively involved in hands-on/minds-on science, asking questions and designing experiments to answer and solve the questions. *Science for All Americans* produced by the American Association for the Advancement of Science (1989) describes it this way:

> Teaching related to scientific literacy needs to be consistent with the spirit and character of scientific inquiry and with scientific values. This suggests such approaches as starting with questions about phenomena rather than with answers to be learned; engaging students actively in the use of hypotheses, the collection and use of evidence, and the design of investigations and processes; and placing a premium on students' curiosity and creativity.

Gordon Wells in *The Meaning Makers* (1986) eloquently argues that "it is not possible, simply by telling, to cause students to come to have the knowledge that is in the mind of the teacher." He rejects the "transmission" model of teaching. Instead, he states that "knowledge can only be constructed by individual knowers and that this occurs most effectively when they have an active engagement in all the processes involved. . . ."

While Wells was speaking of young children and their teachers, we saw supreme value in these statements for our own students and for the teaching/learning environment we wished to create for them. Our goal was Wells' goal: "The aim [of teaching], therefore, should be to foster the development of students' ability to take control of their own learning so that eventually they can assume these responsibilities for themselves." Wells' statement was further intensified for us because the control we wanted our students to learn to take was in the decision-making process as a *teacher*.

Research in undergraduate teacher education has validated Wells' argument against "transmission" models of preservice education. Barbara Spector in *Focus on Excellence*, a National Science Teachers' Association document (1987), states:

> Educational institutions with teacher preparation programs must identify and propagate practices that relieve science anxiety, and provide teachers with the attitudes, skills, and knowledge to teach science effectively at the time when children's minds lend themselves most readily to inquiry, exploration, and discovery. It is easier to prepare teachers properly than it is to provide remediation once they have been certified and are teaching.

Coming from different disciplines, with no built-in common planning time or even any particular reason to begin collaboration, too often professors of education *tell* undergraduates how to teach while providing very poor models of what they profess. We committed ourselves to a very different model of teaching and learning. We decided, before the first semester, truly to *practice what we preach*. In that spirit, we share with you a composite of the structure of our integrated classroom as it evolved over three separate semesters. Many components fit into each semester, but often with new twists, adaptations, and battles with the reality that all of us face: changed teaching schedules, changes in the room(s) we teach in, lack of understanding on the part of administration (who control scheduling), and other faculty (who continue to expect the same amount of committee work, etc., from us). Such issues became a constant challenge to us to retain our philosophical commitment. In the long run, we are thankful for such battles because they made us become more articulate about what we believe. Despite difficult odds, we persevered. The message in this might be, *"If we can, you can, too."*

## COURSE SYLLABI

The first task just before the semester began was to collaborate on a course syllabus. That proved relatively easy as we read over each other's syllabi, adding and deleting to our own. In the first semester, we decided upon the following list of course goals (these hardly changed at all over the three semesters):

1. Develop observational strategies as learners and teachers in science, reading, and language arts.
2. Understand the beginnings of literacy and how they relate to literacy instruction. Also, literacy across content areas.
3. Understand and experience the writing process as authors and teachers of writing, K-8, especially in science.
4. Understand and experience the reading process as readers and teachers of reading, K-8, in narrative and content materials.
5. Examine textbooks and other resource materials for each area and determine their place in instruction.
6. Understand the process of creating interdisciplinary units of study.
7. Observe and teach in a number of classrooms to experience, firsthand, specific teaching/learning philosophies.
8. Learn how to incorporate the language arts into science: reading and writing across the curriculum.
9. Learn to use the computer for word processing, for themselves and as teachers of writing.
10. Examine and critique representative samples of computer software across the three areas of reading, language arts, and science.

11. Develop the knowledge, skills, and attitude necessary to bring science process skills to the classroom.
12. Develop a valid understanding of the nature of science, reading, and language arts, i.e., the processes and products of each.
13. Most importantly, be actively involved in the transition from college student to classroom teacher, i.e., thinking and acting as a teacher.

The heart of our course was in the hands-on/minds-on discovery learning, literate-rich environment we provided on a daily basis for our college students. But the core of any college syllabus for students is the list of assignments. As we easily decided upon those just before our first semester together, we made the first of many discoveries of how much we actually had in *common* as teachers and learners ourselves. What we initially, intuitively agreed upon and what we came to articulate over time was that we were using the write-to-learn philosophy as the main vehicle for our assignments. Within that philosophy, we also explored aspects of the writing process: brainstorming, first drafts, conferencing, and so on. The course assignments included:

1. Keeping a learning log of reactions to activities and discussions during the course, reactions to readings from assigned texts and self-chosen professional journal articles in each field, and overall personal reflections.
2. Creating a "teaching file" of handouts, journal articles, materials from newspapers and magazines, etc., as well as relevant materials from course work from previous semesters in education and science courses.
3. In small groups, creating an interdisciplinary unit of study based on one of four science themes, such as meteorology, astronomy, physical science, and marine science, suggested by Warren. These were to include hands-on science activities and reading and language arts applications.
4. Keeping an extensive journal of field experiences during a four full day teaching experience.
5. Developing through multiple drafts a response to "How would you teach reading and language arts and science?"

## TIME AND ROOM SCHEDULES

Each semester had a different time and class configuration. (See the chart below.) Each had its merits and drawbacks, but we poured into each the essence of our beliefs about integrated, interdisciplinary, process education.

| Semester | Time | Room | Other Factors |
|----------|------|------|---------------|
| Spring 1987 | Mon./Wed./Fri. 8–12 o'clock | Science lab room | |
| Fall 1987 | Tues./Thurs. 8–4 P.M. | One room in the morning, the science room in afternoon | |
| Spring 1988 | Tues./Thurs. | Same as Fall 1987 | Warren had a second section of science methods, only scheduled in the middle of the block: 9–11 A.M.* |

*We chose to handle this dilemma this semester by grouping both classes together for science class in the morning, followed by a one-hour integrated debriefing time, followed by a three-hour reading/language arts class which often built directly upon the science process skills and content discussed in the morning.

## OUR ROLES DURING ACTUAL CLASS PERIODS

The most critical, yet unexpected, role for each of us was that of being a real learner in each other's discipline. We both started out our collaboration with fears, misconceptions, and misinformation about the other's discipline. Like some of our students, Warren, as a scientist, feared writing and had avoided doing much of it. Phyl mirrored many of the scared-of-science students when she wrote during one of the first writer's workshops of the semester:

### First Draft

I feel frightened about science—about what *I* don't know, and how I am not sure *how* to know.

I am currently subscribing to several magazines just to help me "get a handle" on science. As a family, we continue to get *National Geographic* which quietly enters our family life, usually by finding its way to the right hand end table in the livingroom after the wrapper is torn off, the cover admired, and it has been moved several times from diningroom table to side table to. . . . *National Geographic* is an old friend, one to pick up in an odd moment, and now something to be shared with my 7 year old paleontologist son. We *love* looking through the pictures (who doesn't?). In fact, there are two volumes we come back to regularly. I now get *Smithsonian*, a wonderful coffee table addition, but it often sits unopened for months. However, it has become a crucial household reference at times for reports my boys need to do for school.

*Science 86* was devoured from cover to cover, but it changed to *Discovery*, perhaps a bit glitzier. I still enjoy reading that, and marvel at the new horizons of scientific minds. Finally, I continue to wait for and read cover-to-cover, a newsletter called *Brain/Mind Bulletin*. Sometimes it's frightening; sometimes it sounds just like science fiction; sometimes I absolutely don't believe it, and sometimes it totally agrees with my intuitions. It gives a cross-disciplinary approach to "on-the-edge" topics that truly boggle the mind.

That's my reading diet. My working knowledge of science, however, seems awfully thin, especially when my 7 year old starts asking questions. Being a quiet, thoughtful first grader, he is into observing the world. His questions are very real and very deep but at times, it takes me several minutes to uncover what his real question is. Being a first grader, his world is still pretty egocentric so his question comes out of *his* stream of consciousness. Without offending him, I need a few minutes to question *around* his question, to see where he has been looking, or to grab a phrase and relate it to what he had been doing earlier. When I finally uncover his question, I am usually in the dark as to how to *begin* to answer—first of all, my knowledge of the subject is usually very limited. Second of all, I have learned that he does *not* want an extended answer. He needs a short, concise explanation that can fit into what *he* already knows about the world. The best I can do in many instances is to say, "I don't know, honey. Let's look it up." The good thing about this response is that it reinforces his emerging view of *adults* as learners. The bad thing is that we often don't get to it, because we don't have the resources at hand. I am trying to build up our home library of science-related books, but it's too slow a process. So, I fear, is my own emerging knowledge of science—content knowledge.

Each of us was always willing to expose our ignorance or our misconceptions in front of each other and our students, because in doing so we therefore modeled our philosophy of lifelong learning. Initially, we also modeled the asking of questions that our students had also been mulling over but were often too shy to ask. As the semester progressed, their voices became stronger and their questions more confident.

A second valuable role that we played for each other was that of metacognitive pedagogical reflector: while one was teaching, the other was always on ready alert to discuss the other's decision making *as the teacher*.

In the middle of one hands-on science experiment that Warren and the students were involved in, Phyl realized that the students were only responding to Warren as if he were their elementary or junior high school science teacher. They were *not* simultaneously considering Warren as a role model of how to *teach* science. In the middle of the lesson, Phyl intervened and asked students to think for a moment about the teaching and management decisions Warren, as a teacher of science, had just made with them. Phyl and the students made a list on the blackboard, at that moment, verifying and clarifying with Warren (an experienced science teacher!) the rationale behind each of his decisions.

Such spontaneous intervention occurred frequently as we worked to move our students from thinking merely as students in a soon-to-be-forgotten isolated course to thinking as teachers-to-be who would soon be in charge of planning and teaching.

## CLASSROOM ACTIVITIES THAT PROMOTED INTEGRATED CURRICULUM THOUGHT

We often centered our day around a hands-on science experiment. Warren would lead us in *doing* the experiment. Then Phyl would demonstrate how reading and language arts could be woven into the science activity, thus demonstrating that the communication arts come alive for students when they are used as meaningful tools in the pursuit of interesting information. This also provided wonderful opportunities for discussing the *teachable moment* that is so much a part of whole language and process teaching. Again, from Phyllis' log:

Warren began today by asking us to participate in a hands-on lab experience. He brought in gummy "Swedish fish" candy for us to use to begin to explore "doing science." His objectives for the day were: (1) to develop and recognize the process skills involved in doing science, such as observation, classification, data collection and analysis, measurement, and interpretation, (2) to consider the role of prior knowledge in doing science, and (3) to identify the open-ended nature of doing science, i.e., where does this activity take us? We each took a fish and were asked to write down what we observed about it. He quickly introduced us to equipment available to use in the lab room to help us in our observations, and then he set us free.

What I noticed was that my mind and the minds of several other students seemed somewhat rigid in the kind of categories we could come up with. I realized that my observation abilities (and most likely, those of some of the students) were severely limited by my background of experience concerning the kinds of categories I already had in my head (such as color, length, weight) and that Warren had made some assumptions that the class did, in fact, already have some slots available. I realized that one thing Warren was probably going to do was to "pool" the categories of the whole class after a certain amount of independent observation time, but several of the students and I felt very limited in our think-ing. I also realized that what I was coming up with was a list of *ad-jectives*. Those from the combined class included:

| | |
|---|---|
| soundless | sticky |
| immobile | chewy |
| edible | scaly |
| malleable | bumpy |
| sinkable | smooth |

I immediately realized: what a natural place for an ensuing discus-sion to come up about "describing" words! Kids could be led to notice that many of the words the class collectively came up with were *-ible, -able* words or *-y* words. These endings are important syntactic cues for readers. Teachers should help kids discover this language pattern or help them "notice" it, not in isolated work-book exercises but on-the-spot when the teachable moment arises. Also, there were several words which contained Greek and Latin word parts that could be briefly highlighted (*immobile, translu-cent, transparent . . .*) as an additional syntactic cue. The lesson to be learned for our students was to take advantage of such words and the syntactic cue patterns they represented as they naturally arose during a science experiment conversation.

I also realized that it would be absolutely natural with very young students to create a Language Experience text from this science experience later in the day or at the end of the science experiment itself. "Today we studied . . ." After the text was created, the first draft written, the teacher could help the student to engage in Bill Martin's (1967) sentence expansion concept focusing on the ad-jectives generated by the class:

Today we observed gummy fish.
Swedish gummy fish.
malleable Swedish gummy fish.
malleable Swedish gummy fish that are chewy and sticky.

I modeled this for the class, right in the middle of Warren's science class, thus demonstrating in a meaningful way the concept of the "teachable moment."

I also realized that another natural language "lesson" from this science experience for the teacher to capitalize on could be turning to a collection of thesauruses to explore synonyms, additional ad-jectives, nuances of words and multiple meanings of words during the actual list creation, the point of most need of such language tools. The class could develop its *own* thesaurus after having the chance to thumb through junior, intermediate and adult the-sauruses.

We tried to model for our students team teaching in an integrated, interdisciplinary fashion in our own teaching on campus. We also tried to provide many "during" class opportunities for our students to see *us* teaching public school students (in front of them) and to teach students *themselves*, under our guidance and support. We provided many on- and off-campus opportunities for such field-based teaching and learning to occur.

We offer a sample of them:

1. Take advantage of public school breaks that occur when university classes are still in session. Public school children can then come for the morning or for the whole day.
2. Take advantage of classrooms of former and current graduate students for visits and for opportunities for undergraduates to see good teachers in action.
3. Take advantage of former methods students from the integrated block who are currently student teaching. Invite them and their cooperating teacher in for the day to discuss the concerns that are uppermost in the minds of undergraduates who themselves will be student teaching the next semester.

TAKING ADVANTAGE OF PUBLIC SCHOOL BREAKS

This opportunity occurred each semester. Phyl easily persuaded her own two sons and several of their friends to come for the day and to participate with the undergraduate students and Warren as teacher in hands-on science experiments (such as dissecting owl pellets), followed by readers' and writers' workshops and interviews with the children about their individual reading, writing, and science habits and backgrounds. Included in that group of public school student visitors each semester were children of some of our nontraditional students. Often, the assembled group of public school students ranged in age from preschool to high school, thus allowing our undergraduate students access to a wide range of developmental ages.

TAKING ADVANTAGE OF CLASSROOMS OF FORMER
AND CURRENT GRADUATE STUDENTS

Warren began class one semester with a physical science experiment to illustrate the concept of density. He placed small jars of hot and cold colored water in large jugs of hot and cold clear water. He asked our students to observe and predict.

The next class meeting, we traveled to the second-grade classroom of one of Phyl's graduate students. This time, Warren performed the same experiment with the second graders, asking them to respond to the same questions he had asked our students the previous day. Our students sat outside the group of second graders, observing their responses and Warren's teaching. Our purpose was multifold:

1. To have our students see Warren as a successful and interesting science teacher across a wide range of levels
2. To have our students see how universal and adaptable many science experiments can be

3. To have our students begin to see *themselves* in Warren's shoes
4. To have our students begin to examine their own science knowledge

For many college professors, what Warren did would be a tremendous risk. We felt the demonstration (as Frank Smith describes it) was well worth the effort (1981).

Another time Phyl provided a variety of pen pal experiences over the semesters. She identified a primary and an intermediate-age classroom from amongst her current graduate students and arranged with the students in those classrooms to be pen pals with the undergraduate students. Among other benefits, this provided the methods class with fresh, current, rich writing samples over time and across grade levels from process writing classrooms to see how writing develops. It also provided access to real teachers who were implementing many of the ideas Phyl shared in the undergraduate class. Each pen pal experience culminated at the end of the semester in a full-day classroom visit by the college pen pals. This experience usually included a science experiment with related reading and writing activities. Teaching duties for the day were often shared by the classroom teacher, Warren, Phyl, and the college pen pals. For a number of students, this was their first real taste of what a classroom teacher's *full* day is like. We usually arrived at the school of our pen pals by 8 A.M. and left, exhausted, by 3 P.M.!

TAKING ADVANTAGE OF FORMER METHODS STUDENTS

These former students and their cooperative teachers spoke directly to our current undergraduate methods students, who will face, as part of our course, a four-day teaching experience two-thirds of the way through the semester. Providing student teachers to talk to gives our methods students who are full of "first-time" fears the chance to converse with peers who are just slightly ahead of them in course work and teaching experiences.

Such opportunities lessen the potential problem Wells refers to in his discussion of conversations between participants who "differ greatly in their level of cognitive and linguistic maturity—as is the case in interactions between children [preservice methods students] and their parents or teachers [professors]" (1986). The student teachers help "translate" between us and our methods students. Sometimes the student teachers help us and our methods students face the reality of the schism between the real world, where whole language and process science education aren't yet in full swing, and our professional convictions.

## STUDENTS SPEAK

Since we started working together, we have learned a great deal about our students and about our class through their writings. Many statements are validations of what we set out to accomplish in setting up our team taught, integrated, interdisciplinary methods block. Other statements make us pause, reflect, reconsider, and revise what we are doing. Here is a sample of the students' voices over the three semesters:

> I can picture myself as a teacher. I am anxious to have my own class, however, so I could be free to experiment on how I want to teach. I feel that until I do have my own class, that I won't have a true feeling for teaching.

> The dimensions of my view of teacher have changed. The notion of student-teacher as a vertical relationship is fading. I see the role not only more horizontal but interactive. Although the responsibility for what is taught is still mine, I am more aware of assessing student needs and interests. I also see the horizontal dimensions widening to a team approach to relationships with other teachers. . . .

> I think this semester has really brought about a transformation in my thinking from student to prospective teacher. The full day experiences in the field as well as these methods classes have changed my thinking to view myself in more of a teacher role. I look at things around me differently, as to how I could use it in the classroom. I find myself making mental lesson plans or ideas to use in the class all the time. While I'm eating, I think of how many activities such as science, math and language arts that I could do with cereal for example.

> Each of you respected one another, and allowed your opinions to be put into each person's teaching time as an idea of how to integrate what is being talked about. You both offered additional ideas to each other while one was speaking which kept the class flowing.

> Each of you respected the other's subject area and professionalism. You both were concerned about the quality of your teaching.

We have shared with you glimpses of an innovative undergraduate interdisciplinary elementary methods courses. As with any rich context, we could not describe it all. It is our hope, however, that what we have presented does, in fact, represent and respond to the following quote from Harold Burbach (1987):

> An emerging world order is placing a premium on integrative thought . . . in the real world, all the problems are interdisciplinary and all the solutions are inter-departmental, interprofessional, interdependent, and international; and for this reason, "those who would lead must, therefore, get used to thinking integratively."

This information is offered in the hope that it could be a model for other undergraduate methods instructors and to demonstrate to practicing teachers, administrators, academic peers, and communities that, while the fault of the education system is ultimately laid at the door of the undergraduate teacher preparation professor, maybe its solution needs to *start* there!

## POSTSCRIPT

Warren left the University of Maine two years ago to join the faculty of Plymouth State College in New Hampshire but is carrying the spirit of this collaboration into his efforts with both his elementary and secondary science teaching methods courses. The integrated approach has also become a critical component of his earth science content course as well—a real sign that the whole language approach is pervasive!

Phyllis has since team taught with another science educator, Dr. Jennifer Dodd. And now with social studies educator Dr. Lynn Nelson, they are carving out new versions of the integrated, interdisciplinary elementary methods block. They invite your questions, stories, and suggestions.

# 26

## PRACTICING WHAT WE PREACH: WHOLE LANGUAGE WITH TEACHERS OF BILINGUAL LEARNERS

### David E. Freeman / Yvonne S. Freeman

The social context is crucial to the way we construct meaning inside and outside of school. For example, students will respond differently to what they read because of the differences in their life experiences. Margaret Meek (1988) points out that reading experts "often fail to remind themselves that reading doesn't happen in a vacuum. The social conditions and surroundings are important too" (p. 6). The social conditions of literacy development are a major theme in the writings of Paulo Freire (1987), who claims that we must first read the world before we can read the word. As he puts it, "Reading does not consist merely of decoding the written word or language; rather, it is preceded by and intertwined with knowledge of the world. . . . The understanding attained by critical reading of a text implies perceiving the relationship between text and context" (p. 29).

What Freire claims for literacy can be extended to all learning, as Frank Smith (1985) has argued. Reading is just one form of perceiving the world, and we use what we already know, as well as the new things we perceive, to develop a theory of the world in our heads. The social conditions and experiences students bring to their learning have a profound effect on how they respond to class activities and assignments.

In the English as a second language and bilingual education courses that we teach, our teacher education students show us their perceptions of the world through their responses to different readings. Often the responses written at the beginning of the semester reflect the social context of their previous experiences, which, for many students, includes the conservative influences of the Central Valley of California.

Steve's written response during the first week of class to a reading in *California Tomorrow*, a publication on immigrant students in California, reveals the effect his background has had on his reading:

> Well, when I first started reading the article, I knew I wouldn't change my stance on the subject of immigration. Sure, I feel a little for the children, but they're in the U.S. and thus it is up to them to adapt. I feel it's up to them to learn the language and be able to communicate on their own. They decided to come over here, so they should be prepared.

Phil, a former police officer, admits the influence of his past experiences as he expresses similar sentiments in his response to the same reading:

> I have delivered every type of minority I can think of to a correctional facility. My contacts with immigrants have been negative. . . . I really feel that society is ignorant to the amount of drugs that these immigrants bring with them. . . . I am biased in my opinion of immigrants. In fact, I may be ignorant to the good side of the refugees. Hopefully, this class will change my view of immigrants and their influence on society.

When we read responses like Steve's and Phil's, we realize we need to organize our teacher education classes in a way that will encourage our students to explore their own beliefs about the potential of immigrant students; that is, we need to create a context in which students can critically examine their own beliefs and practices. As we organize for whole language in our teacher education classes, we attempt to create a social context where students may be led to change the way they view their students. We believe that the context of the learning is as crucial to change as the content.

If the social context in which our students were educated had been the same as the context in which they are now teaching or will teach, there would be less conflict to resolve. If we wanted them to use the same methods in their classes that their teachers used as they went through school, we could teach in a traditional manner. However, we see our job as preparing students to teach a growing number of language minority students using a new approach that will empower all students. For that reason, we try to organize our classes in ways that allow us to demonstrate how we would like our students to teach their students. In other words, we try to practice what we preach.

School populations throughout the country, and especially in California, where we work, have changed dramatically. Most of our teacher education candidates will teach minority students. Since 1978, the number of immigrant students in California has increased two and a half times. This is the largest migration ever to California. In 1988, one in six children in California schools was an immigrant (Olsen, 1988). Fresno, in the middle of California, has a large

Hispanic population and also a large Southeast Asian population, including the largest Hmong population in the United States. In Fresno Unified School District, 60 percent of the students are minorities, and the percentage is projected to increase. In fact, the term "minority," as Freire (1987) points out, is somewhat misleading when that group is larger than the majority.

Our students will need a new approach in order to teach this new student population. The approach we advocate is whole language. We believe that whole language is important for all learners but especially for bilingual learners. Our beliefs have been shaped by the social contexts of our own lives—by living in Colombia and Mexico, by teaching ESL to adults in this country and abroad, and by our reading (Cummins, 1989; Edelsky, 1986, 1989; Freire, 1970, 1987; K. Goodman, 1986; Goodman, Goodman, and Flores, 1979; Halliday, 1975; Krashen, 1982a, 1982b; Vygotsky, 1987; Wells, 1986). Our personal responses to these readings, the meanings we have constructed, have been further influenced by those around us, including our families, friends, and teachers. Realizing that the way we have reacted to reading was a result of our previous experiences, we reasoned that we needed to provide for our teacher education students like Steve and Phil experiences that would influence their reading and their learning in general.

Our attempts to shape the social context of learning for our students take different forms in different classes. In all our classes, however, we are guided by four principles:

1. Learning is not simply a transfer of knowledge from teachers to passive students; instead, learning occurs when students and teachers construct knowledge actively as they explore topics together.
2. Learning takes place most readily in a supportive community of learners during social interaction.
3. In learner-centered classes, teachers provide choices so that students can find purpose, build on strengths, and take ownership of their learning.
4. Through reading, writing, and discussion, learners think about and come to understand concepts in new and very personal ways.

As we organize for whole language, we attempt to put these principles into practice. We include activities such as lesson shares that allow us to explore ideas with the students. We involve the students in cooperative activities to build community, which often extends to organizing teams for refreshments. We ask students to choose a language minority student and carry out an individual case study. We have students respond in writing to what they read and use their responses as the basis for what we do in class.

In the following sections, we examine more closely some of these activities and assignments that we use to organize our classes as we attempt to follow our own principles and practice what we preach. These activities include lesson shares, case studies, position papers, and responses to readings.

## LESSON SHARES
The first principle we follow as we organize our classes states that students are not passive. Learning occurs as students and teachers explore topics together. In our teacher education classes, we explore techniques for making content area lessons understandable for students who speak English as a second language. We begin by providing short demonstration lessons consistent with whole language (Freeman and Freeman, 1988). We ask students to evaluate the lessons we teach using a whole language checklist we have developed. This helps serve as a guide for the lessons they prepare.

### Whole Language Principles and Checklist
1. Lessons should progress from whole to part
   Does the lesson move from the general to the specific?
   Are details presented within a general conceptual framework?
2. Lessons should be learner centered
   Is there an attempt to draw on student background knowledge and interests?
   Do students have choices?
3. Lessons should have meaning and purpose
   Is the content meaningful?
   Does it serve a purpose for the learner?
4. Lessons should promote social interaction
   Do students work together cooperatively?
   Do students interact with one another or only react to the teacher?
5. Lessons should include all four modes
   Do students have opportunities to read and write, as well as speak and listen, during the lesson?
6. Lessons should reflect the teacher's faith in the learners
   Does the teacher demonstrate a belief that students will be successful learners?

Then we ask our students, most of whom are already experienced teachers, to share a lesson idea that has worked for them with second-language students. Class members who have less experience sign up to share their lesson later in the semester. Often, this activity encourages them to observe in classrooms of the more experienced teachers in the class to get ideas to share. In this way, the lesson shares also follow the second principle, that learning takes place during social interaction. The social interaction that begins in our classroom continues in other classrooms in the city, and our students begin to see one another as resources.

The lesson shares our students do are limited to about ten minutes. We encourage the people presenting the lesson actually to have us participate in the activity as though we were their students. This gets everybody actively involved. The lesson might be a shared big book, a song, or a hands-on math activity. The students bring in materials and samples of student work from their own classrooms. Stacey showed us how she had set up a class post office for exchanging letters, Teresa got class members up to act out "Three Billy Goats Gruff," and Bob had us work in cooperative groups to solve a language problem.

Although teachers often comment that they are nervous about presenting to their colleagues in this way, we always applaud the presenter, and during breaks classmates make a point of being positive and asking questions about lessons shared. In addition, several teachers have developed enough confidence to present their ideas to a broader audience during local reading conferences. The presentations in our class also help them organize their ideas and refine their presentation skills. The lesson shares allow students to experience firsthand the potential for learning from other students. At the same time, all the students like getting practical ideas from one another.

In fact, students frequently comment on how they have tried out an idea they first saw in a lesson share. After Linda explained how she had the students in her high school Spanish class draw a family tree and then write about their family, Rose Marie adapted the exercise for her elementary ESL students. Linda, in turn, has used ideas from others. When Teresa shared a rhythmic poem with movement that she used for elementary ESL children, Linda translated it and used it successfully with her Spanish high school students and then shared the Spanish version with the entire graduate class. Charlene brought in materials and books she had used for a literature study with her fourth graders, and soon afterwards, several other students decided they would try literature studies too.

## METHOD SHARES

An extension and more elaborate version of the lesson share that we use in our ESL Methods course is the method share. In ESL Methods, we study a number of different methods that have been used to teach a second language. In order to provide a demonstration for our students, we begin by teaching a sample lesson using one of these methods. We emphasize that we want everyone to feel what it is like to be taught using the method. By the time we have drilled the teachers for twenty minutes on simple sentences with the verb *be* in the present tense, they know how students in a classroom where a structured oral method is used would feel. We explain that this is to be a demonstration, not a report. As with the lesson share, we want students to involve members of the class, having all of us participate as though we were their students.

After we give an initial demonstration lesson, we ask the students to sign up in teams of three or four to teach the class using one of the other methods to be studied. Here, again, as with the lesson share, we are able to follow our third principle and provide choice so students can find a purpose and build on their strengths. At the same time, by having teams organize the presentation, we are able to promote the kind of social interaction our second principle calls for. Finally, by having them become the experts and teach us, we follow the first principle: we explore these methods together.

Each team becomes a group of experts on one of the methods we study, such as TPR, Suggestopedia, or the Natural Approach. Each week one team teaches us a sample lesson using the method they have studied. If team members speak a second language, they teach in that language to provide a better understanding of what it is like to be the student of a teacher who uses this method. Mary and her team taught us about Suggestopedia using Chamorro. Kathy and Liz put us through an ALM lesson in Armenian. Ellen had us buy magazines, gum, or postcards at a German kiosk in a Natural Approach lesson.

The lesson shares and method shares give students a chance to be teachers in a graduate class. They see that they can teach, as well as learn, when we explore together the best ways to teach second-language students. Their experience in being experts on a topic and sharing their expertise helps them to begin to visualize how to allow their own students to become experts on topics in different subject areas.

All the students, not just the experts on each method, come away with a deeper understanding of how lessons are taught using each method. The lesson shares and method shares give students a chance to be learners, especially when the lessons are presented in a language students are not familiar with. These experiences affect what the teachers do with students in their own classrooms. The teachers begin to realize that their students don't lack intelligence but that even the simplest tasks can be confusing in the context of a new language. After making errors during a simple substitution drill in a demonstration lesson in English, several teachers have commented that they will never again put their students through such repetitive, confusing nonsense.

As these teachers experience this new context for learning—that of having to learn in a second language—they often revise their attitudes about their bilingual students and the methods best suited for teaching them. The teachers become more sensitive to the struggles their students are going through and, at the same time, begin to understand that some approaches to teaching a second language make learning much easier and more meaningful than others.

## CASE STUDIES

Lesson and method shares create a social context in which our students come to realize that they can learn from one another. To further expand the context for learning, we also include activities that involve teachers in learning from their own students.

Often, our teacher education students, like Steve and Phil, have had limited or negative contacts with language minority students. To expand their contexts for learning and to provide a more positive experience, we ask these future teachers to observe a second-language student in a school setting, take notes, and write up a report. In our language acquisition classes, we ask our graduate students, many of whom have already been working with language minority students, to do a more extensive study. We want them to become teacher/researchers and complete a case study which involves them in a critical examination of their own practices. In our syllabus, we state:

> This course focuses on how students acquire English as a second language. You should choose one student and study his or her acquisition of oral and/or written English. In your case study you should analyze the acquisition of English in your student by using data you have gathered and by using information from your class readings.

In preparing their case study, students write their results following the general procedures of process writing (Graves, 1983). They also share their findings with one another by making an oral presentation as part of a panel. Each panel is composed of three or four teachers who have studied similar students. As they give their oral reports, all of us come to understand better both the similarities and differences among second-language learners.

The case studies, like the lesson and method shares, support our attempts to organize our classes around the four principles outlined previously. Teachers become experts as we explore the topic of language acquisition together. The panel reports and peer reviews during process writing provide the social interaction called for by the second principle. Students choose who they want to study, and they take ownership of their own learning. As they collect data, they read, write, and talk about language acquisition. Their personal experiences with second-language learners in their classrooms help them to understand the concept of language acquisition in new and personal ways. We find that, as the teachers study individual second-language learners carefully, they respond to readings and class discussions in new ways. Their attitudes often change as the social context for their learning changes.

In class we read articles about first- and second-language acquisition by Krashen (1982a, 1982b), Cummins (1981), Ellis (1986), Vygotsky (1978), and others. At the same time, our students choose a student to observe. They keep anecdotal records and samples of the student's work. They become informed teacher/researchers—what Yetta Goodman (1978) calls kidwatchers. The time they spend analyzing how one child learns a new language gives our students important insights into language acquisition generally. This experience often changes their attitudes toward immigrant children as well.

Once students have collected information, they write a rough draft. In class, students pair up and exchange drafts for peer revision. To guide the review process, we provide a checklist with the following questions:

1. Is there background information about the student? Is the student adequately described so the reader gets a feel for who the student is and where the student is from?
2. Is there a description of how the student behaves in a classroom or other social setting, including interactions between teacher and student and student with peers?
3. What kind of data has been collected: written, anecdotal?
4. Is there an analysis of that data that reflects what we've been reading about second-language acquisition?
5. Is there a conclusion that includes a plan of instruction for the student consistent with what we've been reading and talking about in class?

Answering these questions helps students, who have seldom shared their written work with peers, respond to one another. We also find that some students who are having difficulty in their own writing pick up useful ideas from reading a classmate's paper. Again, one of our goals is for our students to regard one another as resources. Students turn in a revised version of the paper to us for our comments. Then they write a final draft and edit it. In this way, we are able to provide our students with firsthand experience in process writing. They come to appreciate getting comments from classmates and teachers and learn how to revise. They realize that the final case study is much better than what they would have produced if they had written the traditional, one-draft college paper. And they are more apt to implement process writing in their own classes.

Since many of our teachers choose to study children in their own classes, we also ask our students to propose a plan of instruction for their students. We want the teachers to find purpose in the assignment, so we ask them to use the information they gather to guide them in teaching their students. This helps make the case study something more than just another assignment to be written for the teacher.

Katie's report provides an example of the power of the case study for providing new contexts for teachers. She decided to study a Cambodian girl, Mony, who had been her student but had transferred to another school. Katie was concerned about Mony when she transferred and wanted to follow up on her progress.

Because Katie teaches at a year-round school, she was able to visit Mony in her new school, which was on a different schedule. During each visit, Katie spent time reading and writing with Mony. She also talked with Mony and observed how Mony interacted with other students in her new class. Katie already had insights into Mony that were developed while Mony was in Katie's class. These insights were supplemented by the new data Katie gathered.

Writing her case study allowed Katie to synthesize the information she had collected. In her case study, Katie included samples of Mony's writing and drawing. She also included extensive anecdotal records, based in part on the interactive journal she wrote with Mony. In her written report, Katie made connections between what she had learned from Mony and a number of the readings she had done in our class and on her own: "In connecting what I've experienced with Mony to research, Krashen/Terrel's Natural Approach and Ellis' Variable Competence Model come to mind. . . . The difference in Mony's expressive language lends incredible support to Krashen's Input Hypothesis as well."

We had hoped that doing a case study would help our students develop new attitudes toward their second-language learners. We were excited to read Katie's conclusion:

> In terms of the influence this Case Study will have on my teaching, I plan to:
>
> 1. Expend more effort in getting to know my students personally.
> 2. Provide individual time for each student as often as possible.
> 3. Never again assume that "what I hear" is "what they know."
> 4. Arrange my classroom/curriculum around whole, real, purposeful, meaning filled experiences.
> 5. Find, value, and exploit each student's contributions and talents.

When we read responses like Katie's, we know that our students are gaining new ideas and new attitudes that will help them teach all their students, and especially their second-language students, in new ways. Observation, reading, writing, and discussion provide new contexts for Katie and our other students that help them understand concepts in new and very personal ways.

## POSITION PAPER

A case study lends itself naturally to a course in language acquisition, but, as we organize our ESL methods course, we plan a different sort of major writing assignment. We ask students to write a paper in which they state their position on the best way to teach a second language. Of course, for most of these teachers, that second language is English.

Our goal is to create a social context that will allow students to construct new understandings of the teaching and learning processes with second-language students. As with the case study, our students find themselves involved in activities that support the four principles of whole language: they explore the best way to teach language minority students; they work together in a supportive community;

they form new concepts as they talk, read, and write; and they are encouraged to choose a position that fits their teaching situation.

The position paper is a major focus throughout the course and not just an assignment to be done at the end. We begin by talking about the paper in the first class and encouraging students to talk with one another about what they might write. We try to make writing the position paper a social activity that benefits the learner. As we study each new method, students consider it in terms of how it fits in, or fails to fit in, with the position on teaching that they are developing.

Early in the course we present Anthony's (1963) distinction between approach, method, and technique. Anthony defines an approach as a set of beliefs teachers have about teaching, learning, and curriculum. These beliefs guide teachers in their choice of method. A method is a long-term plan for organizing teaching. During the course we study a number of methods that have been developed for teaching second languages, such as the Audio-Lingual Method and Suggestopedia. Finally, a technique is a particular activity a teacher may do in class on a certain day. Brainstorming or reading a predictable book are examples of techniques.

Anthony's distinction is important, because many teachers claim to be eclectic, choosing whatever works. We encourage teachers to be eclectic at the levels of technique and method but consistent at the level of approach. We then present what we view as a whole language approach, a set of principles or beliefs about how people learn. This discussion helps students develop their own set of principles as a framework for evaluating the methods and techniques we study in class throughout the semester.

The position paper encourages students to outline their beliefs about learning and the methods and approaches they would like to use to support their beliefs. As with the case study, students write drafts, do peer editing, and get feedback from us. When students bring a draft of their paper to class for peer editing, we hand out a peer review sheet with questions that help students explore their position on language learning:

1. Does the paper clearly state the writer's basic approach; that is, is there an explanation of general principles that govern how language should be taught?
2. Does the paper also include a specific explanation of what a lesson or a series of lessons would look like? Can you picture this class?
3. Is there support for the approach being taken? Specifically, is there reference to the methods and techniques we have studied in class? Are readings properly referenced in the paper?
4. Is the paper organized and written in a clear style? Other suggestions that would help the writer?

Often students who are struggling with developing their position paper get a clearer direction as they read these questions and apply them to their partner's paper. The peer review also leads to good class discussion of different ways to write the paper. We encourage students to view writing the position paper as an authentic activity with a real audience. As they complete the peer review, some students, for example, decide to write the paper in the form of a letter to a principal or to the ESL resource teacher at their school.

Too often, we have waited until the end of a course to collect papers. At that point, there is no time for revision, and, since they can't respond to our comments, students spend little time considering how we do respond other than looking for the grade. We use a different approach with the position papers. After the peer review, students revise their papers and give them to us for our comments. We spend considerable time reading and commenting on papers at this stage because our feedback comes at a point where students have a chance to revise. If time permits, once students have made the revisions we suggest, we have them pair up to read one another's papers a final time for minor editing before turning their position papers in. This allows students to experience all parts of the writing process, and they often get a better perspective on their own writing by reading a classmate's paper.

There are constraints in implementing the writing process. We can't ask for drafts too early, since students haven't studied very many methods at that point in the course. On the other hand, if we wait too long, there is not time for revision. In a typical twelve-week graduate class that meets once a week, we have found the following schedule works quite well:

Bring draft for peer review week nine
Bring revised draft for teacher review week ten
Teachers return the revisions week eleven
Bring final copy of paper to class for editing and turn in week twelve

Students continue to revise in significant ways throughout the process because they are continuing to study new methods each week.

Students have commented that, although the position papers are "a lot of work," they like doing them. Merilee explained that when she interviewed for a new job, she could answer the questions quite well, because she had thought them all through as she wrote her paper. Sam presented his paper on the importance of bilingual education to his principal. As a result, he was made chair of the school ESL committee and continues to work to implement a program consistent with his position.

## RESPONSES

While the position papers, case studies, and lesson and method shares all help us to organize for a whole course, student responses to their reading provide us with information we can use to plan on a

**359**
*Practicing What We
Preach: Whole
Language with
Teachers of Bilingual
Learners*

class-by-class basis. When students raise questions about an article or relate experiences triggered by their reading, we can use the insights we gain from reading the responses to plan the next class. Our responses might range from talking to an individual student to planning a whole class activity.

Though our goal in assigning responses to the reading is not to test students, at first, some students see the response as a sort of quiz in disguise. For this reason, we sometimes ask students to give us a brief summary of the reading as well. This often frees them up to really respond to the reading. What we are interested in is their reaction—what they liked or disliked, agreed or disagreed with, the personal experiences the reading reminded them of, and the questions it raised.

The responses also help us organize for whole language around the four principles. Students teach us as they write their responses, so we truly explore topics together. The responses provide us with an opportunity to build community through personal interactions, especially in large classes that meet only once a week. Students may respond to whatever interests them in an article or to one of a series of readings, so choice is provided. And we have seen that, as they write about what they read, students develop new understandings of the concepts they are studying.

In many instances, responses give us insights into what's happening in our students' classes. We find many instances of students putting ideas from their reading into practice in their own class. Linda responded to a chapter on affective activities by commenting, "It was nice to have some confirmation that affective activities have an important place in the classroom. Often LEP students have self-image problems that can be dealt with in a positive way within the classroom. I use the dialogue journal as a way of dealing with feelings." She then went on to explain how the dialogue journal and other writing activities have helped the students in her pull-out ESL classes feel better about themselves:

> One student this year had to deal with her best friend moving away to another part of the city. She wrote about it in her journal for several weeks. Each day she drew a sad face and a broken heart. After about three weeks she drew a happy face and a heart with the words "Happy again" in the journal. It was a good opportunity to acknowledge her feelings and point out some positive ways she could ease the loss.

Other times, students simply share experiences that the reading reminds them of. In responding to another article about the problems immigrants have living in two cultures, Vince told about the writing one of his students had done: "One of my students wrote a beautiful story entitled 'Someday.' In it she chronicles all the things she is going to do and be someday. She speaks of important and common hopes such as protecting her family, making lots of money and sadly, this beautiful Laotian child, looks forward to the day when she can dye her hair blonde and wear blue contact lenses. What a strange and mixed message she is receiving."

When students share what happens in their classes the way Vince did, we can share his powerful story with the class by reading the passage aloud (with the author's permission), and all of us can learn from one another.

While the readings often cause our students to reflect on their own classrooms and their own students, some readings lead them to share more personal memories. Angelina began one response by writing, "I'm very sorry Yvonne and David, I can't read this. . . . The feelings that were stirred up in me as a result of the reading are too painful." She went on to describe her own experiences in school as a second-language learner. Through writing the response to her reading, Angelina came to understand her own experiences better. As a result, she is more sympathetic to the second-language students in her own class. She vows never to treat them as she was treated.

At times students use the response paper as a way of commenting on the class in general. Linda finished one response with a note:

> I would also like to share with you some of the feelings I have about this class. Being a new teacher, I'm really searching so much to find ways to be effective and to resolve what I consider to be difficulties in my teaching methods. I'm finding that when I come to class with issues on my mind, that somehow the direction that I need to go appears.

She went on to explain how a lesson share she had seen and some reading she had done had given her new ideas for her class.

We write back to our students each week, putting comments directly on their responses, in the margins, and at the end. This allows us to answer individual questions and concerns. Because we are reacting to concerns they have raised, we find this a good way to provide instruction at a point where students are ready to listen. Carol had begun to implement change in her reading and writing program and was asking for some advice, as her response indicates:

> . . . we were reading "round robin." I've stopped that and am allowing the students to read on their own. They really are enjoying it much more. . . . At the end of reading time, we discuss. Last week one student mentioned he thought the story was boring. When I asked him what he liked and disliked about it, a wonderful discussion followed. . . . I sometimes feel, as a teacher, I have to control everything. When I gave the kids the lead, I was greatly impressed. My students are now asking what something means instead of asking only what a word is. After reading, I have the kids write several sentences about what they liked or disliked about the part they read. Is this good, or should I wait until the end of the book for this type of activity?

In her written response to Carol, Yvonne encouraged her and also gave a suggestion: "Not every discussion works out this well, but those that do make 'letting the child lead' worthwhile. . . . You have started the equivalent of a literature log! Great! Start having them keep these in a journal to look back on."

However, if all we did was to respond to individuals, we would be missing an opportunity to create community. So, in addition to the individual responses, we type and run copies of a response to the whole class. In this response, we include comments particular students made that we think the whole class would find helpful. For example, Yvonne began one of our responses with a quote from Susan's paper, "I am retarded!!! I speak two languages and therefore, I am retarded. O, woe is me! This chapter infuriates me to no end." Yvonne went on to share the ways others in the class had responded to a chapter on intelligence testing for bilinguals.

We also include in the group response further comments on any part of an article that students are having trouble with. After one class read an article that dealt with linguistics by Paul Gee (1988), for instance, David began his class response by saying, "I was pleased with the quality of the responses to quite difficult reading. The key seems to be to take something fairly specific in each article and think about it on paper rather than trying to cover everything. I'll try to do that with some further thoughts on the Gee article." He then clarified some of the linguistic concepts the article presented.

In our individual and group responses, we encourage real dialogue. We encourage students to continue the dialogue by responding to our responses—either the individual or the group responses. Some students begin to feel empowered enough to write back to us in the same way we write to them. This allows us to really explore topics together, each learning from the other. Sometimes students respond by writing in the margins or at the end of our whole class responses, just as we often do in our personal responses to them.

When Yvonne started one response by saying, "I really enjoyed reading your responses this week," a student wrote back, "I appreciate how positive you are—I look forward to your comments and enjoy our dialogue in class and as pen pals." Then, at the end of the same response, she wrote nearly a page reflecting on her own children and the prejudices she carried as the result of being raised in the South. Yvonne continued the dialogue by adding, "I really appreciate your openness and the way you are approaching this class."

It takes time for us to respond to our students individually and as a group. However, the written dialogue creates a social context on both an individual and a group level that allows our students to come to a new understanding. Students come to realize the importance of having a real audience for their writing. When they see us taking the time to respond, a number of them choose to initiate similar writing activities with their own students.

## CONCLUSION

In our classes for teachers of second-language students, we attempt to practice the whole language philosophy we preach. We choose activities and assignments that we think will change our students' understanding and their attitudes. Our students write responses to their reading, share lessons and methods, conduct case studies, and write position papers.

As we organize our classes for whole language, we attempt to create social contexts in which real learning and change can take place. In these classes, students and teachers construct knowledge actively as they explore topics together in a supportive community of learners. We try to provide choices so that our students can find purpose, build on strengths, and take ownership of their learning. Within these contexts, students can come to understand concepts in new ways through reading, writing, and discussion.

Our schools are filling with a new wave of bilingual students. Immigrants with a variety of cultural and language backgrounds present new challenges for our teachers. What teachers need is not a notebook filled with notes on new methods, techniques, or materials; they need new approaches to learning and new attitudes toward their students. We see our job as creating contexts where those new approaches and attitudes can develop.

When Steve and Phil started studying, they brought with them strong feelings about the students they soon would be teaching, and they reflected those feelings in their early responses. Over the course of a semester, immersed in a supportive classroom community where they continued to read, write, and talk about teaching second-language students while they also had opportunities to observe immigrant students, both Steve and Phil began to reexamine their attitudes and beliefs.

Steve had begun his first response by saying, "I knew I wouldn't change my stance on the subject of immigration. Sure, I feel a little for the children, but they're in the U.S. and thus it is up to them to adapt." By the middle of the semester, however, his stance had begun to change: "No matter what subject, you must use dialogue that's going to be understood by your students, and something that they'll be able to understand when they get home and have to do their homework." He has started to see that teachers, as well as students, have to change. By the end of the semester, he had more fully developed his idea: "Kids don't want stagnant instructors either. They want someone fresh, invigorating, someone that they can look up to, and more than this, someone they can also respect as a human being. This is what teachers have to do also, look at the students as human beings, and respect their ideas too, because they are our future."

Phil's experience with immigrants had been confined to carting them off to jail. His attitudes, formed in that context, were changed in the new context of the class. One of his last responses shows the difference teacher educators can make. He wrote: "In being teachers of the future, we are going to have to accept some simple facts. First, we will have in our classrooms immigrant students. Second, we are going to teach these students and help them learn regardless of their situations. . . . We make judgments about people everyday and it really isn't fair. We are educators, not educators of only those who appear to want to learn."

Such dramatic changes of approach and attitude are possible when we, as teacher educators, view our job as one of practicing what we preach.

# 27

# REFLECTIONS ON DESIGNING A K-12 WHOLE LANGUAGE CURRICULUM: IMPLICATIONS FOR ADMINISTRATORS AND POLICYMAKERS

**Fredrick R. Burton**

## PRELIMINARY THOUGHTS

Occasionally, I am asked by bright, enthusiastic teachers and principals to recommend books that will help them along their way toward more informed, whole language teaching practices. I usually hesitate, because I believe that problems are best solved by those who own them, that teachers do not need to wait to be "empowered," and that nothing quite takes the place of the reciprocal processes of action and reflection as one lives through teaching experiences. However, I almost always give in and recommend the following three titles in the following order: John Dewey's *Experience and Education* (1963), Elliot Eisner's *The Education Imagination* (1979), and Michael Armstrong's *Closely Observed Children* (1980). Reactions have ranged from embarrassed disappointment to passive hostility: "Oh, but I mean a book about the writing process or children's literature or the reading process." And, in my view, *that* is part of the problem—at least with regard to developing conceptions of curriculum that support rather than undermine and frustrate the whole language practices of teachers.

Until the names of Perrone, Apple, Carini, and Duckworth become as familiar to us as Smith, Goodman, Graves, and Calkins, we will be a bit like a professional tennis player having an overdeveloped

Our committee is greatly in debt to Dr. Robert Donmoyer and Dr. Susan Kidd for their curriculum development work. The committee, chaired and inspired by Dr. James Allen, was comprised of the following members: Mona Anderson, Joetta Beaver, Frank Cole, Diane Driessen, Eleanor Goldsmith, Jane Hubbard, Jini Hushak, John Kingsboro, Randall Pfeiffer, Peg Reed, Rachel Reinhard, Liz Richmond, Marsha Shulman, Kevin Stotts, and Kathleen Taps.

"literacy" arm and an underdeveloped philosophical one. And it is the philosophical arm—tempered by practice and tailored to the social and political context of a school—that I have found most helpful in the development of our K-12 curriculum.

## ALTERNATIVE CONCEPTIONS OF CURRICULUM

There is a great historical divide between the field of curriculum and that of language learning. Since the 1960s, there has been a renaissance in what we know about how children learn language; yet, in the field of curriculum development—how what we teach is framed, displayed, developed, and communicated to parents—has changed very little. The skill and drill exercises found in language workbooks are reminiscent of the practices inspired by the "mental discipline" theory (i.e., mind as muscle) that dominated our conception of the curriculum prior to the 1900s. Moreover, the cult of testing and efficiency that Thorndike and Watson fueled in the early 1900s and the applied behaviorism of Skinner (and later Mager and Popham) continue to shape teaching and administrative practices today.

With regard to curriculum development itself, no one has had more influence on the way we design curriculum than Ralph Tyler. Tyler's little book, *Basic Principles of Curriculum Instruction*, was published in 1949 and describes in detail the "Tyler rationale." The Tyler rationale has "the logic of an industrial production system [and] underlies the most widely prescribed model for teacher planning" (Clark and Peterson, 1986). It views the curriculum from an ends-means perspective, in which objectives are always precisely formulated prior to an activity. When studying curriculum history and examining the assumptions that undergird textbooks and the omnipresent curriculum guide that can be found in classrooms across the United States, it is clear that the Tyler rationale, as well as a legacy of behaviorism, is still very much with us.

This mismatch between how children learn language and the historical grounding of how we continue to frame and display the curriculum was very much on my mind as I participated in reforming the K-12 language arts curriculum guide in the Upper Arlington public school systems.

## RECONCEPTUALIZING THE
## TRADITIONAL CURRICULUM GUIDE

The original Upper Arlington K-12 language arts guide was about the size of a telephone book of a reasonably large city. However, it wasn't nearly as useful as a telephone book. A telephone book contains numbers important to its users. It can also help someone in trouble and save its user valuable time. Our curriculum guide had none of these features.

The most striking way that the new guide (which can be obtained by writing Dr. James Allen, Upper Arlington City Schools, Upper

Arlington, OH 43221) differs from the old one is in the number of objectives it contains. The original guide contained approximately 1,200 objectives. Now, some would argue that 1,200 objectives is really not that much, especially if you break it down into 13 grade levels: that would only be about 92 objectives per grade level or about 23 objectives for reading, writing, speaking, and listening, respectively. Spread this over 184 school days and you have 0.5 objectives per day. That's not too bad. Is it? However, the new guide, rather than containing 1,200 objectives, has only 10 *policies*. That's 10 policies *K through 12*.

Figure 27-1 is the complete text of Policy Statement 1 as it appears in our K-12 curriculum guide. Each of the ten policy statements contains the following: a policy statement; a rationale; policy statement objectives (PSOs); suggested learning experiences; assessment opportunities; and intervention possibilities.

I will briefly discuss each dimension of this fully developed statement in hopes that it will illuminate the constraints, as well as the possibilities, of this particular curriculum. I would also like to note that we asked an official of the Ohio Department of Education to be a member of the district's language arts committee. This person proved to be invaluable and at times frustrating as she pointed out language that we would need to use in order to satisfy state requirements.

THE POLICY STATEMENT

There is nothing really very complicated about a policy statement. A policy is simply a broad statement that implies action without over-specifying details. It sets forth a *direction* that has, in the case of our language arts curriculum guide, a literacy theory and research base. Although a policy is intentionally written to be broad in its scope, it need not be vague or unclear. I think it would be helpful to point out to critics who ground their curriculum development procedures in behaviorism that, while a behavioral objective is very specific about actions, a policy statement is grounded in a very specific point of view. In parentheses you will note the words "program objectives" and later on, under the PSO, "subject objectives." This was language that the state department required us to use for the purpose of helping them to understand our curriculum guide during the times they conduct their periodic evaluation of our school district. Although the committee reluctantly included the terms, we have since found it a small sacrifice that satisfies the state requirement without really affecting the intent and practice of the guide.

RATIONALE

The rationale is a concise statement that elaborates on the policy statement itself. It answers for us the "why this policy" questions and

**Figure 27-1**  *Policy Statement*

## Policy Statement 1
(Program Objective)

Students will engage in meaningful reading, writing, and speaking activities for a variety of purposes and audiences.

"Each of us is like a desert, and a literary work is like a cry from the desert, or like a pigeon let loose with a message in its claws, or like a bottle thrown into the sea. The point is: to be heard — even if by one single person."

François Mauriac

### Rationale

When students have a purpose for, care about, and can make sense of reading and writing activities, they become better and more prolific readers and writers. Their literacy is further enhanced when students communicate with numerous real audiences. [References: Arthur Applebee, Nancie Atwell, James Britton, Lucy Caulkins, Ken Goodman, Donald Graves, Donald Murray, Louise Rosenblatt, Frank Smith]

### Policy Statement Objectives: the core curriculum
(Subject Objectives)

| K—2 | 3—5 | 6—8<br>(See additional objectives) | 9—12<br>(See additional objectives) |
|---|---|---|---|
| A. Participates daily in reading and writing processes. | A. Participates daily in reading and writing processes. | A. Participates daily in reading and writing processes. | A. Participates daily in reading and writing processes. |
| B. Reads, writes, and speaks for a variety of purposes and audiences | B. Reads, writes, and speaks for a variety of purposes and audiences | B. Reads, writes, and speaks for a variety of purposes and audiences | B. Reads, writes, and speaks for a variety of purposes and audiences |
| C. Begins to relate one literary work to another | C. Begins to relate one literary work to another | C. Begins to relate one literary work to another | C. Begins to relate one literary work to another |
| | D. Reads prose, informational literature, and/or poetry for a sustained period every day | D. Reads prose, informational literature, and/or poetry for a sustained period | D. Reads prose, informational literature, and/or poetry for a sustained period |
| | | E. Identifies purpose for reading, writing, and speaking | E. Identifies purpose for reading, writing, and speaking |

### Suggested Learning Experiences/Events

| K—2 | 3—5 | 6—8 | 9—12 |
|---|---|---|---|
| ◆ Discussions<br>◆ Imaginary stories and poems<br>◆ Observations<br>◆ Letters, thank you notes<br>◆ Presentations<br>◆ Graphs, lists, charts<br>◆ Author's circle<br>◆ Content area logs<br>◆ Informational reading/ writing<br>◆ Reading/writing workshop | ◆ Discussions<br>◆ Imaginary stories and poems<br>◆ Observations<br>◆ Letters, thank you notes<br>◆ Presentations<br>◆ Graphs, lists, charts<br>◆ Author's circle<br>◆ Content area logs<br>◆ Informational reading/ writing<br>◆ Reading/writing workshop | ◆ In-depth book discussions<br>◆ Imaginary stories and poems<br>◆ Observations<br>◆ Letters, thank you notes<br>◆ Presentations<br>◆ Reader response journals<br>◆ Brainstorming<br>◆ Checklist for writing folders<br>◆ Essays<br>◆ Information articles<br>◆ Poetry journals<br>◆ Sustained silent reading of whole pieces of poetry, prose, and informational literature<br>◆ Oral response, both individual and group<br>◆ Reader's theater<br>◆ Student publications | ◆ In-depth book discussions<br>◆ Imaginary stories and poems<br>◆ Observations<br>◆ Letters, thank you notes<br>◆ Presentations<br>◆ Reader response journals<br>◆ Brainstorming<br>◆ Checklist for writing folders<br>◆ Essays<br>◆ Information articles<br>◆ Poetry journals<br>◆ Sustained silent reading of whole pieces of poetry, prose, and informational literature<br>◆ Oral response, both individual and group<br>◆ Reader's theater<br>◆ Student publications and contests |

### Assessment Opportunities

| K—2 | 3—5 | 6—8 | 9—12 |
|---|---|---|---|
| ◆ Writing portfolio<br>◆ Literacy folder<br>◆ Teacher observations<br>◆ Teacher-pupil conferences<br>◆ Student written work<br>◆ Anecdotal records<br>◆ Holistic scoring | ◆ Writing portfolio<br>◆ Literacy folder<br>◆ Teacher observations<br>◆ Teacher-pupil conferences<br>◆ Student written work<br>◆ Anecdotal records<br>◆ Holistic scoring | ◆ Writing portfolio<br>◆ Literacy folder<br>◆ Teacher observations<br>◆ Teacher-pupil conferences<br>◆ Student written work<br>◆ Anecdotal records | ◆ Writing portfolio<br>◆ Literacy folder<br>◆ Teacher observations<br>◆ Teacher-pupil conferences<br>◆ Student written work<br>◆ Anecdotal records |

### Intervention Possibilities

| K—2 | 3—5 | 6—8 | 9—12 |
|---|---|---|---|
| ◆ Risk-free environment<br>◆ Shared reading and writing<br>◆ Teacher-pupil conferences<br>◆ Home support<br>◆ Author's circle<br>◆ Self selection of books and topics | ◆ Risk-free environment<br>◆ Shared reading and writing<br>◆ Teacher-pupil conferences<br>◆ Home support<br>◆ Author's circle<br>◆ Self selection of books and topics<br>◆ Interest inventories | ◆ Teacher-pupil conferences<br>◆ Home support<br>◆ Self selection of books and topics<br>◆ Reading, subject, or interest inventories<br>◆ Peer instruction | ◆ Teacher-pupil conferences<br>◆ Home support<br>◆ Self selection of books and topics<br>◆ Reading, subject, or interest inventories<br>◆ Writing intervention Workshop<br>◆ Family or peer instruction |

makes more explicit the point of view that undergrids the policy.
Particularly important is the list of names of prominent language
researchers and theorists whose work support the policy. At the very
least, these names tend to legitimate the policy for some (especially
the skeptics), and, in the best of cases, they provide a starting point
for those who want to follow up on this professional work. For those
who do, we've included not only a complete bibliography of these
researchers and theorists, but have provided teachers with a Professional Development File, which includes sample articles by the people listed in the rationale.

POLICY STATEMENT OBJECTIVES (PSOs)

PSOs came about in part because of state department requirements.
PSOs were developed to suggest actions for grade level groupings
(i.e., K-2, 3-5, etc.) without overspecifying or suggesting that literacy can actually be broken down and "mastered" by grade level. The
state department required us to add the words *see additional objectives* for the middle school and high school in which case specific
courses were being taught. This "constraint" proved to be minimal
because the state does not actually require a large number of objectives for the courses, and the language used to write them is not
overly prescriptive.

SUGGESTED LEARNING EXPERIENCES/EVENTS,
ASSESSMENT OPPORTUNITIES, AND
INTERVENTION POSSIBILITIES

Each of these dimensions is designed to guide teachers in creating
and assessing whole language experiences for children. The state
department's language requires that Ohio schools "assess and inter-
vene." When looking over these three sections, you will note that
there is almost identical overlapping at each of the four grade level
chunks: K-2, 3-5, 6-8, 9-12. In fact, the Assessment Opportunities section completely overlaps. This is viewed as desirable.
Furthermore, the words *suggested, possibilities,* and *opportunities*
intentionally imply a flexibility that would allow teachers to develop
additional ways to create literacy experiences for children.

## IMPLICATIONS FOR ADMINISTRATORS
## AND POLICYMAKERS

School districts wishing to break free of traditional approaches to
developing curriculum must continually keep in mind the influential
forces of the larger community context. I am in no way suggesting
that the Upper Arlington Guide is transferable in its completed form
to other school districts. Yet, having worked on this guide for almost
three years, the following ideas seemed to be critical to the curricu-

lum development process and might be helpful for others undergoing curriculum work.

## 1. ADMIT THAT CURRICULUM MAKING IS A POLITICAL ACT.

We designed expert testimony sessions in which central office staff, teacher groups, board members, and community members discussed their perspectives on what it meant to be literate and how their view related to the school curriculum. Also, having a state department official work on the committee (one who was informed about language learning but also was informed about the limits and possibilities of state regulations) proved to be extremely helpful. We continually tested our initial ideas out on these various constituencies.

## 2. COMMITTEE MEMBERS SHOULD STAY SOMEWHAT NAIVE.

Naivete and humility were great assets to committee members. I worry a bit more about people who know *too* much about whole language than those who know only a little. Our committee itself remained a community of learners that shared whole language principles but enjoyed entertaining the multiple ways these principles could be played out, given the problems and possibilities inherent in the values of our school, community, and state.

## 3. SPEND AN INORDINATE AMOUNT OF TIME ON PHILOSOPHY.

We lived by the ground rule that Ann Cook (at the Progressive Education Conference in Chicago, 1989), a teacher in New York City, shares with her high school students: "Attack ideas, not people." It was the act of deliberation over time that enabled us to *become* a community of learners. Communities are built as members affirm and test their values against one another and the larger group. Taking time to wallow in ideas may appear to be wasting time, but in fact is essential. This principle of community building not only applied to the language arts curriculum committee itself but also was especially important for the constituencies that the committee served.

## 4. CREATE A COLLEGIAL SUPPORT NETWORK.

The committee created formal organizational structures that supported teachers willing to risk to create whole language experiences in their classrooms. For example, a Colleague Support Network was created. A portion of this is shown in Figure 27-2 (p. 370).

In my view, it is critical that such a network should not only be a core of expert whole language teachers (who may be perceived as the "in" group) but also include those who are at various stages of

---

**Figure 27-2**   *Colleague Support Network*

### COLLEAGUE SUPPORT

As teachers/learners, we learn much from one another. The person who shares as well as the one who receives input gain through the process of sharing. Sharing ideas, resources, time, processes, and insights strengthens and enhances our understandings.

The following individuals have agreed to share their present understandings and practices. You may contact them by phone or arrange to visit their classrooms. Please use the Staff Directory to locate phone numbers. If you desire to observe in the classroom, you will need to follow procedures suggested by the implementation team.

**Author's circle**

Missy Lawson
John Kingsboro
Maureen Reedy
Peggy Harrison
Debbie Houser

**Author/illustrator focus**

Elizabeth Clark
Karen Boreman
Missy Lawson
Peggy DeLapp
Jeana Hodges
Peggy Harrison
Diane Driessen
Sue Bauchmoyer
Terry Trubiano
Donna Donovan
Jini Hushak
Shelley Hanahan

Amy LaRue
Bonnie Darrow
Cheri Slinger
Maureen Reedy

**Big books**

Kathy Helmrath
Jeana Hodges
Donna Donovan
Debbie Houser
Sandy Miller
Sherilyn Harrison
Amy LaRue
Karen Boreman
Cheri Slinger

**Choral reading**

Kathleen Taps
Myra Dull
Debbie Houser

Kathy Helmrath
Amy LaRue
Cheri Slinger

**Comparison charts**

Peggy DeLapp
Amy LaRue
Jini Hushak
Sue Bauchmoyer
Maureen Reedy
Jeana Hodges
Karen Boreman
Cheri Slinger
Cindy Perkins
Debbie Houser
Terry Trubiano

---

ability. In this way, peer observations become genuine opportunities for teachers to deliberate in a way that benefits both the "expert" listed in the network as well as the observer.

### 5. CROSS-REFERENCE PEOPLE, PROFESSIONAL WRITING, AND POLICIES.

Scope-and-sequence charts, as antithetical as they are to how children learn language, *do* provide teachers with a sense of structure and support. Since we had eliminated the scope-and-sequence chart, what sort of guide and support could be provided for teachers who would certainly react negatively (understandably so) to having something taken away that they had come to rely on so heavily? In answer to this dilemma, a Policy Statement Cross Reference Guide was developed. A portion of this guide is shown in Figure 27-3.

Teachers who are new or need more guidance than the Suggested Learning Experiences/Events section provides can use this cross reference guide not only to see how their current practices contribute

**Figure 27-3** *A Portion of the Policy Statement Cross Reference Guide*

### POLICY STATEMENT CROSS REFERENCE GUIDE

| Learning Experiences/Events | Policy Statements |
|---|---|
| Artistic Response (painting, dioramas, collage, sewing, songs, dances) | 5,6,7,8 |
| Author's circle | 1,3,5,6,7,8,10 |
| Author/Illustrator Focus | 1,4,5,6,7,8,9,10 |
| Big Books | 1,2,3,4,6,8 |
| Book promotions | 1,4,6,7,8,10 |
| Book theme parties | 5,7,8 |
| Brainstorming | 1,3,6,9,10 |
| Buddy reading | 1,2,3,4,6,9 |
| Character analysis | 5,7,,8,10 |
| Charts, graphs, lists, drawings | 1,2,6,7,8,10 |
| Choral reading | 1,2,3,4,6 |
| Class observation walks | 2,6,7,9,10 |
| Classroom cooking | 1,2,4,5,6,8 |
| Comparison charts (theme, author, observations, opinions) | 1,2,4,5,6,7,8,9 |
| Comparison of predictions with findings | 2,3,7,8,9,10 |
| Content area logs | 1,2,3,4,5,6,7,8,9,10 |
| Creative movement | 2,5,6 |
| Critique Groups | 1,3,5,6,7,10 |
| Diary kept as book character | 3,5,6,7,8,10 |

to the implementation of the ten policies of the district but also to find help in "how to" essays written by teachers in the district and included in the guide itself.

## 6. LESS IS MORE.

Debbie Meier, speaking at the 1989 Progressive Education Conference in Chicago, shared that the less is more principle has helped her staff create a New York City high school that draws on the best features of a good kindergarten classroom. Often in the name of "excellence," school boards and administrators attempt to add numerous standards. By trying to "cover" so much material in discrete, short time periods, the addition of standards actually has the opposite of its intended effect. Consequently, moving from 1,200 objectives to 10 policies allows teachers to develop classrooms that are experience-centered instead of objectives-centered. It is a "living" document that will continually be revised as teachers share knowledge which can only arise over time through shared experiences.

## CLOSING

Lawrence Cremin, in his book *The Transformation of the School* (1961), believes that one reason the Progressive Education movement died was because its members became overly preoccupied with themselves as a group and forgot to look beyond to what was happening in the larger context of society. Whole language teachers must not only critique existing practices but also develop alternative conceptions of school practices while remaining cognizant of the forces that shape their professional lives. There is a great temptation to create an "us/them" dichotomy. But it is a false dichotomy because ultimately "them" *is* "us."

# 28

## TEACHER SUPPORT GROUPS: REACHING OUT, BRINGING IN

### Dorothy Watson

A few months ago I got a letter from a fourth-grade teacher who had just attended a professional conference—her first introduction to whole language theory and practice. What Julie heard and saw in those few conference days shook her beliefs about teaching, especially about how she taught reading and writing. All the new information—presented with great enthusiasm—caused her to do something she had never seriously done before—question what was going on in her own classroom.

Julie left the conference a bit dazed but very excited. She was loaded down with articles and books to read, lists of children's literature, ideas for thematic curricula, and innovative suggestions on how to encourage and celebrate children's reading and writing. What she didn't leave the conference with was someone to talk to about the storm of ideas buzzing in her head.

In Julie's letter, she told of the exhaustion and discouragement built up over ten years of teaching, and then in contrast she told of the excitement and enthusiasm generated during the three-day conference. And now that she was committed to further whole language study and was seriously planning curriculum revisions—she was scared. The excitement of the conference was gone, the discussion groups were over, the confident whole language teachers were miles away, the keynote speaker's tape had been played a dozen times, and the message was no longer enough—she felt terribly alone.

In response to her letter, Julie received two letters: one from a fourth-grade teacher in our TAWL group and one from me. We stuffed our envelopes with articles, bibliographies, and encouragement. We issued invitations, advice, and suggestions. We told Julie how hard it was to go it alone, and we both told her that she needed a support group.

Yesterday Julie phoned. She had taken our advice and was encouraged when she found two other teachers in her school district who were eager to study whole language and to share their ideas and concerns with her. The teachers decided to meet after school every other Friday. Julie's telephone conversation was filled with reports of her student's growth and love of language, and filled with questions about the care and keeping of her teacher support group that, according to Julie, "amazed us by growing so fast we can barely fit into my front room."

Like Julie, other whole language teachers from across Canada and the United States are asking for information about forming groups of teachers who are practicing whole language theory. The following ideas, from members of support groups in Canada and the United States, might be of help not only to Julie who teaches in a small rural community but also to teachers who are members of larger, well-established groups in urban settings.

## WHAT'S IN A NAME?

Teacher support groups are known by a variety of names. TAWL (Teachers Applying Whole Language) is an often used acronym, but there is also CEL (Child-Centered Experience Based Learning), SMILE (Support, Maintenance, and Implementation of Language Expression), and a dozen or so others. Any group calling itself TAWL should be prepared to hear a few jokes about TAWL teachers who are short and TAWL teachers who are tall; we endure. The A in *TAWL* has caused some confusion. The Bloomington, Indiana, group calls itself "Teachers Attempting Whole Language"; it seems that Jerry Harste, one of the founders of the group, heard *Attempting* for *Applying*, and the name stuck. The members think that it not only distinguishes them but also describes their efforts, especially when the going gets tough.

The groups in Edmonton, Alberta, are CAWL, not "Canadians Applying . . . ," but "Children and Whole Language." Mid-Missouri TAWL is faced with the problem of a location name; happily we are no longer the only group in the middle of Missouri. In fact, the other mid-Missouri group has grown so rapidly that our TAWL may soon be eclipsed.

The name is up to the members. Politically, it's a good idea to let the name reflect your purpose and what you stand for.

## YET ANOTHER ORGANIZATION?

Over the years I've heard teachers tell stories about what it was that brought their group together. For the most part, the histories are similar: teachers unite because they need to be with others who are experiencing similar professional concerns. Whole language educators have issues and problems that simply are not addressed by other professional organizations. There is an eagerness to learn more about the theory and practice of a "new" and exciting way of teaching and learning. Add to that urgency a burning need to break out of professional isolation, and you have the makings of a whole language support group.

In addition to growing professionally by studying and sharing with each other, many teachers also want to share their own research and practices with potential whole language educators. TAWL is an organization through which they can offer whole language conferences and in-service workshops and seminars.

Whatever the reasons for starting a whole language support group, those reasons need to be clear to the membership and be reviewed regularly. Such an inquiry provides the criteria on which evaluation of the organization can be based.

## WHO IS INVITED TO JOIN?

In most cases, the answer to this question is any teacher applying or attempting whole language. For a time, our members considered inviting teachers who were riding the fence or who needed to be convinced of the merits of whole language. One member commented that she needed help and that she didn't want to spend TAWL time talking someone out of doing phonics and into holistic and authentic teaching and learning. "TAWL," she said, "was a place where she knew her beliefs would be accepted and strengthened." We decided that this teacher was right—we spent a lot of time, day in and day out, defending our practices—we didn't need that at TAWL, too. Our group opened membership to all professionals who were trying to understand the theory and practices of whole language; potential members needn't have all the problems worked out, but they must have a commitment. The "fence-riders," we decided, would be invited to our annual conference or any special meeting more suitable for "interested skeptics."

We have in our group both private and public school teachers, including a substantial number of special education teachers and teacher educators. A few administrators and state department of education people attend meetings on an irregular basis; we're encouraging greater participation. Many of our members are in graduate school; some, full time. Many members are parents; their children are often placed in skills-based classrooms. As yet we have no librarians; we need to work on that. We are contemplating starting a small TAWL within our group for preservice undergraduate students.

The diversity of professionals in our group adds to its richness. You may choose to identify your group membership more precisely, for example, teachers who work in junior high, ESL, primary, and so forth.

## HOW ARE GROUPS STRUCTURED?

Many groups start small; ours began with six members, a comfortable fit for a living room. A year later, when membership rose to twenty-five, we moved out of our homes and into an elementary school room that holds fifty or sixty. After thirteen years, our membership is one hundred, with about forty attending each meeting. We continue to meet in Stephens College's elementary school, where we often spill out into the halls and other rooms for small discussion groups. This year our meetings will be held in different members' classrooms to see various whole language environments firsthand.

We have an advisory board of thirteen members. Officers are elected for two years; a one-year term is inadequate for our needs. We meet monthly in the evening. The advisory board convenes at 6:00 P.M.; between 6:30 and 7:00, the members check out books, look at new materials, talk with each other; the program starts at 7:00 and runs to around 9:00. We can't meet immediately after school, as many groups do, because of the long distances some of our members travel.

Some groups attempt to hold their numbers constant, say twenty-five, primarily so they can truly get to know and help each other but also to have the luxury of meeting in homes. When groups are kept small, there is often the understanding that, once the membership grows to thirty, the group will split, forming two smaller groups. Dividing a group that has been together for a long period of time is often so difficult that the members decide to stay together and move to larger quarters, or they meet together as a large group every other month.

Some groups have a core group of thirty or so members. This group organizes programs, in-service, and conferences for a much larger group of whole language teachers. Although such an organizational structure appears to work well, it's important that the "inner-group" not become, or be perceived to be, elitist and controlling.

When there is a close relationshp with the local International Reading Association, a whole language special interest group is sometimes formed within the IRA chapter. In such an arrangement members of the interest group meet with the entire chapter but also meet regularly on their own. Such special interest groups within the local IRA add a great deal to the spirit and enthusiasm of the total organization.

Some school districts help with the organization of support groups. Often an administrator, a language arts supervisor, and a teacher will cooperatively start a group. Such an arrangement facilitates good communication between classrooms and middle- and upper-level administrators. Some whole language schools have an active support group within their own faculty.

Size of the group is not the primary concern. Julie started her group with two teachers who met after school every other Friday. Some teachers begin with just one other person whom they phone once a week in order to share successes and struggles. The organizational structure of your group may or may not be similar to the ones described here. Not to worry. The point is to get started; the form will work out naturally.

## THE TERRIBLE TWO'S AND OTHER PROBLEMS

When in the course of human events it becomes evident that things are not going well, do what you do in your whole language classrooms: stop and reflect. Our second year presented pesky problems: the sharing took too long, and people were stifling yawns; three members were doing the majority of the organizational work, while others felt left out; we were losing our sense of history and purpose; we needed some finances and didn't have a penny; other annoyances plagued us. Midway through the second year, we looked at the rut we'd gotten ourselves into and decide that TAWL was worth the effort needed to understand and solve the problems. It became evident that, despite our "we are all leaders" attitude, we did need officers and an advisory board to organize ourselves in a reasonable way and to spread the work around. We also decided to collect dues (mainly for duplicating and mailing notices). We began to rethink our program of sharing and decided to expand (sharing will always be a part of our meetings) to include focused topics.

Your group's problems may not come as they did for us, but if they do, don't ignore them. Give them the attention they deserve. Experiment with new programs, logistics, organizational structures. With foresight, major problems may never arise, but don't be discouraged if they do. When members are consulted, informed, and have representation, and when there is ongoing evaluation, the problems are surmountable; they may even make the group stronger.

## PROGRAMS

Groups that are small in membership seem to have very little trouble planning meetings. The members share—classroom strategies, language stories, research, literature, students' accomplishments, their own writings, gains, and losses. Members study together. They are renewed by each other.

When groups get large, programs need to be rethought. Even the backbone of many support groups—sharing—undergoes changes. Seven members sharing successes and problems is not the same as thirty teachers doing so. Such sharing may be informative and confirming, but it can also get tiresome. Guidelines are needed. Most groups don't want to give up sharing but have found it to be a richer experience if volunteer members are designated prior to each meeting. Time, of course, is available for those who have something that just can't wait. Some large groups divide into interest or grade levels for sharing.

Many groups plan their programs two or three months in advance, and a few try to schedule a full year. Typically, members volunteer to present something they are particularly interested in: dramatization, literature study, student as researcher, whole language evaluation, reading and writing across the curriculum, parental involvement, conferencing procedures—anything immediately important and compelling. To enrich these programs, the presenters give members appropriate articles to read prior to the presentation and ask teachers to bring examples from their own classes that illustrate the points being made.

Opportunities to piggyback on the visit of an author, illustrator, publisher, or teacher are explored. Sometimes local resource people, such as an administrator, a member of another support group, or a parent, are asked to speak. One of our most memorable meetings was when a seventh-grade poet presented her work to us. Many of us will never forget her lovely poetry and her last piece of advice to teachers: "Don't give kids topics. They can think of wonderful things to write about on their own, with just a little help from you or from a friend."

Some groups have *Small TAWLs* (we got the name from the Tucson TAWL) within their large organization. Our Political Action Small TAWL leads us in our political education and awareness. This group planned a meeting in which all the candidates for the board of education gave answers to five predetermined questions concerning literacy. All nine board candidates took their responses (two minutes for each question) very seriously. The meeting closed with a brief presentation of the TAWL point of view. Another meeting planned by this subgroup involved the study of the governor's advisory committee report on literacy education. After gathering suggestions from the entire membership, the subgroup met on the following Saturday morning to draft recommendations. They then sent TAWL members to the six state meetings in which the literacy report was deliberated. In the Phoenix area, a group calling itself WILD was organized for the purpose of orchestrating district-wide change in the curriculum.

Many groups spend some part of every meeting in study sessions discussing something they have read. Professional articles and books are usually studied, but literature for children and youth is also explored. Members receive the books and articles prior to the meeting in order to prepare for the discussions. In Tucson, Small TAWL members share their own writings with each other.

Whole language teachers are great at adopting and adapting good ideas, but be careful of focusing too long or too intensely on a single age group or a specific subject. Most importantly, consider the interests of all members—the high school teachers, the elementary school principal, the nursery school aide. Explore all potential resources, and keep the meetings lively.

## FINANCES AND PROJECTS

During our first two years, we resisted collecting dues. After awakening to the realities of printing and postage costs, our dues rose

gradually over the years to $20. This may seem like a big invest-
ment, but members get their money's worth. New members receive a
folder of "classic" whole language articles and a copy of Ken Goodman's *What's Whole in Whole Language* (1986). Those renewing
their membership get new articles and a copy of a newly published
whole language book. Dues defray the cost of the monthly newsletter and a booklet of members' addresses and school affiliations.

Our first money-making project involved writing and selling a little
book of strategy lessons that had been used successfully by TAWL
teachers. That book evolved into *Whole Language Strategies for
Secondary Students* (Gilles, 1988) and is now published by Richard
C. Owen. The prepublication copies of the strategy book not only
provided good suggestions for teachers but also financed our first
Renewal Conference. The topic for that first conference was chosen
just as we choose themes today—ten years later. At that time,
because we felt a need for information about the writing process, we
invited Ben and Beth Nelms to talk about writing theory and practice. We were delighted when a whopping forty people showed up
for the conference. We were also relieved to learn that we actually
covered our expenses and made a little money, and, just as importantly, we were delighted to know that we had established a reputation for having a substantive conference. The following year 350
attended, and this year 675.

TAWL kids are a part of TAWL. At the Renewal Conference,
children sell copies of books they have written and illustrated. The
money received from the sales goes toward buying books for Rainbow House, a local shelter for abused children. TAWL kids also write
book reviews for our newsletter.

Baby-sitting at our meetings is provided if needed. Parents and
TAWL share the cost.

Support groups invest in their members. An amount is set in the
Mid-Missouri TAWL budget to help finance two or three members to
attend a conference. We have a growing library of professional
literature to lend to our members. Two years ago we began buying
sets of children's and young adult literature. These sets consist of
seven or eight copies of a single title; these can be checked out for
classroom use. We have a few big books.

We order large quantities of professional literature and some
children's books to sell to our members at a slightly reduced rate.
This is also a money-maker for the organization.

When members travel to appear before the state legislature or
represent our group at a political meeting, we pay their expenses,
including hiring a substitute teacher.

## GROWING

Along the way, it became apparent to our members that we needed
to elect officers, establish an advisory board, circulate a monthly
newsletter, conduct a conference, enliven our programs, and be-

come more politically active. When we realized we had a substantial treasury, we needed to establish our tax-free status. These are all benchmarks. Your group will have its own major moments.

Some groups have grown to such an extent that help exceeding an active member's role is required. In such cases, the groups employ one of its own members as a part-time director. It is vital to plan and to think carefully about this person's role. The executive director is not to take over the duties and chores that should be handled by the membership at large, but rather to enhance the organization and facilitate members in their professional development through their membership in TAWL. An executive director works closely with the president, offering assistance when and where needed. Perhaps one of the most important tasks of a director is to be a constant source of information to the board about membership.

Occasionally teachers attend TAWL a few times and are never heard from again; they may even continue to pay dues but don't attend meetings. Apparently, TAWL isn't meeting their needs. Why aren't they returning? Other activities, such as planning workshops and visitations to outstanding classes and organizing a newsletter, might be coordinated by the executive director.

### THE WHOLE LANGUAGE UMBRELLA

On February 18, 1989, the constitution of the Whole Language Umbrella (WLU) was ratified in Winnipeg, Manitoba. There is now an international network that makes communication between individuals and groups possible. The WLU provides a mechanism for whole language advocates to get in touch with each other; a way to share across states, provinces, and countries; a way to break out of our isolation. WLU, in its first year, has organized conferences, meetings at IRA and NCTE, sent out articles and bibliographies to members, established a newsletter, provided information to whole language educators concerning sociopsycholinguistic theory and practices, and organized for political awareness.

Local, state, and regional support groups are encouraged not only to join WLU but also to contribute to its operation through creative ideas, work, and finances. CEL in Winnipeg almost single-handedly financed WLU's birth. It has done so by adding a $5 fee to its annual conference registration; this surcharge is donated to WLU. Other groups have promised to support WLU in a similar way. Members of TAWL in Detroit have taken over the writing and production of the WLU newsletter. Members of the Whole Language Teachers Association in Massachusetts answer the stream of letters that come in asking how to start support groups. Members of the Mid-Missouri TAWL try to keep up with letters from teachers such as Julie, from those who ask, "Can you help me? I'm trying to become a whole language teacher."

Groups in the United States may write to Debbie Manning, 4848 N. Fruit, Fresno, CA 93705 for WLU membership information.

Canadians may write to Lorraine Krause, P.O. Box 1688, Huntingdon, QC JOS 1HO. Debbie and Lorraine are the WLU membership co-chairs.

## NEED MORE INFORMATION?

If you need more help, pick up the phone and call a whole language teacher. If you don't know a whole language teacher, write to Debbie or Lorraine for addresses. The newsletter, called *Teachers Networking*, published by Richard C. Owen Publishers, will put you in touch with some. You can subscribe for $12 a year from Richard C. Owen Publishers, 135 Katonah Avenue, Katonah, New York, 10536. Several articles have appeared in the newsletter about organizing a support group. Those and other articles giving information about starting or maintaining a group are listed in the "Helpful References."

## THE BEGINNING

Nothing happens by itself. If a support group is organized and flourishes, it will be because of your commitment and through your effort.

## HELPFUL REFERENCES

Areglado, N., and L. Stevick. "Suggestions for Organizing a Whole Language Networking Group." *Teachers Networking*. Katonah, NY: Richard C. Owen Publishers (May 1988).

Goodman, D. "TAWL Topics." *Teachers Networking*. Katonah, NY: Richard C. Owen Publishers (May 1988).

Hood, W. "Whole Language: A Grassroots Movement Catches On." *Learning* (April 1989).

Teachers and Research: Language and Learning in the Classroom. IRA, 1989.

Watson, D. "Support Groups." In *Developing Teachers: A Celebration of Teachers Learning in Australia*. Methuen, Australia: Ply Ltd., 1987.

Watson, D., and M. Bixby. "Teachers! A Support Group Needs You." *Georgia Journal of Reading* (Spring 1985).

Watson, D., C. Burke, and J. Harste. "Invitations and Encouragements." In *Whole Language: Inquiring Voices*. New York: Scholastic, 1989.

Watson, D., and M. Stevenson. "Teacher Support Groups: Why and How." IRA, 1989.

# BIBLIOGRAPHY

Ahlberg, A., and J. Ahlberg. *The Jolly Postman or Other People's Letters*. Boston: Little, Brown, 1986.

Allen, R. V. "Reading Is Creative Living." *Claremont Reading Conference Yearbook* 22 (1974).

American Association for the Advancement of Science. *Science for All Americans: A Project 2061 Report on Literacy Goals in Science, Mathematics, and Technology*. Washington, DC: American Association for the Advancement of Science, 1989.

Anthony, E. "Approach, Method and Technique." *English Language Teaching* 17 (1963): 63–67.

Areglado, N., and L. Stevick. "Suggestions for Organizing a Whole Language Networking Group." *Teachers Networking*. Katonah, NY: Richard C. Owen Publishers (May 1988).

Armstrong, M. *Closely Observed Children*. London: Chameleon Books, 1980.

Atwell, N. *In the Middle*. Portsmouth, NH: Boynton/Cook, 1987.

Bakhtin, M. "The Problem of Speech Genres (1929)." In G. S. Morson (Ed.), *Bakhtin: Essays and Dialogues on His Work*. Chicago: University of Chicago Press, 1986.

Baratta-Lorton, M. *Mathematics Their Way*. Menlo Park, CA: Addison-Wesley, 1976.

Barnes, D. *From Communication to Curriculum*. New York: Penguin Books, 1976.

Bauer, C. *This Way to Books*. New York: H. W. Wilson, 1983.

Bean, J., and J. Ramage. *Form and Surprise in Composition: Writing and Thinking Across the Curriculum*. New York: Macmillan, 1986.

Bemelmans, L., *Madeline*. New York: Viking, 1967.

Bird, L. B. "The Art of Teaching: Evaluation and Revision." In K. Goodman, Y. Goodman, and W. Hood (Eds.), *The Whole Language Evaluation Book*. Portsmouth, NH: Heinemann, 1989.

_____. *Becoming a Whole Language School: The Fair Oaks Story*. Katonah, NY: Richard C. Owen Publishers, 1989.

Brathwaite, E. *Rights of Passage*. Oxford, England: Oxford University Press, 1967.

Britton, J., et al. *The Development of Writing Abilities (11–18)*. School Council Research Series. London: Macmillan Education, 1975.

Bronte, C. *Jane Eyre*. New York: Random House, 1848.

Burbach, H. "School Leaders—New Kinds of Thinking Needed to Lead Education into New Age." *National Association of Secondary School Principals Bulletin* 71:502 (1987): 1–7.

Calkins, L. *The Art of Teaching Writing*. Portsmouth, NH: Heinemann, 1986.

_____. Keynote speech presented at the Colorado Council of the International Reading Association Convention, Denver, 1988.

Callahan, S. *Adrift*. Boston: Houghton Mifflin, 1986.

Cambourne, B. *The Whole Story*. Sydney, NSW, Australia: Ashton-Scholastic, 1989.

Carle, E. *The Grouchy Ladybug*. New York: Harper & Row, 1977.

Clark, C., and P. Peterson. "Teacher's Thought Processes." In M. Witrock (Ed.), *The Handbook of Research on Teaching*. New York: Macmillan, 1986.

Clarke, J., R. Wideman, and S. Eadie. *Together We Learn*. Scarborough, Ontario: Prentice Hall, 1990.

Clay, M. *What Did I Write?* Portsmouth, NH: Heinemann, 1975.

Cleary, B. *Ralph S. Mouse*. New York: Morrow, 1982.

Cochrane, O., D. Cochrane, S. Scalena, and E. Buchanan. *Reading, Writing and Caring*. Winnipeg, Manitoba: Whole Language Consultants Ltd., 1984, pp. 3-15.

Coles, R. "Grade Eight Students Cope with Today and Get Ready for Tomorrow." In K. Goodman, Y. Goodman, and W. Hood (Eds.), *The Whole Language Evaluation Book*. Portsmouth, NH: Heinemann, 1989.

Colorado Communicator. "The Colorado Communicator Interviews Jane Hansen." *The Colorado Communicator* 12 (1988): 1, 21, and 23.

Cossey, R., J. Stenmark, and V. Thompson. *Family Math*. Berkeley, CA: Lawrence Hall of Science, University of CA, 1986.

Cowley, J. *The Meanies*. San Diego, CA: The Wright Group, 1983.

Cremin, L. *The Transformation of the School*. New York: Random House, 1961.

Cummins, J. *Empowering Minority Students*. Sacramento, CA: California Association of Bilingual Education, 1989.

_____. "The Role of Primary Language Instruction in Promoting Educational Success for Language Minority Students." In *Schooling and Language Minority Students: A Theoretical Framework*. Los Angeles: Evaluation, Dissemination and Assessment Center, 1981.

Dalphins, M. Keynote address to National Anti-racist Movement in Education, Birmingham, England, 1988.

Dalrymple, K. " 'Well, What About His Skills?' Evaluation of Whole Language in the Middle School." In K. Goodman, Y. Goodman, and W. Hood (Eds.), *The Whole Language Evaluation Book*. Portsmouth, NH: Heinemann, 1989.

Dewey, J. *Experience and Education*. New York: Collier, 1963.

Eckert, A. *Incident at Hawk's Hill*. New York: Dell, 1971.

Edelsky, C., and S. Harman. "The Risk of Whole Language Literacy: Alienation and Connection." *Language Arts* 66 (1989): 329-407.

_____. *Writing in a Bilingual Program: Había Una Vez*. Norwood, NJ: Ablex, 1986.

Egan, K. *Teaching as Story Telling: An Alternate Approach to Teaching a Curriculum in the Elementary School*. Ontario: Althouse Press, 1986.

Eisner, E. *The Educational Imagination*. New York: Macmillan, 1979.

Ellis, R. *Understanding Second Language Acquisition*. Oxford, England: Oxford University Press, 1986.

Ende, *Momo*. Garden City, NY: Doubleday, 1985.

Ferreiro, E., and A. Teberosky. *Literacy Before Schooling*. Portsmouth, NH: Heinemann, 1982.

Fielding, L., P. Wilson, and R. Anderson. "A New Focus on Free Reading: The Role of Trade Books in Reading Instruction." In T. E. Raphael (Ed.), *The Contexts of School-Based Literacy*. New York: Random House, 1986.

Forbes, K. *Mama's Bank Account*. Chicago: Harcourt, Brace and Company, 1943.

Foucault, M. *Discipline and Punish*. New York: Penguin Books, 1977.

Frank, M. *If You're Trying to Teach Kids to Write, You've Gotta Have This Book!* Nashville, TN: Incentive Publication, 1979.

Freeman, D., and Y. Freeman. "Whole Language Content Lesson." *Elementary ESOL Education News* 11 (1988): 1-2.

Freire, P., and D. Macedo. *Literacy: Reading the Word and the World*. South Hadley, MA: Bergin and Garvey, 1987.

_____. *Pedagogy of the Oppressed*. New York: Seabury, 1970.

Gardiner, J. *Stone Fox*. New York: Harper & Row, 1980.

Gee, J. "Dracula, the Vampire Lestat, and TESOL." *TESOL Quarterly* 22 (1988): 201-225.

Gentry, R. "Learning to Spell Developmentally." *The Reading Teacher* 34:3 (1981): 378-381.

Gilles, C. *Whole Language Strategies for Secondary Students*. Katonah, NY: Richard C. Owen Publishers, 1988.

Goodlad, J. *A Place Called School*. New York: McGraw-Hill, 1984.

Goodman, D. "Family Community Studies." In K. Goodman, Y. Goodman, and L. B. Bird, *The Whole Language Catalog*. New York: American School Publishers, 1990.

_____. "TAWL Topics." *Teachers Networking*. Katonah, NY: Richard C. Owen Publishers (May 1988).

Goodman, K. "Dialect Barriers to Reading Comprehension Revisited." *Reading Teacher*, October 1973, pp. 409-417.

_____. *What's Whole in Whole Language?* Richmond Hill, Ontario: Scholastic TAB, 1986. (Distributed in the United States by Heinemann.)

Goodman, K., Y. Goodman, and B. Flores. *Reading in the Bilingual Classroom: Literacy and Biliteracy*. Rosslyn, VA: National Clearinghouse for Bilingual Education, 1979.

Goodman, K., Y. Goodman, and W. Hood, Eds. *The Whole Language Evaluation Book*. Portsmouth, NH: Heinemann, 1989.

Goodman, Y. "Kid Watching: An Alternative to Testing." *National Elementary Principal* 57:4 (1978): 41-45.

Goodman, Y., and C. Burke. *Reading Strategies: Focus on Comprehension*. Katonah, New York: Richard C. Owen Publishers, 1980.

Goodman. Y., D. Watson, and C. Burke. *Reading Miscue Inventory: Alternative Procedures*. Katonah, New York: Richard C. Owen Publishers, 1987.

Goody, J. "Language and Dialect: A Discussion Paper for Secondary Schools." London: *ILEA* (1981).

Graves, D. *Final Report: A Case Study of Observing the Development of Primary Children's Composing, Spelling, and Motor Behaviors During the Writing Process*. Durham, NH: University of New Hampshire, 1978-1981.

_____. *Writing: Teachers and Children at Work*. Portsmouth, NH: Heinemann, 1983.

Greene, M. "Research Currents: What Are the Language Arts For?" *Language Arts* 65:5 (1988): 474-480.

Halliday M. A. K. *Learning How to Mean: Explorations in the Development of Language*. Wheeling, IL: Whitehall, 1975.

Hansen, J. *When Writers Read*. Portsmouth, NH: Heinemann, 1987.

Harste, J., V. Woodward, and C. Burke. *Language Stories and Literacy Lessons*. Portsmouth, NH: Heinemann, 1984.

Heller, R. *Chickens Aren't the Only Ones*. New York: Scholastic, 1981.

Hendrickson, J. "Human Bingo." *Livewire*. Urbana, IL: National Council of Teachers of English, August 1986.

Hewitt, R. "White Adolescent Creole Users and the Politics of Friendship." *Journal of Multilingual and Multicultural Development* 3:3 (1982): 277.

Hill, E. *Spot*. New York: Putnam, 1980.

Holdaway, D. *The Foundations of Literacy*. Sydney, Australia: Ashton-Scholastic, 1979.

————. *Independence in Reading: A Handbook on Individualized Procedures*. Portsmouth, NH: Heinemann, 1980.

Holden, L., and A. Roper. *Pattern Factory*. Oak Lawn, IL: Creative Publications, 1980.

Holm, A. *North to Freedom*. New York: Harcourt Brace Jovanovich, 1965.

Hood, W. "Whole Language: A Grassroots Movement Catches On." *Learning* (April 1989).

Howard, D. "The Wonderfilled Lessons." Unpublished handout, 1984.

Howe, D., and J. Howe. *Bunnicula*. New York: Macmillan, 1979.

Howe, J. *The Celery Stalks at Midnight*. New York: Macmillan, 1983.

Hunter, M. "Madeline Hunter in the English Classroom," *English Journal* (September 1989).

Jones, R., and A. Lunsford, Eds. *Report of the 1987 English Coalition*. In press.

Juster, N. *The Phantom Tollbooth*. New York: Dell, 1961.

Kasten, W. *The Behaviors of Selected Third and Fourth Grade Native American Children*. Unpublished dissertation. Tucson: University of Arizona, 1984.

Kasten, W., and B. Clark. *A Study of Third and Fifth Grade Students' Oral Language During the Writing Process in Elementary Classrooms*. Ed 227 025, July 1986.

Kirby, D., and T. Liner. *Inside Out: Developmental Strategies for Teaching Writing*. Portsmouth, NH: Boynton/Cook, 1981.

Krashen, S. *On Course*. Sacramento, CA: California Association of Bilingual Education, 1982.

————. *Principles and Practice in Second Language Acquisition*. Oxford, England: Pergamon, 1982.

*Language Arts for the 21st Century: Crossroads of Possibility and Practice*. Unpublished report. Queenstown, MD: The Elementary Strand at the Conference of the Association of English Coalitions, July 7–24, 1987.

Lee, H. *To Kill a Mockingbird*. New York: Harper & Row, 1961.

Leigh, J. "Whole-Language Approaches: Premises and Possibilities." *Learning Disability Quarterly* (1980): 62–69.

Lewis, C. S. *The Lion, the Witch, and the Wardrobe*. New York: Macmillan, 1950.

Lipsitz, J. *Successful Schools for Young Adolescents*. New Brunswick, NJ: Transactional Books, 1984.

Lloyd-Jones, R., and A. Lunsford. Eds. *The English Conference: Democracy through Language*. Urbana, IL: National Council of Teachers of English, 1989.

Lobel, A. *Frog and Toad*. New York, Harper & Row, 1974.

Macrorie, K. *The I-Search Paper: Revised Edition of Searching Writing*. Portsmouth, NH: Boynton/Cook, 1988.

Martin, B. *Sounds of Home*. New York: Holt, Rinehart and Winston, 1972.

————. *Sounds of Jubilee*. New York: Holt, Rinehart and Winston, 1973.

_____. *The Sounds of Language*, Teachers Edition. New York: Holt, Rinehart and Winston, 1967.

Martin, N., et al. *Writing and Learning Across the Curriculum 11-16. Schools Council Writing Across the Curriculum Project*. London: Ward Lock, 1976.

Mayer, M. *There's a Nightmare in My Closet*. New York: Dial Books for Young Readers, 1968.

McCracken, R., and M. McCracken. *Reading, Writing, and Language*. Canada: Peguis Publishers, 1979.

Meek, M. *How Texts Teach What Students Learn*. Avonset, Bath, England: Thimble, 1988.

Moffett, J. "Rationale for a New Curriculum in English." In M. Myers and J. Gray (Eds.), *Theory and Practice in the Teaching of Composition: Processing, Distancing, and Modeling*. Champaign, IL: National Council for Teachers of English, 1983.

Morris, V. *Existentialism in Education*. New York: Harper & Row, 1966.

Munsch, R. *I Have to Go*. Scarborough, Ontario: Firefly Books, 1985.

_____. *Thomas' Snowsuit*. Scarborough, Ontario: Firefly Books, 1985.

Musgrove, R. *A Study of Prespelling Kindergarten Children's Constructions of Writing. An Unpublished Dissertation*. Sarasota: University of South Florida, 1987.

National Council of Teachers of Mathematics. *Curriculum and Evaluation Standards for School Mathematics*. National Council of Teachers of Mathematics, 1989.

Newkirk, T., and N. Atwell, Eds. *Understanding Writing: Ways of Observing, Learning, and Teaching*. 2nd ed. Portsmouth, NH: Heinemann, 1988.

O'Dell, S. *Island of the Blue Dolphins*. New York: Dell, 1960.

Olsen, L. *Immigrant Students and the California Public Schools: Crossing the Schoolhouse Border*. California Tomorrow Policy Research Report, 1988.

O'Neill, S. "Gluskabe Tames the Wind." *Cricket Magazine* 11 (1983): 30-36.

Ong, W. J. *Orality and Literacy*. London: Methuen, 1982.

Parry, J., and D. Hornsby. *Write On: A Conference Approach to Writing*. Portsmouth, NH: Heinemann, 1985.

Paterson, K. *Bridge to Terabithia*. New York: Harper & Row, 1977.

Paulsen, G. *Hatchet*. New York: Puffin, 1987.

Peck, R. *A Day No Pigs Would Die*. New York: Dell, 1972.

Ponsot, M., and R. Deen. *Beat Not the Poor Desk: Writing: What to Teach, How to Teach, and Why*. Portsmouth, NH: Boynton/Cook, 1982.

Porter, R. *Black Ink*. London: Black Ink Collective, 1968.

Powell, A. G. "Being Unspecial in the Shopping Mall High School." *Phi Delta Kappan* 67 (1985): 255-265.

Raffi. "More Singable Songs." Troubador Records, 1977.

Rey, H. A. *Curious George*. Boston: Houghton Mifflin, 1941.

Rich, S. "Restoring Power to Teachers: The Impact of Whole Language." *Language Arts* 62:7 (1985): 717-721.

Richards, J., and T. Rodgers. *Approaches and Methods in Language Teaching: A Description and Analysis*. Cambridge, England: Cambridge University Press, 1986.

Rigg, P., and S. Hudelson. "One Child Doesn't Speak English." *Australia Journal of Reading* 9 (1986): 116-125.

Rius, M., and J. MaParramon. *El Campo*. Woodbury, NY: Barron's, 1986.

_____. *La Ciudad*. Woodbury, NY: Barron's, 1986.

Robinson, B. *The Best Christmas Pageant Ever*. New York: Avon Books, 1979.

Rosen, B. *And None of It Was Nonsense*. Portsmouth, NH: Heinemann, 1988.

Rousseau-Clark, L. "My Family History." In K. Goodman, Y. Goodman, and L. B. Bird (Eds.), *The Whole Language Catalog*. New York: American School Publishers, 1990.

Sendak, M. *Chicken Soup with Rice*. New York: Scholastic, 1962.

Seuss, Dr. *Green Eggs and Ham*. New York: Random House, 1960.

Sharmat, M. *Nate the Great*. New York: Dell, 1972.

Slavin, R. E. *Cooperative Learning: Student Teams*, 2nd ed. Washington, DC: National Education Association, 1987.

Sleator, W. *The Green Futures of Tycho*. New York: Dutton, 1981.

Smith, P., and C. Daniel. *The Chicken Book*. Boston: Little, Brown, 1975.

Smith, E. B., K. Goodman, and R. Meredith. *Language and Thinking in Schools*, 2nd ed. New York: Holt, Rinehart and Winston, 1976.

Smith, F. "Demonstrations, Engagement, and Sensitivity: A Revised Approach to Language Learning." *Language Arts* 58 (1981): 103–112.

_____. *Insult to Intelligence*. New York: Arbor House, 1986.

_____. *Reading Without Nonsense*. New York: Teachers College Press, 1985.

_____. *Understanding Reading*, 3rd ed. New York: Holt, Rinehart and Winston, 1982.

Smith, K. Oral presentation. National Council of Teachers of English Annual Conference, Baltimore MD, November 1989.

Sonntag, L. *Eggs*. New York: Putnam, 1980.

Spector, B. "Excellence in Pre-Service Elementary Teacher Education in Science." *Focus on Excellence*. Washington, DC: National Science Teachers' Association, 1987.

Spencer, Z. *Flair: A Handbook of Creative Writing Techniques for the Elementary Teacher*. Stevensville: Educational Service, 1972.

Stauffer, R. *The Language-Experience Approach to the Teaching of Reading*, 2nd ed. New York: Harper & Row, 1980.

Taylor, D. *Family Literacy*. Portsmouth, NH: Heinemann, 1983.

Taylor, D., and D. Strickland. *Family Storybook Reading*. Portsmouth, NH: Heinemann, 1986.

Taylor, M. *Roll of Thunder, Hear My Cry*. New York: Dial, 1976.

Taylor, T. *The Cay*. New York: Avon Books, 1969.

*Teachers and Research: Language and Learning in the Classroom*. Newark, DE: International Reading Association, 1989.

Trelease, J. *The Read-Aloud Handbook*. New York: Penguin, 1982.

_____. "Turning on the Turned-Off Reader." Audiocassette recording. New York: Reading Tree Productions, 1983.

Volosinov, V. N. *Marxism and the Philosophy of Language*. Cambridge, MA: Harvard University Press, 1986.

Vygotsky, L. *Mind in Society*. Ed. by M. Cole et al. Cambridge, MA: Harvard University Press, 1978.

_____. *Thought and Language*. Ed. by A. Kozulin. Cambridge, MA: MIT Press, 1987.

Wadsworth, B. J. *Piaget for the Classroom Teacher*. New York: Longman, 1978.

Walshe, R. "The Learning Power of Writing." *English Journal* 76 (1987): 22–27.

Watson, D. "Support Groups." In *Developing Teachers: A Celebration of Teachers' Learning in Australia*. Methuen Australia Ply Ltd, 1987.

Watson, D., and M. Bixby. "Teachers! A Support Group Needs You." *Georgia Journal of Reading* (Spring 1985).

Watson, D., C. Burke, and J. Harste. "Invitations and Encouragements." In *Whole Language: Inquiring Voices*. Richmond Hill, Ontario: Scholastic, 1989.

Watson, D., and M. Stevenson. "Teacher Support Groups: Why and How." In G. S. Pinnell and M. Matlin (Eds.), *Teachers and Research: Language Learning in the Classroom*. Newark, DE: International Reading Association, 1989, pp. 118–129.

Weir, L. "Using a Whole Language Approach in a Transitional First Grade." *Early Years* 15 (1985): 52–54.

Wells, G. *The Meaning Makers: Children Learning Language and Using Language to Learn*. Portsmouth, NH: Heinemann, 1986.

Wood, A. *The Napping House*. New York: Harcourt Brace Jovanovich, 1984.

Wurtenberg, J. *Helping Children Become Writers at Home and at School*. Tulsa, OK: Educational Development Corporation, 1982.